Saving the Waifs

AMERICAN CIVILIZATION

A series edited by Allen F. Davis

Saving the Waifs

Reformers and Dependent Children, 1890–1917

•

LeRoy Ashby

Temple University Press
Philadelphia

Temple University Press, Philadelphia 19122
© 1984 by Temple University. All rights reserved
Published 1984
Printed in the United States of America

Library of Congress Cataloging in Publication Data

Ashby, LeRoy.
Saving the Waifs

(American civilization)
Bibliography: p.
Includes index.
1. Children—Institutional care—United States—History—Case studies.
2. Abandoned children—United States—Case studies.
3. Social reformers—United States—Case studies.
4. Church and social problems—United States—History—Case studies.
5. Child welfare—United States—History—Case studies.
I. Title. II. Series.
HV741.A83   1984   362.7'32'0973   83-18209
ISBN 0-87722-337-8

For Mary
with gratitude and affection

Contents

•

Preface
ix

CHAPTER 1
Dependent Children and "the Gospel of Child Saving"
in the Progressive Era
3

CHAPTER 2
"The Child at the Door": E. P. Savage and the
Children's Home Society of Minnesota
38

CHAPTER 3
Saving the Church by Saving the Children: The Orphanages of the
National Benevolent Association
69

CHAPTER 4
Rescuing the "Newsies": John Gunckel and the
Toledo Newsboys' Association
104

CHAPTER 5
The Ford Republic: Dependency, Delinquency, and Democracy
133

CONTENTS

CHAPTER 6
Aiding the "Left-overs": G. W. Hinckley and Good Will Farm
170

CHAPTER 7
Epilogue
206

Notes
221

Bibliographical Note
289

Index
299

Preface

•

This study examines some neglected dimensions of child saving—a cause that surged with energy at the turn of the twentieth century. In recent years the subjects of juvenile delinquency, child labor legislation, and educational experiments during the progressive era have inspired excellent historical work. The focus of this book will be on some of the institutional and organizational responses to the problems of dependent children, a category that in the thinking of most child rescue workers often included neglected, delinquent, and "unfortunate" youths, not merely orphans or even half-orphans.

Five case studies provide the core of the book. They demonstrate the enormous diversity and complexity of child rescue campaigns in the late 1800s and early 1900s. Moreover, they deal with the theme of reform as it existed "in the trenches." Familiar figures such as Judge Ben Lindsey and Jane Addams have traditionally, and justifiably, received attention. But if they were the generals of progressive youth work, numerous troops in the field devised their own blend of strategies. Sometimes these people in the lower ranks labored together; sometimes they disagreed. None of them, or their institutional and organizational creations, represented simply a type. Instead, each dealt in individual ways with real and perceived problems.

A recurrent theme concerns the vitality and diversity of Protestant voluntary activity that shaped essential aspects of progressive child saving. This interpretation echoes that of scholars such as Clyde Griffen, who have stressed the strong legacy of American Protestantism to the progressive reform era. Although the case studies generally emphasize Protestant opinion and action, it should nonetheless be clear that large numbers of children received care at the turn of the century in religious institutions that were not Protestant. The Children's Home Societies were markedly Protestant, for example, but the Catholic Bureau of Dependent Children also sought to place neglected and needy children directly in foster or adoptive homes. Among the era's leading child savers was Monsignor William J. Kerby, a Catholic University professor who devoted much of his life to helping youths in the Washington, D.C., area, and Father Peter Joseph Dunne of St. Louis. There were also numerous Jewish orphanages and agencies for children, some of which historian Peter Romanofsky wrote about before cancer cut short his larger work on the subject.

Social control was undeniably an important object of many progressive reforms but was hardly the whole story. Many child savers responded to genuinely tragic conditions with considerable sensitivity, empathy, and a driving desire to "do good." While their point of reference was invariably an American past that was rapidly disappearing, time and again they showed that nostalgia—as historian Robert Crunden has argued—could also encourage innovation. Certainly this was so in the Minnesota Home Society's quest for home placement answers to child dependency; in the National Benevolent Association's transition from an "anti-institutional" to an institutional setting; in the remarkable experiments in youthful self-government that were basic to the Toledo Newsboys' Association and the Ford Republic; in the Ford Republic's blending of practical and academic psychologies for dealing with troubled youngsters; and in the fusion at Good Will Farm in Maine of traditional farm experiences with a forward-looking educational system.

By examining several specific institutional and organizational examples, this book attempts both to chronicle some important but little-explored child saving efforts and to capture some of the texture and ambiguity of those efforts. The assumption is that concrete examples, as social historian Robert Bremner has argued, are necessary to test and provide the basis for generalizations. Ultimately, it is with matters of context, nuance, circumstance, and individual response to perceived and changing situations that historians must deal.

Where possible, this study tries to get "inside" the institutions and organizations in order to acquire some sense of what life was like for the children—the "clients," or objects of child rescue activities. In most cases, however, because of a lack of information and details, this has been difficult. Regrettably, with the possible exception of Good Will Farm, the focus is thus undoubtedly too much on the "savers," rather than the "saved."

Another problem concerns numbers. Census figures indicated that by 1910 there were approximately 110,000 children living in 1,151 institutions in the United States. Of these, slightly over 100,000 were classified as orphans, half-orphans, foundlings, homeless, neglected, and indigent. But that figure only hinted at the total number of dependent children across the nation. One writer estimated in 1907 that there were "probably 25,000 homeless children" in New York City alone. The *Juvenile Court Record* guessed in 1911 that there were over 120,000 homeless *babies* in America. Complicating the situation were the substantial numbers of "street arabs" and newsboys whom many reformers viewed as dependent. Although there were scattered census figures for the number of "newsies," they were much lower than the estimates that muckraking observers offered.

Even the definition of child dependency was unclear. Wide-ranging laws concerning dependency and delinquency overlapped considerably. A common conclusion among child savers was that many so-called delinquents were really dependents, and vice versa. Nor did it help to say that homeless children were those who had no families. Strong feelings existed among reformers that many children with families were in fact homeless: the youths lacked parental love or were victims of neglect and abuse. In this sense, dependency (or delinquency, or neglect) was not simply a statistical fact in official records; it was very much in the eye of the beholder.

My own dependency upon many people was abundantly clear to me as I worked on this book. Dozens of individuals in various libraries, archives, and children's institutions provided indispensable services. I am particularly indebted to Clifford Jones, assistant director of the Allendale School for Boys; museum curator Douglas Fernald and former executive director John Plummer at the Hinckley Home-School-Farm; Clyde Reed, retired superintendent of the Ford Republic; Roger Toogood, executive director of the Children's Home Society of Minnesota; Nancy Wahonick, director of communications of the National Benevolent Association; Roland and Kitty Huff and David McWhirter of the Disciples of Christ Historical Society; Lamar Cosby, executive director, and Judith Traband of the Children's Service Society of Wisconsin; the Reverend William Hammitt, former director of the Baby Fold; Mrs. Michael William Cramer, who, while helping me collect materials at Father Dunne's Home for Boys, called my attention to the National Benevolent Association; Mrs. Patricia Kruger of Lad Lake; and William J. Causer, assistant director of the United Methodist Children's Home in Mt. Vernon, Ill. A number of Good Will Farm graduates kindly shared their memories with me, as did the family of Bert Hall in Milwaukee; Emma Blackman, the first county social worker in McLean County, Illinois; and Floyd Starr, who in 1913 founded the Starr Commonwealth for Boys in Albion, Michigan.

Robert H. Zieger of Wayne State University, an unfailing friend, read the entire manuscript in its early stages and offered his usual perceptive suggestions and encouragement. I am also grateful to Allen Davis of Temple University and Robert Bremner of Ohio State University for their critiques of a later version. The newsboy chapter benefited from a session of Washington State University's history seminar group. Raymond Muse and, more recently, David Stratton have been superior departmental heads, invariably doing everything possible to facilitate research and writing schedules. Another colleague, David Coon, offered useful suggestions regarding organizational problems. As always, Sam and Marion Merrill gave their encouragement, friendship, and timely support. Joe Hawes at Kansas State, Jack Holl of the U.S. Department of Energy, and the late Peter Romanofsky also deserve my deepest appreciation. I am thankful as well to the American Council of Learned Societies for a grant-in-aid, and to Washington State University for several travel grants. Diana Cochran typed a complete draft of the manuscript, and Diane Triplett typed the final revisions. The editor of *Mid-America* kindly allowed me to quote from material originally published in that journal.

My greatest debt by far is to my wife Mary. It was she who gave me the idea of writing about dependent children, and she has helped immeasurably with the manuscript by sharing ideas and endless amounts of time and energy. I am, of course, profoundly grateful to

her for much, much more. To our son Steve I owe many thanks—
simply for being who he is. I wish that our son Eric, killed at age nine,
were also here to share my satisfaction in completing this book.

Saving the Waifs

· 1 ·

Dependent Children and "The Gospel of Child Saving" in the Progressive Era

In 1895, as the countryside around Fox Lake in northern Illinois began to show the influence of early autumn, thirty-four-year-old Edward L. Bradley listened as six boys pleaded to remain with him at their rudimentary campsite rather than return to a Chicago orphanage. The boys' arguments elicited from him a commitment that had perhaps started developing at least a year earlier when he first accompanied homeless youths on summer outings. Stay they would. The little group began immediately to construct a shelter against the approaching winter winds. Two years later, Bradley and his young charges moved to a permanent location on the west shore of nearby Cedar Lake, just outside the town of Lake Villa. The result was Allendale Farm, a home for dependent boys predicated on the belief that placing a city waif in a rural environment, and raising him in a setting that contained a sense of family and community, would make it possible to "recreate this boy."[1]

Several years later in Milwaukee, Marion Ogden responded to a newspaper advertisement asking for volunteers to visit children in the local jail. In the municipal courtroom the young woman watched incredulously as a judge sentenced a fifteen-year-old to thirty days in jail for vagrancy. Her anger grew when she discovered that children as young as eight were receiving jail sentences up to sixty days. Dedicating herself to child rescue work, she adopted a three-year-old boy (an unusual step at the time for an unmarried woman) and in 1902 was a founder and first secretary of the Wisconsin Home and Farm School, outside Milwaukee, "for Neglected, Destitute, Homeless and Orphan Boys."[2]

When Edward Bradley and Marion Ogden decided in their own ways to work permanently with dependent youths, they not only started dramatic chapters in their own lives; they joined many other reformers who felt the pull of what the famed juvenile court judge Ben Lindsey described as "the gospel of child saving."[3] Between the 1880s and America's entry into World War I, fascination with the needs of children ignited an explosion of activity that produced juvenile courts, child labor laws, child guidance clinics, babies' health contests, free lunch programs, kindergartens, the playground movement, experiments in progressive education, numerous child study groups, a profusion of organizations (such as the Big Brothers and Big Sisters, the Boy Scouts, Girl Scouts, and Lone Scouts), the formation in 1912 of the United States Children's Bureau, and—as the work of Bradley and Ogden made clear—new institutions and associations concerned with the special needs of dependent children.

Yet however much Bradley, Ogden, and other child rescue workers liked to distinguish their efforts from those of preceding eras, they in fact demonstrated again and again that they owed far more to the nineteenth-century society of their roots than to the emerging twentieth century. In important ways they struggled against the currents of the modern world. Or, perhaps more accurately, their experiences manifested the ambiguous nature of the social and cultural transition to that world. A dominant trend of the post–Civil War period was the steady erosion of the "island communities" that had traditionally defined America's social terrain;[4] in contrast, Bradley and company sought to revitalize traditional village values. A major shift toward professionalism and certified expertise marked early twentieth-century social welfare history, but virtually all the organizers of new associations and institutions for dependent (and delinquent) children were amateurs, lacking formal training in child care. And while the growth of governmental power and responsibility—often with the concurrence of the child savers—characterized public affairs, Ogden, Bradley, and their colleagues pointed up the continuing importance of voluntarism and private control.

The controversy among child rescue workers came not over goals but over how to achieve them. They agreed, for example, that traditional asylums were outdated and needed to give way to more family-oriented settings; that "street arabs" who lingered in back alleys and peddled newspapers on crowded city streets needed protection; and that solutions to children's problems had to be flexible, alert to individual differences, and cognizant of environmental influences on human conduct.[5] But at that point, consensus quickly broke down. Some reformers favored an enlarged governmental role; others worried that increased state involvement would sap the volunteer spirit of citizens and would prove far too susceptible to political corruption. Some hoped to save street urchins by banning them from sidewalk trades such as selling newspapers; others argued that much good might come from learning to hustle on the streets and that reforms should simply channel tough survival instincts in constructive directions. On the issue of asylums, some groups concluded that the best solution was to eliminate them as much as possible and move toward immediate placement of dependent children in foster or adoptive homes. Other child rescue workers, perceiving weaknesses in such a strategy, established or endorsed "anti-institutional institutions" that could recreate the values and emotional bonds of an idealized traditional family. Some, such as John Gunckel in Toledo, worked within urban confines; others, such as Bradley and Ogden, believed that a rural environment was essential for raising children.

Although a strong sense of standing on the edge of a bold new era marked this "quickening interest in the child" at the turn of the century,[6] the interest itself was far from new. It has been evident for some time, growing slowly for several generations and accelerating rapidly in the nineteenth century. Since at least the 1700s, significant changes within the emerging bourgeois classes in parts of Western society had been underway, reflecting a profound cultural shift toward the "rationalization" of human affairs. The tendency to systematize, categorize, and divide according to roles and functions picked up speed in the 1800s along with industrialization, urbanization, and immigration. This massive social and cultural transformation altered with seismic force the roles and images of men, women, children, and families. One result was an inclination among middle-

and upper-class families to see children as unique beings with special importance who needed careful preparation for adulthood. Ironically, as children (and animals) became less important in terms of economic productivity, concern for their welfare grew. By the 1800s an emerging cult of childhood clearly existed, drawing on the romantic ideals of English writers such as William Blake and of the French philosopher Rousseau. The child as a source of freshness, innocence, and spontaneity was appealing to a world that seemed increasingly mechanistic.[7]

In antebellum America the spread of an urban, market society not only transformed the workplace but also popularized a domestic ideal that vitally affected perceptions of women and children. As the cities swelled with newcomers and the rapidly fluctuating economy shifted from home to factory, there was considerable uneasiness about the disappearance of traditional cohesive bonds, of republican virtues, and of civic responsibilities. On one level, this anxious mood proved especially fertile for the cult of "true womanhood." In a world of extreme flux, Motherhood and Home symbolized moral stability; as society tore itself from older certainties, at least some things remained sacred. The ideal of domesticity not only placed the middle-class woman on a moral pedestal; it also helped to elevate one of the primary objects of her attention: the child. By midcentury there was an outpouring of books on child care, and in 1855 the first National Baby Show was held in New York. For middle-class urban residents who moved away from the traditional family's role as a working unit, and who limited the family size in order to save financial and emotional resources, children became increasingly conspicuous and precious. Sweetly innocent and redemptive child figures populated the pages of mass literature: Harriet Beecher Stowe's Little Eva, imparting Christian virtues as she died of consumption; the martyred Elsie Dinsmore, instructing her father, whose mind was too much on business; Timothy Shay Arthur's pathetic Mary, imploring, "Father, dear Father, come home with me now," only to become yet another young victim of the saloon; and the orphaned, or half-orphaned, Horatio Alger youths who prevailed through pluck and luck.[8]

As urban, middle-class culture became more child-centered, other trends also enhanced the position of youth. Evangelical ministers, for example, displayed an expanding interest in young people because the emotional stresses of the teenage years seemed to make them especially susceptible to conversion experiences. In addition, the fact that an urban environment allowed youngsters to gather easily with their peers made them more visible as a social group. Thus, by the close of the nineteenth century, YMCA workers and other Christian youth organizers were seeking out a constituency that stood somewhere between childhood and adulthood, and psychologist G. Stanley Hall initiated a child study movement in which he traced natural stages of development and gave a scientific respectability to the emerging concept of adolescence. There were also Americans, Hall among them, who worried that modern life was softening the fiber of the white Protestant middle class, cutting it off from "life," replacing its original vigor with comfort and convenience, and overburdening it with "civilized" rationality and technique. This group championed a strenuous, active life-style (proof of toughness) and also praised childhood, in which vitality and immediate experience offered a welcome contrast to the perceived emotional shallowness of modern culture. From this view, childhood symbolized a momentary respite from the increasingly rigorous and stuffy prescriptions for bourgeois success. The "street-arab" was alluring because of his rugged survival qualities and fearsome because of those same qualities.[9]

In 1911, when the judge of Kansas City's newly formed juvenile court announced, "This is the age of citizen building," he expressed sentiments that had been growing for some time.[10] Children were indispensable in the battle for the nation's destiny. They were embryonic citizens who represented the cutting edge of the future; insofar as society neglected them, they became symbols—lonely, ragged, unloved—of the limits of the American dream. At the same time, they loomed as potential threats of crime and violence. As the well-known muckraking journalist, Jacob Riis, advised, child rescue work was society's "chief bulwark against bankruptcy and wreck."[11] Reformers at the turn of the century thus recognized the special place of children in an urban, industrial age and mounted powerful, widespread campaigns to protect them.[12] Dramatizing the plight of needy youths was also an effective way to mobilize public opinion against a host of social problems. When social worker

7

Robert Hunter compiled his 1901 report, *Tenement Conditions in Chicago,* which described a world of poverty and filthy, crowded, unsafe housing conditions, he illustrated his point with more than forty photographs of slum children. Similarly, in an age that decried corporate exploitation of workers, few documents were more compelling than the photos by Jacob Riis and Lewis Hine of stunted, grimy youngsters in factory mills and mines.[13]

From this perspective, children represented a major weapon in the progressive struggles for reform that helped to define the nature of twentieth-century America. Progressivism was a label—then and later—for the dynamic burst of reform energy that swept over the nation in the late 1800s and early 1900s. It consisted of numerous campaigns to bring America into the modern world of industrialization, urbanization, and ethnic diversity without losing the nation's traditional ideals. Indeed, a central goal was to protect and refurbish such deeply rooted ideals as a classless society, popular government, the Melting Pot, an economy free of strife and open to talent, and the primacy of the public interest above special interests or factions.

Far from being a monolithic movement, progressivism consisted of numerous floating coalitions that gathered around specific reforms. The nature of the various coalitions depended on the issues involved. Battling for tenement housing reforms, for example, were health enthusiasts, moralists alarmed by the apparent spiritual corruption of slum residents, construction industries attentive to new building opportunities, and city boosters concerned that ugly urban settings would drive away customers, tourists, and investors.[14]

Running like a riptide through the coalition-building process, however, was sharply divergent opinion regarding strategies and priorities. On one side, some progressives displayed democratic inclinations, evident in their struggles for direct primary laws, direct election of senators, the initiative, referendum, and recall, and woman suffrage. On the other side, reformers with a marked elitist bent favored "management" in place of "politics" and placed utmost value on credentials, expertise, social efficiency, social uplift, and correct values. Much of the time democratic and elitist tendencies competed within the same person. Humanitarianism— aiding disadvantaged groups, battling inequities and injustices, arousing the public to confront very real social problems—thus blended shakily with a kind of cultural imperialism, that was sometimes racist, nativistic, and concerned with controlling the "dangerous classes."[15]

The progressive generation also took an ambiguous view of the challenges that faced it. Optimistic, chest-thumping salutes to virility and adventure, so characteristic of the age, may have found strident expression precisely because a sense of panic nagged at many reformers as they entered a new century. Theodore Roosevelt had exulted that life was "bully" even though the jarring tragedy of his mother's and his first wife's death on the same day had momentarily raised the specter of a random and disorderly universe. Ben Lindsey, one of Colorado's best-known progressives, similarly spoke effervescently about life's challenges, although when he was nineteen, such challenges had driven him to a suicide attempt. The muckraking journalist and novelist David Graham Phillips pushed himself at a furious pace because, as he admitted, "I could not trust myself in luxurious surroundings for fear they would soon eat all of the manhood out of me." Urban reformer Raymond Robins plunged ahead with his work to improve society even as he lamented that he was among "the men of the last advance." Josiah Flynt, one of the originators of "realistic sociology," pursued an active life obsessively, only to die of drink and cocaine at age forty. Writer Ray Stannard Baker "praise[d] God for the struggle," yet increasingly tumbled toward disillusionment. When William James, one of the age's most important thinkers, urged people to "believe that life is worth living and your belief will help create the fact," he perhaps did so with special urgency because of his own earlier doubts. "Light out after [life] with a club," advised a frenetic Jack London, who in 1916 killed himself. The shock with which so many progressives encountered urban slums and corruption, and their gravitation towards the ideals and values of an older America, provided further evidence of apprehension about the social order.[16]

If ambivalence marked the progressives' assessment of modern conditions, so too did it characterize proposed solutions, especially regarding the role of government. From one perspective, the history of progressivism unquestionably involved the growing role of state responsibility and the formation of a large-scale organizational society that very much accommodated corporate structures.[17] From another perspective, however, the story was far less one of consensus than of disagreements and unintended consequences.[18] While well-known progressives such as Theodore Roosevelt championed governmental intervention, a substantial body of reform thought was deeply suspicious of a more vigorous state. "The State is being put forward too prominently. This is a mistake," warned an editorial in the *Juvenile Court Record*.[19]

Many progressives suspected that government was too much a prisoner of smoke-filled rooms and corrupt bargains. Reform rhetoric pitting "the people" against "the interests" undoubtedly fired up political campaigns to throw the rascals out, but it also kindled citizens' efforts to work outside government—to avoid the taint of politics. Alongside reformers who sought to increase the interventionist powers of the state were those who placed their hopes mainly in volunteer citizen groups, nothing less than "the public" in action. Whereas critics of such groups saw just another example of factions at work, the participants viewed themselves as representing the general interest. Such optimism and innocence helped to define the era. Reasonable, informed people could genuinely agree upon values and social goals—or so it seemed to resolute, confident progressives. A major product of such assumptions was the formation—or, in some cases, invigoration—of countless volunteer organizations. Their agendas ranged from rescue work to consumer protection, social purity, municipal planning, moral uplift, and health. Here was a potent display of the tradition of voluntarism, whereby individuals rallied collectively through private organizations to meet specific crises or peceived social needs. From this vantage point, a more active state was not necessarily good at all; in fact, it could offer more liabilities than advantages. A social welfare government might reduce the public's sense of responsibility to suffering people. One result could be state agencies that were political pawns. Another could be citizens who assumed erroneously that the state was effectively solving society's problems.[20]

Progressive child savers, like many of their reform-minded colleagues, were far from unanimous about the appropriate role of government. There was, of course, considerable expansion of government activity—at the federal level, with the creation of the U.S.

Children's Bureau (whose charge was to investigate and report on all issues regarding child welfare), but largely at the state and the local level, in terms of child labor legislation, compulsory school attendance laws, the establishment of municipal playgrounds, and various educational and health programs.[21] Between 1911 and 1919, forty-one states adopted mothers' pension laws, by which needy and morally "fit" widows (or deserted wives) received payments to enable them to stay home and care for the children. (Significantly, the pensions were quite small and went only to a small percentage of families; funding and administration were purely local matters, and many counties simply ignored the laws.) However limited the mothers' pensions were, they—along with the juvenile court system—provided some of the era's most conspicuous examples of governmental probing into individual life-styles. Some investigators of pension recipients intruded quite deliberately into family lives, searching for evidence of immorality, "unfitness," and even inadequate child-rearing techniques. Juvenile court judges and probation officers candidly inquired not just into specific instances of dependency and delinquency but also into family habits and values.[22]

Yet despite the obvious increase of governmental powers as the twentieth century opened, there was no agreement among child rescue workers as to how far a state or municipality should go to protect children. This was evident in the sharp difference of opinion between, for example, John Gunckel, founder of the Toledo Newsboys' Association, and advocates of laws to bar children from street vending jobs.[23] It was also apparent in the opposition of leading charity workers (such as Edward T. Devine, Josephine Shaw Lowell, Frederick Almy, and Mary Richmond) to mothers' pensions. Devine, editor of *Charities and the Commons* (one of the era's prominent reform journals), urged federal studies of child labor, orphanages, dependent children, illegitimacy, infant mortality, and other child-related problems; yet he and others resisted the pension movement as an attack on both private charity and the family (the latter because it allegedly encouraged husbands to desert their families).[24]

Mixed feelings also existed about the state's responsibility for dependent children. In the late 1800s several types of state systems had developed. Michigan had set a significant precedent in 1874 by establishing a State Public School to which probate courts could temporarily assign children as wards of the state. Governor-appointed county agents were responsible for finding private homes in which to place the children. By 1900 nine other states had adopted modified versions of the Michigan plan. Another program, which Massachusetts set in motion in 1882, provided for the state board of charities to pay private families who boarded neglected and dependent children. In 1910, according to noted child saver Hastings Hart, Massachusetts had pressed "farther than any other state in substituting the family home for the institution."[25] Pennsylvania and New Jersey had by 1900 taken similar steps, although Pennsylvania relied heavily on a private organization (the Children's Aid Society) to find families in which children could live. Meanwhile, Ohio had in 1866 pioneered another approach: a system of county homes to serve, at public expense, as temporary refuges for dependent children.[26]

Although state recognition of the needs of homeless and wayward children generally gratified child savers, it also raised problems. From the outset the institutional approaches of the Michigan and Ohio systems battled sentiments that had grown since at least the 1850s when Charles Loring Brace, founder of the Children's Aid Society of New York, had declared that "public institutions are dull and lifeless." According to one observer in 1897, the county children's homes in Ohio tended to encourage "abnormal institutional growth," and the Michigan system, as some individuals had feared, fell victim to partisan politics. On the other hand, the boarding-out plan failed to gain much public support outside Massachusetts; indeed, in 1912 a legislature-appointed commission in Ohio specifically rejected the Massachusetts idea: "We believe that most institutions are infinitely to be preferred to a loose and careless system of placing children in homes."[27]

In all this confusion, Father Thomas Mulry, president of the Catholic Home Bureau for Dependent Children, spoke for many child savers when he said that it was more and more difficult to answer definitively the question of "how far a State or municipality may interfere in behalf of its wards." Too much interference could slip into paternalism, but insufficient governmental interest could leave needy children without adequate protection. Not surprisingly, given Mulry's own organizational base, he preferred that churches and private organizations, not legislators, should take the initiative.[28]

The remarkable outpouring of voluntary private activity in behalf of dependent children at the turn of the century indicated that Mulry's preference was widely shared. Census statistics demonstrated an impressive growth of Humane Societies, Children's Home Societies, and various organizations that aided needy, neglected, and orphan children. In the 1870s, twenty-two such societies had organized; in the 1880s, thirty-three; in the 1890s, forty-nine; and in the first decade of the twentieth century, seventy-seven. Even these census figures were incomplete, omitting such organizations as the Boy Conservation Bureau of New York and the Toledo Newsboys' Association.[29] The number of institutions for dependent children also rose dramatically.[30] The 1890s may in fact have been more prolific in this respect than any other decade in American history. At least 247 institutions were incorporated during those ten years.[31] In Mississippi, for example, where responsibility for dependent children was purely a local matter and where abominable conditions prevailed in county poorhouses, three church groups established orphanages. By the early 1900s these three institutions, run by the Baptists, Presbyterians, and Methodists, had cared for around four hundred children. And it was in fact the superintendents of two of these asylums who in 1910 appealed to the National Children's Home Society to start adoption services in the state, an appeal that successfully produced Mississippi's first professional adoption agency two years later.[32]

During the first decade of the twentieth century, the number of new institutions declined somewhat, to 214, but this in no sense suggested a diminishing concern for dependent children. The notable jump in the number of home placement societies more than made up for the somewhat slowed momentum of institution building; and, even with the shift toward home placement, the number of new institutions for homeless and wayward children averaged twenty-two per year between 1886 and 1909. In only three of the years during that time (1897, 1901, and 1905) were as few as thirteen institutions established, and the number as late as 1908 was twenty-two. The 1,151 institutions that reported to the Census Bureau in

1910 cared for a variety of dependent children. "Orphans, half-orphans, and foundlings" were admitted into 915 of the institutions; "delinquent, wayward, or truant" children into 129; "other homeless, neglected, or indigent" youths into 561; "newsboys or other working boys and girls" into 30; and "defectives or invalids" into 129.[33]

Such statistics failed to convey how vague distinctions were between dependent, neglected, and delinquent children. As one writer argued, some children who had families were in fact "homeless."[34] According to the National Benevolent Association, which sponsored several regional orphanages, the key to determining dependency was not "whether the child has living parents but whether he has need. . . . A child is an orphan in the truest sense when denied the blessing of . . . sweet pure love." In 1904 the president of the New York Juvenile Asylum argued that classifications of dependency and delinquency were utterly useless: "As a matter of fact, the line between good and bad, between contaminated and contaminating does not run at all on the legal distinction between dependency and delinquency." A youth guilty of a minor crime was technically delinquent, but in fact that label might apply less to him than to a dependent child who had committed no crime but "whose mind [had] become thoroughly polluted" through associations with drunken and immoral people. The dependent child, though not legally delinquent, might actually be "a fountain head of immorality and evil for all of his companions." By 1914 the state of Washington had what one child rescue worker said was "probably as complete a definition of juvenile dependency as is contained in the statutes of any state in the Union"—eighteen categories, some of which were common to the classification of delinquency in other states, and in Washington as well (for example, habitually visiting poolrooms, using liquor or drugs, engaging in immoral or dissolute activities, continually being truant, and wandering the streets late at night). The rationale was that sometimes the use of, say, alcohol reflected less on the child than on unfit guardianship, which in effect made the child dependent. Most child rescue workers probably agreed with the statement that "the best way to deal with delinquent children is closely allied to that of dependent children."[35]

Additional evidence of the tendency to treat delinquency and dependency as aspects of the same problem marked the early history of the juvenile court system, which started in Illinois in 1899 and by 1920 had spread to all but three states.[36] The *Juvenile Court Record*, a monthly journal,[37] regularly featured photographs, articles, and poems about dependent children. "DEPENDENT!" announced the journal as it displayed a large photograph of a pathetic-looking child in the attic of a shabby tenement house. Rhetorically, the editors asked whether it was the child's fault that his father was dead or whether the mother was to blame for having to work to support herself and the tiny boy. The ringing answer leaped at the reader: "It was your fault! Not you personally, but all of us" who allowed inhumane conditions to exist.[38]

One response to the needs of such children came in the form of groups like the Big Brothers and Big Sisters, both of which emerged in the early 1900s. The major premise of these organizations was that needy youngsters benefited enormously from contacts with solid, stable adult citizens.[39] An outgrowth of this view was a "Caddie Camp" in New Hampshire's White Mountains. During the summer months at least from 1912 to 1914, fifty boys from Malden, Massachusetts, some as young as ten and all selected on the basis of financial, physical, and moral need, journeyed to a plush resort. There they slept in tents and served as golf caddies for "successful business and professional men; primarily good types of the 'man of action.'" These men supposedly influenced the youngsters greatly: "The inspiration from such friendship fires the boy with ambition and resolution." The youth might even secure future employment. At the least, because he was paying for his own board and room, he reportedly took pride in knowing that he was no charity case. He also supposedly looked forward to swimming, hiking, and receiving "the coveted permission of playing on the regular links"— presumably walking in the footsteps of his new-found Big Brother and thereby establishing new and challenging goals for himself. Society gained as well. Caddie camps reputedly provided an imaginative answer to "the Summer Problem," when tenement youths poured out of schools and into hot, rowdy city streets.[40]

Such social-control designs in one form or another characterized child saving from its beginnings, as the orphan asylums and

15

reformatories of the early and mid-1800s clearly illustrated. Institutional efforts to inculcate "habits of industry" in young residents was a prominent theme in William P. Letchworth's voluminous study in 1876. Letchworth, commissioner of New York's state board of charities, observed that children in New York's asylums tended to come from families without good work habits. He described approvingly a few of the routines that some of the state's institutions used to make children "methodical, self-reliant and independent."[41]

A number of new homes and organizations that took shape at the turn of the twentieth century continued to make social control a chief objective. Purity Industrial Home in Marionville, Missouri, was a prime example: "Our great curse is impurity," claimed one of its pamphlets. The more than seventy boys and girls who lived there by 1905 pledged themselves to spurn forever whiskey, tobacco, profanity, obscenity, and the idea that males need not be as morally pure as females. Prayers and the reading room, with its literature on temperance and hygiene, provided sources of instruction. So too did "the Industrial Department," which included jobs for girls such as sewing, cooking, and washing; the boys engaged in farming, printing, wood cutting, blacksmithing, and making brooms that sold for thirty cents apiece. The people in this so-called "Industrial Family" wore blue hats with the words "Industrial Home" on the front.[42]

Across the country, in Nashua, New Hampshire, the Reverend G. W. Buzzell sought support for a series of farm homes and trade schools with the same goals as those of the Purity Home in Missouri. In 1900 Buzzell had established an interdenominational organization known as the Good Will Institute to help save the state of New Hampshire from moral disintegration. Evidence of growing social disorder in the Granite State terrified Buzzell, who described with alarm the rapid shift "from Native to Foreign population," from agriculture to industry, from piety to Sabbath-breaking, "from a home making to a home wrecking people" who popularized divorce, and from "Prohibition to License." To counter "the invading army of immigrants" with Christian ideals, Buzzell advocated settlement houses and missionary departments for the poor, as well as compulsory labor laws for "idlers and drinkers." But he also wanted to deal with children's problems through a juvenile court system and institutions that would provide both practical and spiritual instruction. By 1913 Buzzell was actively campaigning throughout New Hampshire to open a farm home for neglected, homeless, and underprivileged boys and girls in the state.[43]

At the very time that Buzzell appealed to New Hampshire citizens for support, Josie Curtiss published a book touting her accomplishments in rescuing children from alcohol, tobacco, and "the virus of unhallowed sexuality." Curtiss, a well-to-do volunteer in child welfare work, recommended the "scientific remaking of citizens," which involved placing needy children in rural homes and recognizing the importance of eugenics. In the early 1900s she had started Curtiss Place in northern Illinois—a "Samaritan home and temporary distribution station for children from darkest Chicago." By 1912 she claimed to have sheltered some four hundred children, whom she had ultimately placed—on a temporary or permanent basis—with rural families. One of her purposes was to provide a moral environment that would produce patriots and socially pure citizens. "We cannot sow pigweed and thistles and raise giant oaks," she argued. At the same time, she hoped to reduce the numbers of "defenseless" children through eugenics: "Every human being has a right to inquire whether primary race instincts of his neighbor are going to put a burden of unjust taxation on him or his home." In her view, social control was thus not only a matter of guaranteeing proper training for children but also of getting responsible taxpayers to scrutinize "the kind, quality and number of children" in their communities.[44]

While few child savers shared Curtiss's fascination with eugenics,[45] in varying degrees they—like Curtiss, Buzzell, and the founders of the Purity Industrial Home—stressed the need to implant values of honor, honesty, industry, and morality in youth. The Hershey Industrial School, which chocolate magnate Milton S. Hershey started for dependent boys in 1909 in rural Pennsylvania, took as one motto, "He is best educated who is most useful." In the orphanage, each boy would learn truthfulness and "habits of economy and industry." To this end, manual and farm training received highest priority. According to Hershey, "We do not plan to turn out a race of professors." One of the school's first pamphlets noted that serious economic crises plagued the nation because "the trades and professions are overcrowded with men seeking employment in urban occupations." This did not bode well for the future: economic depression, labor turmoil, and "more idleness and want" would result. The Hershey orphanage proposed to offer needed alternatives.[46]

At the Wisconsin Home and Farm School, which Marion Ogden helped to establish, the first superintendent's report in late 1903 contained a specific section on "control." The six boys at the farm were reportedly obedient enough, "yet inwardly they fiercely resent[ed] any interference with their untrammeled action as dictated by their own untrained wills." To increase their "respect for law and order" and to "inculcate habits of neatness and industry," the superintendent used several tactics. He had the boys do chores in pairs and rearranged the partnerships weekly in order to discourage "too close chumming." Although he conceded that sometimes he had to hand out punishments for "insubordination," he tried to show the practical benefits of cooperation. He also set up an incentive plan: "Credits for work well and willingly performed" earned privileges, such as time off and the right to ride the newly acquired horse. The boys' progress at the farm had been somewhat slow, but the superintendent reminded the board that it was difficult to counter "habits of their 12 or 14 years of life." A motto that developed at the institution was "Safety First," meaning that "proper influences" would protect the youths from the eroding forces of social change. The hope was also that the farm would produce worthy patriots—like the nine-year-old immigrant child who scaled a thirty-five-foot flagpole in a windstorm to save "the Red, White and Blue" from tearing. [47]

The Wisconsin Home and Farm School's goal of "reclaiming boys"[48] resembled that of "recreating" youths at Allendale Farm. Edward Bradley, like the founders of the Wisconsin institution and numerous other child rescue workers, was committed to instructing needy children about values. He wanted the ideals of labor and service to be as natural as "supreme play" to Allendale's residents.[49]

To this end, Bradley and several other child savers embraced one of the most original and imaginative concepts of the time: the junior republic. Few ideas captured so well the progressives' desire to expand democratic principles and build good citizenship. A junior republic was, in effect, a miniature state in which the young residents governed themselves. They elected leaders, established their own laws and courts, and in some cases based their local economy on their own scrip. The tiny society thus looked like a scaled-down model of the "Big Republic" of the United States. Presumably, by actually participating in the legislative and judicial processes that governed them, the youths would learn firsthand the challenges and responsibilities of conscientious citizenship. And because the economy rewarded those who worked hardest, the citizens would come to respect the virtues of labor and the worth of property.

Most famous of all the junior republics was that of William R. "Daddy" George in upstate New York, but others ranged from the very democratic Ford Republic outside Detroit[50] to the greatly modified version at the Wisconsin Home and Farm School. Daddy George launched his celebrated Freeville Republic in the mid-1890s, shortly before Bradley started Allendale Farm.[51] George, who urged "that the young people of all countries be given a year or more practical experience as citizens or subjects in a village by themselves," was determined to build a network of junior republics across at least the United States. In 1908 his newly formed National Junior Republic Association included miniature commonwealths in Maryland, Connecticut, and California; and he wrote excitedly about the prospects of putting together "a Colony of Pioneers for a new state," probably in western Pennsylvania. "The 'Republic Microbe'" was, George believed, quite contagious. By 1911, after the association had opened the western Pennsylvania republic, as well as one in New Jersey, George optimistically envisioned a republic in every state and territory within five years. Although his original Freeville Republic existed primarily for delinquent boys and girls, George's efforts also benefited dependent youths. One individual claimed that his "own interest in homeless and friendless street boys" began when he heard George deliver a speech. And a New Haven judge was quick to send two fourteen-year-old "homeless and friendless" boys to the Connecticut Republic.[52]

Meanwhile, apart from George's association, other junior republics took shape. There was, for example, the Junior State, located eight miles outside Athens, Georgia. The parent organization was the Atlanta-based Juvenile Protective Association, which grew out

19

of a 1904 investigation of imprisoned children in Georgia. The investigation had unearthed discouraging information: some of the children in jail had committed only minor offenses, such as playing on revolving doors or hunting game on private lands; others had committed no crime at all, including a number who had simply been lost and at least one who was epileptic. The Juvenile Protective Association had incorporated in 1908 in order "to uplift the chanceless child." It endorsed juvenile courts, laws protecting children, and junior republics. Its own "small commonwealth" opened in 1908 as a home, a school, and a self-governing community. Scrip money in the Junior State bore the legend, "Love, Law, Labor, Liberty." Residents received salaries for their work and paid their own board and room, laundry costs, fines, and taxes of ten cents per month. The first junior legislature banned tobacco products, profane language, cruelty to animals, and gossiping about or slandering other citizens. Although the initial residents included only twenty-five white boys, the association contemplated future departments for white girls and for black children. The Junior State opened to considerable fanfare, including plaudits from Atlanta's mayor, Courtland S. Winn, for its "reclamation of wayward children." Daddy George was also pleased because the Georgia people kept consulting him, and two products of his Freeville Republic were assisting the "little colony" in the South.[53]

George was also interested in the system of self-government at Allendale Farm and hoped that Bradley would join the National Junior Republic Association.[54] Bradley, however, had his own plans and by 1909 talked of buying land in southwestern Colorado for "a western Allendale."[55] By then the Lake Villa venture was breaking even financially, had grown to include five cottages for about sixty boys, and had received praise from the noted Cook County Juvenile Court judge, Julian Mack, as "doing the best work for dependent boys that is being done in this country."[56] Bradley was convinced that this success rested largely on the fact that from its beginnings Allendale had been a junior republic with its own mayor, court, police department, and scrip money system. Like George, he enjoyed comparing the early history of his own little commonwealth to that of the United States. The first eighteen Allendale citizens had been "freeholders," establishing residence around "our Plymouth Rock"—the old hickory tree next to the barn. The constant challenge of survival that "we pioneers" faced had provided "great days of peril and adventure."[57] Although Bradley never adopted a motto like that of William George's Freeville Republic—"Nothing Without Labor"—the miniature economy at Allendale did much resemble that of the New York experiment. "Each citizen put in his weekly bill against the community for all work done," as Bradley explained the operation, "and board and clothing were charged against his account. They were likewise fined for infringement of the law. It was a stiff game. It was something of a fight to keep out of pauperism."[58]

The Allendale boys always knew that conduct unbecoming a citizen bore its price, often exacted by a judge and jury of their own peers. Daily court sessions of the boys' judiciary at Allendale handled a gamut of cases running from disagreements to theft and libel. Without doubt, the court was one of the liveliest centers in Allendale's tiny municipality. In a "decoration of character" case, the claimant won damages of five cents for every time his slanderers used an offensive nickname. On another occasion, a boy had to pay fifty cents when found guilty of breach of promise; the court rejected his claim that a bite of apple was sufficient to cover the fee for a mouth organ that he had rented.[59]

An aspect of Allendale Farm that intrigued William George was Bradley's admittance of boys as young as eight. George, whose Freeville Republic accepted only older children, contemplated a set of "junior colonies." He hoped that youngsters could gain instruction in self-government at colonies like Allendale, and then move to Freeville at age seventeen. But Bradley was quite willing to let the younger boys enjoy full citizenship rights at Allendale without waiting for such privileges to come with age. And he was not inclined to use his institution as a training ground for Freeville. Instead, he considered opening Allendale's western branch in Colorado for older youths who had left Lake Villa but who, in Bradley's opinion, still needed a rural alternative to urban life.[60]

Other child savers, such as Julius Wengierski, looked to both Freeville and Allendale as models for their own self-governing experiments. Wengierski, a young lawyer who for a while had directed the Northwestern University setttlement house and had

21

been a probation officer for Chicago's juvenile court, hoped to convert the Winnebago Farm School outside Rockford, Illinois, into a junior commonwealth.[61] Judge Ben Lindsey contemplated duplicating Allendale Farm in the Denver area but worried that he might not find someone of Bradley's talents to run it. In Connecticut, Judge Albert Matthewson of the New Haven City Court told George that he wanted to open a self-governing home for working boys; and in Utah, several individuals proposed a junior republic near Salt Lake City but doubted that they could obtain sufficient financial backing. The Wisconsin Home and Farm School initially adopted a self-government plan—calling it the "Town of Home"—but quickly scaled it down so that, although the boys held regularly scheduled meetings and elected officers, the superintendent controlled the judicial process of fines and punishments. By 1910, however, the directors were considering reinstituting the republic system for the boys who had reached age sixteen.[62]

Besides places that housed dependent and delinquent youths on a permanent basis, a host of other organizations and agencies adopted various forms of the junior republic idea. This was especially true of newsboys' organizations, the most significant of which was in Toledo.[63] But several boys' clubs as well experimented with self-government. The Boys' Brotherhood Republic, incorporated in Chicago in 1914 for boys of fourteen to eighteen, had a constitution that established a miniature municipal government with an elected mayor, city clerk, police chief, city council, and supervisor. The Chicago organization operated a boys' savings bank, looked for lost youths, and ran an employment bureau. In San Francisco, the Columbia Park Boys' Club by 1904 set up a series of summer camps as "The State of Columbia," replete with constitution, president, legislature, standing committees, uniforms, and an official yell: "C-O-L-U-M-B-I-A, HIP, HIP, HOORAY." And in the Pacific Northwest, Washington's Pierce County Juvenile Aid Society sponsored the United States of Tacoma Junior Republic. In this organization, however, the officers were apparently not youths who had taken "a false step"; they were instead "earnest clean cut young Attorneys" and "High School professors" who worked with the youngsters.[64] Although the Tacoma Republic was a far cry from Allendale or— even more—the Ford Republic, it nonetheless attested to the extensive use of the junior republic approach to "reclaiming" disadvantaged children.

Among child savers, however, another idea was even more popular than self-governing institutions: the farm school. Some of these (like Allendale and the Ford Republic) were also miniature republics, but most were not. Ideologically, they were rooted deep in the American past. A fascination with the positive influences of rural life had long characterized national attitudes. During the revolutionary era the ideal of the sturdy yeoman farmer was central to republican thought and left an indelible imprint on the American imagination. In the nineteenth century, founders of asylums quite deliberately sought out bucolic settings conducive to nature's regenerative powers. Child rescue workers increasingly extolled the advantages of getting city youths into the countryside. Examples abounded: the Ohio Reform School, drawing upon the model of the French agricultural colony Mettray, became a State Reform Farm in the 1850s; Charles Collins Townsend, a decade later, founded a short-lived Orphan's Home of Industry outside Iowa City for "poor and friendless" eastern children; and numerous highly publicized "fresh-air" summer camps sprang up in order to place slum children at least briefly amidst brooks and meadows.[65] As counterpoint to the rapidly expanding cities, the idealized memories of a rural nation became ever more important to many citizens. Predictably, many reformers of the progressive era, themselves often rural products who had moved to urban locales, felt strong emotional ties to the environs of their childhood.[66]

By 1912 editor Lyman Beecher Stowe gratefully sensed that "a real movement countryward" had started. He pointed not only to the "Country Life" campaigns, which had secured the endorsement of President Theodore Roosevelt, but also to the growth of university agricultural programs, and to YMCA gardens and "chicken schools" (where young people learned to raise plants and poultry). Joel Foster's Million Egg Farm in New Jersey (on which a city-born man reportedly built the largest egg business in the world and trained "green city youths" to work with his ninety thousand chickens) offered further proof to Stowe. The editor expressed special enthusiasm for the growing popularity of agricultural training "as a means of character development for dependent and lawbreaking city boys." He singled out several examples: Lincoln Agricultural School, which cared for "homeless and worse than homeless New York street boys" on six hundred acres in Westchester County; the New York state reform school near Rochester, which had replaced its rigid military structure with agricultural training; the National Farm School near Philadelphia; the George Junior Republics; and the Good Will Farm in Maine.[67]

There were many other farm-oriented institutions for dependent and wayward youths that Stowe could have mentioned. Several in the Midwest included Allendale Farm, the Wisconsin Home and Farm School, and Lake Farm, outside Kalamazoo, Michigan, designed specifically "for homeless and dependent boys." There was also the Illinois School of Agriculture and Manual Training for Boys, which opened near Chicago in 1887 with "ten dependent boys, picked up on the streets, neglected waifs with nothing to live on," and several years later moved to a 300-acre property in Glenwood, Illinois. Outside Cleveland was the Hudson Boys' Farm, on 300 acres of municipally owned land. In the decade after its opening in 1902, Hudson had reportedly taught 130 boys "the dignity and necessity of good, hard labor" without any suggestion of servitude. Among farms in New York state were the Charlton Industrial Farm School, which started around 1896, and the Berkshire Farm School. The Boston Farm and Trades School and the Kurn Hattin Homes for homeless and neglected boys in Westchester, Vermont, were two New England examples. In North Carlina's Montgomery County the Junior Settlement, founded in the early 1900s, claimed to have taken "Nicotine boys" from city streets and turned them into "Oxygen boys" of the farm who filled "the woods with laughter and song."[68]

Advocates of farm schools argued that a rural social environment, by providing "an atmosphere which is physically healthy, which is morally wholesome and which is socially uplifting," could transform city urchins into vigorous new individuals. When millionaire candy manufacturer Milton Hershey opened his industrial school, he obviously had this ideal in mind. But besides teaching youths to desire and respect rural life, he also wished (in the words of an early publicity pamphlet) "to check urban growth, one of the most ... alarming features of our modern civilization."[69]

Edward Bradley shared all these sentiments. In his opinion, "a normal boy's appetite for primitive conditions" could never find satisfaction in a city like Chicago. An urban setting lacked "legitimate opportunities to build and construct, to chop and gather, sow and range a wide field." With obvious delight, Bradley quoted a letter from a boy soon to join Allendale: "Every morning I wake up I think *one day* less in Chicago."[70]

But Bradley believed that his farm offered more than fresh air, good food, exercise, and sunshine; it also offered the virtues of home and family. When a youth who had been visiting in the city wrote that he was "the happiest kid in Chicago tonight—one that is coming home to Allendale," he offered what Bradley regarded as the highest compliment. To the superintendent, a reunion of former Allendale residents was something special—"a family gathering in the highest sense, a harvest home."[71]

Bradley's celebration of family life—like his sentimentalized version of rural living—bore the stamp of the progressive era. Few if any goals were more compelling to turn-of-the-century America than the preservation of the family ideal.[72] "Home is the nearest earth-point from which one may step into heaven," said a speaker at a huge conference of the National Congress of Mothers, a quintessentially progressive organization. Congressman Morris Sheppard told a thunderous House of Representatives in 1911 that "the touching cadence and the simple majesty of 'Home, Sweet Home'" far surpassed the greatest symphonies. Two years later, as a symbolic gesture of support for the integrity of the home, Congress unanimously and solemnly designated that each year Americans would set aside a special day in honor of mothers.[73]

But beneath these celebrations of motherhood and family—indeed, undoubtedly helping to explain them—was considerable fear. "The good old-fashioned home has absolutely broken down," said a child rescue worker in Boston, articulating what many Americans suspected was a terrible truth. For a variety of reasons the traditional family—intact, close-knit, and affectionate—seemed in trouble. The evidence was all too clear: "the diminution of the birth rate among the highest classes" (as Theodore Roosevelt phrased it); an accelerating divorce rate; growing numbers of women who worked outside the home, entered college, or joined clubs; and

25

parents who appeared unable (or unwilling) to control their children. The disruptive effects of urbanization and immigration had seemingly precipitated a breakdown in morals, turning city tenements into what one reformer described as "a lodging house plus a Baltimore dairy." A speaker at a state welfare conference in 1916 warned that the family, "the foundation on which the very structure of Society rests," was falling victim to "a reign of moral laxity." The corrosive influences of a sensational press, alley gangs, "lurid" moving pictures, and reprehensible literature were nothing compared to the "rank soil" of godless, profane, intemperate, morally degenerate homes. Efforts to save children through playgrounds, boys' clubs, municipal theaters that offered wholesome children's entertainment, and curfew laws were useful up to a point. But if social workers wanted to help youngsters "steer their little barks aright among the shoals and quicksands of the voyage of life," they would have to deal with the heart of the problem: "the lack of righteousness in the home."[74]

Organizers of the Wisconsin Home and Farm School were among many reformers who guessed that American homes were less disciplined and tightly knit then they had previously been. This, they assumed, reflected in major ways "the extraneous influences of modern life" that relentlessly undermined parental responsibility.[75] The evolving family institution was apparently less a gathering place for loved ones than a revolving door through which members occasionally bumped into each other as they headed in different directions. One consequence, according to the directors of the Wisconsin school, was that parents did not supervise their children sufficiently: " 'Young America' has 'Old America' by the nape of the neck and the old fellow may as well croak for mercy, for he is whipped." Some champions of the juvenile court suggested that a breakdown in traditional family authority had created the need for a new system of juvenile justice. This at least was the tacit message of a poem implying that the new court system was a modern equivalent of the old woodshed meeting between parent and child.[76]

By implication, however, the message also seemed to be that reform agencies such as the juvenile court were in fact improvements over the old ways. A photograph of a sobbing youngster in the *Juvenile Court Record* was captioned, "Father has just held a private session of our family juvenile court. As usual, I lost my case." The inference to be drawn, apparently, was that the child could expect fairer treatment at the hands of a sympathetic judge. Ironically, this view facilitated the very trend toward surrogate parents (clubs, schools, societies, and professional elites) that many critics saw as a primary cause of the family's weakened role. Directors of the Wisconsin Home and Farm School, for example, who fretted about what "Young America" was doing to "Old America," stated confidently that they were helping to improve the situation. At the farm, a "hardened youth" who either lacked a family or had only irresponsible parents was changing for the better. Likewise, Edward Bradley proudly contended that the citizens of Allendale were "more selfpossessed and selfdirective" than "the children of the average home."[77]

Certainly, child rescue workers at the turn of the century were convinced that their responses to the needs of dependent children were vast improvements over earlier reforms, particularly over the asylums for disadvantaged and delinquent children that had seemed so promising in the early and mid-1800s. Among progressive child savers a favorite whipping horse was the aging institution that housed dozens of youths under the same roof in congregate, or barracks-style, living conditions.[78] From such emotionally barren and military style buildings, orphans and other helpless children had typically marched in columns and sometimes in uniform to school and church. By the end of the 1800s, the chief complaint against such relics from the past was that their cold, sterile settings denied young residents the close ties of a family circle and, especially, a mother's love.

Nor were such assessments uninformed or incorrect. Although the large congregate institutions had once filled a vacuum in child welfare work and provided thousands of children with shelter that might not otherwise have been available (in half a century, for example, the New York Juvenile Asylum cared for 36,000 youngsters),[79] the physical confinements of the buildings and crowded conditions all too often severely limited what even gentle, well-meaning matrons and superintendents could accomplish.

The Protestant Orphan Asylum of Detroit, founded in 1836 to care for poor, destitute, and orphan children under the age of twelve, illustrated the point. During the mid-1890s, a matron confided to her diary some of the frustrations and fatigue that came with housing more than seventy children. There were nagging discipline problems—when, for example, some of the boys threw mud wads against the fence and building. There were stormy days when all the residents had to stay inside, leaving the matron and her small staff with the large challenge of trying to "divert them" in the best ways possible. There were the difficulties of sending the children to church, school, or public ceremonies. On one hand, this assignment could be a source of pride and joy. During Rally Day in 1894, for instance, the children marched in procession, carrying flags and eliciting praise from bystanders. "I felt glad they appeared well," said the matron. "We all had a delightful time." But the task of getting the children ready for such appearances was staggering. Sunday was "the hardest day of the week." The matron had to "inspect ears, buttons, neckties, caps, shoe strings . . . tell them how I expect them to act at church," and keep track of the special Sunday handkerchiefs: "I have instituted a roll-call of handkerchiefs and am trying to have the children keep them and not destroy so many." Her statement that the children went to church looking "as well as I could make them" conveyed more exhaustion than satisfaction. The day, moreover, was far from ended. All too often, some of the children misbehaved in church; sightseers visited the orphanage in the afternoon; and in the evening interested "ladies and gentlemen" sometimes stopped by to meet the children, give them "scripture cards," and listen to them—in uniform and waving little flags—sing hymns such as "Keep to the Right, Boys." School presented its own challenges: "I shall try to be very careful to have them always early, punctual, regular in attendance, and tidy. Will help them at home with their lessons all I have time to." Then there was the need to satisfy the orphanage's board of directors, treat sick children, deal with runaways, and simply get through the day. In such a setting it was no wonder that children like little Willie ran away several times and, in turn, that Willie's departures "disturbed" the matron because "we already had all we could attend to." And no wonder that the matron closed one diary entry by noting wearily, "We . . . go to our restful white beds."[80]

By the late 1800s such asylums were clearly on the defensive, as reformers virtually declared open season on them. An article, "Where 100,000 Children Wait," in a popular journal in 1908 forcefully summed up the sentiments of reform-minded child rescue workers. "Nineteenth century methods of philanthropy are called sternly to the bar by the twentieth century," the author charged while sadly describing how young "victims of oppressive routine and discipline" still lived in old-fashioned orphanges. Within cold, loveless walls the old-style asylums relentlessly smothered individuality and initiative. Their cheerless inhabitants, sealed off from the outside, could not possibly learn how to survive in the larger society. The institutional child was not only unhappy; he also had within him the makings of "dangerous dynamite. . . . At first, when nobody cares for him, he is only sad. Later, when he cares for nobody, he is unsafe." Even if he were not a potential criminal, he would be a candidate for the almshouse—once a dependent, always a dependent.[81]

Progressive child savers measured success in terms of how far they had moved from such hated institutions. Edward Bradley, for example, contrasted the strong individualism of Allendale Farm's residents with the passivity of youths who lived in large boarding-houses and orphanages. "Laughter," he wrote, "is the supreme affront to the institutional." Whereas typical institutions tended to sacrifice individuality to inflexible routine, Allendale favored "elemental chaos from which to bring to light a man." Its young citizens were anything but meek, polished conformists. A thirteen-year-old resident represented a "splendid type of boyhood" precisely because he was "sturdy, straightforward; lovable; not too good." Old-fashioned asylums might reduce the child to "the deadly trance of a continuous wearing of the medal for good conduct," but Bradley looked "for some hopeful, lifeful signs of naughtiness." And at Allendale, the youths knew how to laugh—while sledding down the lake bank and across the ice, plotting mischievously to call a strike, using wooden swords to chase an imaginary Pancho Villa around the farm, launching the "annual reform wave" in early December to make way for Santa Claus, and simply having "a lot of fun." Joining the boys was none other than the ubiquitous Bradley himself—"Cap," as the youths called him—running a footrace and getting a charley horse, showing Pathé thriller movies on crisp fall evenings, and engaging in snowball fights. When T. H. Bushnell, an attorney who worked with the Cleveland juvenile court system, visited Allendale and remarked that "there is no air of 'institutional' about it," Bradley was assuredly gratified.[82]

Nor was Bradley alone. Daddy George believed that his junior republics were anti-institutional rebuffs to the old asylum system. The Wisconsin Home and Farm School announced, "There is nothing institutional about the place, the home idea being carried out most perfectly." One of the first five boys to reside at the Hershey Industrial School recalled years later that "there was little about the School when I was there to make it appear as an institution." The residents dressed differently, there was never "any semblance of military methods in discipline," and the atmosphere resembled "a not-too-large, family-like home."[83]

In order to establish a family-oriented environment, all of these "anti-institutional institutions"[84] adopted the increasingly popular "cottage-home" system. The young residents lived in small groups rather than in a congregate arrangement. Each cottage had a matron or supervisor. Typically, the children in each group were of different ages, and they shared various chores in the kitchen, laundry, dining room, or yard. According to R. R. Reeder, superintendent of the New York Orphan Asylum and one of the leading advocates of the cottage system, the youths thus learned to cooperate "in the welfare of the home, just as the child serves or should serve in a well-ordered family." A number of institutions, including Reeder's, shifted to the cottage plan at the turn of the century. Among them were the Albany Orphan Asylum, which had provided congregate quarters for some seventy-five years; New York City's Colored Orphan Asylum, founded in 1836; the Philadelphia House of Refuge; the New York Juvenile Asylum; and the reform school at Rochester. Many of the new residences for needy and dependent children that emerged in the late 1800s and early 1900s adopted the cottage format: the Baptist Orphanage in Hopeville, Georgia; the Methodist orphanages in Macon and Atlanta, Georgia; a Presbyterian home in eastern Alabama; Starr Commonwealth in Michigan; Good Will Farm in Maine; the Hershey Industrial Farm, and numerous others.[85]

Edward and Maud Bradley lived at Allendale Farm in a cottage with the younger children. Chores that might have seemed routine carried titles of distinction; "citizens" belonged to the "Pick-up Squad," the "Pantry Squad," the "Dairy Squad," or the "Ancient and Honorable Order of United Scrubbers," for example. At Good Will Farm in Maine, competition between the cottages resulted in friendly rivalries, especially during the annual Thanksgiving gathering when the various groups assembled, giving cottage cheers.[86]

Even though Edward Bradley, G. W. Hinckley of Good Will Farm, Daddy George, and other champions of "anti-institutional institutions" believed that they were replicating the traditional well-ordered family, a major group of child savers had doubts. To this group, no institution could successfully meet the demands of parenthood. The only sensible approach, they believed, was to place dependent children directly in family homes—through indenture, foster care, or adoption. This idea, of course, was not new. During the colonial period it had been common procedure to bind out orphans and strays as domestics or apprentices; in return for their services, the youngsters received food, clothing, and shelter. In the 1850s the New York Children's Aid Society had once again popularized the idea of home placement by sending its famed "orphan trains" full of waifs to farms in the Midwest.[87] By the turn of the century, home placement was an idea whose time had indeed arrived. The National Home Finding Society, which started in 1883 in Illinois and by 1914 included a federation of thirty-two state organizations, was unquestionably one of the largest of the voluntary associations of the era.[88] The home placement concept also received considerable praise at the 1909 White House Conference on Dependent Children.[89]

Much to the irritation of child savers who had ties to institutions, some of the home placement people seemed bent on proving that their methods were the only ones acceptable in an enlightened society. The superintendent of the Children's Home Society of South Dakota pronounced bluntly that orphan asylums were "unnecessary," and his counterpart in New Mexico asserted grandly that with home placement "we have solved the problem of the homeless and dependent child absolutely, scientifically and sympathetically, and by a general principle which can never be improved upon." At a national convention in 1898, one speaker recommended formal abolition of all children's institutions except those for the ill or feebleminded.[90]

Such arrogance infuriated the founders and directors of institutions.[91] For one thing, many "orphanages" housed relatively few orphans, and most directors did try to place these children in foster or adoptive homes.[92] Increasingly, however, institutions provided a refuge for children of unfortunate, sometimes broken, families. At one point in 1904, for instance, the Protestant Orphan Asylum in St. Paul had only two real orphans among some forty residents. Most were children of widowed or abandoned working mothers who could not provide adequate domestic care for their offspring. The St. Paul asylum sought to provide a helping hand until the homes could be reestablished. On at least one occasion, an unexpected union had occurred: a widower and widow, while visiting their children in the institution, had ended up merging into "one happy family."[93]

The boarding of children for small sums of money from family members or friends formed an ever more important aspect of institutional services across the country. It was misleading for critics of asylums to contend that all the residents needed placement in individual homes. For example, William Letchworth found that at one institution in the mid-1890s, only two of 138 children qualified for placement. Relatives or guardians were paying to board some of the youths temporarily; the local superintendent of poor relief had committed other children for a while in an effort to help families to get through difficult financial times; and a few of the youngsters had mental or physical liabilities that made them unacceptable for placement in most families.[94]

Defenders of institutions, however, argued that they in fact helped to save families and were no less committed to that goal than anyone else, including the Home Societies. Such contentions provided further evidence of how powerfully the family ideal gripped the progressive imagination. Indeed, in this context some advocates of institutional care could not resist the temptation to assume the offensive against home placement. One of their central points was that insufficient supervision of adopted or foster children sometimes allowed terrible abuses to occur. In such cases dependent youngsters ended up in "wretched exile," not affectionate homes.[95] Directors of the Wisconsin Home and Farm School seemed anxious to state that they were not "a home-finding society" and implied that their approach was superior to immediate home placement: "When the boy enters our doors, he is at home, and we try to teach him to realize that fact. We want him to leave the home only when he has reached a self-supporting age." Observers should make no mistake: the Farm School was "a HOME in which the HOMELESS boy is given a REAL HOME, by which we aim to make of him a home-loving boy, and in time a man of character."[96]

Despite the inflated rhetoric that defenders of institutions and home placement aimed at each other, an important fact remained: on a day-to-day basis, the different groups often accommodated one another—indeed, depended on one another—in significant ways. As several individuals wisely observed, the institution-versus-placement debate was often exaggerated and misplaced. It dealt with excesses on each side. The idea, for example, that "any home is better than any institution" had grown out of a recognition of failures in the older asylum system—a recognition that progressive child savers of every persuasion shared. Arguments over appropriate means were no doubt divisive, but the realities of child saving nonetheless pushed many groups together. Hence the Protestant Orphan Asylum in St. Paul not only got along with the Children's Home Society of Minnesota but for a while even temporarily boarded children whom the society was trying to place. Likewise, J. P. Dysart, founder of the Wisconsin Home Society, endorsed the Wisconsin Home and Farm School as "rational," "timely," and "in safe hands"; the school happily publicized his endorsement. "Uncle Bert" Hall, a Milwaukee resident who was engaged in virtually every child-saving project in the city, made the connection specific: he served on the executive boards of both the school and the society. So too did the Reverend Judson Titsworth.[97]

In Chicago, as Hastings Hart pointed out, several organizations had offices in the same building: the Illinois Children's Home and Aid Society, Allendale Farm, a Catholic children's aid society, St. Mary's Training School for Boys, and the Illinois Industrial School for Girls (a private institution for dependent girls, which received some public money). According to Hart "there is a very kindly spirit of harmony and cooperation between those different organizations"; indeed, they had reportedly sought offices in the same building so that they might work even more closely together.[98]

Hart had touched upon an important point. Although divisions, disagreements, misunderstandings, suspicions, and heated arguments marked progressive child saving, so too did a strong sense of being part of a large, united movement. Never before, contended Hart, had "people engaged in child-saving work . . . been so close together and understood each other so well." In this context, even disagreements were unifying: they implied that there were common concerns and that people cared about the issues involved. All of this provided a sense of excitement for child rescue workers. It helped to confirm the feeling that at last society really was moving toward a square deal for children. According to Samuel McCune Lindsay, political scientist and director of the New York School of Philanthropy, the progressive discovery of a "new world for children" resembled Christopher Columbus's pathbreaking explorations some 400 years earlier.[99]

Such feelings of accomplishment, of being at the cutting edge of social progress, did more than define the mood of progressive child savers. The sense of optimism, purpose, discovery, and fighting for social justice also provided an emotional buffer as they left the convention halls and plunged into a world of neglect, abuse, poverty, suffering, and tragedy. The George Junior Republic, the Good Will Farm in Maine, the Wisconsin Home and Farm School, the orphanages of the Christian Church's National Benevolent Association, the various state Children's Home Societies, and other turn-of-the-century endeavors on behalf of homeless, neglected, and delinquent youths were the products of substantial commitment and personal sacrifice in the face of formidable odds.

On many fronts, child savers sallied forth in their battles for America's youth. In 1896 John S. Hawley opened an Industrial Farm School near his home town of Charlton, New York, where he could care for up to thirty homeless or wayward boys. He did so after watching in horror as a small boy—perhaps age eight—tried to steal candy from a wagon, slipped, and died under the wheels of a passing truck. According to Hawley, he decided at that point to rescue youths from surroundings that encouraged criminal acts. Two years after the Charlton School opened, Gottlied Germann, a harness-maker in Rock Island, Illinois, discovered an abandoned boy in a woodshed. Germann, already known for helping poor people in the area, established a residence for orphan or neglected children. By 1899, he had not only founded the home, but he and his wife were operating it without salary. When they left Rock Island in 1902, the institution known as Bethany Home was well established and receiving support from a local women's group and other area residents.[100]

South of Rock Island, in Normal, Illinois, Nancy Mason observed with dismay what happened to some of the smaller children who came from the East on the much-publicized "orphan trains." One of the distribution centers was in Normal, and Mason, who was active in the local Methodist church, learned that farm families preferred boarding or adopting older youths who could help with the chores. Tiny children thus sometimes ended up with nowhere to go—except into the temporary care of the local jailer. In 1902 Mason donated a house for the care of retired deaconesses of the church and orphans of preschool age. For years, the Mason Deaconess Home and Baby Fold (later known simply as the Baby Fold) barely survived on the basis of small donations from the Methodist congregation and sympathetic area citizens. Financially strapped, the institution was forced to rely initially on the help of volunteer schoolgirls, paroled patients from state hospitals, and blind and mentally handicapped people. A number of children died (eight in 1913, seven in 1914); most of them were only a few months old and terribly malnourished before coming to the home. The Baby Fold prevailed nonetheless, largely through the efforts of a widow, Tompie Witten Asher— "Mother Asher" to the children—who served as superintendent for twenty-seven years and, at least as late as 1915, received no salary.[101]

Father Peter Joseph Dunne's interest in caring for street boys in St. Louis grew in part out of his own unsatisfying personal acquaintance with life in an orphan asylum. Orphaned at age twelve, Dunne had for two years observed firsthand the situation in a Kansas City orphanage for girls, where two of his sisters stayed and he worked. Later, as an ordained priest serving one of the more fashionable areas in St. Louis, he had befriended a small, dirty newsboy named Jean

Peter Fleming. When Dunne discovered that Fleming was an orphan, lived in a cave, and depended on newspaper sales for his food, he appealed to Archbishop John J. Glennon for permission to care for the "Little Jimmies" of St. Louis. The sympathetic Glennon allowed Dunne to transfer to the city's tenement district and released him entirely from parish duties so that he could work with homeless boys. In early 1906, Dunne—with $65 and three youths, including young Fleming—established his News Boys' Home. Pressure from unfriendly local residents forced several moves, and limited funds threatened the institution from the outset. Still, by 1913 the home had received over 1,300 boys and was then caring for 148—25 full orphans, 84 half-orphans, and 38 neglected or abandoned. "It matters not whether he is 12 years old or 15 or even older," said Dunne; "if he is homeless . . . the doors of the News Boys' Home are opened to him. . . . I have never refused admittance to any boy."[102]

For Dunne's News Boys' Home, the Baby Fold, and many other institutions and organizations, the "pioneer years"—as Bradley described them—were typically full of crises and precarious financial situations. In most instances, however, by the time of America's entry into World War I, these institutions and organizations were moving from their formative periods to new stages in their development. In retrospect, Bradley believed that "a very special Providence" had allowed his junior republic to weather its shaky first years: "Like our great progenitors who dared the wilderness, there is among us the feeling that we are also a peculiar people set apart for particular benefactions."[103] Such words captured well the feeling of perhaps most of his colleagues.

Even though they had won significant battles for dependent children, however, they had not necessarily won the war. In 1900 the superintendent of the South Dakota Children's Home Society had declared, "Society is in a transition state; old things are passing away." Embacing the future, he had urged reformers "to blaze the way for better methods of child-saving,"[104] and child rescue workers had rallied to that cause with zest, imagination, and serious purpose.

But despite notable successes, a problem remained. Society was still in "a transition state," and some of those "old things" that were in jeopardy included valued aspects of the world of the child savers themselves. If the modern world called for experts, what did this portend for volunteers?[105] If an expanding commercial society promised numerous benefits, did it also threaten community values? If the public sphere necessarily had to assume greater responsibilities, what lay ahead for private autonomous organizations aimed at "doing good"? Or what if, as John Gunckel and William George feared, child labor laws cut young people off from work experiences that reputedly molded character and taught entrepreneurial skills? If new theories of child care moved steadily toward classifying youngsters according to types and temperament, what would happen to the perception that basically the roots of dependency and delinquency were the same and were so closely intertwined that it was virtually impossible to separate them? If the future demanded fresh definitions, priorities, directions, and programs, what would be the fate of those goals that Bradley, Ogden, George, Hinckley, and the others had struggled so hard to reach?

"We are very jealous of traditions," wrote Bradley in 1925. "Into our past is wrought a very large element of sentiment of which we are entirely unashamed."[106] The problem was that those traditions and sentiments proved as vulnerable as any others in a rapidly changing society.

• 2 •

"The Child at the Door": E. P. Savage and the Children's Home Society of Minnesota

There's a child outside our door." Such was the news of an anonymous poet who urged readers to open their doors and admit the "little wandering waif."[1] This advice summed up the underlying sentiment of home placement, one of the major trends in child rescue work at the turn of the century. Home placement attracted considerable popular attention, enjoyed a favored position at the 1909 White House Conference on Dependent Chilren, and inspired a host of organizations that were dedicated to finding families for orphans and neglected children. Especially important in this context were the Children's Home Societies, which started in Illinois in the mid-1880s and by 1908 included organizations in twenty-nine states.[2]

A pivotal figure within the Home Society movement was Edward P. Savage. In Minnesota he founded, and directed for almost twenty years, one of the oldest and most influential of the state organizations. He unquestionably agreed with a Pennsylvania colleague who announced happily in 1906 that "the home-finding idea has won. . . . [It] is the new, modern scientific and true solution of the child problem," firmly shoving "to the lumber chamber of effete social furniture the old institutional methods."[3] Yet Savage's own bitter-sweet experiences showed that, however joyful the work of home placement, it was far more difficult than the popular conception of bringing together homeless children and childless homes suggested. And changing perceptions of what was new, modern, and scientific ultimately helped to relegate Savage himself to the growing heap of outdated "social furniture." Still, at least for a while, he was in the vanguard of the drive to place dependent children directly in family environments.

While Savage and founders of the Children's Home Societies in other states sought to substitute family for institutional settings, the strategy did not originate with them. As early as the 1850s, Charles Loring Brace had pointed the way. Brace, a deeply religious man who early in life declared his intention of helping disadvantaged people, created the New York Children's Aid Society in 1853. Over the next four decades alone, the Society's famed "orphan trains" took some 25,000 youngsters out of the city to rural areas, mostly in the Midwest. Other organizations—such as the New England Home for Little Wanderers in Boston and aid societies in Baltimore, Buffalo, and elsewhere—adopted Brace's techniques and sent thousands of additional youths westward. Although these eastern organizations stirred criticism that they were dumping criminally minded youths in western states, and although the checks against exploitation of the young emigrants in their new "homes" were terribly inadequate, this method of child-placing became increasingly popular.[4] The well-known progressive journalist Jacob Riis was among reformers who extolled the Children's Aid Society. In a highly sentimental account, he described how an agent took into the countryside a "little troop" of children, each "comfortably and neatly dressed in a new suit" and carrying a Bible. "Big-hearted farmers" came from miles away to choose a child. If there were weaknesses in such a system, Riis downplayed them: "Night falls upon a joyous band returning home over the quiet country roads, the little stranger snugly stowed among his new friends, one of them already, with home and life before him."[5]

Ironically, Martin Van Buren Van Arsdale, who started the Home Society movement in 1883 in Illinois, was apparently unaware of Brace's work when he began his own efforts at placement. While attending Hanover College in his home state of Indiana, he conducted Sunday School at a county poorhouse. Among the children was a small girl who begged him not to leave. At this time he pledged that "if time is given me, I will with God helping, deliver children forever from such places." Following his graduation from Hanover and military service in the Civil War he moved to Chicago, where he completed a theology degree and organized a newsboys' home. From 1868 until 1882 he held six pastorates in Indiana and Illinois before leaving the ministry in order to keep his earlier vow to help needy children. When he asked Dwight Lyman Moody for advice, the famed evangelist suggested that he get someone to give him $10,000 to build an orphans' asylum. Such advice only disappointed Van Arsdale, who had no access to that amount of money. Moreover, he favored placing youthful dependents in private homes because, in his words, "The Bible tells us that God setteth the solitary in families." He thus started what was initially a lonely enterprise, trying to gain support for the placement of homeless children. At one point, after his appeal to one congregation received only silence in response, he returned to his hotel "almost sorry that I had been born." The family into which he first placed orphans was, consequently, his own. As his spouse remembered, "I did all my own work, washed and cared for the children. When I heard a carriage drive up at night I knew there were children coming."[6]

Finally, in 1885, after months in which Van Arsdale sometimes peddled a patent window fastener door to door in order to finance his travels in quest of orphans and homes for them, he returned to Chicago and took out a state charter for the American Educational Aid Society. Several years later he changed the name to the Children's Home Society. From the beginning, Van Arsdale hoped to establish a national organization with branches in every state. His first effort to enlarge the society failed, however, when the board of directors in Missouri formed an independent association and rejected home placement in favor of the traditional asylum. Van Arsdale had better luck in Iowa. He succeeded in forming the second state Home Society there in 1888; in the process, by winning over Edward P. Savage, he planted the seed for the Minnesota organization as well.[7]

Savage was born in 1844 in Bristol, Connecticut, to a Baptist preacher's family. In the late 1850s the family moved to Joliet, Illinois, where they were living at the outbreak of the Civil War. Savage, at the age of eighteen, joined the 100th regiment of Illinois volunteers and plunged into battle. He was taken prisoner in November 1862, after injuring his foot and falling behind his unit. During an agonizing three-day march to a Confederate prison, he almost died; then, shortly before his pardon, he received a death sentence for allegedly being a Union spy. Despite these close calls, he survived the war, returned to the Midwest, graduated from the old University of Chicago in 1868, and held Baptist pastorates in Wisconsin, Illinois, and Iowa. In 1870 he married and started raising a family that eventually included two sons and two daughters.[8]

He was preaching in Clinton, Iowa, in 1886 when Van Arsdale stopped in town to publicize the Home Society idea. As Savage recalled, Van Arsdale's speech was profoundly moving: "His methods were so sensible, so natural, so in accordance with the divine plan that it took hold of my conviction as the true way to care for homeless children."[9] Savage likened Van Arsdale's efforts to those of a pioneer, trying "to blaze his way through an almost untrodden wilderness; that is, no one had done anything just like it before." In Savage's opinion, Charles Loring Brace had simply "brought the little street urchins out in car loads and distributed them to the farmers who took them largely for help"; Van Arsdale, on the other hand, was the first who "ever started out with the one great thought burning in his soul, 'there is a home in a good family for every homeless child, and woe be to me if I do not find it.'"[10] In the late 1880s, Savage accepted a pastorate in St. Paul, but he continued to think about what he had heard in Clinton. "The thought of saving homeless little ones had taken complete possession of me," he remembered.[11] In the spring of 1889, after visiting Van Arsdale in Chicago, he initiated efforts to set up a Home Society in Minnesota.[12]

On September 11, 1889, following several months of preliminary work, a small group of people, including Savage and Van Arsdale, convened in the Minneapolis YMCA building to launch the new organization. Savage emerged as superintendent; heading the board was the president of the University of Minnesota, Dr. Cyrus Northrup. A critical decision concerned the group's relationship to Van Arsdale's society. At first, Savage and others in Minnesota strongly considered independent status. Ultimately, however, the choice was to join Van Arsdale, partly to avoid repeating the mistakes that had marked the failed attempt to form a maverick group in Missouri. Also decisive was Van Arsdale's argument that Minnesota's membership would inspire other states to climb aboard.[13]

State Home Societies did proliferate, in part because of the Minnesota organization. J. P. Dysart, who initially worked with Savage, eventually formed a Home Society in Wisconsin; and Savage was instrumental in establishing agencies in the Dakotas. By May 31, 1900, seven years after Van Arsdale's death, the efforts of people like Savage had extended Home Society organizations into twenty-one states. These organizations had, since the start of the first society, cared for almost 25,000 children. In a twelve-month period at the turn of the century, the combined societies received 1,828 new children for placement. The Minnesota group, which claimed 139 of that number, was particularly active, trailing only Illinois (255), Missouri (209), Iowa (150), and Wisconsin (140). Together, the various Children's Home Societies resembled a loose federation, with the state offices enjoying complete autonomy. Only a shared name, a national office, voluntary cooperation, and an annual national conference tied the organizations together. [14]

In this respect, the Home Society movement resembled a larger trend during the progressive reform era: the attempt to find a middle ground between localism and national control—to arrive at uniform standards across the country without sacrificing to nationally centralized authority the perceived benefits of a state-centered system. W. B. Sherrard, superintendent of the South Dakota Children's Home Society, spoke directly on this subject. He emphasized that varying local conditions made clear the need for states' rights. Yet he was optimistic that individual Home Societies, through national conferences and cooperative efforts, could nudge one another to the point where "state superintendents would see eye to eye."[15] Savage undoubtedly agreed. At first he had preferred stronger national ties, but during the 1890s he had watched in dismay as politics turned the central Chicago office into "a storm center." By the early 1900s Savage was grateful that the turbulence of national organizational politics had (largely through the able work of Hastings H. Hart in Chicago) become only "a painful memory."[16] By then, also, Savage's own state society enjoyed somewhat firmer legal footing than it had during its first decade.

As was generally true elsewhere, Minnesota's laws regarding dependent and neglected children developed piecemeal. Indeed, as late as 1917 the state still had not established firm standards of home placement, although the situation had improved. The move toward even minimal state responsibility for needy children had not really started until the last two decades of the nineteenth century, the time when the Home Society was taking shape. To that point, except for the establishment of a Soldiers' Orphans' Home (which was limited to the offspring of soldiers who had died during the Civil War), the state had assumed that several church-sponsored private orphanages could deal with Minnesota's dependent children. E. P. Savage's Home Society was approaching its fifth year before the legislature, in 1893, officially provided it with legal status. Under the new law the society reported to the state board of corrections and charities (itself having been established only in 1883, when the state first intimated that the care of dependent children was not purely a local matter). Despite the enhanced status that the Home Society derived from the 1893 statute "relating to the Societies organized for the purpose of securing homes for orphans," Savage quickly recognized the law's limitations. A key liability was that the statute granted private, certified organizations the power to place in family homes only children younger than two years. For this reason, in 1897 the Home Society reincorporated under an 1866 act for orphan asylums, which meant that the organization could gain custody of orphaned, abandoned, or neglected children to age twenty-one. Only in 1899, when the legislature amended the 1893 law by giving placement societies legal guardianship of children up to age ten, did the society revert to its original form of incorporation. Ironically, for several years the society thus took advantage of the legislation that had originally given life to the asylum system, which was anathema to Savage and his colleagues.[17]

The placement process itself also moved along confusing routes, largely because of a lack of a clear direction from the state government. One alternative—indenture—harked back to the Elizabethan poor laws. It had dominated colonial policies concerning children and defined Minnesota's first response to the needs of young dependents. According to state law in 1864, indentured youths were supposed to receive an education and some remuneration, and they were not to suffer cruel treatment or neglect. Supporters of indenture had long argued that it was inexpensive and that it trained children in the virtues of thrift and hard work. In fact, of course, it was difficult to guard against exploitation of "apprentices." An alternative to indenture was for the Home Society to find free foster homes, in which families (without payment from outside sources) agreed to care for children. A third possibility was for the Society to seek an adoptive family for a dependent child. Sometimes, adoption grew out of a foster placement.[18] Printed records of the society dealt only with the numbers of children "placed," "returned," and "replaced" and thus did not specify whether indenture, or free homes, or adoption were involved. Apparently indenture was not uncommon in the early years, but the main approach as late as 1920 was free home placement. Adoption may have involved less than one-fourth of the children whom the society placed.[19]

In the society's view, the critical goal was placement itself. The aim was to find a deserving, worthy family for a dependent child—on whatever basis was possible. For some reason, however, the Minnesota organization did not design an application blank, requiring references and information about income and occupation, until 1895.[20] Perhaps Savage was lackadaisical in this respect because of his emphasis on personal contacts during the society's first years. Not only did he himself travel throughout the state—building a support network, checking homes, and personally placing children—but he also leaned heavily on local advisory boards composed of ministers and other church activists. Savage's clerical background may have predisposed him to rely on such sources. South Dakota's W. B. Sherrard revealed this tendency; despite his disclaimer that "we are not reflecting in any way on those not identified with churches," Sherrard pointed to "a recognized fact . . . that the churches form a social center for a larger percentage of our best people."[21]

The problem as Home Society leaders saw it was less to obtain information about children and families than it was to secure legislation that facilitated home placement. Laws were invariably vague and inadequate. Typically, in 1900 the national group resolved to seek legislation that would "strengthen the hands of our workers in the various states." Yet at the same time, Home Society advocates did not want public officials moving too far into the field of home placement. Sherrard, with whom Savage worked closely to establish the South Dakota agency, warned against state management of home-finding work. The great strength of private charity, he argued, was that it was independent of politics: human interests, not political favoritism, dominated. Government action must not supplant voluntarism, which appealed to neighborhood cooperation and offered "the privilege of giving."[22]

By the early twentieth century, although the legal position of most of the Home Societies was still somewhat tentative, the public climate was increasingly hospitable to home placement. "Our method has won a complete victory in ten short years," proclaimed one enthusiast. "There never was any logic in the institutional care of placeable waifs."[23] Other ringing endorsements prevailed in a host of conferences and publications—including a melodramatic book written in 1899 by one of Savage's own recruits, J. P. Dysart.

Dysart had been a Presbyterian preacher in St. Paul when Savage approached him to help organize the Minnesota Children's Home Society. Although Dysart was in his late forties, he had already decided to abandon the pulpit for child saving. For two years he worked with Savage in Minnesota, primarily as financial secretary and the organization's agent in the Twin Cities. But in 1891 he shifted his attention to Wisconsin, then without any organized child-placing system. Laboring entirely on his own and without financial support for several months, he placed forty children in family homes. Well aware that the expanding job required more than one person, he formed the Children's Home Society of Wisconsin, which he supervised until his retirement in 1922, due to failing health at age eighty-one.[24]

Dysart wrote his book on homeless children, *Grace Porter: A Jewel Lost and Found*,[25] at the end of his first decade of work for the Minnesota and Wisconsin organizations. Indeed, one appreciative reviewer said that "the story could never have been told by any person who had not been through the field of practical work."[26] Although the characters and general circumstances in the narrative were true, Dysart took considerable license, embellishing his account with emotional scenes. The philosophy informing the volume came, he contended, from no one less than God. But if the ideas were God's, the prose was surely Dysart's. ("Breakfast over, the family carriage is at the door." "Let us honor the 'little red school-house' and keep our 'bonnie flag' waving over it." "She holds Grace in her arms. The heaving of her bosom shows Ruth that she is swayed by a tempest of emotion." "Their wee hearts are starved. . . ." "The whole audience was melted into tears.")[27]

A progressive reform perspective suffused the book. *Grace Porter* bubbled with optimism about education and the value of nonpartisan experts; celebrated new philanthropic ventures that used "rational methods," practical efficiency, and humanitarianism; endorsed rural village values as antidotes to urban malaise and chaos; assumed that the public interest would prevail over petty, selfish concerns; railed against liquor as the source of myriad social evils; viewed the working class with a combination of nervous sympathy and condescension; and expressed fierce loyalty to the family as the bedrock of society. Dysart's book served mainly as an attack on "institutionalism" and a declaration of "social revolution" aimed at allowing children to "enjoy the blessings of home-life."[28]

The central characters were a midwestern family, the Porters: Pauline, the mother, "an intelligent, noble, cultured, Christian woman"; David, the father, a university graduate and farmer who, according to his spouse, had a heart that would "bleed at the sight of even a bird with a broken wing"; and Grace, their adopted child. One delighted reviewer, noting that little Grace was "a transforming genius for a household, a community, a state," believed the book "ought, like Uncle Tom's Cabin, to be the creator of an epoch."[9] That epoch, if Dysart had his way, would be about "our great deliverance" from "the blight and burden of 'institutionalism.'" Time and again, he had his seemingly flawless protagonists inveigh against emotionally cold, loveless, repressive institutions as they celebrated the beauties of home placement. While conceding that a small percentage of children—"the feeble-minded, the badly crippled, and a few (very few) who are terribly criminal"—would have to live in institutions, David Porter envisioned a time when most children would "never see the inside of an institution."[30] The social impact of the book was impossible to measure, but perhaps the Reverend Judson Titsworth, a founder of the Boys' Busy Life Club and the Wisconsin Home and Farm School and a board member of the Wisconsin Children's Home Society, was not the only reader who "cried over its pathos, laughed at its fun and nodded . . . in approval of its philosophy."[31]

Edward P. Savage may nonetheless have read the book with mixed emotions. Certainly he respected Dysart immensely and appreciated the zeal with which his friend articulated the virtues of home placement.[32] Yet he may have had trouble recognizing in Dysart's flowery prose some of the realities of homefinding that marked Savage's own experiences. Dysart's effusive account presented the idealistic backdrop against which the actual organizing of Home Societies took place, but Savage had encountered unpleasant circumstances, grinding schedules, and discouragements about which *Grace Porter* gave no hint. "We do not exactly sail to heaven on flowery beds of ease, in our work for the children," the Minnesota superintendent once said in what was a marvelous understatement.[33]

Savage's responsibilities were staggering, especially in the early years. With only one assistant he covered Minnesota's 84,000 square miles, gathering and delivering children, raising funds, checking on earlier placements, publicizing the society, appearing in court for cases involving neglected children, and editing the *Minnesota Children's Home Finder*, which started as a bimonthly publication in 1899. For a while he also carried the society's work into the Dakotas.[34] At the end of 1903, a weary and discouraged Savage pleaded that "there is a limit to human endurance." In his opinion none of the other state societies had cared for as many children with so few trained fund raisers. "Night and day I have toiled for this work," he wrote. "I planned the methods, wrote the literature that gave the society a legal status in the state, prosecuted the establishment of an efficient service organization extending to all parts of the state." If he had not accomplished enough, or had made mistakes, at least no one could blame his intentions or accuse him of failure to try.[35]

Competing sentiments of love and fear helped Savage deal with the disappointments and sheer drudgery of his work. His commitment to Christian benevolence and his concern about social disorder found expression in two quotations that appeared in each issue of the *Home Finder*. One was the scriptural injunction, "It is not the will of our Father which is in Heaven that one of these little ones should perish." The other was from the French novelist Victor Hugo: "All vagabondage has its origin in neglected childhood."

Hugo's statement raised the specter of crime as a consequence of public apathy toward injustice and suffering. The threat of social breakdown was clearly much on Savage's mind—and the minds of most reformers—as the twentieth century approached. The Minnesota superintendent worried considerably during the economic turbulence of the 1890s about children who were learning to be "beggars and waifs of the street." "I am not a prophet and cannot tell what the future has in store for our strangely disordered country," Savage wrote in 1895. "It is passing through a period in which all previous standards of value have been destroyed and no one can tell where this turmoil and upheaval will end."

There were some encouraging signs nonetheless. Frederick Wines, the nationally known prison reformer, said that Minnesota was one of the few states where crime had actually decreased. "I attribute this largely," Wines added, "to the excellent care that you have taken of your dependent children," especially through home placement work. To Savage, the message was clear: "Does any-one dream that if all the children had been reared in Christian households with reverence for God and respect for constituted authority, that this reign of lawlessness and anarchy would have been possible?"[36]

Certainly Savage saw enough evidence of social malaise. He continually dealt with a world of pain, grief, suffering, abuse—of "sorrow and sin and want," as he described it. One of his cases involved a young girl so badly neglected that "vermin had eaten through the skin and flesh to the skull in places." In another instance a woman drove her spouse from home with an axe and then allowed the three children, covered with sores, to roam the streets. There was also the time when three motherless youngsters found their father, who had been missing for several weeks; he was in jail, and as Savage sadly watched, they tearfully bade their parent farewell. "It was a scene that the writer will never forget," said Savage. On another occasion a woman brought a three-month-old baby to the superintendent's office. The father had just killed his

wife, two of his in-laws, and then himself, leaving the baby cold and crying on the bed until the woman discovered what had happened.[37]

These were pathetic examples of irresponsibility and perhaps insanity, but sometimes even love produced tragedy. Such was the case when parents gave up their children out of affection, hoping that the youngsters would elsewhere receive opportunities unavailable in their own natural families.One abandoned woman, who was in the poorhouse following unsuccessful attempts to wash clothes for a living, turned her two daughters over to Savage and pleaded with him to find someone who could care for them. As the superintendent took the two girls from their weeping mother, he felt the "deepest sympathy" for her.[38]

Sometimes the work could be harrowing as well as sad. Once when Savage tried to rescue two terribly mistreated children, their drunken father drove him away, warning him not to come back. On another occasion, a mother who had been in jail threatened to shoot Savage for taking her child.[39]

After the society had succeeded in rescuing children, it still faced the often arduous task of finding temporary or permanent homes for them. Again and again Savage tried to arouse public concern for "the homeless little ones." Once, as he prepared his regular report to the board, he seemed to forget that he was not writing for public consumption and lapsed into a plea for help: "Dear friend," he asked, "might you open your home to one of these needy little ones?" He wondered plaintively, "Who will care for the baby boys and girls and the older ones now helpless and homeless?"[40] These were distressing questions for a man who firmly believed that somewhere there was "a good family for every homeless child."[41]

When the society did find homes for children, there could still be misfortunes. More than once Savage had to separate siblings despite his efforts to keep them together. Sometimes a new family sent back the child it had received. One man and woman returned a youth because he engaged in "self abuse"; they were willing to take him again if some hospital could cure him of "the disgusting habit." After three months with a little girl from the society, one woman wrote, "I do not wish to keep her." Another family concluded, "He is not the boy we want." Some people were shocked when the

children they received were "sickly" or "frail"; at least once the child died shortly after joining its new parents.[42]

In some instances Savage himself wavered regarding the suitability of placement. This was particularly the case with illegitimate children whom mothers wished to give up. Savage had little difficulty responding favorably when the young mothers were too poor to give their babies adequate care; organizations that refused to place illegitimate children were, from his viewpoint, guilty of "positive inhumanity." But when unwed mothers seemed anxious mainly about their own disgrace, Savage hesitated. He did not want the society to facilitate vice, or to help immoral people "hide the consequences of sin." The dilemma was real, and Savage finally looked to the board of directors for suggestions: "What shall we do?"[43]

Despite such problems, Savage found evidence that he was doing "a blessed work." Once, for example, he took a group of children around the state and successfully placed all but one; "Johnny, I'm afraid, is always left," the superintendent noted sadly. But when Savage showed Johnny to a church congregation in St. Paul, a little girl asked her mother, "Why can't we take that little boy?" The story had a happy ending. Johnny ended up with a loving family, graduated from college, and became a college professor.[44]

Savage's assistants sometimes had equally satisfying experiences. Ellen Thompson, who worked in child placement for several years, laughingly described her reputation among children in southern Minnesota as "the Stork." One little boy who wanted a sister looked at some of the pamphlets that Thompson had left for his parents and said joyfully, "Now we can have a baby, for here is a baby catalog." A. H. Tebbets, who started placing children for the society in 1900, said that whenever he began to have doubts about the "chosen work of child saving," events invariably reassured him. For example, a responsible and happy adult who years earlier, as an orphan, had received help might stop by the office; or a letter might arrive reporting the success of a former ward of the society.[45]

There were traces of martyrdom in all this—perhaps understandably, given social priorities in which corporations thrived while organizations such as the Home Society went begging for funds. Savage believed that the society gave something more important to

nation than the great riches of manufacturing and commerce: "a
andard of life and service" that had found expression at Valley
orge and in Civil War battlefields. Against such examples of dedication, U.S. Steel's millions of dollars paled. But for some reason the
Home Society labored in relative obscurity, struggling "humbly,
modestly, without clamor and display," depending on individuals to
sacrifice themselves for "helpless little creatures." According to one
of Savage's assistants, humanitarian causes required a "consecrated
personality . . . less sordid, less selfish, giving as God gives." Savage
agreed: "I am persuaded that we who are in the work have not
placed as high an estimate upon the worth of it as we ought."[46]

For Savage, it was not enough merely to place children in homes.
He turned his attention as well to the problems of child desertion.
Nearly one-third of some six hundred children who came to the
Home Society in its first five years were victims of desertion. At the
request of the National Conference of Charities and Correction in
1894, Savage prepared a paper on the topic. Over the next year,
amidst his regular duties, he sent out questionnaires to institutions
in every state and in Canada. In his subsequent report he declared
that the number of deserted children in the United States was at
least 60,000, and perhaps more than 200,000. Nine of thirty states
for which he received information had no laws against desertion,
and in states where such statutes existed, the penalties were minimal and often ignored. In light of such information, Savage urged
legislatures and law enforcement officials to act forcefully to halt
this "gigantic evil."[47] He later pointed with pride to the fact that he
had been a moving force in Minnesota behind legislation that for a
while made desertion a felony, not just a misdemeanor.[48]

To help end desertion, he favored not only harsher laws but also
the "institution of boards of examination for the procuring of a
license to marry." Why not, he asked, examine the candidates for
marriage just as candidates are interviewed for the ministry or
medical practice? Careful attention to physical, mental, and moral
qualifications might help to ensure happier marital unions. Savage
even saw the teaching of "domestic science" to girls as a partial
remedy. He favored a practical school curriculum—manual training
for boys and home economics for girls—not only as a way to
diminish pauperism and crime but also as an aid to happy marriages.

Men sometimes turned to drink, according to Savage, as an es
from "insufferable" households: "When I have gone into
wretched dens kept by . . . slovenly wives; when I have seen
abominable stuff that they prepare for food; I have not wonder
that men fled to the saloon for some relief."[49]

It was, however, the subject of nursing babies that inspired some
of Savage's most vigorous action. Here was the grimmest aspect
of child rescue work for the superintendent. In a moving appeal to
the state legislature, he described the horror of observing infants
lying in cribs—"the pale, colorless lips," skin that seemed "to be
drawn tightly over the skull," tiny hands resembling "bird claws,"
shrunken limbs that were "mere bones," and "little ribs that stand
out."[50] Savage had no trouble isolating the major cause of such
tragedy: 80 percent of the babies died who had not been nursed
during the first thirty days or so of life. To guard against this, the
Home Society refused to take a child under the age of one month
while its mother was physically able to nurse it.

The problem was that some destitute mothers received unfortunate advice—namely, that they should not nurse their babies
because it would then be harder to give up the infants. People who
offered such advice were no less than "baby killers" from Savage's
viewpoint, and he proposed a law that would make it a misdemeanor punishable by a fine up to $50 for any person outside the
family to induce a physically fit mother not to nurse her child
during at least its first month. In 1907 Byron H. Timberlake, a
Republican serving his first term, introduced Savage's bill in the
Minnesota legislature.[51]

To Savage's chagrin, the legislature responded to the introduction
of H.F. 362 with laughter and jeered that it was a "wet nurse bill."
One representative derisively suggested that the House should refer
the bill to its author rather than a committee. Responding to such
ridicule, Savage asked, "Has it come to this, that a laugh counts for
more than a life?" The superintendent labored mightily to marshall
support for his cause. He delivered impassioned addresses to the
legislature and to various groups, such as the local Women's Federation. There were, he argued, compelling economic and moral reasons for such a law. He thought it strange that the state encouraged
immigrants to move to Minnesota but ignored its babies—who were

in fact "little immigrants," representing future economic growth, and who did not need to shed foreign customs.[52] The superintendent perhaps used such arguments on the assumption that only matters of dollars and cents moved legislators.

It was with the moral argument that he seemed more comfortable. Writing to Theodore Roosevelt for help, he asserted that the bill would call public attention "to a very great and growing evil," the tendency for mothers intent on social pleasures to refuse to nurse their children. The symbolic implications of the proposed law were from this perspecive very significant. As a statement that Savage cosigned made clear, "the moral effect of such a law *even if no prosecution should take place* would be very beneficial, as it lifts a legal standard where none has existed before."[54]

Ultimately, the issue involved what Savage described as the "God-given rights" of the child, "the sovereign right of the child to the food that God provided for it." What sense, he wondered, was it to have antiabortion laws protecting unborn babies if society subsequently ignored them after their births? One thing was certain: he did not want to accept children for care who had not been nursed during their first month, because to do so could make him nothing less than an "accessory to . . . murder." Hoping to stop "the slaughter of the innocents," he pleaded with the legislature "to wrap about these helpless little ones the shield of the State."[54] He stressed that H.F. 362 would not require any mother to nurse her child. It would simply instruct those outside the immediate family, "Hands off, let that poor mother nurse her baby if she wants to."[55] In early 1907 the House passed the bill by a vote of 71 to 24. By the end of the session, however, it died without a vote in the Minnesota Senate.

Savage's "wet nurse" bill failed, but at least the ideal of home placement—to which he had by then dedicated almost twenty years of his life—had found a large and growing audience. One of the clearest signs was the famed "Child Rescue Campaign" of the *Delineator* magazine from 1907 to 1910. In October 1907, the *Delineator*, a popular journal under the editorship of Theodore Dreiser, published an emotional essay, "The Child without a Home," which focused on the plight of dependent children and criticized orphanages for not supplying the crucial element in a child's life—love. A matching essay, "The Home without a Child," appeared in the next issue, along with an announcement that the magazine was launching a major campaign to bring homeless children and childless homes together.[56]

For the next several years the "Child Rescue Department" was a regular feature in the magazine. It included photographs and brief sketches of dependent boys and girls in need of homes. "The Delineator family this month receives an addition of four little ones," the January 1907 issue announced. "Allow us to introduce you to Marion and James from Washington, D.C., Janet from New York, and Ernest from Newark, N.J." While the campaign sought homes for children, it included as well a series of attacks on the "machine charity" of orphan asylums. Mabel Potter Daggett's "Where 100,000 Children Wait" was a devastating critique of orphanage life, replete with photographs and pathetic-looking children who lived in institutions.[57]

The journal's avowed goal of convincing the public to restrict "institutionalism in favor of the home-placing movement" was a major boon to the Home Societies. South Dakota's W. B. Sherrard, who in Savage's opinion was "a true child-saver," praised the magazine for publicizing "the good results of the child-placing movement." Such support would, in Sherrard's opinion, make child-placing "the best movement for the uplift of humanity the world has ever seen." The *Delineator* also provided the president of the National Children's Home Society with an opportunity to discuss the contributions and history of his organization, from the initial labors of Van Arsdale to the founding of the various state societies. In November 1908 the magazine criticized states that had not yet established home-finding associations. Two months later, the prestigious White House Conference on Dependent Children endorsed home placement as "the best substitute for the natural home."[58]

While Savage surely applauded the favorable publicity that the movement was enjoying, he may have had some reservations. What if the public concluded that finding homes for children was easy? Readers of the *Delineator*'s articles, editorials, and monthly profiles of dependent children could easily get such an impression, just as they could from Dysart's earlier tale, *Grace Porter*. Savage had simply traveled too many weary miles with groups of children, trying to place them with families, and he had seen too many youngsters return to the society following their placement to believe that finding homes was effortless. Moreover, from the beginning of his work, Savage had observed a growing problem about which *Delineator*-style campaigns said nothing: the need to provide suitable temporary quarters for children while they awaited placement.

Initially, the Savages kept some children in their own home for as long as several weeks, and the society paid the Protestant Orphan Asylum of St. Paul to care for the older youngsters on a temporary basis. A more serious puzzle was where to keep the growing number of babies, because few existing institutions were prepared to deal with them. Until the late 1890s the society boarded many of the infants at $2.00 per week in private homes in the Twin Cities. The disadvantages of such a policy were numerous. It was difficult to find homes for this purpose; it was terribly inconvenient for a family interested in adopting a child to travel around the area visiting houses in which children were staying; and it was hard to check on the quality of the care the children received. Savage knew that the care was not always adequate; indeed, he suspected that several deaths had resulted from improper treatment. When several infants were placed together in a home, the death of one sometimes led to the demise of others; in fairness, however, he admitted that some of the children were not in good condition when they were taken to their temporary homes. The truth was that "nearly the only recommendation of the plan was its cheapness."[59]

Finally, in late 1897, the society designated one Minneapolis residence—in which some children had already stayed—as its first temporary receiving home; shortly thereafter a second was set up in St. Paul. Still there were difficulties. Several children died and a number fell sick in the St. Paul residence because of a bad cistern. Although renovation work brought the property to the standards of the local health board, the incident pointed up the need for more supervision.[60] This need remained clear when an inspector found the Minneapolis home "unsanitary" and "decidedly unfit."[61] In the early 1900s, consequently, largely through contacts that Mrs. Savage had made, the society secured in the early 1900's some property in St. Paul and sufficient contributions for the construction of a new receiving home for approximately fifty children.

Kate Snoad Savage, a native of Plainfield, Illinois, and a schoolteacher before marrying in 1890, had already demonstrated her importance to the Minnesota organization. For a while she had administered the society's Minneapolis office. She took care of some of the children and was consistently effective in raising funds. In a three-month period in 1891 alone, she wrote 1,060 letters, took three children to homes, brought four to the society, kept records, and traveled 1,500 miles. Illness forced her to resign from formal duties in October 1903, shortly after the opening of the receiving home that she had been so instrumental in obtaining.[62]

The new facility undoubtedly represented a critical step in the society's development, but the number of babies who died there continued to perplex Savage. His reports to the board had always candidly included death statistics: of 150 children received in one year in the early 1890's, nine had died; in a particularly distressing quarter in 1896, ten out of thirty-three succumbed—half within a week as the result of an epidemic.[63] The superintendent believed that the number of fatalities among the society's infants was due in part to the acceptance of babies who were already on the brink of death, or sickly babies who paid for their mothers' sins. Such infants increased the society's expenses and added to its grief. Still, as Savage recognized, "to refuse to take them would subject us to the charge of neglecting the very class that we are organized to provide for." Even the newly opened receiving home could not solve this problem. Inspectors found it in excellent condition—neat, clean, and with "a marvelously well conducted nursery"—but there were twenty infants deaths (out of two hundred children) within a year.[64]

The disposal of the bodies further complicated the situation for Savage. Upon returning from several days on the road trying to place children, he learned to his horror that the undertaker had carried off a dead child without providing a coffin. The superintendent complained immediately. According to Savage, the mortician replied that he had taken the child on a streetcar because it was very cold, and he had to travel eight miles. The undertaker promised that in the future he would bring a coffin in a carriage to pick up a body.

When the society's board of directors heard what had happened, its members were deeply concerned that this child—and perhaps others—had not received even a small funeral service. The board also wanted information about where such children had been buried. Savage obtained assurances from "an honorable Christian man," whom he had no reason to doubt, "that the babies had all been buried in the Union Cemetary [sic]." The superintendent explained that his heavy duties had often kept him away from the home at the time of a child's death. Rather defensively, he added, "If there have been deficienties [sic] in ceremonies as to the dead there has been faithfulness in the care of the living." Shortly thereafter, the board resolved that dead children had to leave the home in a casket, following a simple prayer service, and that someone must accompany the body to the grave site.[65]

The need for such arrangements was disturbingly frequent. Even the board's decision in 1904, made upon the recommendation of the attending physician, to protect the infants by restricting visitors at the nursery did not change the situation greatly. That autumn nine out of ninety-eight children died in the society's charge.[66]

There was another matter that bothered Savage. Although the construction of the receiving home assuredly pleased him, he also had feelings of uneasiness. Day-to-day needs had in his opinion forced the desirability of such a building on the society, but he emphasized that it must become nothing more than a clearing-house. He warned of "certain evils" that came from keeping many children together, especially when some of them had "exceedingly immoral" backgrounds. "*But* the Receiving Homes," he conceded, "are likely to be a permanent feature of our work and it behooves us to make the best and most carefully guarded use of them that we can."[67]

A disconcerting sign was that each year in the early 1900s there were usually some twenty-five to forty children in the home.[68] Ironically, at the very time that the idea of home placement had acquired such favor among child savers, the Home Society was coming dangerously close to establishing an orphanage. Several decades later, one of the society's publications saw this as evidence that "the drift away from institutional care for children to life in a family home had not yet set in strongly." It was at least partly an example of realities undermining ideals. The several dozen children living in the receiving home at any one time attested all too well to the difficulties of finding satisfactory families for them.

Some individuals contended that this problem derived partly from a screening policy that was too rigid, especially regarding liquor; the society stated emphatically that applicants for children had to be "strictly temperate." From Savage's point of view this requirement was essential, but he complained that drinking had become so widespread "that we are often looked upon, even by members of churches, as being much more strict than necessary." He admitted that a more flexible standard would facilitate the placing of children, but he opposed making any concession to immorality: "We cannot be untrue to what we regard as among the most sacred interests of the children."[70]

Ultimately, the pivotal question was what constituted a good home. By the turn of the century, child savers tended more and more to celebrate the natural family. The 1909 White House Conference concluded, for example, that communities should do everything possible to maintain the integrity of the family as a child-rearing unit. "Except in unusual circumstances," the conference resolved, "the home should not be broken up for reasons of poverty, but only for considerations of inefficiency or immorality."[71] The Minnesota Home Society agreed. As early as 1894 the board had discussed ways of aiding needy families in order to keep them intact, and the possibility of providing short-term care for the children of poor mothers came up at several meetings.[72] With the opening of the new receiving home, the board ruled that—room permitting—the society would accept children "for temporary care in emergency cases." Over the next several years, ten to twenty of the children in the home at any one time were there not for placement but as temporary boarders.[73] In this way the society hoped to buy time for endangered families and thereby to help save them. Here were the rudiments of the emerging "social service" attitude that transformed charity work in the twentieth century.[74]

There was no doubt, however, that the society still intended primarily to place dependent children in new families. In many cases, where the child was an orphan or obviously neglected, there was little question about the need for placement. But in some instances, where there were surviving natural parents, the situation was less clear. Exactly what constituted a "worthy" family was, after all, open to interpretation.[75]

Savage was pulled in two directions: preserving the natural home and placing the child elsewhere. He regretted that communities had sometimes broken up poor families too quickly; when he observed mothers relinquishing their children under duress, he felt pain and indignation. In his opinion, the need to guard society was the only justification for taking "a child from that divinely constituted agency . . . the family home." Because the welfare of children and the best interests of the community were inseparable, families exercised momentous responsibilities. Parents influenced their children in the same ways that a cannon's barrel determined the flight of a projectile. The direction in which each home sent its offspring had profound implications for the future safety of the nation. Sometimes—"in the line of self-protection"—it was necessary for society to split up a family.[76]

With considerable trepidation, Savage recalled the unsettling descriptions of London's slum life in William Booth's famed study, *In Darkest England*, and he worried about the baneful effects of dependent classes on communities. He stressed the importance of removing children from "the pauper and non-productive elements of our population" and placing them with a "purer" and a "more thrifty and industrious" part of society. Such children, "snatched from the great army of dependent ones," could join "the noble army of producers."[77] In this context, courtroom battles to save children from "degraded" families were painful necessities. They might be "tedious" and open to "scenes of protest and lamentation and tears" from the parents, but they allowed unfortunate youths to become useful citizens. The superintendent believed that 90 percent of unwed mothers were unfit for parenthood. "A carefully selected Christian home, remote from the place of . . . origin," could provide an illegitimate child with a new destiny.[78]

From this perspective, child placing could slide easily into a design for social control. W. B. Sherrard, a man for whom Savage had the greatest respect, argued that home placement would "largely solve the tramp and habitual pauper problem," would help to "overcome the evils of immigration from the slums of Europe," and would possibly even resolve the southern race problem by uplifting "the dregs of that race [blacks]" until "the heinous crimes now committed by them will be unknown."[79] According to Sherrard, youngsters trapped in evil settings needed more help than did orphans. If society hoped to check the growth of criminal classes, it must recognize the primacy of a good environment.[80] At one point he urged lawsuits against entire communities for contributory negligence if, by failing to rescue children from bad environments, they helped to create lawbreakers.

Savage considered the proposal "food for serious thought." Like Sherrard, he hoped to save children before they were "hopelessly contaminated."[81] In Minneapolis alone, he noted, there were "perhaps thousands of little children growing up in rags and wretchedness . . . drink and vice and crime." The society should not wait for people to report such cases but should instead send someone "throughout the slums . . . constantly seeking out the needy ones." In the early 1900s the society hired a "city visitor," presumably for that purpose.[82]

By 1909, while admitting that authorities had once been overly eager to break up troubled families, Savage wondered if the pendulum was swinging too far in the other direction: "It has seemed to me for a time past that the tendency has been to keep the child in the unworthy and the unfit home, sometimes to its great injustice." What if the "earnest and laudable desire to secure the permanency of the family home" grew at the expense of the rights of the child and of society? Certainly he wanted those parents who had repented their sins and now sought a better life to keep their children. And he understood the "sorrow and despair" that accompanied the removal of children from some families.[83] But competing with these sentiments were his views of the dangerous "pauper classes" and his worries about social disorder. He may thus have leaned toward moving children from poor, presumably immoral, families to pious middle-class homes.

This inclination resulted not merely from the fact that Savage, like most reformers, approached lower-class groups as an outsider; his own experiences tended to confirm his suspicions and fears of life at the knife's edge, where he encountered so much brutality, so much abuse, and so many children who were helpless victims. "The work in behalf of the homeless little ones brings us in contact with the extremes of life," he wrote. He sometimes worried that so much sadness, disappointment, pain, and ugliness might pull child savers too relentlessly into "the dark side" of human experience, turning them into "hopeless pessimists." On one occasion the prospects of yet another court case—this one involving a woman who loved her children but who lived a "drunken and immoral life"—made him almost ill. "A kind of sickening sensation" came over him, and he dreaded "the thought of again plunging into these scenes of wretchedness and filth and crime." Yet though he shuddered at what lay ahead, he forged on. "Saving children is a beautiful thing to talk about," he observed, "but the work that does it is not all romance."[84] No one could charge Savage with being an armchair reformer.

Because of Savage's high hopes that children and society would benefit from home placement, he must have felt particularly distressed by the number of families who returned boys and girls to the society. However diligently the organization worked to find stable, loving homes, the discouraging truth was that one-fourth to one-half of the children came back. The replacement record was good, tending to match the number returned; still, there was a rather large population of children who floated from place to place. By late 1908, however, Savage could take great pride in the fact that the society, on the eve of its twentieth anniversary, had placed more than 2,500 children.[85]

Then suddenly, like "a clap of thunder from a clear sky," as one observer described it,[86] a scandal broke, driving Savage from the superintendency and threatening to ruin his reputation as a child saver. In November of that year, three employees complained formally to the society's board of directors that Savage's administration was corrupt and hypocritical. The leader of the protest was A. H. Tebbets, a Congregational minister from Danson, Minnesota, whom the board had hired in 1900 as assistant superintendent to replace Daniel B. Jackson (a Presbyterian pastor who had died after taking cold while delivering a boy to his new home).[87] Joining Tebbets in the attack on Savage were Anna Adams, who had served as a matron for twelve years, and Mrs. E. E. Lundgren, a fund raiser.

The charges against Savage were serious: graft on the part of the superintendent and his wife, especially involving some $500 in donations that had allegedly disappeared; failure to check on children whom the society had placed and who were consequently "wholly lost sight of"; "generally unbusiness-like, unmethodical management of the work"; betrayal of the Christian principles of the society; and a policy of accepting illegitimate children, "thus making vice easy." Lundgren broke all connections with the Society on grounds that she could not in good conscience ask for contributions "to maintain an unworthy administration." Tebbets claimed that he had initially tried to fight "graft and maladministration" without making the issues public, but events had ultimately forced him to jeopardize his family's economic well-being and his own "long service in a self denying ministry." He had decided to enlist "with other friends of righteousness" in order to combat "the graft and abuse that have thus far been carried on in the name of Christian charity."[88] The board of directors, facing a crisis that jeopardized the very existence of the society, immediately opened an investigation.

Undoubtedly, the most serious charge was that of graft. On this, however, the board had no difficulty establishing Savage's innocence; it was able to account for all funds and found no evidence of misuse of money. On the other hand, the board conceded that the superintendent had not been the most effective of administrators—hardly surprising, given Savage's rigorous schedule in which he did a little of everything.[89]

Most of the other accusations came down to matters of perspective. Savage had reportedly admitted sickly babies in order to swell the society's statistics about children in its care. Many of the unfit infants had subsequently died or ended up in unsuspecting families. From Savage's viewpoint, this was hardly a fair appraisal. He had candidly discussed how the deaths of babies hurt the society's record; indeed, he had said that if the organization's primary concern was its reputation, it should not accept sick children. The real question, he believed, was who should help them. In his opinion, the society had a moral responsibility to do so.[90] A related complaint of Tebbets and the others was that Savage had doomed many babies to an early death by removing them prematurely from their mothers' nourishment. This must have struck the superintendent as grossly unfair. Had his critics so soon forgotten his own strong feelings on the matter—feelings which had motivated his campaign for the so-called "wet nurse" bill?

Similarly, Savage must have winced at the charge that, by accepting "children of vice," he had facilitated immoral activities and sent "diseased bastard babies" into respectable families. The superintendent had, after all, agonized over this very issue and wanted to act only where the mother was too poor to care for the illegitimate child. Moreover, he did not consider it fair to penalize the baby for its parents' wrongdoing. Tebbets and the others seemed at least implicitly to resent the class of people from whom Savage accepted children. Savage, in his own defense, might have countered that the Home Society, as he conceived it, was supposed to aid needy people. He was clearly apprehensive about the "criminal class," but balancing these fears was his genuine desire to provide humanitarian services for that very group.

Savage's accusers believed that he had sullied the society's reputation as a Christian institution by not providing appropriate burial services or a Sunday School in the receiving home. "It was," Tebbets and the others said, "a common practice for the undertaker to take away a dead body in an old grip sack or telescope, or wrapped in a newspaper." Yet when this problem of burials had surfaced five years earlier, a horrified Savage had acted to correct the situation. He perhaps should have been more aware of what had happened in the receiving home while he was away; still, was it unfair of him to assume, until he learned differently, that undertakers provided coffins and did not simply remove the tiny bodies in grip sacks or newspapers? The lack of a Sunday School was an issue that the board had remedied by the time the Tebbets faction lodged its complaints. The fact that a school had not existed earlier may have been unforgivable to someone interested in church rituals, but Savage had left a pastorate to apply what he saw as practical aspects of Christianity. Moreover, he had considered the receiving home only as a clearinghouse where children stayed a very short time.

As for the charge that Savage had engaged in "deception," "falsehood," and "scheming"—who really could know for sure? The board found that "unfriendly" feelings existed between the superintendent and his assistant, so both men may have been prone to intrigue. Savage might in all justification have seen the accusations of Tebbets and the others as examples of their own "scheming" to unravel his good work and advance themselves.

Although the board essentially vindicated Savage and concluded that Tebbets had exaggerated administrative problems, it realized that the society's name had suffered. A Duluth resident noted that in his area the society had "always enjoyed a standing of the highest among people who are at all interested in this class of work," but that its supporters were "simply amazed" at the charges: "We hardly know what to think." The board thus decided to take both Savage and Tebbets out of the central administrative office and assign them to fieldwork in different parts of the state, a recommendation that Savage himself had offered.[91] Tebbets subsequently left the society. Savage resigned from the board, where he had served for almost two decades, but asked to continue his work in the field. For one thing, he believed that he was still invaluable to the organization as a fund raiser. He indicated that his many friends throughout the state still respected him and, in fact, had made his collections larger than ever. Also, he reasoned that if he left the society, his reputation would suffer irrevocably. However disillusioned his removal as superintendent left him, he continued to serve the society for another decade. On March 1, 1921, he died of heart disease, culminating some thirty years of child rescue work.[92]

The Reverend S. W. Dickinson succeeded him as superintendent from 1909 to 1927. "An able, high-minded Christian man," as the board of directors described him, Dickinson had previously headed the Chicago district of the Illinois Children's Home and Aid Society.[93] Like many people of the era, he was apprehensive about the apparent decline of the American family, "with its high ideals, its standard of morals, its patriotism and solidarity." Whereas the nation's pioneering first century had been one of "home building," the family had, in Dickinson's opinion, fallen victim to a series of lamentable trends: fewer births among the better classes, rising divorce rates, industrialism, and commercialism. Because of the "general hustle for money," more family members than ever before were on the job and outside the home. Dickinson worried about the growing number of women and youngsters in the labor force. To him it was "inevitable that wherein the influence of the family is lacking it becomes the duty of society to supply."[94] Here he echoed one of the strongest justifications for enlarged social services that marked progressive reform thought.

Far more than Savage, Dickinson, who represented the second generation of Home Society work, tilted the Minnesota organization toward a broad social role and a close relationship with the emerging network of professional groups. Shortly before becoming the new superintendent, he had visited several child-saving institutions in Massachusetts and Pennsylvania.[95] And immediately after assuming his duties, he attended the White House Conference on Dependent Children. The conference "virtually gave a new direction to child welfare," wrote Dickinson. He returned to the Twin Cities committed to strengthening the society's "standard ideals" while introducing "new methods suggested by popular advances in child welfare." He cited specifically the conclusion of the White House Conference that there had been a tendency to remove children from their families for insufficient reasons. The "broad social views" that excited him included temporary relief for the poor and mothers' pensions.[96] He also favored strict legislation making fathers responsible for the support of their illegitimate children; this would enable more young mothers to keep their babies and would provide the children with "equal moral standing" in the community.[97]

At the Home Society, Dickinson expanded the temporary care services for children of distressed parents and for unwed mothers. He also worked closely with Margaret Lettice, head of the Baby Welfare Association, which was fighting strenuously to close the "baby farms" in St. Paul. The society set up a special "Baby Welfare Room" in the receiving home for infants whom Lettice's organization had rescued. "The plan worked well," in Dickinson's estimation. Many parents were reunited with their babies, and poor unwed mothers often turned their infants over to the guardianship of the society.[98] Dickinson was especially responsive to the new "scientific" approach to charity, with its emphasis on formal knowledge and trained experts. In 1912, for example, he employed "a scientifically trained Nurse" for the society's nursery. "Scientific feeding of babies was begun and the children brought up to standard according to weight." To Dickinson, this method symbolized a "revolution" in child care at the Home Society, and he went on to help open a

six-month course at the nursery to train women for nursing assignments in private families. Trainees received free board, room, laundry, and instruction while they learned "the latest in scientific
methods in feeding, in value of foods, in the study of anatomy,
biology, first aid." In 1914 six young women formed the first
graduating class. Demand for such nurses was reportedly high, and
the society itself benefited as the health of infants in the nursery
improved. "It was a big innovation in institutional work for children," according to Dickinson, "the first of its kind in a Children's
Home west of Chicago."[99]

He praised social welfare agencies that educated young mothers
in home nursing, and he very much supported the emerging public
health movement—the use of visiting rural nurses, for example.
These nurses could bring valuable knowledge to country mothers,
"lonely, often inexperienced, and obliged to work hard." This kind
of work, along with that of the Home Society, made families more
adept at child rearing. "It is," he wrote, "a terrible arrangement of
home conditions when the arm of the law must interfere and say to
the home, 'You are unworthy to have charge of your offspring.'" He
firmly believed that correct information was also the key to social
and sexual hygiene. In his estimation, a large majority of young
unwed mothers became pregnant out of sexual ignorance, and he
urged public schools to provide "sane and scientific" instruction
about human reproduction.[100]

Like some other progressive social reformers, Dickinson was
keenly interested in "the science of eugenics" as a method of "race
maintenance." While the birthrate of "the better class" declined,
that of "feeble-minded, insane and degenerate parents," seemed to
increase. Dickinson observed that the intelligence test of the French
psychologist Alfred Binet had revealed the existence of a surprisingly large number of abnormal children. Children of "morally
degenerate" parents were particularly susceptible to "physical de-
fects." In order to deal with the problem, Dickinson advocated "an
institution of detention." It would, by examining children of diseased, feebleminded, and degenerate parents and by providing
"scientific remedies," represent "another step forward in modern
charity."[101]

The Home Society needed to make sure that it did not place abnormal children in unsuspecting homes. To this end Dickinson introduced what he described as an "important change in the method of the Society." Children who seemed "retarded, queer or socially unfit" received psychological tests. If a child was indeed abnormal, "the case was settled then and there. The child must be returned to the county or sent to the [state] school at Faribault. It was diagnosed as 'unplaceable.'" Dickinson saw these as necessary steps. They conformed with what the president of the National Children's Home Society, Charles Redmond Henderson, had described as "the scientific principles of education, the discoveries of biology in relation to heredity, nutrition and environment."[102]

Implicitly critical of Savage's administration, Dickinson indicated that the society's placement activities would become more systematic. The new superintendent interpreted the large number or children who came back to the society as a clear indication of the need for greater deliberation in the first placement. "It requires courage," he told the board of directors, "to deny people who may be kind, who love children, but whose conditions of home life are not suitable." He instituted rigorous investigations of prospective families to insure that the home matched the child—something that Savage had presumably not done very effectively.[103] By 1916 Dickinson estimated that he had rejected annually an average of one-third of the applications for children.[104]

Unquestionably, there had been a change in the society's tone following Savage's departure as superintendent. He had launched an organization, guided it for nearly twenty years, and then stepped aside under pressure to watch while it entered a new era. The situation was not unique to Minnesota. The National Home Society had also undergone a momentous shift from the days of Martin Van Buren Van Arsdale. Charles R. Henderson, the new national president, stated in 1908 that, just as "exact science" was influencing the business community, so too should charity agencies adjust to modern realities. Whereas Savage had some five years earlier said that any of his mistakes had been "of the head and not of the intentions," Henderson asserted that "superintendents and agents should eventually stand or fall by their efficiency and achievement." It was, according to Henderson, essential to have precise answers for a practical world. "The loose methods of earlier days on the frontier" would no longer suffice.[105]

Savage—a representative of those frontier days—had once remarked that "a true child saver" resembled a poet. Both had a "natural instinct" for their callings; both were "born and not made."[106] In many respects, Savage's own career had demonstrated that he himself had a touch of the poet. If the changes of the early twentieth century dictated that "exact science" should inform child saving—bringing to it higher and more uniform standards, greater efficiency, and the stringent application of expert knowledge—there were nonetheless dangers. Method could easily supplant sentiment, turning child rescue work from a "calling" into a job—a transformation that was not without its own liabilities. Somewhere between the poetry of a Savage and the science of a Dickinson, the Children's Home Society of Minnesota—indeed, the home placement movement generally—would need to chart its future.

· 3 ·

Saving the Church by
Saving the Children:
The Orphanages of the
National Benevolent Association

For St. Louis's saloon districts one late summer day in 1899, it was not quite business as usual. Children from the Christian Orphans' Home passed through, booming out the hymn "Dare to Be a Daniel," challenging tavern patrons to reform themselves. The youngsters' mission to the saloon areas may have amused the customers. But those who read about the incident in the *Orphan's Cry*, monthly publication of the National Benevolent Association of the Christian Church (NBA), were undoubtedly pleased. As Fannie Shedd Ayars, a founder of the association and the Christian Orphans' Home, asserted, the orphans were "an army for God and for good. 'Save the children and you save the world.'" From the point of view of the NBA, nothing less was at stake than the soul of Protestant Christianity. The expanding philanthropic work of the Catholic Church, fraternal organizations, and secular agencies threatened to leave the once-proud benevolent forces of Protestantism in shambles. By plunging into what one minister described as the "dark continent of unexplored child suffering," the association hoped to do great good—for the children and for the faith.[1]

In early 1887 the National Benevolent Association had emerged primarily through the efforts of a small group of women within the Christian Church (Disciples of Christ), despite the denomination's conservative conception of gender roles. The organization's declared purpose was to aid the helpless, house the homeless, care for the ill, and comfort the distressed. But significantly, the NBA pressed far beyond the isolated and separate local benevolent activities of most Protestant churches of the time and established a protective network of institutions across the nation. The Christian Orphans' Home in St. Louis was only the starting point. Within thirty years the NBA founded eight orphanages with a combined capacity of five hundred children, four homes that could care for seventy-five elderly citizens, a training school for nurses, and a hospital for the poor. By the fall of 1915, the association's annual expenses exceeded $170,000, and its assets were over $400,000. "We had not the experience of any like association to help us," recalled Mrs. J. K. Hansbrough, an NBA organizer. "There was no national benevolent association in any of the denominations. We were pioneers in this work."[2]

Although originally intent on providing personalistic Christian charity without elaborate organizational structures, the NBA ultimately demonstrated how even anti-institutional groups at the turn of the century increasingly found their charitable impulses bureaucratized. Just as the Disciples of Christ adjusted their benevolent activities to meet the problems of a mass industrialized and urban society, so the forms that charity took became ever more emulative of the corporate, industrial world. By the 1920s the early vision of the NBA founders seemed quaint, as the association concentrated on professionalism, financial accountability, and tighter administration. Also left to memory were those formative years when the NBA's pioneers had worried that the association might itself be a kind of orphan—not just in the larger society but, because of the deeply rooted anti-institutionalism of the Disciples of Christ, within the church itself.

A strong suspicion of institutions had marked the Christian Church since its origins in the nineteenth century. The church was very much a product of, and a contributor to, the powerful democratizing forces that shaped America from the 1780s into the 1830s. During that turbulent postrevolutionary era, a "crisis of confidence in a hierarchical, ordered society" had rocked virtually every aspect of the new nation—from medicine to law, the theater, politics, and religion. Popular speakers and mass publications had lambasted special privilege, artificial social distinctions, and elitism. These vigorous challenges to traditional authority, along with celebrations of the simple virtues and the wisdom of the common people, very much influenced religious reformers such as Alexander Campbell. A Scottish immigrant who arrived in America in 1809, Campbell urged "the declaration of independence of the kingdom of Jesus." In place of religious organization, he optimistically posited a form of radical individualism that left each person with the inalienable right to discover God's word in the New Testament. His diatribes against "clerical aristocrats" echoed the preaching of Elias Smith in New England, James O'Kelly in the South, and Barton Stone in Kentucky—all of whom founded sects with the name "Christian." In the 1830s Stone joined Campbell's wing of the Christian Church, the Disciples of Christ, a merger so successful that within thirty years the Disciples claimed 200,000 members and were America's fifth largest Protestant denomination.[3]

In the antebellum era the Disciples watched suspiciously while other churches established benevolent societies. It was not that the Disciples opposed charity. Indeed, from the outset a deeply felt sympathy for disadvantaged people characterized their world view. They assumed, however, that individuals and local churches should take responsibility for aiding the poor and the helpless in their immediate areas. Strong opposition to privileged elites and to secular influences, along with literal readings of the New Testament, very much helped to explain the Disciples' viewpoint. Campbell and Stone feared that establishing separate "societies" for charitable purposes would invariably lead to a network of organizations apart from the church. According to Stone, benevolent societies, however good the intentions behind them, resulted in "sectarian establishments," nothing less than monopolies that controlled "the wealth and power of the nation." Even the idea of a church-supported orphanage drew the wrath of one prominent Disciple in 1856. "Orphan homes," he contended, "are attempting to perform, in part, the labor which it is the imperious duty of each congregation to do."[4]

Disciples in Midway, Kentucky, had established a girls' orphanage and school in the 1850s anyhow, but they hardly set a trend; a proposal in 1855 to open a boys' orphanage got nowhere. Nor had the formation in 1849 of the American Christian Missionary Society (the Disciples' first national missionary organization) signaled a grass-roots shift in sentiment. The arch individualism and anti-aristocratic, anti-institutional biases of the Disciples persisted into the late 1800s, ironically stirring the very kinds of debates over New Testament doctrines that Campbell and others had hoped to avoid.[5]

In early 1886, while these debates still raged, a small group of women in St. Louis gathered informally around a gas-lit table in the basement of the First Christian Church on 17th and Olive Streets to discuss how they might deal with human suffering in their city. In May, after subsequent meetings in the church and in their homes, the women formed the Benevolent Association of the Christian Church. By the end of the year, however, the group could claim no tangible accomplishments. On January 10, 1887, in hopes of galvanizing the little organization to more action, the members formally incorporated as the National Benevolent Association to aid the sick, the distressed, the helpless, and the homeless. Essentially without funds, and dependent on annual dues of $1.00 and life memberships of $25, the association initially distributed food and clothing to poor people in St. Louis.[6]

Throughout 1887 the association increasingly focused its attention on another goal: "the building of a *'Home'*" for orphans.[7] On January 24, 1889, with less than $50 on hand, the NBA rented a five-room house. Here was an important but tentative step. During the first year, thirteen dependent children, including the infant of the widowed cook whom the NBA employed, received care at the home. By 1897, following several moves to larger facilities in St. Louis, the home had a population of ninety-five youngsters from seventeen states. The next year, in order to provide better care for the infants, the association opened a separate institution in the city, the Babies' Home and Hospital, which accommodated seventy-five children and provided space for as many as twenty-five working or needy mothers.[8]

From 1900 to 1914 the association enjoyed its period of greatest growth, adding ten institutions to its roster. It established four homes for the aged: in January 1900 one that opened in St. Louis before moving a year later to a permanent location in Jacksonville, Illinois; in 1903 one in East Aurora, New York, and another in

Jacksonville, Florida; and in 1907 one in Eugene, Oregon, which moved shortly thereafter to Walla Walla, Washington. These institutions together could house seventy-five elderly residents. The number of dependent children under the NBA's care jumped to five hundred with the addition of orphanages in Cleveland, Atlanta, Dallas, Denver, Omaha, and, for a while, Walla Walla.

The Cleveland Christian Orphanage represented the first NBA children's institution outside St. Louis. At first the situation was far from ideal. In late 1902 the association took over the In His Name Orphanage, which an individual member of the Christian Church had operated for two years; it was in serious financial trouble, overcrowded, and so dilapidated that city officials were ready to declare it unsafe. Not until 1906 did the NBA find a new location: a nineteen-room residence on six acres overlooking Lake Erie. Although the Home specialized in caring for orphans under age fourteen, it accepted older youths as well. The number of children in residence averaged sixty.[9]

The smaller Southern Christian Home in Atlanta, like the Cleveland institution, was initially an NBA salvage effort. In 1902 the Woman's Society of Georgia Missions had opened an "Industrial School" in the hill country of Baldwin, Georgia, some seventy-five miles from Atlanta. The school, whose goal was to prepare "the hands as well as the minds of our children for future work," enrolled from sixty to one hundred students and provided a residence for twenty-nine orphans. When the NBA took responsibility in late 1905, it emphasized the care of dependent children. Until 1911, when it moved the orphans to a rented house in Atlanta, it used an old, decrepit hotel with twenty-two rooms. The move to the city was essential; Baldwin was simply too small to provide access to funds, emergency medical care, and the range of educational experiences that the association deemed necessary. But the Atlanta site had its own problems. Citizens, angry when they heard that the orphanage was slated for their neighborhood, protested. Although the anger soon abated and the institution became an accepted part of the area, the building, by the NBA's own admission, was "poorly adapted to the needs of its work." It had insufficient playground space, inadequate fire protection, crowded rooms, and furniture that by 1916 was "little better than a collection of junk." Despite numerous appeals for funds, the NBA was not able to build a new home until 1927.[10]

In contrast, the Juliette Fowler Home in Dallas was substantially better off, thanks to a bequest in 1898 of fifteen acres on the eastern side of the city to be used for orphans and old folks. Convinced, however, that a farm setting would make the orphanage self-sufficient, the NBA in 1904 purchased two hundred acres some ten miles outside Dallas, at Grand Prairie. The farm failed even to approach self-sufficiency—despite the optimistic publicity photographs of sixteen happy boys lined up in the fields at "the Hoe Brigade," ostensibly chanting, "Big weeds, little weeds, you must go." In 1910 the NBA sold the farm and moved the children to the Fowler property, where construction commenced on a new orphanage that ultimately housed 125 children. A smaller residence for old people was built on the same lot.[11]

A brief effort to have a self-sustaining farm orphanage on some two hundred acres outside Loveland, Colorado, ended in a similar move to an urban area. In 1902 J. W. and Mary Warren, a childless couple who had for years dreamed of building an orphanage, deeded farm property to the NBA. Three years later the home opened and housed an average of ten children. But in 1907 the association, concluding that the children were too small for farm work and in need of a good school system, moved the institution to Denver, temporarily in a rented home under the direction of the Warrens, and in 1910 to a new building. By 1917 there were forty-three children, ages three to sixteen, and the home was turning away as many as five needy youngsters per day for lack of space.[12]

One of the most impressive additions to the NBA network was the Child Saving Institute in Omaha. In this case the association did not have to coax an institution through its precarious formative years. A. W. Clark, pastor of the Calvary Baptist Church in Omaha, had established the institute in 1892 because, in his words, there was "no recognized work on behalf of little children" and "the 'cry of the child' appealed to me." With no financial backing and only an abandoned livery stable as a building, Clark searched through Omaha's streets—especially its saloon area, Ram Cat Alley—for neglected and homeless children. His main objective was to place such youngsters as soon as possible in permanent homes. By 1900, a year in which Clark aided 190 children, ranging from infants to twelve-year-olds, the average length of residency in the orphanage was only thirty-four days before placement. Relying almost entirely on voluntary help, Clark also ran Sunday Schools, a free kindergarten (with support from the Women's Christian Temperance Union and the Omaha Free Kindergarten Association), a cooking school (again with help from the WCTU as well as the Woman's Club of Omaha), a reading room, a Nurse Maids Training School (with an enrollment of fifteen), and an employment bureau (which in 1900 found jobs for 105 boys and girls). The years of shoestring budgets finally ended in 1912 when a $25,000 gift sparked a drive resulting in a new, modern $100,000 building. At that point, however, Clark moved to California for other church work, and a group of Omaha business people began to operate the institute. But after several months the new administrators decided that the project needed the supervision of a benevolent organization. One of the directors reportedly expressed concern that financial success threatened to make the institute "a benevolent institution commercialized, and what we want is to find some organization that can run it without the commercial smack."

At a quiet dinner on October 31, 1913, the NBA became that organization. By then the institute had an endowment of $35,000 and a new building with a capacity of ninety. The association continued to emphasize quick but careful placement. Children of any faith were welcome, but the institute was closed to blacks on grounds that it could not "keep them separate from the others." In 1916 the Omaha institution, which housed a considerable number of infants (averaging thirty-five babies at any one time), reportedly broke the world's record for low mortality: 0.75 percent over a twelve-month period.[13]

The smallest of the NBA's children's institutions, the Northwestern Christian Home, opened in Walla Walla, Washington, in 1910, but its development was more tentative and complicated than that of the other homes. Although for several years the association had planned to establish an orphanage in the Pacific Northwest, events forced the decision. In 1905, a congregation of Disciples in Eugene, Oregon, had established a small home for aged church members in their region. Two years later the local group turned the project over to the NBA. The NBA preferred to leave matters at that point for a while. The national group worried about extending itself too much too soon but "yielded," as its publication, the *Christian Philanthropist*, later said to "insistent pressure" from that region. Seeking a central location that would serve the needs of Oregon, Washington, Idaho, and Montana, the NBA purchased a nineteen-acre farm outside Walla Walla. Five orphan children were the first residents. Within a few weeks the association sold its Eugene property and moved the five elderly occupants to the farm. The challenge of caring for both small children and aged, infirm people in a five-room house quickly proved too much. In fact, conditions were so crowded that the harried couple in charge of the home lived for a while in a tent in the yard. Hard choices confronted the NBA; ultimately, it chose, in the words of the *Christian Philanthropist*, "to suspend the work for the children for a time because of the pressure from the churches to care for the aged." In late 1913 it exchanged the farm for an eighteen-room sanitarium in Walla Walla. Although the NBA indicated that the new property had ample space for the future construction of a children's home, the northwestern institution became solely a place for needy, aged church members in the region.[14]

By the end of 1913, the period of rapid NBA expansion had ended. "Homeless and penniless in the beginning," it had acquired holdings worth $300,000 in ten states. In its twenty-seven years of existence, it had provided institutional care for 197 aged citizens, trained 27 nurses, helped 1,151 destitute women (who stayed and worked for periods of time at the orphanages), and "fathered and mothered" 7,104 dependent children.[15]

Looking back, the organization liked to celebrate the emergence of "a vast army of brethren eagerly seeking to restore the spirit and practice of apostolic benevolence." But this interpretation downplayed early difficulties and obstacles. The simple truth was that the origins of the NBA owed far more to the tenacity of several dozen energetic women who battled considerable odds than it did to enthusiastic recognition from Christian congregations across the country. Years later there was a lingering hint of bitterness in an article recalling that the NBA had been "almost friendless at its birth," and "born in weakness and obscurity."[16]

The association's founders had contended not only with the

denomination's anti-institutional inclinations but also with critics of women who dared exert their influence outside the home. David Lipscomb, one of the powerful voices within the church, had argued that men who encouraged females to venture from the home worked "against God, the church, womanhood, the interest of the family, motherhood, and against true manhood itself." Another Disciple, John T. Poe, maintained in 1874 that mothers of delinquent and sinful youths were "most often" the leaders of organizations such as the Women's Christian Temperance Union.[17]

Poe probably would not have been surprised to learn that Martha Hart Younkin, who more than anyone molded the NBA in its formative years, looked to the WCTU for inspiration. "I owe them much," she claimed. "They have done more for womankind than any other organization; my work has constantly been in line with theirs." Her friend and colleague, Mrs. J. K. Hansbrough, recalled how Younkin had gone "tirelessly . . . up and down the land—as much as a woman could in those days—preaching the gospel of help for the needy. From house to house, from church to church, day after day she went, urging cooperation in organizing for benevolent work." Mrs. W. D. Harrison, another of the NBA organizers, credited Younkin with acquainting her with benevolent action: "She was a pioneer not only here in our city, but through the state of Missouri. She won hundreds to the cause of the orphan."[18]

"Mattie" Hart Younkin's early years in many respects resembled the lives of the poor, dependent children she later sought to help. In 1847, when she was four, her parents had moved from Eaton, Ohio, to Peoria County in Illinois, only to have robbers steal what little money they had. Six years later her father died, leaving a large family unable to fend for itself, and Matilda Hart went to live with her grandparents, under whose influence she became a devoted reader of the scriptures and joined the Christian Church. After graduating from Abingdon College in Illinois, she taught school for a while in Illinois and Iowa. In 1861 she married Edwin Younkin, a college classmate who entered the medical profession and, in 1875, moved to St. Louis where he later became Dean of the American Medical College. Mattie gave birth to two daughters and busied herself with the duties of wife and mother. Perhaps it was nagging memories of her own earlier hardships that made her so sensitive of the city's poverty. The human misery in St. Louis's slums disturbed her greatly, and she could not understand why so many local churches seemed oblivious to such suffering. As one friend recalled, Younkin personally decided to initiate "some concerted method for caring for the helpless and the needy." She not only took the lead in organizing the National Benevolent Association but also served as its voluntary fund raiser and "missionary," soliciting food and clothing which she distributed to unfortunate people.[9]

Younkin undoubtedly needed no urging to focus on the plight of homeless children. It was nonetheless an incident involving one of the other organizers of the NBA, Sophia Robertson Kerns, that provided the specific impetus behind the association's efforts to establish an orphanage. In 1886 Kerns found a small boy, hungry, ragged, and with no family, on the streets of St. Louis. She gave the boy a meal and some clothes and took him to the police, only to learn that the authorities had no way of dealing with him except to place him in a Catholic orphanage. Kerns, certain that her own church should sponsor an orphan's home, broached the idea of such a project at several of the meetings out of which the NBA evolved.[20]

While the small group that formed the NBA had no trouble agreeing upon its central purpose, Younkin quickly learned that enthusiasm for an orphanage—and for the association itself—was quite limited within the Disciples of Christ as a whole. At first she could not even get a hearing at the Christian Church's General Conventions. Once when she sought to speak at a state convention, a preacher dismissed her request: "There is not time to hear you; we are here to preach the gospel!" On another occasion, she gained the platform at a state gathering only when a pastor, sympathetic to expanding the church's benevolent work, yielded part of his time to her. In 1895, she successfully got the General Convention in Dallas at least to consider a petition to recognize the NBA as an official agency of the church, only to have a hostile majority table the resolution. The sarcasm she confronted in Dallas grew partly out of opposition to establishing a national organization separate from the church, but the fact that Younkin was a female unquestionably sharpened the hostility of her opponents. According to the association's magazine, "elders, ministers and convention managers, who saw no place for a woman in the program of the church," battled her again and again. She nonetheless persisted and finally, in 1899—several months before she died of cancer—gained official status for the National Benevolent Associaton within the Christian Church.[21]

Memories of the sexual discrimination that marked the NBA's early struggle did not easily disappear, however. In 1914 the association dedicated an entire issue of the *Christian Philanthropist* to the "splendid women"—the "royal sisterhood"—who had started the organization. Mattie Younkin's photograph appeared on the cover between two columns of words: "The N.B.A., Born in Woman's Loving Heart" and "The N.B.A., Led by Woman's Skillful Hand." An article noting that Younkin had successfully pressed her ideas upon "a preoccupied brotherhood" emphasized that "the work of child redemption has been essentially a woman's work." Women not only had founded the NBA, but dominated its management and, in numerous ways, its institutions. An essay, "Woman's Control through Committee Work," pointed out that females ran the association's various homes: "They have control of almost every phase of the life of these institutions through their committee service." With obvious pride the anonymous writer indicated that "men have nothing to do with what we might call the domestic phase of the work . . . it is the privilege of the women to rule, as they should, as queens of these households of Christian love and service."[22]

This was, of course, in many respects a very traditional kind of feminism. It attempted, in a society still with quite limited gender roles, to use the expected responsibilities of women in the home as a cultural lever to gain additional breathing space. In retrospect, such a tactic may have been a "a comfortable revolution,"[23] but to the participants it was no small matter. The *Christian Philanthropist* in 1914 stressed the importance of the association's "fixed policy . . . to recognize the place and power of the women in its work." A few months earlier, when the NBA assumed control of the Child Saving Institute in Omaha, the institute's officers and board members were all males. The NBA promptly placed women in office and on the governing board.[24]

The general trend, however, was in the other direction. Once the NBA gained official recognition from the church, the place of men in the organization grew noticeably. Officers of the association had been overwhelmingly female in its formative era, but when Fannie

Shedd Ayars stepped down in 1908 after three years as president, the executive position went to a man, the first of a long, uninterrupted line. J. W. Perry, vice-president of the National Bank of Commerce of St. Louis, assumed the position because, in Ayars's words, "it seemed wise, for the present, to call to the leadership of this great work a thoroughly seasoned and tested business man."[25] It made good strategy, of course, for the association to broaden its base. But over several decades this shift made it possible, as one unhappy individual complained in 1934, to forget that the "tender, beautiful ministry" of the association was "essentially woman's work in its beginning." The writer believed that, "in recent years especially," the organization had not sufficiently recognized the contributions of women.[26]

Unquestionably, to overlook the role of women was to blot out nothing less than the early history of the National Benevolent Association. The list of females who had founded and carried the NBA through its first years was impressive, starting with Mattie Younkin but including Sophia Kerns, Emily Ivers Meier (orphaned daughter of a St. Louis steamboat captain, a founder of the St. Louis Women's Club, and first president of the Christian Orphan's Home), Rowena Mason (who published the *Orphan's Cry* and the *Christian Philanthropist* until the early 1900s, when the NBA assumed financial responsibility), Mrs. J. K. Hansbrough (first editor of both journals and, for more than fifty years, corresponding secretary of the NBA); Fannie Shedd Ayars (the organization's first recording secretary, its president for three years, and an instrumental force behind the Christian Orphan's Home and the Babies' Home and Hospital), and others.[27]

Ayars's explanation of why she and the other women labored so hard to found the NBA was simply that they had found "the low wail of our orphan children or the pitiful sob of our old saints" more compelling than the theological debates that dominated the church at the end of the 1800s. "So many feeble, pleading, outstretched arms . . . were pointed toward us that our mother hearts could no longer endure the strain."[28]

While Ayars's account of her motives, and those of the other women who organized the association, was undoubtedly partially correct, the story surely had other dimensions. The life of Isadora E.

S. Dowden, who in the early 1900s helped establish the northwestern auxiliary of the NBA, suggested an additional concern: that of finding a useful position in a society that offered few culturally acceptable public roles for females. When Dowden described her childhood by saying, "I was only a girl" and "I knew of no work I could do," she expressed poignantly the frustrations of a growing number of women in the late nineteenth century. She had fiercely hoped to serve her church and society, only to find continual reminders of how effectively the larger Victorian culture into which she had been born limited her choices.[29] According to the expectations of that culture, strong men inhabited and forged the world of public affairs, while gentle women tended the domestic sphere of hearth and home and exerted moral influence upon their husbands and children.

For Dowden, growing up in a very religious family on the ranch outside Davenport, Iowa, the pressing question was how she might apply Christian principles to the world around her, other than by sitting as a "silent listener" in church or by occasionally visiting a sick friend. Her dissatisfaction continued as she entered public school teaching, an occupational field which a few bold and imaginative women, such as Emma Willard and Catherine Beecher, had carved out in the antebellum era as suitable for women because it was an extension of motherly duties. While teaching in rural Iowa schools, Dowden remembered looking at the boys and considering how they "would grow to manhood and enter into various callings, including the holy ministry." Such opportunities were not available for the girls. "What of their womanhood and service for the betterment of the social and religious problems?" Dowden wondered. Invariably, that question served only to underline her own lack of options. She felt certain the Lord wanted her help, but she fretted about what she could do. To become a foreign missionary, an acceptable woman's role within the church, would take years of preparation. Then, as she later recalled, God suddenly "presented the opportunity." A minister came through town trying to organize a Children's Home Society. Dowden immediately signed on and helped to establish Home Societies in Iowa, Missouri, Texas, Montana, and the Pacific Northwest before allying herself with the National Benevolent Association. Child rescue work provided her with a socially acceptable route along which she could channel her creative talents, establish herself as an organizer and administrator, find personal rewards in her work, and fulfill her ambition to serve Christianity in a practical way.[30]

In a major sense, of course, child saving—like teaching—was simply an enlargement of the nineteenth century's domestic sphere for women. For Isadora Dowden, its promise and its opportunities nonetheless came with the force of a revelation. A whole new world had opened up for her—a world of travel and increased recognition. Child rescue work was a career and a calling; it offered a chance to be socially useful and to enhance her own life. Dowden's experience was hardly unique. It was an individual variation of themes familiar to Jane Addams and many of the other women who dedicated at least parts of their lives to settlement house work and reform activities at the turn of the century. Presumably, Mattie Younkin, Fannie Shedd Ayars, and the other women who pioneered the National Benevolent Association found the urge to live socially purposeful lives no less compelling than did Dowden. The fact that they found such purpose in answering "the low wail of the orphan children" told as much about the large cultural setting in which the women worked as it did about the women themselves.[31]

Although Younkin and her associates initially had considerable difficulty finding a sympathetic audience, the fact remained that over several decades the NBA's support grew considerably. Evidence of this was the fact that even though the association invariably was strapped for funds, it extended its institutional network at an impressive rate, especially in the early 1900s. Moreover, the organization's monthly publications—the *Orphan's Cry*, from 1894 until 1903, and the *Christian Philanthropist*—were welcome in a growing number of homes. By 1906 the subscription list had reached 15,000.[32] If these journals were any indication, the association drew its energies from an electric blend of Good Samaritanism, a desire to salvage remnants from a disappearing village world, a fear of growing social disorder, and a search for converts to the Christian Church.

Like most denominations in the late nineteenth century, the Disciplines of Christ felt deeply the effects of the Social Gospel movement. As early as the mid-1880s, some of the church's leaders had attended interdenominational conferences that discussed social reform and had expressed strong sympathies for such socially minded ministers as Washington Gladden, Walter Rauschenbusch, and especially George Herron. A gospel that recognized social ills and human needs appealed strongly to those Disciples who had tired of theological debates within the church. To them, the model of Christ ministering to the poor captured best the original spirit of Christianity, as well as the animating sentiments that underlay the founding of the Christian Church itself. Christianity, they contended, had prevailed in its first centuries against "the united powers of the world" because of its compassion for the downtrodden. It was only when Christians of later eras elevated creeds over loving deeds that their religion had fallen "easy Prey" to movements such as that of Islam.[33]

Supporters of the NBA believed that the association represented a major landmark in church history precisely because it refocused attention on "the orphan's cry and the aged's sigh." "I love organs and stained glass windows," said Ira Boswell, minister of Chattanooga's First Church, "but I love orphans and stranded saints more. . . . A church that does not serve is not Christian." Time and again advocates of organized benevolence within the church argued that the time for "applied Christianity" had surely arrived. "This is the age of doing things," declared Omaha's A. D. Harmon in 1913.[34]

In the early 1900s the *Christian Philanthropist* bubbled with progressive reform sentiments about "doing good" and fighting corruption. "This is above all others a philanthropic age," asserted editor George L. Snively. Indeed, the twentieth century was witnessing nothing less than the dawning of "the golden age of human brotherhood." Snively, general secretary of the association from early 1903 until mid-1906, had been pastor of the Christian Church in Jacksonville, Illinois, and was reputedly a superb stump speaker—"a born preacher." He was an enthusiastic follower of Theodore Roosevelt and Missouri's Joseph Folk, "that princely Reformer" who represented "civic righteousness" in the battle against corrupt "St. Louis boodlers." Snively's editorials inveighed against Senate "stand-patters," "old barons," saloons, the "unparalleled greed" of the meat-packing industry, "unholy trusts," and child labor. ("How many little ones," he wondered, were "deformed" so that a J. P. Morgan or John D. Rockefeller could be multimillionaires?) Although he was sympathetic to labor unions, in predictable progressive fashion he condemned labor violence and championed "the general public." "Christian Philanthropy," he wrote, "is loving class hatred out of human hearts and obliterating all American caste lines." Brimming with optimism, Snively echoed the belief so basic to the progressive reform generation: "There is no room for doubting that the world is growing better."[35]

Such optimism, like that of many reformers entering the twentieth century, may well have masked an underlying uneasiness about the nature of social change in the country. As the *Christian Philanthropist* made clear, Snively and others in the NBA were certainly alert to the disappearance of an earlier America. The journal summoned forth an image of the way the nation used to be: a land of farmers and villagers who were more or less equal. One individual recalled that "in little villages, everybody knew everybody else"; as neighbors they were willing to help each other in times of crisis. But the coming of cities, industry, and millions of immigrants had altered irrevocably this bucolic past. By the late nineteenth century, "the demoralizing influences of crime-breeding poverty" threatened to paralyze the nation. Additionally, the once-stirring philanthropic message of Christ had given ground to the Darwinian theory that the strong should survive and the weak should perish.[36]

The NBA regretted that Protestant churches—including the Disciples of Christ—had generally not met the challenge. While building houses of worship for the affluent, they had ignored the slum districts. Many poor laboring people had consequently turned from religion to fraternal organizations that offered insurance plans and other programs for dealing with hardship. It was "the church's neglect of its social opportunity" that had encouraged the growth of lodges, explained one person. Fannie Shedd Ayars quoted a woman dying of consumption who said sadly, "I wish I had joined a lodge instead of a church."[37]

If any one denomination had responded to the needs of the urban masses, it was the Roman Catholics—a fact that gave the Disciples of Christ little comfort. The only way to diminish "the power of the pope," advised a *Christian Philanthropist* editorial, was to "dispoil [*sic*] him of the monopoly he has upon the ministry of the good Samaritan." Fannie Shedd Ayars stated that she had helped organize the National Benevolent Association in part to stop orphans and old people from being "taken 'over the hill to the poorhouse,' [or] to the Catholics."[38]

Child saving, in this context, assumed special significance. Of all needy groups, disadvantaged children seemed particularly vulnerable and weak. The "empire of childhood," as George Snively described it, was hardly a match for the growing "nest of enemies" that included poverty, saloons, and other organized agencies of America's lower life. The Reverend Harry Minnick of Worcester, Massachusetts, told several Christian conventions in 1910 that "there is not a dirty dance hall, a reeking doggery, a gambling parlor, a low vicious theater, a salacious moving picture exhibition but what is a foe to childhood." Another minister evoked a heart-rending scene in which children, "gaunt with hunger," shivered in the cold and struggled in the markets of modern commerce. This was especially the case with dependent children or orphans— "Nobody's Darlings," according to one poem."[39]

More was involved here than pity and compassion, although certainly such emotions were strong. The NBA insisted that to work with children was to influence nothing less than the future. They were, as a poem said, "the little to be's": "Our soldiers and sailors to come, / Our Generals and Presidents, too, / Our lawyers and doctors and merchants and priests, / And our patriots, all good and true." Future doctors and patriots they might be, but without proper care they were also potential criminals. Citing statistics, the *Christian Philanthropist* claimed in 1917 that "about five-sevenths of all criminals in the U.S.A. have come from homeless and neglected children."[40]

By answering the children's cry, the NBA believed that it could meet a number of pressing social needs. To a child who might other wise fall victim to a harsh Darwinian struggle for survival, the association could say, "Bless your heart, you precious little one . . . we will protect you from the bitter contest that is offered in this awful world." To people who fretted that close village ties had given way to the cold, impartial relationships of an industrialized urban world, the association could fulfill the old ideal of "good, old-fashioned, neighborly helpfulness." To patriots who worried, as the NBA did, about the influx of millions of immigrants—"Christless hordes seeking our shores . . . godless multitudes pressing upon us"—the organization offered the ideal of peaceful assimilation.[41]

Perhaps most important, however, was the promise that child saving held for the church itself. Of course, the act of benevolence brought rewards to the giver. But there was another factor, one about which the NBA talked most excitedly and which had momentous implications for the nature of the care the children received in its homes. As one of the association's boosters said bluntly in 1910, "Training the dependent child is the cheapest and most effective kind of evangelism. . . . Our records show that, almost without exception, children placed in homes of our selection come into the church."[42]

Here was a point that brought together a variety of concerns about children as the hope—or threat—of the future and the role of the Christian Church as a viable religious force in a rapidly changing society. By rescuing dependent children, the Disciples could in a most practical way further their own mission and enlarge their membership. From this premise flowed the primary agenda of each of the NBA orphanages—an agenda that in September 1899 sent the children on their hymn-singing expedition to St. Louis's tavern areas. According to a *Christian Philanthropist* editorial, "The well-conducted Christian orphanage is a most fruitful home missionary agency"; it trained neglected and homeless youths "for country and for Christ." "God's future army will be the boys and girls of to-day," reported the director of the Cleveland orphanage. Children whom the church helped were nothing less than "little ambassadors from the poor to this institution."[43]

With undisguised enthusiasm the NBA homes reported on the spiritual progress of their charges. In 1908 the Juliette Fowler officials happily counted "twenty-five confessions and baptisms since our last year's report," and a St. Louis minister who visited a chapel service at the Christian Orphan's Home was delighted: "Such singing, such Bible lessons from memory, such close attention, such ready responses!" With equal excitement, one matron reported that six-year-old Jake, "a Jewish lad, a fact of which he is not very proud," had said "he'd rather be 'a 'Merican' than a Jew!" Such encouraging signs stirred hopes that the NBA would soon wrest "first place in charity from the Roman Catholics," and lure people from fraternal lodges.[44]

It was, of course, hardly surprising that a church-sponsored organization expressed concern about saving souls or enlarging the denomination's membership. A legion of orphanages under the aegis of various church groups around the nation had similar goals. Certainly, more than one home for dependent children grew out of the competition for souls as well as pity for the disadvantaged.

But the NBA's efforts in this respect pointed up something else: the organizational revolution that was reshaping American life. In an effort to bring order out of the fearful drift, even chaos, of unregulated economic and social change, a host of groups at the turn of the century drew upon the organizational model of the modern corporation. As Jane Addams pithily observed, "The trust is the educator of us all." Across society there was a vastly accelerated willingness to intervene in human affairs with new institutions—public and private—or with dramatically reconstructed older organizations. Watchwords for this resolve to control events were efficiency, expertise, coordination, and centralization. Progressive reformers were especially conspicuous among people trying to reconcile traditional ideals with a society in rapid transformation by using new forms of organization. The NBA, like so many reform groups of the era, adapted numerous viewpoints and techniques from what a historian later described as "the new interventionism."[45]

One of the association's most persistent claims was that it could focus scattered benevolent impulses behind major projects. In a complicated, sprawling society, the efforts of isolated congregations simply could not be as effective as a coordinated, collective attack on a problem. According to its executive director, J. H. Mohorter, the NBA existed to apply Christian sympathy wisely—to "harness the mighty Niagaras of wasted heart-power." The association, in other words, would combine the benevolent impulses of individual Disciples around the country "into one organic union." Mohorter's advice was heady stuff, considering the individualistic, anti-institutional traditions of the Christian Church. But he persisted, noting that when it came to charity most people were amateurs who misapplied their good intentions.[46]

In mid-1909 the *Christian Philanthropist* offered "A Glimpse at the Future," in which the NBA stood "years ahead of any organization in America." And it did so because efficient management, rather than "miscellaneous charity," characterized its work. "Organization and efficiency are two of the watchwords of today," asserted one NBA enthusiast, articulating an increasingly dominant theme in the NBA literature. Chattanooga preacher Ira Boswell was convinced that individual work could seldom cope with local needs. "Obligation demands organization," he said. When the Reverend Henry Minnick described the powerful and unscrupulous enemies of children—saloons, gambling halls, and nickelodeons—he shuddered. A united front against such "giant foes" was mandatory. Through the NBA, Minnick confidently assured his audience, "we meet organization with organization; skilled leadership with skilled and consecrated leadership."[47]

If organization was basic to the association's goals, as Minnick and others believed, so too was expertise. The fact that NBA workers were experienced in benevolent work meant that they could spot impostors and "the unworthy," and could thus pare needless expenses. In 1917 the matron of the Christian Orphans' Home, Betty R. Brown, urged that expertise and efficiency should govern not only the national administrative offices of the NBA but each of the separate institutions as well. Addressing the Missouri Convention of Charities and Correction, Brown aptly titled her speech. "Efficiency in the Care of Dependent Children." Although she conceded that emotions were important for charity work, she insisted that institutions must rely on "the critical scientific method." Brown went on to give detailed advice about the mechanics of good recordkeeping: the advantages of the vertical filing system, 8- by 11-inch cards, and alphabetizing names. Although she did not ignore subjects relating more directly to the atmosphere of children's homes (such as the need to celebrate individual birthdays), she concentrated on the increased accountability of all institutions and agencies in an age "when experts are called in from the outside." Brown, and the NBA generally, clearly hoped to ally the association with such expertise. Appropriately, the *Christian Philanthropist* in

1915 pictured eight of the NBA's nurses on the cover with the caption, "Science and the Christian Religion Are United in the N.B.A.'s Institutions in Child Redemption."[48]

Striving to identify itself with the "new way of treating poverty and crime," the NBA praised its orphanages as part of a spreading web of "preventive agents," ranging from night schools to public baths and juvenile courts. A *Christian Philanthropist* editorial, drawing upon the medical analogy so popular among progressive reformers, distinguished between the old strategy of trying to save an already sick patient and the new approach of using vaccination to stop diseases before they started. Among developing preventive agencies, the orphanage was "one of the most effective of all." And among orphanages, those of the NBA were supposed to be models, taking children who would otherwise threaten society and training them for virtuous and useful citizenship. So important was this view to the association that the *Christian Philanthropist* ran the same editorial, "Prevention Better than Cure," verbatim on three occasions in four years.[49]

An uneasy tension nonetheless marked the association's enthusiasm for the widening collection of preventive agencies, within which the NBA placed itself. At one level the organization unabashedly endorsed the progressive trend in which the state assumed greater responsibility for social problems. Editorials in the *Christian Philanthropist* urged state intervention regarding such issues as prohibition, the Pure Food and Drug Act, vigorous antitrust policies, public arbitration of strikes, and municipal ownership of utilities.[50] On the need for public solutions to the plight of children, the NBA was especially zealous. It applauded, for example, the establishment of the Children's Bureau; the formation of juvenile courts; the passage of child labor laws; state regulation of charity work; medical campaigns to reduce the "slaughter of the innocents" by poverty, dirt, and disease; and legislative aid for mothers of dependent children.

But while the NBA favored expanding the public's social welfare responsibilities, it nervously contemplated what this might portend for private benevolence. Understandably, the association did not want to jeopardize its own philanthropic role. Thus while the broadening of public aid for unfortunate citizens was a satisfying sign of social progress, the NBA's leadership fretted about such a trend. At least three times the *Christian Philanthropist* published an editorial criticizing a woman who reportedly believed that the large number of state institutions had rendered private or church orphanages obsolete. The association warned that state institutions—unlike those of the NBA—were pawns of party politics. Although the Reverend A. D. Harmon of Omaha lauded the juvenile court, he believed that child rescue work was much too vital to be in the hands of politicians. Other warnings appeared in the *Christian Philanthropist* about the danger that dependent children might become the victims of deals made in smoke-filled rooms. Until state services were free of political maneuvering, the NBA had no doubts about the matter: "The dependent child is far better provided for under the Church of Christ."[51]

The association was willing, politics aside, to concede that the state had more money and the capacity to offer better physical care to dependent children than did churches. At issue, however, was not simply the material status of youngsters. Here the NBA and the editors of the *Juvenile Court Record* echoed each other. "The State can never supply and furnish that love and affection that the ordinary parent can give to the child," an editorial in the *Record* insisted. "The State is at all times cold, distant, heartless and irreligious." The NBA could not have agreed more. The nub of the matter, the NBA emphasized again and again, was that love and moral training constituted the heart of child saving. And love did not exist in state institutions with their cold, machinelike atmosphere, and monotonous routines.[52]

To the casual observer, the association's criticism of old-style congregate asylums might have appeared hypocritical. After all, had not the NBA itself established orphanages in which dozens of children lived under the same roof? Obviously sensitive about such judgments, the NBA went out of its way in the early 1900s to justify its labors in light of both the increased public skepticism about traditional asylums and the rising popularity of the home-finding movement.

With considerable care the NBA distinguished its homes from the old-fashioned orphanages that had, for good reason, fallen into disfavor but still existed as state and county institutions. Aligning itself with the growing opposition to traditional orphanages, the association rebuked such institutions for isolating their residents from the outside community, typically dressing them in uniforms, ignoring individual needs, and treating the children en masse. Charles Dickens had effectively captured the tragic aspects of such an environment. Moreover, according to the NBA, there was little that state and country institutions could do about the situation. Politics too often shaped policy, and public employees reportedly thought more about their salaries than about the children under their care. Inevitably, public institutions were emotionally barren and expensive to operate.[53]

"An asylum is not a good place to bring up a child"—here was a popular sentiment with which the NBA agreed wholeheartedly. The disturbing fact, however, was that it came from a man who refused to support the association's work for precisely that reason. The NBA strenuously argued that its homes were vastly different from antiquated asylums: for one thing, they existed only as temporary refuges until individual Christian families could provide permanent care; for another, the loving environment in NBA homes was something very special. The *Christian Philanthropist* could not make that point too often: "It is the presence of love that changes the institution into a sweet home." With pride, the Colorado home reported the judgment of a state official that "yours is the most homelike institution in our city."[54]

Lest anyone think that such opinions were biased, the head of the Christian Orphans' Home cited the testimony of none other than a five-year-old resident. When the little boy, who had no parents, first learned that he would have to live in an orphanage, he was terrified. But after his first night in the St. Louis Home, he told the matron, "I'll stay here with you, but I won't go to the orphan's home." The institution's president summed up the situation: "Bless his little heart. In all the months he has been with us, I don't believe he has ever known he was in that dreaded home."[55]

Despite these descriptions of love and happiness in the NBA homes, the association was quick to assert that "no child should be kept in an institution, no matter how well managed, a day longer than is necessary . . . the right kind of a family home is far better." "We are a home-finding society," avowed executive director James

Mohorter. "We believe it better to find homes for the children than to keep them in an institution, even one of our splendid homes."[56]

Ironically, the NBA's strong advocacy of home placement as the ultimate goal of orphan rescue work diminished markedly when the subject of other home-finding societies arose. In theory, these organizations were fine. The problem, as the association saw it, was that "too often their practice is wretched." "Over-enthusiastic child-home-finders" simply abused a good idea. So intent were they on placing homeless children that they paid insufficient attention to who took the youngsters. The result all too often was a "wholesale giving away of children" that quickly collapsed into "throwing them away." "Promiscuous distribution of children," argued the *Christian Philanthropist*, had little to recommend it, and the fairly common practice of exhibiting "unfortunate little ones" before curious crowds was reprehensible. In one small Missouri town, for example, a carload of children from New York reportedly "went off like hot cakes." On another occasion, a man quickly found takers in the South for a load of New York youths and went back for more. To the NBA, this was little more than "child-peddling" and allowed incompetent adults to gain control of children whose lives were already troubled enough. The NBA staff itself had once rescued a thirteen-year-old Kentucky boy who had run away after a home-finding society had placed him with a brutal farmer.[57]

It was probably not coincidental that in 1910 a rush of criticism of home-finding societies appeared in the *Christian Philanthropist*. In both the White House Conference on Dependent Children the previous year and the much-publicized *Delineator* campaign, there had been strong disapproval of congregate institutions and much praise for home-finding societies. The NBA unquestionably was eager to show that it, too, hailed the passing of the traditional orphanage and that it was in the vanguard of the home-placing movement. Yet the Association anxiously argued that a need still existed for children's institutions and that the NBA, once again, offered a model.

Carefully and emphatically, the Association explained that several types of children did not benefit from home placement and required institutional attention. These included boys between ages of three and ten—"too big to be sweetly innocent of mischief, too small to be of value in service." Another group of "undesirables" included those in "the defective class," who were crippled, physically unattractive, ill, or mentally deficient. Others were unappealing because of fears that they had inherited "tainted blood" from immoral parents. The NBA certainly did not favor turning any of these children over to a "Christless public charity." Given the lack of individual Christian homes for all dependent children, the NBA promised the next best thing: "a well regulated institutional home."[58]

When the association heralded the family as its institutional model, it was engaged in far more than a defensive reflex against the claims of the rising home society movement. Concerns about the fate of the family shaped the agenda of progressive reformers at many levels, and the NBA was no latecomer in this respect. From the outset, the association hoped to provide opportunities that would allow widows to keep their children. Monthly reports in the *Christian Philanthropist* from the various homes were full of references to working mothers who boarded their children in NBA institutions; in many cases the women were employed in the homes themselves. The bleak choices usually available to poor widows, the association said, were patently unfair. If they did not work, they and their children faced starvation. If they did work, it was often at the expense of giving up their children, because most jobs did not allow for the demands of child rearing. Helping widows care for their offspring was not only a Christian duty; it also kept families together. "The almost universal sentiment today," the *Christian Philanthropist* observed sympathetically in 1916, "is that mother and child should not be separated if it can possibly be avoided." When the NBA endorsed state pensions for widows, it argued that this was one charitable function that government could carry out "more effectively" than individual or private organizations. In the meantime, the Disciples hoped to do their part. By opening doors to both mother and child, the NBA allowed them to stay together. Of course, the homes benefited from the labor of these women, but certainly more than institutional self-interest was involved.[59]

In fairness, no one could doubt the NBA's commitment to using its institutions to strengthen family bonds. Where it was impossible to keep parent and child together, or to place a child with foster or adoptive parents, the homes strove to establish a family atmosphere. Reports from the orphanages consistently referred to all the residents as "our family." Descriptions of some of the children, and sometimes lengthy discussions of activities in the homes, represented assiduous efforts to convey a sense of the human dimensions of the institutions.[60]

And there was evidence that the association did successfully establish close ties between children and the homes. One of the first four children in the NBA's care subsequently brought his wife and two offspring to visit the St. Louis home and "Mother Hansbrough." When another of the first residents dropped by twelve years after leaving, Hansbrough answered the door, paused without recognizing him, and then joyfully exclaimed, "Our boy!" when he introduced himself. Sometimes the *Christian Philanthropist* printed letters from former residents. "I so often think of you and your kindness to me and my sisters and brothers," wrote one "graduate" in 1908. Another closed by saying, "I am as ever, your girl." "Tell me all about the home," urged one youth, who enclosed a quarter for the *Orphan's Cry* and sent a special greeting to the matron, "Miss T" (Tena Williamson). In 1904 a young woman who had lived in the Christian Orphans' Home nine years earlier returned as a widow with her child. She had found employment, but she wanted the institution to board her son because her own experience proved that "he could not be brought up better."[61]

Despite such gratifying accounts, there were some signs of how herculean a task it was to run "a well regulated institutional home." One orphan girl who lived in the St. Louis Home for several years ran away. When the president asked why she had left, the girl sobbed, "I wanted to get to 'my people,' I wanted to belong to some one." No matter how hard the homes tried, invariably there were those children who for whatever reasons felt they did not "belong."[62]

More than anyone else, the matrons carried the burden of the "family" setting. They were "the privates in the ranks," in the words of the *Christian Philanthropist*, "unnoticed and unrewarded."[63] While some supporters of the NBA gave money, talent, and time, the matrons often gave nothing less than themselves. Even that was not necessarily enough. So demanding were the duties, so overwhelming the responsibilities, that it was an exceptional person indeed who had any chance of success. Sometimes the homes virtually needed revolving doors to accommodate the coming and going of newly hired matrons.

Most of the association's matrons had at least some college instruction and experience teaching in public schools. All had to be members of the Christian Church. Despite previous experience and dedication, the assignment of matron presented an awesome challenge and paid little. Beyond the constant stress that accompanied the daily routine of supervising dozens of youngsters ranging from infants to teenagers, there were endless other tasks. Each month a report was due for publication in the *Christian Philanthropist*. Visitors could drop by at any time: on one Sunday in 1904, ninety-eight callers were on hand at the Christian Orphans' Home. Broken equpment, illnesses that sometimes turned into epidemics, staff shortages, the need to provide opportunities for children to visit the zoo or attend a circus—all of these duties pressed relentlessly on the matron. One rainy day, Betty Brown, the diminutive ninety-pound matron of the Christian Orphans' Home, wondered, "Did you ever spend a day indoors with a hundred children learning a yell?" Emma Bush, completing her fifth day on the job at the Cleveland Christian Orphanage in 1905, wrote, "I have not one minute to call my own, from five in the morning till eight at night when each of the weary sixty heads is quietly reposing on the pillow."[64]

During the winter of 1908, one of the sixty-two children at the Juliette Fowler Home came down with the measles. Despite precautions to stop the disease from spreading, the staff readied for the siege: "May the Father be with us through this most trying ordeal," read the monthly report. The next year at the Christian Orphans' Home, not only did measles strike "in a most malignant form" but so too did the chicken pox and the mumps. As many as forty-seven children were in bed at one time, some suffering from measles and mumps simultaneously. All schoolwork halted for more than a week, and several children died. "In my three years and six months' work in the Orphan's Home," recorded the weary matron, "it has never been my experience to cope with a situation so trying." The death of a child in any of the orphanages imposed especially wrenching emotional demands. "Dismissed to the angel of death, Robert

Brady, age 11 years," wrote one matron as she described the services, at which a flower rested on the boy's vacant chair in the chapel and the children sang his favorite song. At almost every point, of course, the matrons were able to obtain aid from assistants, volunteer groups, members of the boards, local doctors who donated medical services, and other individuals—such as the "Ole Parson," as the St. Louis children called George Snively. It was nonetheless a rare woman indeed who held up under the strain.[65]

Even the apparently indefatigable and very popular matron of the Christian Orphans' Home, Tena Williamson, fell victim to the pressures of the job. "Miss Tena," as the children affectionately knew her and as she usually signed her reports, served the St. Louis orphanage admirably as assistant matron for four years and then, from 1901 to 1905, as head matron. Her round, cheerful face conveyed both tenderness and good humor—two characteristics that made her a favorite of the children and the board. More than most of the NBA matrons, she infused her reports with a distinctive personal touch. As much as the children, she seemed swept up with excitement about birthday parties, coloring Easter eggs, and going to a downtown toy department to visit Santa Claus. She spoke proudly of the children as her own sons and daughters. She also exhibited a knack for teaching lessons in a gentle, unobtrusive way. And certainly forgiveness marked her view of little Carl who, "sleepy and cross," had punched another child. The chastened Carl sat next to Williamson as she sketched out her "Matron's Letter." "He looks very sorry," she said before asking rhetorically, "Shall I send the scamp to bed?"[66]

Presumably, however, the ebullient tone of Williamson's reports sometimes glossed over the more anxious moments. She described her trip to the 1904 World's Fair with sixty-five children as "delightful," but she must have felt cold dread when four of the children were lost for a while in the huge crowds. Six months earlier a similar incident had occurred. She had taken seventy-three children Christmas shopping in St. Louis's department stores, only to lose Ben, a boy who had moved to the home just the previous day. She had warned him to stay with the group, since there was no way that she or her assistants could watch him constantly. Yet when it was time to go back to the home, Ben was missing. "I left Willie with car fare to hunt Ben and come on," Williamson recalled. She did not elaborate on what thoughts entered her mind as she and the others "were speeding on home and singing as usual."[67]

Williamson's resilient personality unquestionably aided her on such occasions, but so too did her religious faith. Whether she was battling to save a sick child or longing for a large playroom where the children could work off surplus energy, she was convinced of one thing: "This work of caring for homeless children *is* God's work." Indeed, she once conceded, following a particularly frantic period during which 1,000 visitors came to the home within two weeks, "I often think it a most fortunate thing that this work itself is praise to God—for it takes all of the time."[68]

Ultimately the job simply overwhelmed even the dedicated and still young "Miss Tena." In May 1905 she resigned with regrets and returned to her Lebanon, Missouri, home. In the words of the *Christian Philanthropist*, she needed "rest for her tired brain and over-wrought nerves." Her departure had an unsettling effect on the orphanage, however. Three of the smaller girls ran away when she left and were missing overnight before someone found them.[69]

Williamson's successor lasted barely three months. Nannie Gordon, who had taught school for seven years in Lexington, Missouri, was no stranger to working with children, but nervousness and rapid weight loss quickly convinced her to "give up the strenuous life" at the orphanage. Sadie Maxson's spirits were high when she took over in August. Initially, she had felt rather uncomfortable with the prospects "of mothering so large a 'brood.'" After a month she observed hopefully, "I already feel that the family belongs to me." Several weeks later she resigned because the position was too demanding. The next matron arrived September 14, 1905, finding "things in a torn up condition, housecleaning, painting, plastering, etc." Although she claimed that she was "not easily discouraged," she quit the following February.[70]

Finding qualified matrons and keeping them were almost as difficult for the NBA as raising funds. Donations of help, food, clothing, and money came from a variety of sources but were seldom sufficient. At the most basic level, help came in the form of "ingathering"—small contributions from individuals, congregations, Sunday Schools, and various aid societies. Monthly reports of the homes commonly listed donations of such things as canned goods, blankets, dressed chickens, and mittens. This kind of aid did help meet daily needs: "If you had to find something to cover the heads of 102 little ones, you would have a slight conception of how this is appreciated," wrote one matron. Nonetheless, in early 1911 the Georgia home ended one month with $5.09 in the coffers and $173 in unpaid bills, a situation all too familiar in the other orphanages as well.[71]

In order to remind people of the institutions' needs, the NBA continually publicized its work. One technique was to bring some of the children to the annual state and national conventions of the Disciples of Christ. In 1914 six-year-old Ivy Henderson wasted no words in telling the Georgia state conference, "We need some money from you all." Usually the appeal was more elaborate, featuring a delegation of youths singing hymns, reciting poems, or sometimes standing quietly at the front of the hall. The *Christian Philanthropist* was full of calls for money—for example, "Stick Sixteen Cents on This Slip and Add a Foot to a Mile of Pennies for the Cleveland Christian Orphanage." In 1905 the journal published a special Easter supplement containing the script for a program that individual congregations could perform. At one point in the script, "Nellie, the Little Orphan," sings about being "out in the street." As she sinks to the ground, a small group walks on stage with a message: "Take up the poor little one, / Chilled by the night wind so wild; / Out in the streets all alone, / Save her, the poor orphan child."[72]

Campaigns for donations obviously produced results, but while the NBA dutifully thanked the contributors and attested to great accomplishments, its workers often became very discouraged. One of the most frustrating parts of the association's work was all too often a lack of support within the Christian Church itself. One NBA representative, who called on virtually all the Protestant denominations in Missouri, commented indignantly that only in Christian churches had he not received permission to address congregations following the Sunday sermons. Baptists, Methodists, Presbyterians, Congregationalists, and others had allowed him to speak. "This is more than I can say for some of our own churches," he grumbled. "In some places . . . I am entirely ignored."[73]

An especially painful controversy for the NBA involved Easter Sunday contributions. In 1892 the organization decided that Easter would be the day on which it would request "a general offering" from the denomination's churches and Sunday Schools across the nation. Previously, the Disciples of Christ had not paid Easter much attention because of the desire, as the *Christian Philanthropist* explained, "to eliminate all unscriptural forms and ceremonies from our worship."[74] But the NBA Easter appeals caught on and in 1903 alone added $7,000 to the association's treasury. In the meantime, however, the Christian Woman's Board of Missions staked its own claim to the Easter offering. Angrily, Hansbrough, Snively, and others argued that the NBA had, by acting first, preempted Easter as its special day. Snively feared that "partisan politics" would deny the association what rightfully belonged to it. Ultimately, the NBA simply had to hope that individual churches would favor the organization with Easter contributions. In 1910 Fannie Shedd Ayars stressed that the Easter offering "is our bread and butter money." But because Christian Churches as a body were apparently unwilling to award the NBA any special collection day, the association was left to scramble for its own funds.[75]

This only heightened the NBA's sense that it was still on the periphery of the Christian Church's vision and concern. In 1910, when Edgar DeWitt Jones of Bloomington, Illinois, addressed the Centennial Convention of the Disciples of Christ at Pittsburgh, he could not understand why the NBA still had "so small a place in our program of activities." He lamented that so "very few of our thousands of churches give any place to this important work."[76]

Fannie Shedd Ayars angrily concurred. As she described how the Babies' Home and Hospital had used "the basement, the barn, the carriage house, the attic and every inch of space," she fumed that "many seem to forget we exist." She observed that during the past harsh winter months, "our wee babies suffered for lack of clothing and bedding." Thinking about all this did not put Ayars in a tolerant mood. In exasperation, she stormed: "Hide your heads for shame and ask the Lord to forgive you for your sins of omission." The problem of limited funds may have been an important reason why in early 1911 Ayars broke from the association. She had been a prominent figure in the NBA since its origins. A charter member, she had at one point been president of the organization, and more than anyone had created and administered the Babies' Home and Hospital. When she split with the NBA, she maintained control of the Babies' Home and formed a new group, the Christian Woman's National Benevolent Association. The NBA reorganized the Christian Orphans' Home so that it could once again accommodate infants and "worthy" mothers, but for the next several years the organization complained that some contributors confused its work with that of Ayars.[77]

By the time Ayars left the NBA, the association was nearing the end of its boom period of growth. This was true not only in terms of new institutions but also in an emotional sense. Consolidation, rather than expansion, increasingly dominated discussion. An important segment of the Twenty-Seventh Annual Report in September 1913 focused on the organization's limitations. Although it was still considering new possibilities—a regional orphanage in California, a tubercular sanitarium in the Southwest, a home for incurables, and a hospital (which it ultimately opened in Kansas City in 1915)— it was more interested in marking the boundaries of its benevolence. In this context, "good business" became as important a gauge as "good Christian practice" for measuring the association's work. The 1913 report observed that the need to end waste in charitable endeavors required "a modern system of accounting and auditing." With pride, the NBA observed that in Denver, St. Louis, and Cleveland, commercial groups exemplifying prudent business practices had given "unqualified approval" to the association's orphanages.[78]

Developments in the national economy helped to explain the association's growing emphasis on finances. In 1913, for example, the NBA believed that a shaky economy accounted for an $18,000 drop in the organization's contributions during the previous twelve months. Over the next several years, the *Christian Philanthropist* bewailed the fact that the spreading war in Europe further curtailed the tendencies of Americans to think about local charity needs. In early 1915 a special Disciples of Christ Commission on Benevolences submitted a bleak report, based on a six-month investigation of the church's philanthropic activities. Perhaps never in its twenty-nine years, the report guessed, had the NBA "been in such urgent need." Its crowded orphanages were all in debt; indeed, there was the possibility that some might have to close. A few months later the president of one of the homes moaned, "We have reached the limit. . . . God alone knows what is to become of us."[79]

More than ever, the association seemed aware of the sheer enormousness of its task, and the heightened recognition of the limits of what it could do eroded its earlier optimism. In late 1913, following the acquisition of the last of its orphanages (the Child Study Institute of Omaha), the association wondered about "the extent [to which] a Christian institution shall go in its efforts to aid the indigent." At the very time that the NBA continued to worry about the church's relinquishing its charitable responsibilities to secular groups, it was also apprehensive about the church's trying to accomplish too much by undertaking "a burden . . . which really belongs to the state." At this point the association made an astonishing disclaimer: it was not responsible for "people who have no special claim upon the church for physical support, unless it is conceded that the church should bear the whole burden of charity work." Clearly the NBA was torn between the contradictory tugs of financial and practical considerations and its founding ideals—ideals that represented a desire for the church to become a champion of benevolence, not to ignore certain groups. Quite simply, the NBA was narrowing its role: "Experience has taught the Association," said the 1913 annual report, "the necessity of limiting its activities if it would save the church from bearing the state's humanitarian burden."[80]

As the association noted with discouragement that it lacked the funds to meet the needs of even its own members, let alone other groups, it edged toward an uncharacteristically cynical view of philanthropy itself. By 1917 the NBA expressed bewilderment at the apparent increase in poverty and dependency. Human misery was seemingly spreading, despite an unprecedented munificence of charitable work. Private and public aid for unfortunate citizens had never been greater, and new laws established to protect poor and dependent people constituted "one of the outstanding characteristics of our modern civilization." But, mysteriously, human suffering did not appear to diminish. This raised the troubling question, according to the *Christian Philanthropist*, "as to whether much of our philanthropy has been as wise as it has been abundant." Perhaps

101

charity in its own way added to pauperism by undermining "the spirit of independence, of self-respect and of manliness." From this perspective, the act of doing good could all too easily become a misplaced effort that turned the needy into parasites.[81]

Whereas in 1903 the *Christian Philanthropist* had characterized orphans as "little ambassadors from the poor," there was a tendency a decade later to widen the distance between the social classes. True, in 1916, a story in the journal affectionately described the visit of a burly laborer with his offspring, whom he had placed in an NBA home, and suggested what fine bridges the association was building between the worker and the church. At roughly the same time, however, the magazine reflected on the need to isolate "the incorrigibly idle and worthless" class into state-run programs of discipline and "industrial and moral training."[82] The shift in temperament was subtle but significant. There was a substantial difference in emphasis between building bridges to unite social groups and constructing fences to protect worthy citizens from the great unwashed.

In a sense, the NBA was ready for the 1920s. Just as its energies and work at the turn of the century had reflected so well the mood of the progressive reform era, so did its development after about 1913 conform to patterns that marked the waning of progressivism. Like many reform organizations, the association grew more sensitive to the limits of social change than to its possibilities, more attentive to the demands of businesslike efficiency and accounting, less hopeful about narrowing the chasm between social classes.

In another sense, however, the war years marked the successful culmination of the NBA's struggle to gain the recognition that it had sought for so long within the Christian Church. Following several frighteningly lean years, 1916 turned out to be "a truly faithful friend," according to the *Christian Philanthropist.* "The old year found us a little in doubt as to the exact standing of the association as a member of the family of organized activities of the church. . . . It leaves us with all doubt upon this question removed." The orphanages in St. Louis, Cleveland, and Dallas were finally free of all debt. Over the next few months the NBA's pleas that "the din of war" not "drown the cry of the orphan child" brought even more positive results. In 1917 and 1918 the NBA enjoyed its best financial years to that point. Its funds in 1917 exceeded the previous annual high by almost $23,000, and in 1918 jumped by $40,000 more, bringing its total income for one year to a record $265,000. The number of contributing churches increased dramatically, with 207 new congregations participating in 1917 alone.[83]

For a while in late 1918, in the flush of acceptance and an enlarged treasury, the NBA renewed discussion of expanding its "facilities for child-serving so as to be able to provide for our share of all dependent children that may come to us without reference to race or nationality." There was even talk of opening new children's homes, in southern California and the Washington, D.C., area.[84] As a matter of fact, however, the NBA network's period of expansion was over. Nevertheless the organization had established a number of benevolent institutions that would continue their work for decades to come, including children's homes in six regions.[85] And after some thirty years of feeling like an orphan itself within the Christian Church, the National Benevolent Association had at last determined that it was a full-fledged member of the Disciples family.

• 4 •

Rescuing the "Newsies": John Gunckel and the Toledo Newsboys' Association

Ice on the Maumee River was more than a foot thick, and a bitter wind whipped across Toledo that February evening in 1885 when John E. Gunckel, railroad ticket agent, first saw them: two homeless newsboys seeking refuge from the below-zero temperature had curled up under their papers in the vestibule of a nearby store. Gunckel provided them with sandwiches and coffee, and let them spend the rest of the night in his office.[1] Such compassion was merely one expression of the ticket agent's growing interest in the lives of youthful street sellers. By the time of his death, thirty years later, thousands of boys in Toledo and elsewhere knew him affectionately as "Gunck," founder of an organization that received national acclaim: the Toledo Newsboys' Association, or Boyville. One of the most popular photographs of the progressive era showed the gentle-faced, smiling Gunckel with a happy group of small newsboys gathered around him. "This big-hearted man is playing well the part of the big brother," read the caption in the *Christian Philanthropist*, one of many publications that printed the photograph while urging other citizens to follow Gunckel's example.[2]

In the turbulent setting of a northern industrial city,[3] John Gunckel creatively approached a particularly complex and bothersome aspect of America's "boy problem"—the young street venders of newspapers and shoeshines.[4] On one hand the "newsie" tugged at the affections and respect of the public. To middle-class shoppers he symbolized the disadvantaged youngster, invariably with runny nose and ragged clothes, surviving through hustle and ambition, surmounting hardship through pluck. Yet he also represented something disturbing, even frightening; he was a grim reminder of disintegrating forces that threatened social harmony. As one writer observed, "The newsboy is the peculiar product of the modern city; with him environment and association have usually done their worst."[5] From this vantage point, the newsie marked the end of innocence. An inhabitant of pool halls, cigar stores, and saloons, he was "the embryo criminal." "If we do not lift him up, he will pull us down," warned J. F. Atkinson, an organizer of the Chicago Boys' Club. Lewis Hine's memorable 1910 photographs, "Newsies at Skeeter Branch," in which several young newsboys puffed sullenly on cigarettes as they struck tough-guy poses for the camera, captured this threatening image all too well.[6]

Gunckel's solution was that of a philanthropy based on child labor—a solution putting him in conflict with prominent progressives such as those in the Hull House group, and accenting divisions among reformers regarding the newsboy problem. Some argued that the only answer was to get the youths off the streets, to admit that the disadvantages of working the sidewalks far overshadowed the reputed benefits of street vending. To Gunckel and his supporters, however, members of the Toledo Newsboys' Association were "little merchants," emblematic of capitalism on the make and statesmanship on the rise. As the boys honed their entrepreneurial skills, they reportedly carried the shields of self-discipline, respect for law, and civic pride—all part of the armor that Boyville provided against the perils of a disorderly environment.

While reformers debated the subject, the actual status of the newsie remained ambiguous. There was indeed disconcerting evidence of exploitation and misery, but there were also suggestions that at least some of the newsboys, as little "John Q. Workers," were quite willing to develop their own forms of accommodation with the world of the middle class.[7] On this level, an ongoing dialectic between newsboys and reformers helped to shape the Toledo Newsboys' Association. The study of the association thus not only illustrated different reform responses to "the boy problem"; it provided yet another variation on the theme of social class so central to the progressive era.

The organization's origins also fit nicely into a larger national script in which orphans and newsboys seemed one and the same. Gunckel's encounter with two homeless boys during that cruel winter of 1885 appeared to confirm the equation. "The typical newsboy is poor, ragged, dirty and, frequently, homeless or worse than homeless," reported one observer. "Waifs of the street" was what settlement-house worker and muckraking journalist Ernest Poole called them. "Go late to-night down through the narrow streets near Newspaper Row," Poole advised; "you will find over a hundred little chaps, wholly dead to the world." In the cold November hours one evening between midnight and two o'clock, Poole counted "over sixty on two streets alone. They lie in tangled heaps of two's and three's, over gratings, down steps, and under benches . . . all are foul and ragged." Appropriately, Jacob Riis opened his discussion of New York City's homeless children by telling about a small newsboy who had broken down emotionally one wintry day near the Brooklyn Bridge.[8]

Although the vast majority of newsboys in Toledo and elsewhere were actually not orphans, the belief that they were played a critical part in the public's perception of them. Popular literature had for some time presented an image of young street vendors as orphans struggling to survive. The fact that by the early 1900s, in a city such as Buffalo, more than one-fourth of the newsboys were under the age of ten and more than 80 percent were less than fourteen undoubtedly helped to confirm such opinions. In Buffalo, however, closer inspection revealed that all but two of forty-nine boys between five and eight still had both parents; the other two were half-orphans.[9]

Still, there was a touch of reality sustaining the popular view of newsboys as America's Oliver Twists. Ernest Poole, for example, after studying some 5,000 New York City newsboys, claimed that "hundreds" were homeless. Even those who had one or both parents were virtually dependent on their own wages for living expenses. Further, according to Poole, newsboys tended to be restless types who spent hard-earned money in Bowery bookstores on paperback adventure stories and then hit the road looking for excitement; in the process they learned how "to be homeless." Although "the homeless, the most illiterate, the most dishonest, the most impure" constituted only a minority of street workers, Poole believed that they exerted an influence on the streets far beyond their numbers.[10] One writer who conceded that selling newspapers could provide invaluable experience nonetheless felt that those most susceptible to the city's evils were those who had "no home restraint"—who were virtual if not actual orphans.[11] Not surprisingly, when the Boys' Club Association of New York sought contributions, its advertisement showed a very small, apparently homeless ragamuffin, newspapers in one arm and a dog at his side, partially curled up in a box in an alley.[12] The image was as powerful as its designers intended.

It was perhaps appropriate, then, that John Gunckel received tributes as both "father to the fatherless" and "the Father of the Newsboys."[13] Born in 1846 in Germantown, Ohio, Gunckel grew up in the comfort and security that came from belonging to one of the town's pioneer families. After attending public schools, he studied three years at Oberlin College before joining his father briefly in the banking and insurance business. He married his wife, Alice, who was a Canadian by birth, in Germantown. They had one child, a son named Will. In 1871 they moved to Toledo, where John Gunckel tried selling real estate. Eventually, he signed on with the Lake Shore and Michigan Southern Railroad as ticket agent, a position he held for thirty years. Toledo, like most midwestern cities, was booming in the late 1800s, and Gunckel found a social as well as an economic niche for himself. He joined the Rotary Club and, although he never owned a craft larger than a row boat, was very influential in the local yachting association. Gunckel had the energy and personality that might have lifted him into the upper business ranks in the city, but very early he showed a greater interest in the lives of Toledo's street boys, especially those who hawked newspapers.[14]

During the 1890s that interest sparked the creation of Boyville. After observing the needs as well as the shrewd adaptability and tough resiliency of newsboys such as Moses Black, Gunckel decided to take action. Black, whom Gunckel had noticed on a street corner instructing another youth in the art of selling newspapers, supported himself and five younger siblings. In Gunckel's opinion, he "was the greatest little hustler on the streets, a leader, made of the kind of material I wanted." Years later, Moses Black remembered Gunckel's visit in 1892 to a meeting of the Bootblacks' and Newsboys' Union, which had recently emerged out of a disagreement with a Toledo newspaper. The railroad ticket agent surprised the boys by urging them to form an association in which the newsies governed themselves.[15]

Gunckel's proposal became a reality shortly thereafter, in December, when he struck up an acquaintance with a newsboy named Jimmie. Although Jimmie was the "leader of a gang of little toughs," he had revealed, to Gunckel's delight, that he had a social conscience. Gunckel asked the youngster to invite his friends to a Christmas dinner. "I don't want a good boy in the crowd," Gunckel remembered telling Jimmie. "I want only boys who are bad. . . . I want poor boys. . . . they must sell newspapers or shine shoes, and not a boy must come in a dress suit." With the help of several other Toledo citizens, Gunckel fed the 150 poor youths who showed up in what to them was a most unfamiliar setting: the Toledo Yacht Club. Disorder prevailed; at least three fights broke out among the unruly youngsters; and one of seven police officers in attendance ended up on his ear outside the building. Despite that inauspicious beginning, after dinner 102 of the boys followed Gunckel's suggestion and officially formed a newsboys' association based on the principle of self-government. They elected Gunckel president and Jimmie vice-president. A year later the organization more than doubled to 250 members; three years later it claimed 1,520 members—in Gunckel's words, "a little army, and all working harmoniously together for each other's good."[16]

Although Gunckel continued to work until 1906 for the railroad, he spent enormous amounts of time building the association. The fact that his employer, W. R. Callaway, sympathized with such activities helped; so too did aid from individuals like Flora and Bennett Friedman. The Friedmans, who in the early 1900s operated two confectionaries in the area where the newsboys picked up their papers, urged street sellers to join Boyville.[17] Later, there were others such as Edward Gallagher, a product of the association who stayed on to work closely with Gunckel and who, according to an important member of the juvenile court movement, was "one of our coming boy wonders," someone who enjoyed the respect of Toledo's youths.[18] By 1909 Gunckel would also have a full-time assistant, William R. Neale, the son of a local Presbyterian minister.[19]

In the early years, however, it was largely the driving energy of John and Alice Gunckel that galvanized the association. Time and again they displayed a deeply personal interest in the boys. When a newsie named Ben Cohen ended up in the hospital, they visited him. Shortly thereafter, Cohen, back on the streets but still sick, heard from a doctor that he would have to lose his leg. The distressed boy limped to the Gunckel's home, and Alice immediately took him to a neighborhood physician, who said there was no need to amputate. Then came word that Cohen was again in the hospital. A worried John Gunckel, on his way out of town on business, wrote to Mayor Samuel M. Jones, urging that "some one who has influence ought to say a word to the doctors at the St. Vincent Hospital. I would like to have you please 'phone them and see what is the matter." Jones acted quickly and learned that there were apparently no plans to remove the boy's leg.[20]

It was thus not surprising that Toledo newsboys called Alice Gunckel "Mother," or that she in turn referred to them as her boys.[21] John Gunckel became, simply and affectionately, "Gunck." Years later a former newsboy recalled how at the age of ten he had sat on Gunckel's lap, received his membership badge, and listened to personal instructions on the importance of honesty, courtesy, and cleanliness. "As a kid," he said, "that made a terrific impression on me." Another remembered "how we used to come in to see him [Gunckel], and he gave us a nickel or a dime and told us to go out and get some ice cream or a sandwich or something." The important fact was that "he treated us as if we were adults, and he had that personality about him that made us feel as if we counted for something."[22] One Toledo visitor wrote to Judge Ben Lindsey in 1909 that Gunckel was "a prince of fellows. An attractive personality, and the boys love him. He is undoubtedly the biggest man in Toledo today."[23] Brand Whitlock, a leading progressive politician and mayor of Toledo from 1905 to 1913, also stressed the powerful role of Gunckel's personality: "You should see him on the street with a group of his boys chattering about him. . . . you should see him in consultation with them at headquarters . . . teaching them to do justice to themselves. . . . He does not do it by rules, or by following precedents," but instead through the force of his gentle, kind presence. "The work has not suffered from being institutionalized," Whitlock noted, "and it will not, at least so long as Gunckel lives."[24]

While a genuine and deeply felt affection for his young charges inspired Gunckel's efforts, so too did his disturbing sense of the destructive tendencies of modern society—tendencies that tore away at community ties and threatened personal character. "The crowding of population to the cities," he wrote, "is gradually destroying the home feeling" and producing "a dependent class of boys." Indeed, without citing his source of information, he contended that "in every city, with a population of 100,000 or more, thirty percent of the newsboys, the sellers, have no homes or their homes are worse than none at all. . . . they are strayed sheep." They were also particularly susceptible to bad and even criminal influences. Gunckel's personal investigation of the problem over a three-year period convinced him "that seventy percent of our newsboys" received a street education that pointed them toward prison. Compounding the problem was society's inclination to dismiss such children as bad, to bar them from clubs, to "curse and kick them," and then to forget them.[25] The prospects were frightening, unless a change occurred.

To Gunckel, the solution rested with Christian example and self-government. Although he was a long-standing Congregationalist, his references to religion avoided narrow denominational limits; instead, he evoked the model of the Golden Rule—appropriate enough in Toledo, the city of Mayor Samuel Jones, who from 1897 to 1904 governed according to that precept. The scriptural edict to "take this child and nurse it for me, and I will pay thee thy wages" also impressed Gunckel. He noted that Christ had treated wrongdoers as misdirected people who needed help. It was time, Gunckel urged, to "go out upon the streets, work among the newsboys, reach down to those below, and offer a hand to lift them up." Drawing upon the imagery of the famous nineteenth-century speech by Baptist preacher Russell Conwell, but using it as a rationale for aiding others rather than for getting rich, Gunckel maintained that "in your own city . . . at your own doors, are acres of diamonds only waiting for you to help in the work of polishing." It was essential, in order to find those youthful diamonds, to remove "the germs of disorder" that threatened modern civilization.[26] Here was precisely where Christian love and understanding were so essential. Gunckel illustrated the point on his Christmas cards in 1914 which showed two ragged young newsboys leaning on each other for support; part of the accompanying verse read, "The soul of things our heart would see, / If I knew you and you knew me."[27]

One feature of the association in which Gunckel took special pride was "the Popular Sunday School," which aimed its Sunday afternoon meetings at those boys who for various reasons had been unwelcome in established church schools. Preachers who appeared there were at the mercy of the young listeners. Those who were successful reportedly avoided "a tiresome string" of do's and don'ts, must's and mustn'ts; it was "plain talks," aimed at "boys whose veins are bulging with rich, red human blood," that proved most popular.[28] Gunckel was convinced that regular Sunday School workers should pay more attention to the newsboys. He appealed to them to join him in "a field of work in which I have been laboring for many years," that of leading "the boy of the street, regardless of nationality or sect, towards the Sunday School, the Church; making him a good citizen."[29]

In 1913 Gunckel worked closely with the Toledo and Lucas County Sunday School Association. He asked each new applicant for membership in Boyville, "Do you go to Sunday School?" Those who did not promptly received a visit from Sunday School officials. Gunckel was delighted to report that 317 new members had joined the sixty-one Sunday Schools (and eleven denominations) that he had visited: "The good accomplished cannot be estimated."[30]

When Gunckel wrote that it was possible to lead the newsboy bit by bit, "without his suspicion . . . into your Sunday School, your church," he revealed the kind of stratagem that often characterized reformers' work with children.[31] Through subtle adult manipulation, youths who seemed destined for trouble could become good citizens. The stakes in such a venture were high. Gunckel cited Theodore Roosevelt's advice that "if you are going to do anything permanent for the average man you have got to begin before he is a man. . . . That applies peculiarly to those boys who tend to drift off into courses which mean that unless they are checked, they will be formidable additions to the criminal population, when they grow older."[32] From the perspective of Gunckel and other progressive child savers, the most effective technique in this necessary task was that of gentle persuasion, not a cuff behind the ear.

Serving as a hedge against Gunckel's manipulative strategies, however, was his strong endorsement of self-government. The emphasis here was on youths "working out their own salvation," "solving the boy problem themselves."[33] As a small democracy, the "newsboy family" was to rest on "the principle of equal rights for all and special privileges for none," a situation which would allow what Gunckel saw as the basic goodness of children to surface. Moreover, in a self-governing system disadvantaged children would have responsibilities and thus a sense of individual importance and usefulness.[34] Class barriers would dissolve as well. When sellers from the downtown section joined carriers from the residential neighborhoods, the two groups would come to respect each other.[35]

Boyville had a constitution, which Gunckel undoubtedly helped to write. It divided Toledo into four geographically defined auxiliary units composed largely of neighborhood carriers, and another specifically for the sellers on the city streets. Each group held periodic meetings and annual elections. Political campaigning was sometimes robust and included the passing out of literature; in 1915, for example, a 2- by 4-inch card carried the message, "SELLERS TAKE NOTICE!! Vote for MAX BARKAN for Vice President of the Sellers Auxiliary." There were also annual elections to fill the association's central offices—except for the presidency, which belonged to Gunckel. Members did not have to pay dues, and there were no restrictions in terms of race or religion. For a while at least, in 1902, there was a female member, but shortly thereafter membership was limited to boys between eight and seventeen. If photographs were any indication, a very large number of the youths were under age fourteen.[36]

According to Gunckel, the newsboys conducted their monthly auxiliary meetings "with more decorum and intelligence than the average political conventions." This did not mean that agendas were noncontroversial or abstract. One auxiliary secretary recorded that "a heated disscussion [sic]" preceded the adoption of a motion rendering ineligible for office anyone who used tobacco. On occasion, decorum itself broke down. The seller's auxiliary became "so boisterous" at one point that, according to the minutes, "it had to adjourn—in disgrace."[37]

From the beginning, no one could doubt the moral purpose of Boyville. The voluntary oath and the membership card both stated specifically that the member did "not approve of swearing, lying, stealing, gambling, drinking intoxicating liquors or smoking cigarettes."[38] The association's constitution established a "Court of Investigation," comprising the vice-presidents and secretaries of each auxiliary, which inquired into alleged infractions of the rules. This body could suspend guilty parties for up to a year. On December 22, 1910, for example, "after a hot discussion," the court suspended Jake Brucker for sixty days, and decided "after a light discussion" to reinstate Isador Blum. In a striking display of judicial impartiality, the court also showed its willingness to apply standards of justice even to the association's upper ranks. Ed Gallagher, who for several years had held various offices in the organization and was by then a central officer, received a sixty-day suspension and was stripped of his position "for calling the President [Gunckel] a liar, and being a continuous knocker." (Later a redeemed Gallagher held another major office.) The conduct even of members of the court received scrutiny. When one left the courtroom without permission from the presiding judge, he received a summons to explain his conduct.[39] Suspensions reportedly declined in number by 1913; the previous year only three boys received sentences in excess of thirty days, and all of them were reinstated after ten days.[40]

Gunckel kept his own record of complaints that boys brought to him about each other. In a notebook entitled "Saving Waywards," he listed individual offenses such as "Foul Language," "Swears," or "Smokes Cigarettes." The book was open to all members so they could know who needed help. When a boy reformed himself, a blue pencil mark across his name and a comment in the margin such as "O.K.," or "He is a good boy now," duly registered the transformation. On a rare occasion a particularly difficult boy proved so disappointing that Gunckel, out of frustration, took him to the juvenile court. But invariably, if the judge suggested that reform school was the only solution, Gunckel would mellow. "Then

'Gunck' would say," as Judge O'Brien O'Donnell recalled, "'Oh! Don't stain him. Don't send him away. I'll give him another chance.'" O'Donnell could not remember a time when Gunckel recommended the reformatory. "Always, he would say he wanted to try him again. And in nearly every case, he succeeded finally in bringing out all the good there was in a boy."[41]

Around 1912 the association established a volunteer auxiliary to work with Toledo's juvenile court officials. From six to eight boys—known as Probation Officers of the Toledo Newsboys' Association—received appointments from the city's juvenile court judge. Their assignment was to inform youths in public places of state laws prohibiting those under age seventeen from inhabiting saloons or pool rooms, from using tobacco, from swearing and stealing, from wandering the streets at night, and from "growing up in idleness and crime." The Probation Officers had no powers of arrest; they were simply to use "the system of warning" to keep potential offenders from getting into trouble. Their purview extended to all boys and girls in the city, not just to those who belonged to the association. In their first official report, covering sixty days of work, the Probation Officers said that they had visited 108 saloons and found 1,230 boys and 13 girls: "The boys were bad enough; but oh, my, the girls were terrible. We took home twenty-one (21) boys too drunk to know their names." The officers succeeded in sending home 402 of the 1,108 boys in pool rooms and about a quarter of the more than 3,000 boys and girls wandering the evening streets. They also escorted a number of young girls out of "disreputable dance halls" and stopped 274 boys who were "fighting and swearing." Gunckel saw such efforts as opening "a new field to willing workers"; he urged others to "warn the boy and girl of the evils before them." After eighteen months, the officers claimed to "have saved" 450 boys from jail. A photograph showed a Probation Officer, in suit and tie, pointing his finger accusingly at a group of youngsters—holding cigarettes and crouching over rolling dice—and warning them, "Boys, Stop It." As evidence that the "warning plan" worked, one officer claimed that three years after he had instructed a young thief about the dangers of criminal ways, the boy had told him, "Say, pal, that talk you gave me stuck in my gizzard and every time I go to do something I had not ought to do I think of it. I've got a good job now, I've quit stealing and I'm going to stick to it."[42]

Undoubtedly, more than a few youths responded to the Probation Officers with their own advice. At least some of them perhaps resembled the several street workers in New York City whom Ernest Poole described. According to Poole, they listened to one of their members singing, "Don't Drive a Nail in Mother's Face," and then interrupted the song to argue whether or not they would steal $5.00. "Yer would, yer know yer would," a boy said. "So would I. We're bot' crooks. Go on wid de pyanner." Toledo was not New York, but the statistics of the Probation Officers themselves showed that substantial numbers of youths remained in saloons and pool halls after they had received a warning.[43]

Nor was Boyville itself entirely free of recalcitrance. In 1908 a weary and dejected Gunckel walked out of a noisy meeting of the sellers' auxiliary after he had faced an "insurrection." At the raucous gathering of a hundred boys, a small group of insurgents challenged Gunckel after he had declared ineligible their vice-presidential candidate, a youth under suspension for smoking cigarettes. The suspended member shouted at the president, "You cannot prove your charges." But when asked if he indeed smoked cigarettes, he had answered defiantly, "Yes." This provided another boy on the suspended list with an opportunity to complain about unfair treatment, and one member of the "anti-Gunckel" faction announced that nearly all the sellers smoked. As the meeting grew rowdier, Gunckel left, reportedly feeling "keenly the revolt."[44]

Still, one of the most remarkable features of the Toledo Newsboys' Association was the extent to which so many youths found it appealing. Gunckel and his organization undeniably struck a popular chord. Boys—many of whom were clearly from poor, new-immigrant backgrounds quite different from Gunckel's middle-class, Protestant life-style—responded with extraordinary zeal to the moral imperatives of the association.

A prime example of the newsboys' enthusiasm was the way in which rank-and-file members sought to enforce the association's rules. They did not rely only on the organization's established legal network, with its Probation Officers and Court of Investigation.

Instead "justice" often swelled up from below, sometimes with notable fury. A ten-year-old named Buster "licked" one boy "fur swearin'." On another occasion, when a newsboy short-changed a customer, the youth's associates took him (as Gunckel described the scene) "in the alley, bumped his head against the wall of the building, rolled him in the mud, took his badge from him and with a parting word of advice left him." Gunckel's history of Boyville also included an illustration, based on a real incident, showing a small newsboy hitting a much larger youth in the face and saying, "He sweared at a lady and I punked [punched] him." When Gunckel learned the facts of the case, he had an affirmative answer for the little assailant, who asked, "Say pres., wasn't I right in punking him?"[45]

One of the association's information sheets said that the boys had a motto: " 'Make bad boys good. Never give up a bad boy.' They gave no quarters [sic]. They punished a bad boy in their own way, wherever they found him, any place, any time." This was, according to one observer's euphemistic phrasing, "lending a hand for manliness."[46]

Such an approach, by which "bad habits were knocked out of the boys"[47] by other boys reportedly produced results. Gunckel was pleased that the lad who received the beating for short-changing his customer learned a lesson; he recovered his badge, conducted himself admirably on the streets, and ultimately got a job with a company that hired him because of his membership in the association. From Gunckel's viewpoint, "it was a very wise thing to have any boy punish a member, and in his own way." Newsboys, he was convinced, learned to avoid dishonest and immoral conduct not because they feared police or jails, but because they had to answer to their own conscience and to each other, and because they respected the association too much to sully its reputation.[48]

It was, after all, the young street sellers themselves who came up with the idea of turning over to Gunckel all valuables that they found. "You can lose your pocketbook on the streets of Toledo," claimed Brand Whitlock, "and if a newsboy gets it you will get it back the next day." There was more than a grain of truth to this. The association, in the years from 1908 to 1913, returned to original owners lost items adding up to an estimated value of $52,000. The

Newsboys' "Honor Roll" ledger contained brief descriptions of members who had found the gold watch of a Rossford, Ohio woman, or a purse with $8.00 in it belonging to Mrs. Mikolayczak, or a Grand Army of the Republic badge. One visitor to Gunckel's office saw three packages that newsboys had turned in that morning alone. Toledo newspapers notified the public about the newsboys' findings. Even if the boy did not receive a reward from the owner, he could count on joining the association's Honor Roll and receiving a certificate of congratulation from Gunckel: "You have *done something good*. You have sacrificed your self-interest, your own pleasure, to make some unknown person happy. You have obeyed the Commandment of God, to love your neighbors. . . ." The reputation of the newsboys was such that, as Gunckel said, "A lady called me up and asked if any of the boys had found her watch, YET."[49]

These achievements of youthful lost-and-found agents enhanced the newsboys' reputation for honesty, but so too did a remarkable statistic that few commentators missed: by 1908 Toledo claimed the lowest youth crime rate among cities of comparable size. Indeed, according to one journal, "For ten years Toledo has claimed a smaller percentage of boys in court and in the state reform school than any other city in the Union. Its youth has a record for being clean, thrifty, and free from vices. . . . All this and more stands to the credit of John E. Gunckel."[50]

An intriguing question was why "newsboys' government" exerted such influence over the city's youth. Gunckel took special pride in the fact that his first recruits had been "mostly the poorest boys of the streets, little outcasts." More than a decade later, when one of Gunckel's assistants tried to get some of the members ready for a shower, he literally had to cut their clothes from their bodies— clothes that their families had sewed to be worn night and day until the material fell apart. The youngsters also came from a wide variety of immigrant backgrounds. One writer guessed that there were probably youths from every European country in the association, and a publicity photograph showed Gunckel with nineteen young boys "representing Nine Different Nationalities."[51]

Even though the association eventually included a majority of members who were carriers in their own residential neighborhoods, it remained extremely popular among the sellers who worked the city's streets and who were products of the laboring-class and immigrant districts of Toledo. In late 1913 the sellers' auxiliary (by then numbering some 1,300 out of a total membership of about 8,950) had to adjourn an election meeting prematurely because of too much enthusiasm. There were "so many sellers wanting office," according to the minutes, that the group fell victim to an excess of democracy.[52]

But it was not merely the prestige of holding office that attracted youngsters from Toledo's streets—the "flotsam and jetsam of the human race . . . the little lambs of the slums," as one of Gunckel's close friends described them. There was, for instance, the time when a seventeen-year-old from a large family of Syrian immigrants expressed concern to Gunckel about his younger brother, age five, who was already swearing and developing tough habits. Would the association lend a hand? Gunckel successfully recruited the youngster and so influenced his behavior that the father, mother, and other children stopped by on different occasions for advice about their own problems of being poor and trying to adust in a new country.[53]

Another newsboy brought his mother and father to Gunckel in hopes that Boyville's president could prevent an impending divorce. "I'm no court," Gunckel replied, "but if there's anything I can do for you, I'll be glad to help you get your differences settled." During the ensuing discussion, Gunckel learned that the parents took the money the boy made from selling papers, got drunk, and then quarreled. "I lectured them a little and told them what a good boy they had and how he was trying to make the home happy," Gunckel recalled, "and then I gave them each fifty cents and told them . . . to go out and buy each other something nice for Christmas." He also assured them that he could get some of his business friends to provide the boy with decent winter clothes. The results were little short of miraculous: "They went out arm in arm and I know they will try to do better."[54]

The long-range effects of the parents' visit with Gunckel were perhaps less impressive than he thought, and the press's description of the Syrian family which he had helped—"now clean, physically and morally, and prosperous because he has taught them how to earn and how to use what they earn"—may have reflected what the reporters wanted to see. Despite such problems of perspective, however, there was undeniable evidence that large numbers of boys, many of them out of Toledo's slums, rallied to Gunckel's organization with genuine excitement. One of the reasons was unquestionably "Gunck" himself. "Kids who have to scrape and hustle for the penny and the dime," wrote a former newsboy turned poet, "have some feelin's for a feller that's helpin' all the time."[55]

Another reason was the apparent desire of many young street sellers to be respectable. Although Gunckel and his youthful charges generally came from sharply contrasting backgrounds, there was considerable resonance between their worlds. This may have reflected the power of cultural hegemony—the success of the dominant class in persuading less powerful, marginal members of society that they too can benefit from the ruling hierarchy of power and values; however, the situation was probably far more complex, as much the product of a dialectic within social classes and individuals as between them. Historian Paul Boyer has suggested that the impulse to respectability may not have been limited to middle-class reformers and may have had considerable hold upon the poor. Without doubt, members of the immigrant and working classes of late nineteenth-century and early twentieth-century America responded in many ways to existing social and economic conditions, and although they confronted sharply limiting historical circumstances, they were not faceless victims who simply reacted helplessly to the world around them. Indeed, they continually drew upon a variety of personal and collective resources in order to mold as much of their environment as possible. As historian Aileen Kraditor has argued, any presumption that elites and bosses played the "determining role must portray John Q. Worker as a blank page for cleverer people to write their own values on." Perhaps "John Q. Worker's belief-system may turn out to have been neither 'bourgeois' nor 'antibourgeois' . . . but an autochthonous phenomenon."[56]

When workers and immigrant groups collaborated with middle-class reformers, as they did in cities like Milwaukee at the turn of the century to effect changes in public education, they were not necessarily testifying to the strength of privileged elites in enforcing patterns of deference. Instead, such reform coalitions grew because different groups, although often for different reasons, sought similar goals. The quest for higher-quality public education, for example, was not merely something that middle-class reformers imposed upon workers and immigrants. For very good personal reasons, lower-class groups (although far from a monolithic bloc) were interested in shaping schools to meet their own expectations.

While various middle-class progressives sought to construct bridges between social and economic groups, there were also signs that segments of the working class were anxious to cross over, or to build bridges of their own. Assuredly, during the twentieth century, the tentative nature and eventual fragmentation of cross-class coalition have provided notable reminders of social and economic divisions within the nation. Examples of considerable overlap between classes, groups, and individuals have nonetheless been abundant—from John L. Lewis (the coal miner from Iowa who was president for years of the United Mine Workers and the Congress of Industrial Organizations, yet listed his occupation as "executive" rather than labor official or union leader) to the Guardian Angels (New York City street gangs who in the 1970s championed law and order on city subways and in 1981 volunteered to join the search for the murder of several dozen black youths in Atlanta).[57]

The Toledo Newsboys' Association, during the years of John Gunckel's leadership at least, provided additional evidence of the adaptability of marginal or "dependent" groups and the fluidity of social and cultural values. Boys who worked the city sidewalks developed their own variations of such middle-class ideals as individualism, "character," self-discipline, and success. If they hoped to succeed on the streets, they had to be sharply competitive, highly motivated, and shrewdly attuned to the values and expectations of potential customers. Perhaps some of the most revealing statistics of the association were those concerning the subsequent careers of the original 102 members. Those "little outcasts," as Gunckel described them, had included eleven who were homeless and thirty-nine whose parents had drinking problems; almost all of them wore ragged clothes; among the first officers had been a youngster with a feared set of fists and another who was reputedly the worst thief in the area. Twenty-five years later, twenty-seven of those charter members were reportedly doctors, five bankers, two ministers, seven newspaper managers, and twelve traveling salesmen; eleven worked in wholesale houses, fifteen had learned a trade, eleven had joined the navy, and one was a circus clown.[58]

In a very real sense, Gunckel was thus justified in describing Boyville as "a kindergarten in the great school of business and citizenship." With approval he quoted the favorable comments of others: Governor Myron T. Herrick hailed the "boys who represent our little street merchants, boys who are destined to be the good men of the future"; a Toledo editor was happy that an association member learned "to travel on his own merits and not lean on his papa. He is taught that he must paddle his own canoe."[59]

There was also the matter of civic pride and leadership. In 1908 five hundred newsboys served as official guides for the city when veterans of the Grand Army of the Republic held their encampment in Toledo; later the association collaborated with the local civic federation for Clean Up Day. On May 22, 1911, Gunckel made a specific appeal for the boys to back him in a movement to "help make Toledo one of the greatest and best of cities." It was, he declared, "my purpose to use the few years left me for work, to push the Boys into active service, to help the City." Predictably, his request produced a flurry of activity. The association soon had an Information Bureau, complete with "Ask Me About Toledo" badges. Volunteers between the ages of ten and fifteen agreed "to talk Toledo" and aid the city. For newsboys over sixteen there was the Toledo Newsboys' Business Men's Club, organized in October, 1911, and dedicated to assisting the "Toledo Commerce Club and other live organizations to boost Toledo."[60]

Gunckel's success in channeling the energies of Toledo's newsboys into civic responsibility, and their own moral uplift, captured considerable acclaim in Toledo and elsewhere. A 1902 photograph of Gunckel and ten of the youngest newsboys gained national attention in magazines and Sunday supplements; it was reputedly one of the most publicized photographs of the era and the picture from which the vaudeville stage drew its model of the "newsie."[61] The journal *Work with Boys* proclaimed that Toledo had "the most remarkable newsboys' organization in the world," and in 1905 the Newsboys' Band, sixty-five members strong, marched in Theodore Roosevelt's inaugural parade.[62]

121

Around the nation Gunckel grew in esteem as "the Newsboys' Friend." The Chicago *American* called him no less than "the founder of boy work." Civic groups, chambers of commerce, and child saving organizations were anxious to obtain his services as a speaker. At the St. Louis World's Fair in 1904, he addressed the National Association of Managers of Newspaper Circulation and succeeded in establishing August 16 as an annual Newsboys' Day. The *Journal of Education* declared that he was "a man that every teacher and worker among boys should hear." He received invitations to discuss his work with college students and other individuals who were committed to social reform. A representative from one college's sociology department and the director of a Philadelphia boys club visited Toledo to observe how Gunckel dealt with "the boy problem." Denver's celebrated juvenile court judge, Ben Lindsey, had no doubt that Gunckel was "one of the greatest champions of boyhood in this country and his work, especially with newsboys," was "unexcelled." And Brand Whitlock, Toledo's reform mayor, noted with pride that Gunckel had helped the city gain a national reputation as a community that recognized the rights of children.[63]

Paradoxically, however, Toledo lagged at least a decade behind a number of cities in establishing child labor laws regarding newsboys. Not until 1923 did the city adopt such legislation, and even then it was considerably more lenient than elsewhere.[64] The irony was that although Boyville provided a model for some child savers, to others it was—despite its virtues—a reform that missed the main problem. Worse, it obscured essential facts and bolstered an indefensible economic arrangement: the exploitation of children to make a profit. Whereas Gunckel focused on uplifting boys who were engaged in work that he deemed beneficial to later success, child labor reformers such as Florence Kelley attacked the very premise that selling newspapers was a useful experience for youngsters. Here was an issue that divided progressives who had a special interest in the needs of children.

Certainly Gunckel was no apologist for economic injustice. Slum conditions stirred his conscience, and he added his voice to cries for tenement house reform. "If the present cheap-John tenements could be wiped out," he wrote, "it would go a long way towards correcting one of the greatest evils of the day." He considered it sad that "our leading men in business . . . men who stand high in the commercial world," were party to rental agreements that ruined "hundreds of young lives." And he included in his history of Boyville a photograph of a shabby Toledo tenement building in which seventeen poor families had lived.[65]

But he also featured a photograph showing four happy newsboys with a distinguished, friendly-looking businessman who was supposedly saying, "I will buy from the little fellow."[66] It was here that progressives who sought to regulate or abolish child street trades would have demurred, however much they respected Gunckel and his association. For them, it was essential to destroy the overwhelming public impression that newsboys were youthful street merchants. In this respect they faced a monumental challenge. Literature abounded—often in publications notable for their reform persuasion—alleging that young street sellers gained an early schooling in the rules of success.

The *Juvenile Court Record*, for example, was dedicated to helping delinquent and dependent children, and it championed one of the most prized progressive creations: the juvenile court system. Yet in the *Record* one could find a photograph of a bright-looking, neatly dressed newsie hailing a potential customer. The accompanying article, "Boys That Hustle," maintained that today's "Street Urchin" was tomorrow's "Successful Business Man." "Our life today demands something else than butterfly youths," the essay contended, and claimed that the newsboys gained practical experience more useful to "manhood" than college courses. On the streets a young man would adjust "to hard knocks. . . . He won't go home and cry, and tell mama."[67]

The *Newsboys' World*, official magazine of The Newsboys' Republic in Milwaukee, echoed this interpretation. (The Republic was organized in 1912 and, however intentionally, resembled Boyville; it had its own court system, stressed reliance on self-government, and held elections—which in 1915 featured the Peoples, Newsboys, and Independent parties.) A poem called "The Newsboy," set the tone. It was about a ragged but hard-working street seller who completed high school with honors, and then "About five more years have past, / And James has graduated from

Harvard at last, / And his heart is filled with happiness and joy, / But he will not forget the time he was Jimmey the Newsboy." Elsewhere, the journal printed a cartoon demonstrating that "The Newsboys of Today Are the Masters of Tomorrow." An article stressed the virtues of "Salesmanship" and "Grit and Pluck"; it reasoned that the newsboy, through meeting all classes of people, could "develop into an A No. 1 salesman."[68]

Even an article in *Charities* magazine, one of the most important reform publications of the progressive era, wavered. After discussing the dangers that went with street work, the author conceded that experience in handling money and contacts with the competitive side of the business world placed many newsboys "far ahead of the companions who have not had the same experience."[69]

It was precisely this image of the newsboys as independent street merchants—Horatio Algers on the rise—that child labor reformers angrily challenged. Scott Nearing, Secretary of the Pennsylvania Child Labor Committee, and muckraking journalist William Hard, for example, wrote moving descriptions of the pathetic conditions under which they had observed young sellers working at night in Philadelphia and Chicago. They included grim photographs to prove their points. One picture showed a dozen or so newsboys on the street at four o'clock in the morning; another a tired boy, papers under his arm, leaning his head against a lamppost. The narratives, trying to convey a sense of what Nearing described as "the true condition of affairs," told of ten-year-old boys carrying forty pounds of papers at two o'clock on Sunday mornings, and of youngsters lying down on sidewalks to capture a few hours of sleep. The newsboy, according to Nearing, "lives on the streets at night in an atmosphere of crime and criminals, and he takes in vice and evil with the air he breathes."[70]

William Hard poked bitter fun at the kind of thinking that exempted young street sellers from the protections of child labor laws: "The Newsboy does not receive a salary. He is not an employee. He is a merchant. . . . He occupies the same legal position as Marshall Field & Co. . . . Therefore no rascally factory inspector may vex him in his pursuit of an independent commercial career." Hard cited information from the superintendent of a Chicago reformatory that newsboys committed to his institution were generally about one-third below the size and strength of average boys their age. "In the face of testimony of this kind," Hard wrote, "which could be duplicated from every city in the United States, it seems absurd to talk about the educative influence of the street."[71]

Florence Kelley, Secretary of the National Consumers' League, told a meeting of Chicago social workers in 1911 that she had seen a five-year-old child peddling newspapers late at night near the Albany, New York, railroad station; and in New York City she had witnessed "a very ill-fed wretched, shabby litle boy" selling papers shortly before midnight outside a plush hotel. It was time, she urged, to shatter the old romantic stereotype of newsboys as heroes. "Nothing could be worse than their experience. Why do we put up with it? . . . Why do we . . . see this army of children on the streets and encourage them and think that we are starting young merchants on the commercial road?" The answer, she guessed, was that Americans were "a little insane on the subject of legal fictions."

Other social workers and charity groups argued against youthful street trades on grounds that most families did not really need the money; for those who were actually destitute, they said, it would be far better to provide direct aid from the community than to have ten-year-olds working on city street corners.[72]

Gunckel was no less concerned with the baneful influences of urban settings upon newsboys. But his own experience told him that the appropriate response was self-government; group pressure, internal discipline, and a sense of responsibility to others could help youths counteract the temptations of the city's streets. Such a strategy not only uplifted the boys but had vast potential for reforming entire cities. A host of Boyvilles—by training dedicated future citizens, by boosting the Toledos of America, by providing examples of honesty and hard work—could set a higher moral tone in communities struggling against corrosive modern tendencies. Thus Gunckel, "The Newsboys' Evangelist,"[74] had no use for attempts to prohibit youngsters from selling papers on the street; that would be a little like destroying children in order to save them.

Not all child-savers agreed, as Gunckel discovered. In June 1906 he journeyed to Chicago to deliver an address at a Hull House meeting for American and Canadian reformers. While he waited his turn to speak, he listened with growing dismay to J. J. Kelso of

Toronto. In a stirring presentation that evoked loud applause, Kelso attacked the employment of youths to sell papers: "The first step in the work of the juvenile court is to compel the newsboys to keep off the streets and abolish this system. People should be trained to buy their papers in stores." The speech and the sympathetic response it received so rankled Gunckel that he walked out, saying that newsboys had suffered a "black eye." Although he was scheduled to give the evening's banquet address, he returned to Toledo that afternoon instead.[75]

Ben Lindsey regretted that such a misunderstanding had occurred. The judge had himself been aiding a Denver newsboys' association which, although not structured as carefully along self-government lines as was Boyville, had sufficiently influenced the boys' behavior to win praise from the city's chief of police. Following the Hull House affair, Lindsey reassured Gunckel that Boyville was "the real thing and is in fact accomplishing what these people [at the Chicago conference] are trying to get at." Elsewhere—in places such as Bowling Green, Columbus, and Springfield in Ohio—judges and interested citizens initiated efforts to adopt "the Gunckel plan."[76]

In Toledo, Gunckel plunged ahead with his own work, leaving his railroad job so that he could devote his attention to Boyville and the newly formed National Newsboys' Association. A committee of sympathetic business leaders in the city made this financially possible; each person agreed to pay a reported $50 a year "to set Gunckel up in the newsboy reform business," as one of the men phrased it.[77]

The National Newsboys' Association, which Gunckel had originated in 1904 at the St. Louis World's Fair, found a wide audience. To join, a youngster merely wrote to Gunckel, "stating his bad habits" and pledging to stop them. In return he received a badge and a membership card (like those of the Toledo organization). The association existed primarily for newsboys, but was willing to accept any youth who needed moral uplift. "What We Want Is a Boy with a Bad Habit," declared one information sheet. "Here is an easy, successful way of making bad boys good. An honor to you, an honor to your town." By 1913, the organization boasted of 28,000 members and 200 branch associations across the United States.[78]

"Detroit Boys Make Declaration of Morals by Joining the Big Association," read the headlines of one newspaper in 1907. Dallas, Texas, featured one of the more notable branches. B. A. Dunn, a volunteer probation officer who sold his local business in 1911 so that he could become full-time superintendent of the Texas organization, claimed that it had improved the conduct of street boys more effectively than the juvenile court, sheriff, churches, and Sunday Schools combined. One happy observer reported that it was now virtually impossible to find a Dallas newsie smoking a cigarette, a remarkable change from earlier days. Of the eight hundred Dallas members by 1912, sixty policed the ranks as "detectives." Once, six of the detectives apprehended a runaway youth within thirty minutes after the distraught mother appealed for help in finding him. When the newsies gave the youngster a hot bath so that he would be "a nice, clean little boy," the youth tried to escape from the tub, thereby earning a trip to "the spatting machine." Two detectives subsequently returned the much-chastened, and presumably cleaner, youth to his home.[79]

However much the meteoric growth of the national organization pleased Gunckel, he unquestionably took special pride in the Toledo Newsboys' Building, dedicated in 1909 and publicized as the "only structure of its kind in the world." Actually the idea of a building for newsboys' use was not new. As early as 1854, Charles Loring Brace had opened his Newsboys' Lodging House in New York City; and in 1893 the Grand Rapids, Michigan, *Evening Press* started some notable pioneering of its own. A series of informal discussions between the manager and the newsboys about the importance of courtesy and manliness proved so successful that in 1895 the paper's owners established a newsboys' school to provide a basic education for its young workers. Four years later they added a school of dancing and deportment to help direct social activities. When the *Press* opened its new building in 1907, it included a hall that could hold a thousand people. William Byron Forbush, nationally recognized authority on boys, described the *Press*'s achievement as "a wholesale way of uplifting humanity."[80]

What distinguished the Toledo Newsboys' Building from its counterparts in Grand Rapids and elsewhere was the scope and specific purpose of the project: an entire building; constructed at a cost of over $100,000, for the exclusive use of newsboys. Its funding, moreover, came from a dramatic community campaign for donations. At one point a singer at Toledo's Lyceum drew loud applause by requesting the audience to help build that "home for newsboys." By 1908 more than 6,000 contributions, from school children and millionaires, and ranging from pennies to $5,000, made Gunckel's dream a reality. The building opened in February 1909 in the central downtown area; it was three stories high and included a swimming pool, gymnasium, shower facilities, billiard room, kitchen, library (to which Mrs. Russell Sage in New York City contributed 122 books), a meeting hall that held 350 people, and an auditorium for 1,200. There was also a private office for Gunckel and a general office for the association's elected officials. Here, the Toledo *Blade* declared, "was a magnificent monument to the good works of John E. Gunckel . . . commemorating the influence of what one modest, unassuming man can bring to pass." When Gunckel took the stage at the dedication ceremonies, the audience gave him a five-minute standing ovation.[81]

More than six years later, on August 18, 1915, a vast audience again packed the auditorium to pay tribute to Gunckel, but this time there was no joy. Two days earlier he had died in his home after almost a year of illness. In 1914 his health had given way, forcing him into the hospital several times. To the end, however, he continued to demonstrate his affection for Boyville. During the spring of 1915 he had struggled to the auditorium for a surprise visit. When the first boy to see him cried out, "Hey, fellars, there's Gunck," the air had filled with flying hats, whistles, and cheers: "Gunck, Gunck, Gunck." That summer he had for the first time missed the annual picnic. With tears running down his face, he had told a group of newsboys who stopped by his home that it was "a grand day": the water would be warm and they would not have to worry about sunburn. Shortly thereafter, he had left by train for Baltimore to undergo an operation—a last attempt to save his life. Hundreds of newsboys accompanied him, now an invalid, to the railroad station. He had returned to Toledo to die at the age of 68. On August 16, members of Boyville sold newspapers bearing the sad banner headlines of his death. On the day of the funeral, at the mayor's request, all streetcars were shut down for a short time; city offices were closed; and businesses were also urged to shut their doors. At the services, 2,000 newsboys walked behind the hearse, and the newsboys' band played the funeral march. "The feet walk slow / In Boyville," wrote a local poet.[82]

Gunckel was gone, but the association remained. Alice Gunckel continued to work with Boyville until her death in 1931; their son Will also played an active role. Succeeding Gunckel as president, and heading the association in a distinguished way until he died in 1929, was Jefferson D. Robinson, one of the founder's closest associates. Robinson had started as an office boy in the glass industry at the age of nineteen and pulled himself to the top of the Libbey Glass Manufacturing Company. He became one of Toledo's major philanthropists, helping to found the city's Community Chest and at one point giving $100,000 to the local hospital. For years, however, it was Boyville that dominated Robinson's charitable work. He was determined after 1915 to keep the association true to Gunckel's memory. During his fourteen years as president, he personally financed, at a cost of perhaps $100,000, the remodeling of the Newsboys' Home and established a vocational training program in which boys could learn carpentry, shoe repairing, printing, and other trades. Wealthy and aristocratic in appearance, he nonetheless was familiar to the boys simply as "Jay Dee," and he carefully respected the principles of self-government.[83]

Another individual who was important to the continued development of Boyville was John N. Mockett, who for several decades had been one of Gunckel's closest friends. Mockett, like Robinson, was a self-made man of wealth. After shipping out of his native England as a cabin boy on a fishing schooner, he had lived for a while in Toronto before moving first to Detroit and then to Toledo, where he established a lucrative clothing business and became one of Boyville's essential benefactors. Around 1900 he started his annual Christmas donations of coats and clothing to the hundred neediest members of the Toledo Newsboys' Association; following Gunckel's death, he endowed Boyville with $10,000 in honor of his old friend.[84]

In the early 1930s, following the deaths of Mockett, Robinson, and Alice Gunckel, the association began a gradual transformation. In 1936 the requirement that members needed some experience selling newspapers gave way to a policy of accepting all boys over the age of nine. By 1939 the association had a new name: the Boys' Club of Toledo.[85]

Gunckel was not forgotten, however. Annually, Toledo's luminaries, newsboys, and many citizens decorated his grave with lotus blossoms, his favorite flower. In 1917 the city dedicated a monument to "The Newsboys' Friend, John Elstner Gunckel," constructed of 30,000 stones that children had collected. The monument rises some thirty feet in the shape of a steep-sided pyramid, and is located on a hill overlooking a small stream in the Woodlawn cemetery. More than thirty years after Gunckel's death there was even talk about a Hollywood movie tentatively entitled, "A Man Called John." Star entertainer Danny Thomas, himself a former Toledo newsboy, liked the script for the proposed film and took it to Hollywood with the hope that he might get Spencer Tracy to play Gunckel.[86]

Gunckel's life deserved praise. He was one of the genuinely heroic reformers of his era—a man of tremendous dedication and compassion, someone whose work with newsboys displayed a special kind of care and imagination and whose accomplishments were indeed large. It was never money or power that lured him; he spurned several efforts to draft him for mayor of Toledo at times when there were strong feelings that he could win office.[87]

But from another angle, Gunckel's achievements handicapped other reformers who believed that they had the best interests of newsboys in mind. The Toledo Consumers' League, struggling unsuccessfully after Gunckel's death to get the city to ban children under age fourteen from selling newspapers, faced a rugged uphill battle. Members of the league labored against a very vocal opposition and the ghost of Gunckel. It was not simply that Boyville had been so popular and gained so much attention. There was also the powerful public image of the newsboy—an image that Gunckel had drawn upon again and again when publicizing Boyville. One publicity sheet portrayed two very small sellers, obviously poor and disadvantaged with their ragged clothes and smudged cheeks, but nonetheless bright-eyed, cheerful, and smiling broadly as they stood with papers in hand. According to the accompanying poem:

Sellers of the street are we,
Enjoying ourselves where'er we may be,
Leaving all evils behind at recess,
Learning the lesson of true success.
Everyone of us, no matter how we dress,
Remember that we are but boys of the street,
Selling our papers to those we meet.

Following Gunckel's death, J. D. Robinson sustained this view. "You are not street urchins but street merchants," Robinson once told the sellers' auxiliary. "You must conduct yourselves like any business man. Today you are selling papers. A few years from today you will be our governors and statesmen."[88]

Critics of the newsboy-as-entrepreneur thesis battled back with studies and statistics. For example, a 1916 survey of Iowa's Industrial School for Boys revealed that of the 425 residents, 144 had been newsboys and 50 had been bootblacks. There were also the findings of Maurice Hexter, who argued that—in Cincinnati at least—more than 70 percent of the newsboys were on the street despite their parents' wishes; that the popularly conceived newsboy-as-breadwinner was largely mythical; that more than half of the city's street sellers were retarded in their schoolwork; that they had a higher than average truancy rate and triple the normal amount of heart trouble; and that they suffered disproportionately from flat feet and throat problems. In 1919 the Toledo Consumers' League circulated Hexter's information in a small pamphlet, "The High Cost of News," emphasizing that it was erroneous to believe that newsboys were precocious little merchants on their way to prosperous and useful futures. More than likely, the League warned, the boys would grow up "with underdeveloped bodies, empty minds, and shrivelled souls, [and] add to our problem of unskilled labor."[89]

Set against that argument were Gunckel's own statements and the many tributes to him—tributes that irrevocably linked the man with the romantic image of newsboys: "Lift your ragged caps, little newsies." A wrenchingly sentimental poem called "The 'Newsies' Heartache" told of a person who found "one little urchin" mourning for the man whose newsboys' auditorium was "To us 'Boys' . . . known as HOME."[90]

Such drama was material for legends, ready-made for Hollywood. But the story could easily turn maudlin, glossing over some of the real dilemmas that confronted progressive reformers when they turned to the problem of how to save the newsboys.

· 5 ·

The Ford Republic:
Dependency, Delinquency, and Democracy

By the time Fred Bloman was nine, he had no family and was in trouble with the police. But when he died of heart trouble only four years later, on September 6, 1911, he had an enviable reputation as a judge—so enviable, in fact, that the state Supreme Court sent one of its members to attend his funeral at St. Paul's Cathedral in Detroit. Two former justices were also there, along with other distinguished individuals from the city. The Wayne County Probate Court adjourned in his memory.

Followers of the Bloman story had no difficulty accounting for his remarkable turnabout from rootless troublemaker to model citizen—a veritable "genius from the gutters," according to one source. The small, redheaded boy owed his transformation to the Ford Republic, an institution just outside Detroit for delinquent and homeless boys. In the freewheeling environment of that "boy community," he had pulled himself up the ranks to the esteemed position of citizens' judge, where he had served admirably enough to become a Detroit celebrity at age thirteen. To observers, the youth's short but illustrious career was impressive evidence of what the Ford Republic was doing for "the Blomans of our cities."[1]

Perhaps in no other institution was the era's tendency to blur the lines between delinquency and dependency so evident. Indeed, from the viewpoint of the Ford Republic's organizers, any difference between the youthful criminal and the homeless youth was deceptive. According to a publicity pamphlet in 1910, "because the

133

delinquent boy as well as the dependent boy is usually the product of an improper home, it is not necessary to make a distinction in the treatment and care of the two kinds of boys." Later, starting around 1913, the Republic's administrators were more inclined to make such distinctions, as well as others regarding ethnicity and emotional disposition; by then, the supervisors and staff were also expressing growing reservations about the institution's self-governing format. But in its early days, at a time when the junior republic as a child saving technique enjoyed its widest popularity across the country, the Ford Republic was probably more democratic and genuinely self-governing than all its conterparts. This was due in large part to the influence of Homer Lane, the institution's inspired and unconventional superintendent from 1907 to 1912. But it may also have been due to the fact that the Republic admitted not only delinquent youths (at a time when definitions of "delinquent" included young people whose actual connections with crime were quite tenuous) but also homeless boys who were simply "in danger of becoming . . . delinquent."[2]

Aptly enough, the Republic's most famous early citizen, Fred Bloman, was a youngster without a family. When the police arrested him for begging in a Detroit slum, he was a tobacco-chewing, filthy, "foul-mouthed, and apparently incorrigible street Arab," who could not remember his parents or his home.[3] Adding to his symbolic importance was the fact that he was among the first group of boys when the institution in 1909 fully launched its experiment in self-government.

Over the previous two decades, the institution had evolved from a temporary urban residence for released adult prisoners to a boys' home in the county. Mrs. Agnes L. d'Arcambal had founded the rescue home for former convicts in the 1880s. As a young girl in Kalamazoo, Michigan, she had taken flowers, clothing, and fruit to prisoners in the small country jail, and soon she began visiting the state prison in Jackson, befriending the convicts and establishing an extensive library for them. She became a familiar figure in the state capital through her many appeals to the legislature for penal reforms. She opened "Tramps' Rest" in Kalamazoo, a place where homeless men could find temporary lodging. In 1888, she received enough financial support to establish on Willis Avenue in Detroit the Home of Industry for Discharged Prisoners, a residence where former prisoners could live and work as they adjusted to the outside world. She affectionately called the home's residents her "boys," and they referred to her almost reverently as "Mother." In 1896 Agnes d'Arcambal, then in her seventies and in failing health, received commendations from the prison boards of Michigan for her accomplishments. When she died in February 1899, her last request was that she wanted no other memorial than the continuance and extension of the home's mission. Responsibility for this rested with the d'Arcambal Home of Industry Association, which Agnes d'Arcambal had helped to incorporate under a state statute for charitable societies.[4]

But on April 1, 1902, the association's trustees made a decision that, however true to the spirit of Agnes d'Arcambal, substantially changed the character of the group's work. They closed the Home of Industry and shifted their primary attention to the prevention of crime by aiding "neglected street boys." The new priorities reflected several developments. First, thanks to recent penal reforms, there was less need for the kinds of services that the Home of Industry had provided. Second, the trustees concluded that it was "more humane as well as economical to save the first offenders from a criminal life." With this goal in mind, the association had already helped to push into law a system of probation for first offenders who were "not likely to again engage in a criminal course of conduct."[5]

Although the d'Arcambal organization continued to find jobs for some released adult convicts, and paid for their temporary lodging at the city's McGregor Mission, its major activities now revolved around the newly formed Juvenile Court. A representative from the association regularly attended the court's sessions to seek suspended sentences for boys found guilty of such offenses as vagrancy, fighting, and loitering. Because Michigan law at that point limited the Juvenile Court's jurisdiction to thirty days, the d'Arcambal Association served in effect as a probation officer, providing supervision of youths under suspended sentence. During the organization's first year of such work, it supervised seventy-nine boys who had appeared before the Court.[6]

In order to advance "the reformation of the boy," the association in January 1903 opened a "Temporary Home" for boys who were adrift on the city's streets. Located initially on West Congress Street, the home was for youngsters ages eight to fifteen, regardless of race. According to the d'Arcambal people, this "was the first shelter for neglected and wayward boys in Detroit." The residents regularly attended Sunday Schools of their choice and public schools in the area. Any homeless boy was welcome once the association had investigated his situation. Occasionally, the home provided a place other than jail where boys could stay while awaiting trial. The Juvenile Court's probation officer, whom the association furnished at no charge to the city or county, sometimes chose to place youths in the Temporary Home rather than return them immediately to relatives. Among the first residents were an abandoned eleven-year-old; a fourteen-year-old whose father was dead and whose mother was in a mental institution; a nine-year-old who had been arrested for "placing obstructions" on railroad tracks and whose parents were "constant drunkards"; a "typical truant and street boy, and daily patron of cheap theaters," whose parents refused to care for him; and a newboy of nine who was already in trouble for begging and stealing. The d'Arcambal Association proudly noted that the newsboy, after his arrival at the Temporary Home on probation, had not only attended school regularly but had received a class prize for achieving the best record for one month. "No longer associates with his old companions," read the association's report on his progress. "Never on the street after 5:30 P.M. And the indications are that the improvement will continue."[7]

In May 1906 the association formally amended its corporate charter to bring it in line with the direction in which the organization had been moving. The old Home of Industry officially became the Boys' Home and d'Arcambal Association, aimed at "saving . . . boys from criminal ways" and providing "a temporary home for delinquent boys." In line with the organization's preventive goals— "A Fence at the Top of a Precipice is Better than an Ambulance at the Bottom" was one of its mottos—the association's volunteers patroled the city, looking for endangered youths. By March 1907 the association claimed to have sent home more than 3,000 newsboys and beggars who were on the streets and in saloons after 9:30 P.M. It had also reported to schools and the police dozens of truant youngsters, found homes in the country for thirty youths, and temporarily housed 426 boys.[8]

A dominant figure in the association by this time was Fred M. Butzel, a local lawyer and product of one of Detroit's most respected Jewish families. His father, Magnus, had taken an early interest in Agnes d'Arcambal's Home of Industry.[9] Fred, after graduating in 1897 from the University of Michigan, completed two years of study at the Detroit School of Law. Following his admission to the bar in 1899, he practiced law with his brother Henry. Yet his real interests were far less in the world of torts and contracts than in music and sociology. He was both a talented pianist and an indefatigable worker in Detroit's charity groups. At the turn of the century, he taught English and civics classes for boys at the Jewish Institute, opened the first night school for immigrants in Detroit, helped to introduce Boy Scouting to the city, and was instrumental in operating Detroit's first public playground. His courtroom experiences quickly convinced him of the necessity for a separate legal system for youthful offenders, and he threw his energies behind the successful battle to establish a juvenile court system in Michigan. As late as the mid-1950s, almost a decade after Butzel's death in 1948, it was still possible to hear the comment, regarding a boy in Juvenile Court, "Too bad Fred Butzel isn't still alive. He could have helped this kid."[10]

Butzel's early interest in the d'Arcambal Association flowed naturally from his numerous activities in behalf of immigrant and youth groups in Detroit. But by 1906 he was worried. A growing discipline problem in the d'Arcambal boys' home clearly needed attention. The boys, perhaps seeking to demonstrate their independence, were belligerently resisting authority. For example, no amount of persuasion or threats seemed sufficient to induce them to use soap and water on their hands and faces. Ultimately, Butzel turned to Homer Lane, a large redheaded man of about thirty, whom he had known for several years.[11]

The two men had first met in 1904, when Butzel was seeking someone to teach a class in manual training at the Hannah Schloss settlement house. They were a study in contrasts: Lane was invariably restless, impetuous and excitable, probably insecure despite his

137

outward bravado; Butzel was modest, quietly confident, stable to the core. Yet they quickly struck up a strong friendship and shared a deeply felt sympathy for disadvantaged and suffering people. From the start, Lane dazzled Butzel with his innovative ways of working with children. The charming redhead responded to troublesome situations as if by instinct, with a born gambler's intuition. At the settlement Lane not only taught woodworking classes, but also established a self-governing club that spawned a series of successors. The boys, rugged slum kids for the most part, eagerly set up a variety of programs and even imposed a two-cent weekly tax on themselves. Adult participants such as Butzel and Lane also paid the fee and enjoyed very little more status than any of the youthful members. At a joint gathering with the "Knights of the Round Table"— another boys' group that middle-class child savers were forming across the country—the roughhewn, democratic qualities of Lane's young charges were clear. The slum youths' wide-open style and spontaneity differed sharply from the cautious role playing and artificiality of the Knights, whose members addressed each other formally by such names as Sir Galahad and Sir Lancelot. Butzel was delighted.[12]

Not surprisingly, then, when Butzel wanted to shape up the boys at the d'Arcambal home, he turned to Lane. Accepting the challenge, Lane brashly contended that he could clean up the boys if Butzel would simply give him $1.50 and ask no questions. That evening Lane showed up at the home and began to make molasses candy. Nonchalantly humming a popular tune, he got ready to pull the taffy. Sleeves rolled up, he washed his already clean hands and then began to work the candy with his fingers. The boys at the home had been curious from the beginning about what the tall stranger was doing at their place; when they realized that he was making candy, they asked if they could help. Sure, he answered, but they would first need to wash their hands. The eager youths returned from the sink only to have Lane block them again: their hands, thanks to accumulated weeks of grime, were still so dirty that they would poison the candy, he said. After pulling the taffy alone, he shared it with the boys and then got up to leave. One youngster, alert to future possibilities, asked whether Lane might return to make candy in a few days and allow those who had gotten their hands clean to help. "Sure," was the reply, "but I don't believe you can get your hands clean in a month." When he and Fred Butzel visited the home several days later, they found that the boys had used soap and water with commendable diligence.[13]

From Butzel's perspective, his friend had worked another miracle. Lane, ever confident and ready to offer an opinion, pointedly observed that the home's existing superintendent, C. S. Carney, was completely ineffective. Carney, a University of Michigan graduate in sociology, had previously worked for six months in the prestigious settlement house environment of Graham Taylor's Chicago Commons. "Pooh," the unimpressed Lane snorted; the d'Arcambal Home was "a joke" and would remain so as long as Carney was in charge. Lane also urged that the aassociation move the boys' home to the countryside, where the residents could work in the fresh air. Butzel already had his own doubts about Carney. Moreover, he liked the idea of a rural setting for the Home. So he convinced the d'Arcambal board that it was time for major changes.[14]

In the spring of 1907, the home moved to its new location on a seventy-acre farm near Farmington, some seventeen miles outside Detroit, and acquired a new superintendent: Homer Lane. For the next five years, Lane—enigmatic, unquestionably charismatic in dealing with youths, and possessed of almost magnetic charm—moved the institution through its seminal period as a boys' farm and junior republic. He had staked out a heavy claim to Butzel and the board: "Get a farm and let me take 30 of the worst boys your Juvenile Court can pick out, and I'll go out and live on it with them, and I'll clean up their habits of doing wrong just as well as I did their hands."[15]

Lane's expectations were unquestionably grandiose, but his earlier life suggested that in disposition and experience he was well qualified for the assignment. A product of generations of solid Yankee stock, with American origins that preceded the Revolution, Lane had been born in 1875 in Hudson, New Hampshire. He spent his youth in various New England towns. The setting was generally rural and, because of his mother's strong Congregationalism, pious (although Homer himself was only nominally devout). His father worked on the railroad. Homer quickly demonstrated that he had talent, unflagging energy, considerable capacity for work (as a deliv-

ery boy he was regularly on the job at four o'clock each morning),
and imagination. He grew into an attractive young man with the
reputation as a go-getter. Ambitious and bright, he was bent on
excelling, distinguishing himself, being the best at whatever he did.
From his first teaching assignments he derived perspectives that
turned out to be invaluable for his work at the Ford Republic.
Briefly, he studied and then taught a voluntary evening class in the
"Sloyd" system. Sloyd, the Finnish word for skill, was at the time
an exciting concept to many educational reformers. With its stress
on working with the hands instead of books, it represented the
cutting edge of the drive for manual training programs in America.
Lane took very seriously one of the injunctions he had learned from
his instructor, Gustav Larsen, regarding the Sloyd system: "The
child must not be forced to learn." Nor did Lane forget the summer
in which he taught woodworking at the Pennsylvania State Reformatory in Huntington. He came away with a permanent scar—
the result of a boy's having struck him with a tool—and the
conviction that reform schools did anything but reform. In 1902,
following the death of his first wife, he moved to Detroit, where he
taught in the public schools, struck up relations with the local
newsboys' association, took groups of "newsies" to summer camps,
served for a year as superintendent of playgrounds, and established a
local reputation as something of an educational radical because of
his emphasis on personal freedom and spontaneity in the classroom.
His flair for the dramatic, his iconoclastic temperament, his tendency to posture, and his flamboyant defense of unpopular ideas convinced some observers that he was probably a fraud. But to people
like Fred Butzel, Lane had enormous promise.[16]

Among Lane's backers was Charles Cooley, an eminent sociologist at the University of Michigan and a pivotal intellectual among
progressive reformers.[17] Cooley had talked with Lane, and in August
1907 he visited the d'Arcambal Boys' Home. According to Cooley,
Lane had a "remarkable natural aptitude for boys' work" and expressed ideas that reflected "the best psychology and pedagogy." His
knack of winning the boys' devotion astounded the sociologist: "I
have never seen a better man in this regard."[18]

If there was much about Lane that held out the promise of
success, there were also hints that he was almost predisposed to fail.

His carelessness with details and finances marred his superintendency from the outset, but there was something else as well. Competing with his aggressive, even combative nature—indeed, contradicting it—was his fatalistic view that his faults virtually assured disaster. Success brought guilt and foreboding. This pessimism perhaps resulted from a shattering adolescent experience: when he was not yet fifteen, his little sister, supposedly under his watchful eyes, had toddled onto a railroad track and died under the wheels of a passing train. Whether or not this was in fact the root of his fears, Lane—despite his outward confidence and bravado—seemed to expect failure.[19]

Whatever his well-hidden doubts about himself, however, Lane plunged into his new duties with an almost swashbuckling abandon. From the outset, he attempted to involve the boys in running their own affairs. Although he did not implement the miniature government system until 1909, he always tried to make the youths believe they had a stake in the home. The farmhouse that the board had purchased was filthy and in disrepair; in fact, chickens were roosting in the front room. Lane insisted that he and the boys should clean up the place themselves, rather than allow the d'Arcambal Association to prepare it for their arrival. Within the first few weeks, he and the youthful residents started constructing a building that he had himself designed, because the farmhouse was unbelievably crowded: besides Lane, Mabel (his second wife, the sister of his first), and their four children, there were some two dozen boys, a teacher, and another couple. Lane and the youngsters hurriedly dug foundations and mixed concrete for the new structure. The boys also helped with various kinds of housework, including washing and mending clothes.[20]

Lane's personality provided the social glue during these first chaotic months. His sense of humor, and his capacity—which Charles Cooley observed—to show genuine sympathy for the boys and faith in them, certainly helped. He was also willing to impose his own considerable strength on recalcitrant youths. Fred Butzel recalled how Lane had earlier handled one of the tough kids at the Hannah Schloss settlement house: "He took his coat off and gave the boy a thorough licking." Then, when the boy remained unbowed, "Lane went in and gave him another licking." In the early days at the d'Arcambal Home, he sometimes punished boys who ran away by dressing them up like girls and making them walk in public view up and down a path.[21]

But Lane increasingly believed that such tactics were only super-ficial remedies to problems of youthful wrongdoing. The crux of the matter, he decided, was that events and institutions tended to reinforce young people's suspicions that society had conspired against them. It was only natural that maturing boys should seek independence; that was the essence of growing up. A youngster's first "bad act" resulted from a desire to "experiment," not from malice. Taking a puff on a cigarette, for example, was a gesture of defiance by which a youth tried to prove that he was his own person. The cigarette symbolized his self-esteem, showed that he could make certain decisions and define his own life. The guilt that came from knowing he had challenged authority was no match for "the exhilaration of victory." Truancy, another symbolic act, was like-wise a declaration of independence. Tragically, society implicated itself in the sad events that usually followed: adults, trying to protect their dominant position, reacted by asserting their au-thority; typically, they used force. As the boy looked around, he saw the agencies of society everywhere—parents, truant officers, the police—marshaling against him. "It had never occurred to the forces against him," wrote Lane, "that a flag of truce or the discharge of a few volleys of love and friendship would immediately break down his defenses." Society instead intensified its "attack upon his most impregnable point—his new found manhood." And in the process, adult groups only confirmed the siege mentality of the youth; surely adults were at war with him. By defying them, he grew in heroic stature, not only in his own eyes but in those of his peers, as well. What had started as a natural and innocent attempt to assert his rights as an individual thus ended by convincing adults of his supposed criminal tendencies.[22]

Lane pointed an accusing finger at society. More than likely, he charged, "the city had neglected [the boy's] welfare in its great industrial energy and robbed him of his playground that a new factory might be built." The laws and institutions that surrounded youths were invariably the creations of adults. Parents, teachers, law enforcement officers, and other adults necessarily shaped youthful impressions of the way society works. Children who continually encountered regulations that were simply there—arbitrary, inflexible, unexplained—learned nothing about why society needed rules. Grown-ups needed to take advantage of "the flexibility of the boy-mind" and allow youths to learn why particular institutions and laws were necessary.[23]

The question, of course, was how to do this. In a four-part newspaper story in early 1909, Lane sketched out some possibilities. He created a fictitious situation in which an organizer of boys' clubs, Henry L. Parks, tamed a youthful gang and channeled its energies in useful directions. Lane was well aware of the growing public concern over juvenile gangs. He had already cited psychologist G. Stanley Hall's opinion that never before had American boys "been quite so wild." As evidence, Hall had noted the adolescent city gangs that defied the police, terrorized citizens, and provided the "nurseries where the problems of the future are being reared."[24] Into this turbulent social setting, Lane sent his protagonist, Henry Parks, to subdue the notorious "River Gang." A fourteen-year-old boy nicknamed Turkey had organized some twenty slum kids into a rugged street force that harassed neighborhood police officers, vandalized property, spread fear among the city's respectable people, and gained attention in the press. The efforts of a well-meaning minister to form a boys' club made up of Sunday School youths and the "River Gang" ended in a fiasco, but Henry Parks was determined to keep the project going: "I believe," he said, "that if properly directed, their activities which now take the form of lawlessness, may be diverted into a more wholesome channel."[25]

Parks's strategy, and one which Lane was at that very time setting in motion at the d'Arcambal home, was to subvert the gang by becoming part of it. Rather than proving his point by physical force, he resorted to winning over the slum kids through example. Parks obtained permission to use a large room in a deserted factory and then approached Turkey's followers with the prospects of having a warm, well-lighted place in which they could wrestle and box without getting into trouble. By promising that neither police nor preachers would bother them, Parks placed the club beyond the symbols of adult authority—the law and the church. The boys, although initially suspicious of his aims, nonetheless responded to his easygoing manner. He talked directly to them, and was neither condescending nor threatening. "He ain't mushy, neither," observed Turkey. Parks allowed the boys to smoke by saying, "It's up to you. This is your room, not mine. What you say goes." Soon he had them engaged in a shuffleboard game; he mingled with them and shouted his approval. Then Parks challenged a boy named Jumbo to a wrestling match. When Jumbo pinned him, Parks laughingly complimented him for his strength. Jumbo, proud of his achievement, was equally pleased by this acknowledgement of his prowess. But as Parks started to explain the advantages of his proposed boys' club, one of the youths threw a block through a window; the others, quickly sensing an opportunity for more fun, began to break windows also. When the boys then prepared to run from the scene, Parks completely surprised them by himself lofting a block through a remaining pane of glass, and then another. "Come on boys," he told the surprised youths. "Go outside and pick up your blocks and let's finish the rest of them." Whereupon he sent his third missile sailing through the glass.[26]

Readers of the story may well have shaken their heads in doubt when the third installment ended at this point. Had not Parks in the process of trying to transform the gang been himself transformed? A ritualistic theme in much American literature, from Puritan New England onward, had dealt with the need to cross over into savagery in order to defeat barbaric enemies. Whether it was Puritan missionaries dealing with heathen Indians or, later, Pinkerton detectives adjusting temporarily to the life-styles of criminals and radicals in order to destroy them, the story was familiar.[27] But in Parks's case, it appeared that it was he who had ultimately succumbed. Primitivism had apparently won out; the feared juvenile gang was now as victorious in fiction as in the real streets where frightened citizens worried about the shadows.

In the last episode of his story, however, Lane showed how such tactics had in fact "regenerated" the gang. After the boys and Parks had retrieved the blocks and broken the rest of the windows, Parks quietly proceeded to sweep up the broken glass while the youths watched. When they subsequently argued with each other over who had started the trouble, he reminded them that they were all to blame. He and they had equally enjoyed destroying the windows.

Now, because it was their room, they should help to get it back in order. The boys ultimately joined Parks, even to the extent of paying for new windows. Parks had in effect crossed over the line of primitivism, but not at the price of civilized values after all. At the end, he brought the gang itself back into respectable country.[28]

The story illustrated, however melodramatically, what Lane increasingly believed: decent, civic-minded behavior had to come voluntarily. Dependence on external authorities to keep order resulted in dictatorial systems, not democracies. The key to a free society, he emphasized, was the same as for a successful classroom: "*self*-discipline or *self*-restraint."[29] Such logic drew deeply upon a longstanding American reform tradition. Lane simply articulated an idea that had informed a variety of reform movements. Self-control had been, for example, one of the most popular goals of antebellum reformers, including temperance advocates, spiritualists, health champions, builders of sexual utopias, and antislavery people. Here was what a historian later called "cultural voluntarism"—the principle by which individuals choose to conform to values larger than themselves. Choice, not duress, was the major factor. Certainly the dominant theme of the junior republic idea, so popular among child savers in the progressive era, was a variation of cultural voluntarism. Youths, under this system, were supposed to learn the value of cooperation and of harnessing their own impulses. The strategy was intensely American—individualistic, democratic, anti-institutional.[30]

Lane's enthusiasm for the self-government method was clear by the time he took charge of the d'Arcambal home. In August 1907 he shared his thoughts with sociologist Charles Cooley. Lane's "main principle," Cooley observed, "is that the way to bring out the best in [the boys] is to inculcate an ideal or group tradition by personal influence and let it work itself out without interference." Lane believed that youths could, as Cooley phrased it, "develop wisdom and character by free choice and natural self expression." Cooley noted that Lane's "views in this regard are just the opposite of those prevailing in the ordinary institution. . . . He read me an outline of his scheme of self-government, and I have no fault to find with it. . . ."[31]

At first, however, events thwarted Lane's hopes of setting up self-government at the d'Arcambal home. For one thing, during the first year in the countryside, too many boys passed through the institution too quickly. Because of a controversy about the constitutionality of the law establishing Michigan's juvenile court system, the state reform schools were reluctant to receive boys from the court. Rather than see them remain in jail or prematurely end up on the streets, Lane admitted many youths to the home for short stays. The 145 boys who came at various times during the year constituted what Lane described as "a floating population of the very worst boys in the city of Detroit." Although this prevented the immediate establishment of "the machinery of self-government," Lane informed the d'Arcambal board that he had at least adhered to the spirit of the idea; he had supplied each boy "with as many opportunities as is possible to develop his own individuality, to think for himself and to control himself." Lane liked to believe that the youths, however short their stay, were "very much more independent and self-reliant than when they first entered" the home.[32]

Even with his reservations about his accomplishments, Lane was placing those first months in the best possible light. The initial period at the farm location was undoubtedly nothing less than chaotic. Not only was the setting new, but conditions were at times little short of wretched. At one point there were sixty-five boys staying in the old farmhouse; it was a substantial dwelling but hardly capable of holding so many people, plus Lane's family, without considerable discomfort. The ground often resembled a quagmire—"so soggy and wet," Lane reported, "that even respectable weeds would not take root." Lane admitted being "bitterly disappointed," because the farm was in such bad shape—"as unproductive as a city pavement"—that the boys had not been able to grow enough food to meet their needs. The laundry equipment was totally inadequate. Because there was nothing like a gymnasium, more than five dozen boys sometimes milled around in the dining room during bad weather. The farm was located a mile from the end of the streetcar line, and the roads were sometimes virtually impassable. The only form of transportation at the farm was a battered, old one-seated buggy.[33] There was, moreover, the matter of safety. This

came abundantly
apped some fo

Lane atte
successf
relia
Self-g
more in
Lane's par
in the attic
the steps and
onto outstretche
Fortunately, even
dent's fractured wr
boys—bareheaded an
storm—watched flames
dered about the future of t
tion already faced a debt of se
no easy task to save the projec
found temporary lodging in near
the Solvey Guild Association in L
short-term quarters for the boys.[35]

While construction
Ford Hall, in honor of
two months. They bo
order to continue
Lane's point of vie
less important tha
"the blind follow
tion. "What we
development of
this must be
individuality
school syste
personal ho
Time an
sense of s
gangs su
When a
peers,
streng
agenc
At t
self-
Th
in
i

As things turned out, the fire signaled
not the end, of the d'Arcambal home.
scorched clothes, made a dramatic visit to
appeal for funds to finish the building that he
constructing. Earlier, one of Ford's daughters h
describe what the d'Arcambal Association was d
underprivileged boys and had rushed home to ask
contribute to the cause. Now, Lane desperately told t
the very future of the project hung in the balance. He
with a pledge of $45,000, and the institution readied for a
with a new name. Although many people later assumed t
Ford Republic derived its name from Henry Ford, the autom
manufacturer, that was not the case. Henry did serve on the boar
trustees for a while, and he gave a small amount of money to th
d'Arcambal Association, but it was the unrelated E. L. Ford family
that bailed out the project during its greatest crisis.[36]

...astened along on the new building—na...
...he donors—the boys remained in the city...
...rowed books and used pine boards for desks...
...e educational aspects of the program. From
..., the physical setting of the school was always
...the teaching methods anyhow. He objected to
...ng of text books" in much contemporary educa-
...are after," he declared, "is the mental and moral
...the pupil along healthful and thorough lines. But
...ccomplished without dwarfing and destroying the
...and self-activity of the pupil." At the heart of the
...he was trying to implement were "self-reliance and
...or."[37]

...again Lane stressed that youths must first develop a
...lf-respect. This, he argued, was precisely why juvenile
...ceeded and most adults who worked with youths failed.
...oungster's "eats 'em alive" posture won the approval of his
...is self-image was enhanced, and he enjoyed a feeling of
...h and independence. In contrast, by the time most adult
...es dealt with him, he had usually lost his sense of self-esteem.
...at most unpropitious moment, many youths—already full of
...hatred—entered institutions to which society consigned them.
...ese institutions, supposedly designed to convert their residents
...to useful citizens, started at an enormous disadvantage. Most
...stitutions nonetheless made the mistake, according to Lane, of
...mposing even more restraints through rigid rules and routines.
Youths who resided in such places consequently became "institutionalized," mechanically carrying out assigned tasks. When
they eventually moved into the outside world, they could only "fall
and fall hard." Tragically, a typical child saving institution, by
relying on external restraints, did nothing to build a set of habits by
which young people could learn to regulate their conduct.[38] Lane
was not about to make the same mistake.

During his weekly visits to the Juvenile Court, Lane sometimes
used a ploy to start building a youngster's self-worth at the outset: if
the judge claimed that a particular youth really would not benefit
from life at the d'Arcambal farm, Lane would loudly interject, "If
that boy isn't first-rate material your Honour, I'll eat my shirt."[39]

With such a gesture, Lane established his friendship with the youngster and made the boy feel like someone special.

Once the youth arrived at the farm, however, the challenge was to make him recognize that being good was more fun than being bad. To accomplish this, Lane embraced the idea of a self-governing junior republic—"not an institution, but a community of individuals, who, as a result of self-restraint, are welded together into a larger unit of society." Following a visit to William R. George's famous Freeville republic, Lane assembled his own charges to describe what he had observed in upstate New York and to ask if they wished to adopt a similar system.[40]

In early 1909 "the Commonwealth of Ford" became official. The constitution, which Lane presumably wrote, stated that "the people of the Boys' Farm, Commonwealth of Ford" hoped "to build the highest type of manliness, citizenship and public spirit." The population, averaging approximately fifty boys, made up the legislature. Officers were chosen by secret ballot. During the first six months of the Republic's existence, from thirty-nine to sixty-three noisy young citizens gathered daily, with sometimes half a dozen on their feet at one time hollering for the president to recognize them. Despite the rowdy atmosphere, the meetings dealt with a wide variety of issues. Some legislation defined crimes and punishments: "grabbing for food, putting elbows on table, saying 'O Beans!' etc.," became misdemeanors; running around the sleeping area exacted a fifty-cent fine; and leaving the plug in after using the wash basin was illegal. The legislature not only decided on the sheriff's salary ($4.00 per week in Republic scrip) but also stipulated that he could not swear at any citizen. On occasion the citizens established planning committees—to decide, for example, where to locate the baseball diamond. Now and then, confusion prevailed: "Moved by Mr. Bojanczyk that we ought to have manual training started this week. Carried. Moved by Mr. Bojanczyk that we must have manual training this week. Carried. Moved by Mr. Dodd that we have manual training next week. Carried."[41]

The striking thing about the Ford Republic was not just how young its members were (by mid-1911 the average age was thirteen, and some boys were only eight—considerably younger than those at William R. George's famed Freeville project).[42] It was also that the citizens exercised such extensive control over their own affairs. Homer Lane, just like the fictitious Henry Parks who tamed the infamous "River Gang," had no more authority at the legislative meetings than any other citizen. At least once, for example, the president ruled Lane out of order. The legislature also decided that the schoolteacher could no longer "put a dirty cloth around a citizens' [sic] mouth." In fact, the boys had the right to file complaints against Lane, the teacher, or any other adult at the Republic. Adults had to stand trial and, if the judge so decided, to pay fines; in turn, they had to depend upon the court system to impose punishment and discipline on unruly youths. This meant, for instance, that Lane had to file a written complaint in the Citizens' Court if he disliked a particular boy's conduct. As a member of the d'Arcambal board of trustees observed, "The laws are the same for all citizens, adult or young; so adults are forced to set a good example and be on the square."[43]

The Republic's judicial system was extraordinary. A citizen was innocent until the court proved otherwise; all trials had to be public; no citizen faced double jeopardy; each defendant had to know about the charges against him at least two hours before the trial; and all accusers had to state their complaints publicly. There was also the right to appeal to the Republic's Supreme Court: the superintendent. (In that sense, of course, the system *was* rigged in favor of the adults; Lane could have the last word. Yet he, as much as anyone, was aware of the necessity that the system "be on the square" and surely used his prerogative with much discretion.) The jurisdiction of the Citizens' Court was wide-ranging, including crimes of smoking, laziness, disorderliness in school, untidiness, bullying, name calling, tardiness, and "dangerous play." The Supreme Court—Lane's bailiwick—dealt with crimes of lying, stealing, destruction of property, "treason," and "insolence to officers." Again, the balance of power tilted in the superintendent's favor. Still, within its limits, the boys' court was extremely energetic and one of the best-known features of the Ford commonwealth.[44]

Penalties from which the Citizens' Court could choose were numerous but did not include imprisonment, because the Republic lacked a jail. The judge had the authority to place the culprit on "probation." He could impose extra work or make the offender stand in the dining room during meals. A common punishment was called the "Merry Go Round," which meant that the guilty person had to walk around a flowerbed for a prescribed amount of time. According to one publicity pamphlet—which showed three youths, heads down, walking the circular path—discomfort resulted not merely from the monotony of the exercise but from the taunts of the others. "Note the upright citizen 'guying' the prisoners," the Republic's literature pointed out. "That's what hurts." On one occasion the court ordered a boy found guilty of swearing to wash his mouth with soap for three nights. Another youngster, who had thrown paper wads in school, had to spend three days after classes throwing and picking up more of them. Corporal punishment was also a possibility, one which the court assigned to the sheriff, another officer, or the superintendent. Overzealous application of this penalty stirred the citizens' legislature to resolve on March 24, 1909, that the sheriff could not use a strap.[45]

Fines and "state labor" were intimately connected to the Republic's economic system. In May 1909 the commonwealth started using its own aluminum currency in denominations similar to those of United States money. In a fashion resembling William R. George's "Nothing without Labor" scheme, boys at Ford paid for bed and board ($3.00 per week in scrip in 1909), laundry bills, clothing, and taxes; and they received pay for various tasks, including going to school. If they wished to buy something outside the Republic, they could redeem the aluminum currency; in 1909 a dollar in Republic scrip was good for twenty-four cents in "real" money. But without labor it was impossible to pay one's expenses. Nonpayment eventually resulted in trouble with the Citizens' Court. The judge reportedly warned one boy who had fallen behind on his laundry bill, "Get a hustle on . . . 'cause the tax-payers ain't goin' to stand it to support a big, husky lump like you." A youth who spent his time fishing received a warning from the bench: "Fish don't count here. We've got to pay eighty-five cents in taxes to feed you during the week, an' that don't go." Unpaid debts led invariably to the penalty of state labor—working for the commonwealth without compensation. Boys on state labor sawed wood and scrubbed floors, for example; they could not enjoy the normal privileges of citizenship, such as voting and recreation; and they supposedly "lost the respect of the public." Until a citizen had paid his debts, he would also "be frequently reminded by other citizens that he is a dependent." The stigma of dependency thus carried a heavy burden at the Republic.[46]

Most important, according to the Republic's literature, boys learned—on their own—that individual conduct should never occasion public expense. This lesson came not from abstract sermonizing about the virtues of work and honesty but from direct personal experience. After a prudent calculation of self-interest, they were reputedly inclined to reconsider their previous hostility toward authority and government. In this sense, the Republic was engaged in what Lane called "the production of values."[47]

To illustrate how it worked, the Republic publicized what was supposed to be a typical experience. When a newly arrived citizen stepped off a city streetcar at the end of the line he encountered "a barefooted boy about his own age, seated in a dilapidated, rickety old buggy, attached to a venerable gray horse," ready to take him the rest of the way to the farm. The new boy was naturally surprised to learn that his welcoming committee was none other than the "sheriff" of the Republic. Another surprise awaited him at the farm when he found the other residents roaming around with apparent freedom. At this point the new citizen invariably resorted to the kind of activity that had won favor in his old street gang: he attempted something mischievous, assuming that to do so would win approval. But this time, unruly behavior brought rebuke—and not from an adult, but from another boy: "Say, Fellow! That business don't go here; you stan' up against the wall." In this bewildering Alice-in-Wonderland environment, familiar patterns were reversed, and earlier points of reference were meaningless. With his former world turned upside down, the youth had to scramble to get his bearings. Bad conduct brought disapproval, not respect, from his peers. Desperately needing support from the other citizens in order to boost his self-esteem, he learned to control himself in ways that he had never previously considered. He who had formerly resisted adult restraints thus ended up imposing those very restrictions upon himself. He had, through a very natural process of adjustment, internalized values that his larger society held dear. His experiences at the Republic taught him, graphically and unforgettably, to be a good citizen.[48]

After only a few months of the miniature republic's existence, Lane was ecstatic about the results, claiming that the boys' aptitude for self-government had surpassed his grandest expectations. The key to such success, he was convinced, rested in the fact that no mere sandbox democracy existed at the commonwealth. Instead, the young citizens at Ford controlled their own affairs to such an extent that they had in effect "been entrusted with the entire management of an institution." No other experiment in youthful self-government had gone so far. By May 1909, according to Lane, all rules at the Republic had come directly from the boys' legislature. Moreover, he informed the d'Arcambal board excitedly that the youngsters were administering their affairs better than he had done prior to the existence of the junior state. Lane went further: The system of justice at the Republic was, he contended, purer than that in the outside world. This was so because no layers of legal paraphernalia separated court and citizens. In one evening, the elected judge could deal with as many as fifty cases. There were no lawyers to complicate the process and no jury was necessary, because all citizens attended the Court, and frequently, the judge asked them for help in deciding difficult cases. Because the Republic had no attorneys, there was no tendency to obscure issues with technicalities and rhetoric. The result, Lane said enthusiastically, was that justice came "from the heart," and had not "been perverted by technical and legal phraseology into injustice."[49]

To Lane, these were not empty words designed for public consumption. He was a true believer in self-government at the Republic, and his confidence in the boys was genuine. It was not unusual for him to send a youngster into the office to pick up the institutional payroll of some $200. According to one of the adult employees, "Lane tried through affection and understanding, asking nothing in return, to build up respect, confidence and reliance first in self and then toward others by living and working together." He refrained from intervening in young people's affairs, especially in matters of youthful bad judgment. Once, for example, he simply watched while the legislature happily voted to have ice cream with every meal. When the cook demurred on the grounds that the budget could not tolerate such luxury, Lane instructed her to abide by the citizens' decision until the money ran out. Following a three-day orgy of eating ice cream, the week's food money was gone. For the rest of the week the youths survived on beans alone. Presumably, the lesson was clear: actions indeed have consequences.[50]

Lane was not the only person excited about the Republic's accomplishments. Maurice Willows, superintendent of the Birmingham, Alabama, Boys' Club, visited the institution and reported that he had "talked Ford Republic ever since coming back." He subsequently asked Lane to accept an eleven-year-old from Birmingham; the boy, a victim of parental neglect, had burglarized a store. "I think so much of your methods," Willows told Lane, "that we want to have a representative there." The Republic admitted the youngster, to the delight of *Detroit Saturday Night*, a weekly newspaper that served as one of the most zealous boosters of Lane and his junior commonwealth.[51]

Moderately progressive, *Detroit Saturday Night* backed "insurgents" against "standpatters," endorsed reform-minded Chase Osborne for governor, featured photographs of slums in answer to individuals who denied that Detroit had tenement housing problems, and championed better care for needy children. Under such headlines as "How Boys Are Saved" and "Remember the Waifs," it applauded the Ford Republic. The newspaper, agreeing with "competent critics" that Homer Lane ranked with Judge Ben Lindsey as a child saver, printed at least seven of Lane's essays and a long letter. To the editors, the Ford Commonwealth offered nothing less than "a revelation of boy character in the way the youngsters have assumed practically the entire management of the d'Arcambal home." In fact, "Mr. Lane's experiment," stood as "one of the greatest arguments for American democracy yet advanced." It proved "that the spirit of American democracy is inbred in the soul of the unfortunate and immature boy as in the consciousness of the adult and reflective man."[52]

According to H. W. Crane, a sociologist with Charles Cooley at the University of Michigan, the Ford Republic "was the best thing of the kind that has ever been tried." Invariably, some individuals compared it to William R. George's New York institution: J. S.

Williams, secretary of Detroit's Association of Charities, said flatly that the Ford system was "the best example of self-government" he had witnessed, including that of the George Junior Republic.[54]

Daddy George, however, had his doubts. Initially he resented the fact that the Ford Commonwealth "was evidently copied after our Republic without giving us the credit." On the other hand, he admitted that he really knew only what he had read in some of the d'Arcambal Association's literature, and he conceded it was "a pretty good thing," at least in terms of spreading the junior republic idea in Michigan. In 1910, after a sister of one of the trustees of the Ford Republic had visited Freeville, George established communications with the d'Arcambal organization. He described his plan to establish "at least one Junior Republic in each state of the Union. . . . Next year I start one in Illinois, and another one in Wisconsin." George claimed to have had offers of land in Michigan as well. But if the Ford Republic's work matched the standards that George was setting for his own network, he in no sense wanted to duplicate it. Perhaps, he ventured, the Ford Commonwealth might affiliate with George's to everyone's advantage. George and his people could thus "throw all of our influence and personal effort in the way of strengthening the Ford Republic." But George intimated strongly that he would hold the dominant position: "If the Ford Republic were not carrying out the Junior Republic principles fully we would undoubtedly start a real Junior Republic."[54]

In 1912, George's National Association of Junior Republics formally invited the Ford Commonwealth to join it. Lane declined, undoubtedly in part because he was not ready to subsume his project under anyone else's control. Yet more than ego was involved, although surely that was a factor; there were also philosophical matters at stake. Ironically, George said that the Ford institution was "not carrying out the Republic idea fully—at least not according to my idea"[55]—while Lane suspected that it was George who had stopped short of establishing "a real Junior Republic." Lane believed that George secretly manipulated the affairs of Freeville's miniature society so that it did not really provide self-government at all. Moreover, he disliked the fact that Freeville's court system included jails; in Lane's estimation, prison discipline sullied any junior republic. To George, this showed that Lane had fallen victim to a "Utopian fallacy"—a naive, sentimental, and foolish inability to see the harsh realities of the actual world.[56]

Utopian fallacy or not, Lane may indeed have seen things as he wanted them to be, rather than as they really were. Schooling at the Ford Republic was a prime example. From the beginning, Lane asserted that the school was "a success." It had developed self-reliance, individualism, and personal honor. If this was indeed true, the teacher must have worked a small miracle, considering that she had as many as fifty boys between the ages of eight and sixteen in one large room.[57] Leisure time provided additional problems. After the evening meal, chaos apparently prevailed. "There was no kind of planned evening program," recalled an adult employee, "so the boys milled around and the place was a madhouse." Moreover, the miniature economy at Ford may have provided incentives for individual enterprise other than what Lane had in mind: theft. Lane preferred to pay the citizens' hourly wages—for jobs and school time—in the Republic's currency, not in credit. "Unfortunately," recalled an employee some forty years later, "it was unsuccessful then and has failed each time the plan has been revived. There has never been any way in which private possessions, especially money, could be safeguarded and still be in a boy's possession." (Later a system of keeping a simple ledger accounting of each boy's financial status was adopted.) Matters of safety also nagged at the institution. Although Ford Hall was a vast improvement over the old farmhouse that burned down, the problem of safety persisted. In 1912, for example, two of the boys were injured in "terrible accidents" while using the mangle in the steam laundry.[58]

Moreover, the reputed moral transformation of the Republic's citizens may have been far less sweeping than Lane and others suggested. Of the 386 boys who resided at the d'Arcambal home between March 1907 and October 1910, a majority stayed three months or less. How was it possible to reshape a youthful personality so dramatically in so short a time? Fifty-four had stayed for four to six months; nineteen for seven to ten months; and fourteen for one year. Only thirty-six had remained for more than a year, and five for the entire three years. Allowing even for the transitional months immediately following the home's relocation in the countryside—a time when Lane himself lamented the "floating population"—the average stay for any boy in 1910 was five months. Even then, only six of ninety-eight boys stayed during one three-month period. Not only did the youths remain a relatively short time, but their age variation simply had to affect the actual processes of self-government. Some kind of "pecking order" must have separated youngsters who were, say, eleven or younger (totaling 104) from those fourteen and older (totaling 149).[59]

Publicly the d'Arcambal Association argued that the short residency of the boys was a measure of success. Within a few years the institution had supposedly discovered that the majority of boys needed to stay less than three months. "In other words," according to one pamphlet, "it has been found that a boy's attitude toward authority and government may be changed at the d'Arcambal Farm in much less time than is deemed necessary by the authorities in the State Institution." Privately, however, some trustees felt there was evidence to the contrary: "We do not keep boys long enough to really get the best benefit out of their work," wrote one.[60]

Youths who left the home remained theoretically under the superintendent's careful scrutiny for a while in order to make sure they did not go astray. But it was unlikely that the overburdened Lane carried out this responsibility with the necessary diligence. Not a lack of interest on his part, but the sheer grind of his schedule—supervising the farm, visiting the Juvenile Court, writing articles, and publicizing the Republic—surely limited the attention he could award former citizens. Even as late as 1916 there were indications that the board of trustees still worried about keeping better track of boys after they left.[61] Consequently, because the actual effects on many of the boys of life at Ford lacked documentation, the positive assessment of Lane and others were problematical.

If the Republic was even half as successful as Lane and his admirers insisted, it was perhaps because of something in addition to the vitality of self-government and Lane's charm. Many of the boys may not have been as "bad" as that label implied. Adults, after all, defined criminal conduct, and by the turn of the century, reformers were displaying a marked inclination to judge bad tendencies, questionable morals, and victimless infractions as "criminal" in nature.[62] It was at this point that the concepts of dependency and delinquency blurred in the minds of many progressive child savers. What dependent child, for example, did not at least lean toward those actions which some states, such as Ohio, included in their definition of delinquency: "growing up in idleness"; wandering the streets late at night; using "vile, obscene, vulgar, profane or indecent language"; smoking cigarettes; frequenting "any theater, gallery, or arcade where any lewd, vulgar or indecent pictures are exhibited"; gambling; and associating with "immoral persons." According to a Utah newspaper, Judge Willis Brown in Salt Lake City was doing splendid work, whether he was "saving small boys from the curses of the slums" or "sentencing seven-year-olds to the reform school"; he was rescuing them "from themselves and from their parents." Even the gentle and understanding Ben Lindsey once sent a boy to reform school not because he had actually broken the law but because he needed to learn to be more manly. "Frequently," according to Lindsey, "we handle a boy whose only trouble is unchastity."[63]

A representative of the Minnesota state training school regretted the haphazard process by which boys and girls came to his institution. It was apparently not uncommon for the commitment papers to omit fundamental information about the children, including the nature of their crimes. Once, when a sheriff brought two boys to the institution and an official asked what they had done, the answer was simply that they were "two d———d bad boys." The official wrote to the authorities responsible for committing the youths but again learned only that they were "two bad kids." Finally, he determined from the boys themselves that each had stolen several apples and some peanuts. In this case petty theft had apparently provided the clinching evidence for judging the boys as "bad." In other instances youths ended up in the training school for truancy. Here, however, the representative from the state training school had no complaints: "My observation is that truancy is simply a symptom of something worse. . . . Truancy does not precede a criminal act, it usually follows it." The fact remained, of course, that in such cases it was not for previous criminal acts but for truancy that the commitments occurred.[64]

Significantly, the overwhelming majority of boys at the d'Arcambal home were from the Juvenile Court. Of the first 386 residents, 320 were there at the court's behest—and 142 of them were truants.

Fifty-seven other boys were guilty of both truancy and larceny, and three more of larceny alone. The larceny charges were presumably misdemeanors, because the statistical record had a separate category for felons, of which there were only nine. One youngster had been arrested for vagrancy.[65] Many of these boys were thus perhaps not fundamentally "bad" at all. Lane described them as "without exception chronic truants" who did not "fit into the school system of Detroit." Yet given Lane's own aversion to the "the rut" of monotony and lack of imagination in most public schools, such truancy was perhaps not altogether unforgivable. At least it may not really have been an indication of a criminal bent.[66]

There were indications, moreover, that as many as fifty of the first 386 boys had done nothing wrong. Parents had committed twenty-four of them because of poverty; the probate court had rescued eight who were neglected; the police had committed fourteen who were homeless; and several came from other institutions.[67] In sum, many of the Republic's first residents may well have been basically decent youths—promising material out of which to build a junior commonwealth. It was thus perhaps not surprising that in the first three and one-half years only twenty-one came back to the d'Arcambal farm on charges of delinquency, and that fewer than forty ended up in industrial or reform schools.[68]

Even a few months at the Ford Republic undoubtedly provided them with learning experiences quite different from what they would have found in most institutions. This did not necessarily mean, however, that they had gone through a radical "transformation," or been "regenerated"—an achievement perhaps better left to the world of Henry Parks, Lane's fictional counterpart, who so dramatically altered the "River Gang."

Whatever the actual limits of the Republic's influence, it nonetheless provided the setting in which a Fred Bloman could flourish. Yet the commonwealth's most illustrious citizen was special not only because of his abilities but also because he stayed far longer at the d'Arcambal farm than did most boys; his four years there placed him among only a handful of residents. Also, as one of the Republic's pioneer citizens, he and the self-governing system developed together. He became enormously popular with his peers. Mischievous in school, athletic (until his health gave way), and politically active, he formed many friendships. After holding several elective offices, he reached the capstone of his young career when he served two terms as judge of the Citizens' Court. On the bench of the miniature commonwealth, he thrived as never before. According to Fred Butzel, "He helped as much as Lane to give the place the character it developed. . . . His fame grew to be such that people came . . . to watch him administering justice."[69]

Bloman displayed a keen sensitivity, a basic fairness, and considerable ingenuity. He also had a flair for the dramatic; he once brought charges and levied a heavy fine against himself (for using tobacco). When deciding cases against a "greenie," or new citizen, he was usually less severe, settling for a stern warning. But with repeat offenders he had a reputation for toughness. He agreed with the policy of barring attorneys from the Citizens' Court on grounds "that a fellow who had to hire a lawyer to defend him must be a crook." He once fined a citizen who had left a baseball game after the team captain had criticized him; although there was no law against leaving a ball game, in Bloman's estimation "there's a law against quitting." Another of his rulings concerned fighting. In his opinion, adversaries should exhaust all legal remedies before resorting to their fists. If they could not solve their differences peacefully, the court would allow them to fight—but according to strict rules. First, there could be no spectators. Without the "gallery," Bloman reasoned, the battle would lack the excitement of a public spectacle, and the opponents would not be the center of attention. Secondly, the loser had to admit formally that he was "licked" and report the results to the president of the Republic. The responsibility of publicizing the outcome of the battle thus rested with the vanquished. With the possibility of such additional humiliation hanging over the participants, they might be less inclined to fight.[70]

Bloman's death in 1911 was not simply a tragic moment in the history of the Ford Republic; it also struck a sentimental chord across the Detroit area. "Never before in the history of the world," claimed one newspaper, "have the courts of such a large city honored a mere boy in this way." The d'Arcambal Association based a major fund-raising drive upon Bloman's achievements. A flood of banners, letters and news stories used "the late Judge Fred Bloman, aged thirteen," to call attention to the accomplishments of the Ford

Republic and to establish November 27, 1911, as Boys Republic Day. The fund campaign received the support of the Boy Scouts and various civic groups, including Detroit's Associated Charities organization.[71]

The d'Arcambal Association was not attempting to "cash in" on young Bloman's death. Sadly, the organization had been struggling financially all along, especially following the transfer of the boys' home to the farm. "Our removal from the city has placed us rather out of touch with the smaller donations with which the public were so generous while we were in the city," observed Lane. Some of Detroit's major industries and organizations gave only small contributions; in February 1909, for example, Hiram Walker and Sons, Distillers, and the Detroit United Railway sent only $10 each. The Detroit Women's Club contributed $5.00 on several occasions, and the local YMCA provided $2.00 to buy Easter eggs at one point. Wayne County paid sixty cents per day toward the support of those boys whom the Juvenile Court had committed to the Republic. But basically the financial lifeblood of the institution depended upon several generous people, especially Mrs. E. L. Ford and her two daughters (who provided band instruments, holiday dinners, and Christmas gifts, as well as the substantial donation to build Ford Hall); Joshua Hill, who in 1910 gave the association some property in the Hamtramck manufacturing district to sell for a profit; and J. L. Hudson. Undoubtedly, trustees such as Fred Butzel and Rollin Stevens were also generous with their pocketbooks as well as their time. But despite such support, by the end of 1909 the Republic was running a monthly deficit of $200 to $300. Lane was certain that the home was "probably the most inadequately supported charity in Detroit."[72]

Lane's typical inattentiveness to the financial side of the d'Arcambal home did not help, nor did some untimely publicity in 1909 that probably raised more than a few eyebrows. "Boys Smoke with Lane" announced one newspaper, describing how the superintendent had invited several boys, sixteen or older, "to Join Him in Tobacco Parties." Admitting that he had indeed let several of the older youths smoke with him in his room in the evening, Lane argued that he thereby deterred them from sneaking in surreptitious puffs that would set a bad example for the younger boys. Such reasoning failed to convince some vocal skeptics. A county agent, for example, expressed complete amazement and disapproval at such "revelations." There were, after all, laws against furnishing minors with tobacco.[73]

Although Lane successfully weathered the storm over tobacco parties, his luck ran out some three years later. In March 1912, barely six months after the death of Fred Bloman, the Ford Republic suffered another shock: the abrupt departure of its controversial superintendent. As far as the public knew, Lane had simply resigned. That was just as well, for the circumstances could only have rocked the boys' home and the d'Arcambal Association with unwanted press coverage. Behind the scenes, the d'Arcambal board confronted Lane with evidence that he was having an affair with his secretary, a woman who taught at the Republic. For Lane, who apparently had fallen in love with the woman, it seemed advisable to resign the superintendency. He did so, leaving the Republic, his wife, and his children. A year later, still in his mid-thirties, he went to England, where he attracted considerable attention—and notoriety—initially as superintendent of the Little Commonwealth, a new correctional institution for boys and girls based on self-governing principles, and later as a psychotherapist.[74]

Lane's impact on the d'Arcambal home had been profound. More than anyone, he was responsible for introducing self-government at the institution, and he had done so with inimitable style. Yet even among his strongest backers, there had been a growing concern that under Lane's furious leadership the Republic was ready to fly apart. More than likely, even without the adulterous affair that provided the occasion for Lane's resignation, he and the board had been on a collision course for some time. In 1916 none other than Fred Butzel expressed second thoughts about those early days. "Not long ago we found a doctrine obtaining that boys could govern themselves practically," he told a group at the formal opening of a new juvenile court building. The belief had prevailed "that there are no bad boys. . . . Today we are ready to confess that we were too radical in our views." Although Butzel believed that such "radicalism was necessary to bring the work up to a higher standard," he had come to favor "the preventive proposition" over "the curative proposition." Later he said that "while Homer Lane gave a wonderful impetus to boy work in Detroit . . . it was very difficult to keep him, with his unbounded imagination and idealism, from engaging the various institutions for which he worked to undertakings on which it was impossible to make good." Butzel admired "the idealistic, imaginative type of men," but this experience with Lane had made him wary of any "strong tendency to force the millenium [sic]."[75]

In the years immediately following Lane's departure, the d'Arcambal Association and the new superintendent, J. M. McIndoo,[76] focused on making the Republic more orderly and financially secure. The result was a subtle but important shift in emphasis from political democracy in the miniature commonwealth to economic and moral lessons. At this point the institution's approach became far more orthodox, drawing upon the traditional American faith in the regenerative powers of a country setting rather than the creative energies of transplanted city youths.

McIndoo, who served as superintendent from November 1912 until 1922, was a product of rural Illinois. He received his B.A. degree at Antioch in 1900, taught English and Pedagogy in two high schools, and served several years as superintendent of schools in Broken Bow, Nebraska (population 3,000). In 1909 he entered Clark University on a scholarship to pursue graduate work under G. Stanley Hall. He was completing his Ph.D. requirements when he accepted the superintendency of the Ford Republic.[77]

Although McIndoo acted quickly to improve the living conditions at the d'Arcambal home—bringing in electrical power in 1913 and declaring the dangerous mangle iron off limits to the boys until a safer model was installed—he was less enthusiastic about the self-government system. "One of the unsolved problems," he informed his mentor, G. Stanley Hall, was "just how much self-government there should be and how much of the parental." Now that McIndoo actually had a chance to be "face to face with the psychology of the [boy] gang," he concluded that the ethnic composition of the young residents limited the efficacy of self-government. "A large per cent of our boys are Polish," he told Hall. "I find that the more Irish, French, and Jewish boys we have the more efficient is our self-government. There is a small per cent of leaders among the Polish boys." To the new superintendent it thus seemed "that a pure republic among boys of the gang age is, in the nature of things, an impossibility"; it evolved "into an oligarchy ruled by the few gang leaders." Convinced that the Commonwealth of Ford needed new directions, McIndoo stressed farmwork and hoped to open an industrial department in which the boys would repair articles and make toys.[78]

Even before McIndoo's arrival, the d'Arcambal board had decided to "concentrate the work of the Association at the farm" in order to increase its efficiency and enhance the reputed benefits of rural living for the residents. In the fields and woods of the Republic, delinquent and homeless boys were supposed to find "a wholesome environment . . . away from the crowded tenement district where the moral atmosphere is sometimes poisonous." The transformation of city boys into "little farmers" was reportedly something to behold. "It may be in the blood, this quick return to farm life," extolled the association's literature, "for many of the boys are only a generation removed from the fields of Europe." Some of the youngsters at the institution worked periodically at neighboring farms. Indeed, on such farms "many a graduate citizen" found "a good home and earn[ed] more money than he would in a factory or shop."[79]

In this context the d'Arcambal people thought they might also provide the impetus for an even larger social revolution. More was at stake than simply transplanting a few urban boys to the countryside. According to the institution's literature, perhaps the Republic was "helping more than we know in solving the problem of getting the younger generation back to the farm where they are more needed than in the congested cities."[80]

Despite such celebrations of rural life, some of the boys probably would have been surprised at the association's claim that "toil on the farm does not mean drudgery to them." Observers could reportedly "watch the smile of enjoyment on the boy's face" when he worked behind a team of horses or cared for the livestock. The youths themselves offered a somewhat less glowing version. One of the citizens' committees stated that "the farm is a good place to work when . . . it is warm but in the winter the kitchen is a better place and the guys that work there have no kick coming." In sum, work was work, and even the bracing outside air had its limits.[81]

Under McIndoo the d'Arcambal Association not only tried to

build up the farm's land but also started a system whereby the boys had individual garden plots, approximately 14 by 16 feet. The association provided seeds. Each boy regulated his own work schedule on the small plot and sold his produce to the institution. Because adults gave scientific advice on how to grow various crops, the youths learned something about "practical agriculture." The association had other goals as well, however. Theoretically, cultivating a garden developed a respect for property: "It was *his* garden and the boy was made to feel that as a good citizen he was expected to keep his little farm in good condition."[82]

This faith in the practical and moral benefits of gardening was far from unique to the Ford Republic. By 1913 there was considerable interest among child rescue workers elsewhere in the redemptive powers of even a small plot of earth. "A garden develops boys as much as boys develop a garden," summed up the superintendent of the New Britain, Connecticut, Boys' Club. In addition to New Britain, New York and Worcester, Massachusetts, were among the cities heralding local projects that involved "boys with the hoe." In Worcester the Social Settlement organization sponsored a "Garden City Plan" by converting some "miserable dumps" and vacant lots into 10- by 18-foot children's gardens. For five cents a youngster between the ages of six and sixteen could work one of the plots and receive five packages of seeds. The gardens together formed a "juvenile city" in which the youthful citizens elected a mayor, a city council, police officers, and various commissioners. One of the laws of the miniature city council forbade swearing, drinking, and smoking. The New Britain scheme lacked self-government but members of the Boys' Club grew and sold a variety of vegetables on five acres of donated land outside the city. The average number of youths at work there on any given day was thirty-five, although on occasion there were as many as one hundred. Boys averaged three hours of labor per day.[83]

Whether the scene was Massachusetts, Connecticut, or the Ford Republic, the objectives of such gardens were moral and social. Because many of the youths came from immigrant backgrounds, an experiment such as Garden City was reputedly "a melting pot, a good citizens' factory." Juvenile crime—including even cruelty to animals—had reportedly almost vanished in the several months following the opening of Garden City. Gardening was ostensibly something that youngsters did naturally: "Who ever saw a child that did not like to make mud pies or dig in the sand?" The lessons that accompanied gardening were, according to one club superintendent, invaluable: "A boy will soon learn in a garden that weeds allowed to grow will give him some puny vegetables. You can make him see that bad habits allowed to grow will give him a slope-shouldered, narrow-chested, flabby-muscled, squeaky-voiced, namby-pamby, mollycoddle sort of man." As in Victorian England, these gardening projects represented a response of middle-class reformers to the jarring social shift from country to city. Gardens provided miniature farms in an urban setting. They were educative in the sense of stressing themes of industry, self-improvement, and respectability while offering an alternative to the temptations of crowded city streets. The gardeners, with their little stakes in society, would presumably benefit personally as well as advance the welfare of the larger community; they could fuse the virtues of privacy with useful activities for the greater good.[84]

Some of this excitement among American child savers about the redeeming powers of gardening reflected the thinking of G. Stanley Hall. In his controversial theory of recapitulation, the preeminent child psychologist of the era had concluded that the life processes of children duplicated in miniature the larger history of civilization. Thus "The Garden City Solution of the Boy Problem" rested on the assumption that "the boy repeats the stages of the race"—in this case, the stage that focused on cultivating the soil. McIndoo's system of private gardens at the Ford Republic certainly reflected Hall's influence, and the superintendent happily informed his mentor that "the boy gardens" had "gratifying results."[85]

The garden plots of the fifty-five boys at the Ford Republic clearly testified to the d'Arcambal Association's commitment to the spirit of private enterprise and moral development, but so too did the Citizen's Bank, another of McIndoo's creations. The boys could deposit earnings and write checks to pay fines or buy personal goods at the store. According to the association, each new citizen quickly learned that industry brought undeniable advantages: "The fortunate possessor of a bank account is accorded privileges and immunities that his indigent neighbor is not. He can run the risk of getting off with a fine while the other 'guy' will have to 'walk the merry-go-round,' be spanked or put 'on close bounds.'" It was reportedly easy to spot "the plutocrats of the Republic. From their new shoes with the shining buckles to the latest in caps on their heads they radiate[d] prosperity." In 1927, well over a decade after the establishment of the bank, the superintendent could point out to visitors which boys evidently had "substantial bank balances" by how many desserts they purchased at meal time.[86]

While some of the youths, thanks to their financial status, may have looked spiffier or eaten more luxuriously than the poorer citizens, all were supposed to be clean. McIndoo, during his first months on the job, launched a cleanliness campaign at the Republic. "There was no such thing as dental hygiene when Dr. McIndoo arrived," recalled one staff member. It was he who provided a special cupboard for individual toothbrushes, and who replaced the community towel with individual towels and washcloths. Before each meal all citizens lined up so that their duly elected "Health Officer" could inspect them. The official not only examined faces and hands but prohibited sloppy dress.[87] Here was additional evidence that the institution was easing away from Homer Lane's approach. Lane had left the decision of clean hands with each boy, who was supposed to gauge his conduct in terms of self-interest: shedding dirt paid off in terms of producing desirable consequences. But with the Health Officer system, individual conduct came more in response to external rules and regulations than from the internalization of values.[88]

As part of the cleanliness campaign, in 1913 the Republic declared war on flies. By killing flies the boys earned money—fifteen cents for every hundred bodies—while learning their responsibility to save the junior commonwealth from filth and disease. According to the d'Arcambal Association's literature, the fly war not only offered opportunities for young entrepreneurs on the make but also presented "lessons in civic biology." The battles even offered the more inventive boys a chance to become virtual Edisons on the hunt as they designed various flytraps. For some youths, the old-fashioned fly swatter was still the preferred weapon, but the body count became such a messy business that the Republic resorted to using an apothecary's scale to judge the number of winged victims.

McIndoo was pleased with the results. "We . . . have almost exterminated the fly from the Ford Republic," he wrote. "Another season I think will finish the fly here."[89]

"Civic biology," "practical agriculture," organizing "primitive gang impulses . . . along right lines," "individual instruction," and "flexibility of courses"[90]—such expressions in the d'Arcambal Association's publications reaffirmed some of the most popular views of progressive child savers. But the idea of self-government was by 1914 more tenuous than it had been earlier, and perhaps not only at the Ford Republic. As self-governing concepts spread in the United States, reaching into middle-class institutions in the form of clubs and student governments in high schools, they may have served less to facilitate the transition from childhood to adulthood than to insulate youths in what a historian later described as "an age-segregated world of peers . . . from which the exits were by no means obvious." In other words, training for future citizenship became less important than simply organizing peer relations.[91] Unlike Homer Lane's view, in which the lessons of the gang could mold individual responsibility, the emerging strategy stressed the mechanics of how to keep the gang orderly. However much the d'Arcambal Association may have reflected such larger social trends, it clearly was in recoil from the perceived excesses of Lane's superintendency. And McIndoo, a new professional fresh out of graduate school, quickly expressed his own reservations about boys' self-government once he actually came "face to face" with the gang.[92]

Demographic changes at the Ford Republic also shrank the democratic impulse. Perhaps as a result of the growth of home placement agencies that dealt with dependent children, the Republic's population was increasingly limited to delinquent boys, many of whom apparently had serious emotional problems. A report to the board of trustees in 1930 showed that of the 1,000 youths who came to the home between April 1922 and September 1929, only twenty-five fell under the "Neglected-Dependent" label; "a large percent of the boys were emotionally unstable and not a few of them definately [sic] psychopathic." Despite considerable enthusiasm in the local press about the miniature commonwealth, the report to the trustees concluded that "a considerable percentage of boys" did not respond satisfactorily to the Republic system. "A much larger percentage of boys" than previously were allegedly becoming "deadweight as far as the active participation in affairs of state are [*sic*] concerned—boys who must be carried along as inactive citizens by more socially minded ones." By this time the d'Arcambal Associaton had introduced psychological testing, hired a consulting psychiatrist, and begun to use terms such as "schizoid type," "dementia praecox tendency," "constitutional psychopath," and "unstable-impulsive."[93] One of the most ardent boosters of self-government at the Ford Republic lamented in 1943 that "instead of self government being an actuality, it is now a very shallow shell with little real governing work being done. . . . We are now a custodial institution instead of a unique institution where real democracy prevails among boys."[94]

In 1950 an investigator for the state of Michigan's Department of Social Welfare reached a bleak conclusion: "My visit to the Boys Republic has left a very vivid picture in my mind; that of a lively spirit residing in a corpse, and at that, in one which is rapidly decomposing."[95] Such a judgment was perhaps far too harsh and hardly did justice to the dedicated people who still very much hoped to revitalize the institution. Still, without question, long gone were those heady days in the early 1900s, when that "lively spirit" had drawn its energy from a distinctive combination of dependency, delinquency, and democracy—days when Judge Fred Bloman's diminutive figure had cast a disproportionately large shadow over the Detroit area.

·6·

Aiding the "Left-overs":
G. W. Hinckley and
Good Will Farm

In March 1909 life seemed to cave in on nine-year-old Celia Jackson, growing up in Seawall, Maine. Her father, after a terrible fall, bled to death in his home as his horrified spouse and four children watched helplessly. The mother was unable to care for the children, so the two younger brothers moved to an orphanage in Bangor. Celia and her brother lived with a minister for a year until local townspeople paid for them to go to an institution for needy children in central Maine: Good Will Farm, located halfway between Fairfield and Skowhegan, on the beautiful but often harsh rolling hills that sloped toward the Kennebec River. For Celia, the first week in her new home was an emotional ordeal, and she cried incessantly. But by the time she left Good Will several years later, she felt a strong attachment to the farm and its founder, the Reverend George W. Hinckley. Celia was only one of several hundred "left-overs" whom Hinckley, according to one popular journal, had salvaged and turned into good citizens. "They do things well in Maine," agreed the editors of a leading child saving magazine as they applauded "the incomparable Hinckley . . . that princely man."[1]

The evidence was indeed striking. In 1888, at the age of thirty-four, the minister started raising funds to rescue children "in need of a helping hand."[2] Twenty-five years later, after an exceedingly difficult beginning, Good Will had become a notable showcase as a child saving institution. It had grown from one building and three boys to thirteen structures for almost two hundred boys and girls.

On its more than five hundred acres were cottage-style residences for the youths, a school, a chapel, and considerable farmland with a dozen horses and thirty cows. Since its origins, almost 1,000 youngsters had lived there, some for as long as ten to twelve years.[3] For all of the residents, Hinckley had stressed not only a family- and community-oriented environment but strong educational training as well. He developed an impressive academic program (surely one of the best of its kind in the country) that included classics, agriculture, and various trades. By 1913, with a library of 10,000 volumes, a high school degree that was acceptable to colleges of the New England Association, and a staff of thirteen teachers, Good Will received attention as "one of the finest college fitting schools in the state." Approximately half of its three hundred or so graduates had by that time gone on to college.[4]

Like many progressive reformers, however, George W. Hinckley was himself a kind of "left-over," a product of the nineteenth century who was never altogether comfortable in the emerging organizational world into which he delivered his beloved Good Will Farm. He thought far less of educating his young charges for the ranks of industry and corporate commerce than of instilling in them the values of an older, idealized America that emphasized the work ethic, moral restraint, love, religious faith, and service to others rather than personal gain. That undoubtedly helped to account for the enthusiasm with which some observers responded to Good Will. According to one individual, it demonstrated the power of "pure philanthropy" in a "commercial age." In the opinion of Hastings Hart, who probably examined more children's institutions than anyone of his generation, the farm was so fine a place "that men and women come, as we have come, from all parts of the United States to see what has here been wrought."[5]

Whereas Hart and other visitors saw all this as the achievement of "a country minister," Hinckley perceived larger forces at work, and he never tired of citing Psalms 37:5—"Commit thy way unto the Lord, trust also in Him and He shall bring it to pass." Good Will's founder never claimed, however, that God had made the work easy. In fact, there had been so many problems and delays that Hinckley had wondered time and again if his long-held dream would ever reach fulfillment. "Good Will was not a mush-room growth," he recalled. "It was the germination of a seed that had long been ready for the planting."[6]

He explained that he had gotten the idea by observing unfortunate youths, but the truth was probably less simple. The sketches he provided of his life, like all autobiographical efforts, were products of selective memory and a desire to publicize, or at least to explain, what he had done. The series of personal incidents that he recounted in 1943, under the title *The Man of Whom I Write*, is a proud tale of his accomplishments—ironically so, considering his pugnacious refusal to mention himself by name. After claiming that he would not use the personal pronoun "I" (because to do so would signify "a hopeless case of apparent egotism"), he chose the even more inflated style of referring to himself throughout the book as "The Man of Whom I Write." However much he tried to dismiss the incidents in his narrative as "apparently insignificant," he left no doubt that they were significant. Despite his announced humility, the selected vignettes from his life conjured up Horatio Alger images.[7]

His early years, as he remembered them, were full of childhood slights and hurts, of having to battle great odds while getting little recognition and continued rebuffs. He had been born in Guilford, Connecticut, on July 27, 1853, to parents of solid Yankee stock for whom life was a constant struggle. Although the Hinckley side of the family traced its American origins back to Plymouth colony in 1635—and in fact claimed Plymouth's last governor[8]—George Hinckley inherited little more than the name and a pious outlook. His parents labored desperately to make a living from a small, uncooperative farm and to raise five children. Despite George's reference to "the humble but happy Connecticut home" of his birth, his childhood was apparently full of disappointment, work, and little praise. In his reminiscences his parents were only vaguely defined figures. His very devout but "overworked" mother, who continually sang hymns as she did her household duties, had reportedly "consecrated him to God's service" when he was still in the cradle and had hoped from the beginning that he would become a minister. Years later, he still prized the small Bible he had received from her on his seventeenth birthday with the inscriptions: "Seek ye first the kingdom of God," and "Godliness with contentment is great gain." His father was perhaps a rather severe taskmaster, for Hinckley remembered arduous hours pulling a plow on horseback and receiving only criticism for his efforts: "Down on my luckless head fell all the curses. . . . I shall never be the boy rider in the field again. But I will not forget the lesson. A kind word when one is succeeding will help prevent opportunities to condemn." George Hinckley also hinted that his parents had been overly protective. As a teenager, for example, he chafed under restrictions that forbade his going camping lest he become sick and die from sleeping in a tent.[9] (Later, at Good Will Farm, he always made sure that the older boys had the opportunity to go on the kind of long camping trips that he, as a youth, had not been able to take.)

Hinckley's childhood education was a source of many of his most unpleasant memories. He recalled tersely that "happiness in school—well, it was not abundant." Playground bullies beat up on him, and he lived in fear of the next fight. He endured teasing and the nickname "Goggy Woggy," suffered a "long series of embarrassments," and put up with "overbearing" students who crowded him away from the stove on wintry days. On several occasions teachers humiliated him in front of the classroom. Once, a principal laughed uproariously midway through what Hinckley intended to be a serious speech; as snickers spread across the class, Hinckley crumbled his paper in his hands and retreated dejectedly to his seat. His decision at age fifteen to join the Congregational church supplied some of the local toughs with additional incentives to harass him. "Their taunts were sometimes cruel," he wrote. "Their sneers hurt. . . . Sometimes they made my heart ache; sometimes my courage almost failed."[10] Later he perhaps found a certain satisfaction in knowing that one of his adversaries had died a drunkard, another had gone to prison, and several had missed "the real sweets of life";[11] but at the time he felt bitter and rejected.

More disappointments awaited him. His hopes of getting a Yale degree, doing seminary work, and entering the clergy disintegrated while he was in his early twenties. He spent only a year at the State Normal School in Connecticut before an inadequate diet, poor health, and a lack of funds forced him out. Later he held jobs in the pulpit and the classroom, but invariably he felt like an interloper; for years he wrestled with an inferiority complex, doubting that he held much status among church and school officials who had degrees and credentials. Once, after he had gotten a preaching position, he agonized in the front row of a Connecticut Baptist convention while the speaker assailed anyone who entered the ministry with less than four years of college and three more of seminary. As Hinckley listened to the "staggering, blinding, damning words," tears ran down his face; at the end of "the ordeal," he could do nothing but "retire, whipped, scourged, driven from the temple."[12]

In a world moving toward certified expertise, Hinckley was always painfully aware that he was an amateur. Without formal training, he relied upon his instincts. For several winters, even though he lacked a degree, he taught school in Connecticut and Rhode Island. The experience was hardly uplifting. At one point he lay in a damp and gloomy room, anticipating that the approaching school term would present him with an unpromising group of students and fearing that the local community was critically scrutinizing him, the new teacher in town. Years later, when children arrived at Good Will Farm with their own doubts and anxieties, Hinckley felt that he understood them because of what he had himself undergone. They might each think, "I'll die if I have to stay here." "But they never die," he said; "neither did I."[13]

Although Hinckley perhaps romanticized his early troubles, his eventual accomplishments were undeniably hard-won and the product of considerable personal struggle and turmoil. His strong religious training and early hardships had obviously enlarged his capacity for empathy. There were also hints that he had very much itched for recognition. His memories of youthful adversity suggested not only personal suffering but possibly also a burning desire to succeed, to prove that he deserved better. And if he continually felt tugs of inferiority, he also appeared anxious to leave his imprint on the world.

Whatever his psychic needs and inner drives, during the late 1870s he experienced a severe identity crisis that ultimately brought on a kind of conversion. Frustrated, viewing his shattered dreams all around him, he rebelled: "I said I had a right to do as others did—a right to make money and take pleasure." He took a job clerking in a country dry goods store. With visions of launching a prosperous business career, he stayed away from church, smoked a cigar and pipe despite his earlier aversion to "users of the weed," and visited the race track. This new life-style brought its own discontents, however, and within seven months he was overwhelmed with "revulsion." One day as he looked around the store, he noted that there were only material goods, not food for the spirit. "I was dead," he wrote. He closed the store; walked about aimlessly, while memories of his life flashed through his mind; and then, in a daze, went to bed. The next morning at the store he fell to his knees, saying, "God, thou art stronger than I." Shortly thereafter, newly committed to entering the ministry, he quit his job.[14]

Such a crisis and "conversion" episode were not uncommon to Hinckley's generation. A number of prominent progressive reformers recalled similar jolting moments during which their lives had turned in new directions. The major turning point for Tom Johnson, Cleveland's acclaimed reform mayor, reportedly came when—as a rising entrepreneur—he first read Henry George's *Progress and Poverty* and then, in 1889, observed through tears the terrible devastation of the Johnstown, Pennsylvania, flood. Convinced that he needed, as he put it, "to escape corruption in living," he denounced "special privilege" and launched his reform career. Similarly, economist Richard T. Ely, after completing his graduate studies in Germany, was nauseated with shame as he walked through the blighted streets of New York City. He even contemplated suicide as he looked at the poverty, squalor, and corruption. "Is this my America?" he wondered. Instead of killing himself, however, he pledged to do whatever was possible to improve conditions. Famed defense attorney Clarence Darrow underwent a similar crisis of conscience during the 1894 American Railway Union strike. And Frederick C. Howe, in his *Confessions of a Reformer*, described his struggle between the lure of wealth and fame, and the suspicion that such success came only through unacceptable means. Thus Howe said that his "life really began in the early nineties instead of the late sixties." Jane Addams also experienced a period of intense inner conflict as a young woman before finding release in the settlement house movement.[15]

Hinckley, like Addams, Ely, and others, was a complex individual with many motives and personal agendas. Like them, too, he felt the

175

attraction of worldly success which, in turn, produced a sense of guilt. Moralistic, introspective, continually questioning his own worth, invariably setting altruistic goals and then castigating himself for insufficiently realizing them, he had by 1879 reached "the end of the rope" and tumbled into his searing emotional crisis. Long-held feelings of isolation, inadequacy, and inferiority bore down upon him. By weathering the crisis and resolving "to minister to the greater needs of humanity,"[16] he not only reclaimed his future but took a positive step toward resolving nagging personal contradictions between the drive to succeed, to make himself known, and the guilt that accompanied such ambition. In this sense, virtue could indeed be its own reward.

Two weeks after quitting his clerking job, Hinckley's life dramatically entered a new phase. Despite his lack of formal preparation for the ministry, he received an unexpected offer to be the pastor of a Baptist church in Allenton, Rhode Island. In September 1879 he delivered his first sermon. Over the next several years he moved to pulpits in three Connecticut towns. On August 12, 1880, he married Elma Palmer, whom he had met in Providence.[17]

At the least, Elma Palmer Hinckley must have been a tolerant and understanding wife. Although she apparently remained on the periphery of the actual development and administration of Good Will Farm, she handled most of the basic day-to-day affairs of her own family, which included raising four children—two boys and two girls. She was "devoted," as Hinckley described her—"a wife who kept house and home for me, while I was trying to solve the problem of more homes for the homeless." A former Good Will resident described her as "warm, motherly, unassuming, quiet, always there but always in the background. . . . He was the star, and she wanted it that way."[18] For a long time she had to make do with a severely limited budget. One morning during the first months of their marriage, the new couple talked about finances. Hinckley owed $400 as a result of his aborted efforts to gain an education; his Hartford pastorate offered only a meager salary; his boots had holes that exposed his stockings; and his Sunday coat was hopelessly worn out. "We sat at the breakfast table," Hinckley remembered, "the brave little woman who dared share my lot with me, and I," and concluded that there was nothing to do but work and pray. That day, when a sympathetic member of the community purchased a new suit of clothes and boots for Hinckley, Elma may have drawn the same lessons as her husband did: namely, that God would provide.[19] Finances aside, for Elma Hinckley there was also the matter of a husband who not only was away a great deal of the time but for a while must have seemed virtually driven to create an institution for needy children.

As Hinckley told it, the idea of building a home for poor boys had first come to him at the age of thirteen or fourteen, when he was weeding onions in his father's garden. A subsequent incident involving a classmate left a profound impression on him. The boy, after going dinnerless for three days because his widowed mother could not care for him adequately, stole food from a laborer's dinner pail and was sentenced to the state reform school. Such injustice outraged the youthful Hinckley. Not long afterward, he became close friends with Ben Mason, a redheaded orphan. They talked about Ben's unhappy experiences in an asylum and about where he might find a home. Hinckley's parents were unquestionably surprised when George invited Ben to live with them; the family house was small and there was little money. But whatever the parents thought about the idea, they did not protest and Ben moved in. Several months later, George recognized the drain on his parents' resources and left home on grounds that he was old enough to care for himself and Ben was not. "It was my first sacrifice for boyhood," Hinckley said later.[20]

Over the next fifteen years, Hinckley's desire to aid needy boys was perhaps obsessive. While he was preaching in Hartford, he visited the city's missions on raw winter evenings, talking with poor youths.[21] Beginning in 1880, he clipped and pasted dozens of articles and poems, many of them dealing with children: "How to Help the Boys," "Teach the Children" (regarding the dangers of liquor), "How the Poor Were Fed" (about boys' lodging houses in New York City), "Working Boys' Picnic," "A House without Children," "City Children in the Country," and others. Several essays dealt with the advantages of moving the urban poor to rural areas where they could have a new start. One piece described a woman's visit to an orphanage, where she watched the well-meaning matron put the children through a drill; when the visitor kissed one child,

177

she was stunned to learn from him that such affection was not part of asylum life: "That isn't in the rules, ma'am."[22]

Hinckley's dream of building a home for dependent boys was clearly much on his mind, and he dutifully formulated strategies—but these were still just ideas. After he moved to Maine in 1883 to do fieldwork for the American Sunday School Union of Philadelphia, he fretted that time was running out. While "'somebody's child' was in moral peril," he was raising money for the Sunday School Union, a galling task so irrelevant to his essential goals that—unbeknownst to his employers—he often deliberately refused to take collections. "Ambitious thoughts of aiding a few [dependent children] . . . fill my head. When? Where? How to begin?" On November 25, 1884, with his old school debt finally paid, Hinckley opened a bank account for what he called "the Boys' Fund." By the end of the year he had deposited $39.83—not much for a project that would probably cost several thousand dollars for the land alone, but a start nonetheless. As he channeled dollars from his own thin purse into the fund, he discussed his plans with other people, some of whom made contributions. By the end of 1886 the total reached $212.54.[23]

Meanwhile, Hinckley kept up a strenuous travel schedule for the American Sunday School Union. In June 1885 he logged 455 miles; in August, 948; in October, 686. He preached, set up Sunday Schools, visited sick people, gave children's sermons, and—always—looked for a possible location for his boys' home.[24]

In early 1888, in its fourth year, the special account edged over $1,000. Certain that it was time for a larger effort to publicize his project, Hinckley in February published the first issue of the *Boys' Fund*, a small monthly journal. "The boy who needs a home is in danger," Hinckley warned, stating his intentions to build "a Home"—not an orphan asylum—that would offer "daily duties, moral training, contact with nature, and strong Christian influences." Quoting Psalms 37:5, he wondered if others might assist him in caring for "boys who need a helping hand."[25]

There was no sudden flood of interest. On February 20, Hinckley lamented that for "the last two weeks the sun has not seemed to shine very brightly on the Boys' Fund. . . . Here's a trial of faith."[26] The next day, however, $300 worth of pledges arrived. This was the pattern for months: anxious days when the mails were "dry," uplifting moments when a dime arrived from a youngster, and the satisfaction of opening a letter with $20 enclosed. Most of the donations were small, but there were encouraging signs. One evening, Hinckley slogged through the rain and mud to address a meeting in Newport, Maine, about the fund; about a hundred citizens had also braved the elements to listen to him and contribute $332.[27]

Hinckley kept searching for a prospective site. One February morning he rode six miles to look at a farm that was for sale; the next week he examined two others. Through all of this he continued his assignment with the Sunday School Union, preaching, playing the organ, and leading the choir at an average of one public religious service each day.[28] He also gave countless talks about the Boys' Fund and each month published another copy of his little magazine, which grew to eight pages.

In June 1889 events moved suddenly. Just one day after Hinckley had suffered a nervous collapse, which a doctor said would perhaps require a two-year respite from all work, he learned by chance of a 125-acre farm for sale some six miles from Fairfield. A few hours later he reined up in front of the farmhouse overlooking the Kennebec river and announced, "Eureka, I have found it; after all these years I have found it." The $2,000 by then in the Boys' Fund was just enough to pay for the property.[29]

This happy turn of affairs energized Hinckley. He rebounded quickly from his exhaustion and began readying the farmhouse for occupancy in September. As things turned out, a group of dependent children arrived that summer. During a trip to Boston in July, Hinckley met George Henry Quincy, a member of one of the city's foremost families. "It was the cry of imperiled childhood that brought us together," Hinckley believed. Quincy offered to send fifteen orphans and two attendants to Hinckley's newly purchased place for a six-week camp. On July 15, "a band of little pilgrims"— twelve girls and three boys—arrived from the Boston Children's Friend Society, with two women to care for them. There were no accidents or illnesses, and according to Hinckley, the children "grew rosy cheeked, brown faced and noisy." One of the brightest moments occurred when a little girl asked if she could sit on the grass, and Hinckley told her proudly, "There are no 'Keep off the Grass' signs." She could go where she wished. At the end of the six weeks, the three boys stayed on to become the first full-time residents of what Hinckley now called Good Will Farm. He thought the name captured the benevolent spirit of the people who had made his work possible. Accordingly, in September he changed the *Boys' Fund* to the *Good Will Record*, and in October he incorporated the Good Will Association. Annual membership cost $2.00; a lifetime membership, $50. The board of directors included Quincy and fifteen other men who had been supportive of the project. Hinckley was general supervisor and editor of the *Record*.[30]

Over the next few years, there was no problem finding needy boys to live at Good Will, but the demands of raising money and managing the operation were staggering. Hinckley secured the services of his sister Jane as the first matron. Until her death in 1914, she was instrumental to Good Will's development. Although she had no training in such work, she managed the first boys' cottage with skill and sensitivity, took care of much of the office work, helped establish and run the girls' department, and organized the library.[31] "Aunt Jane," as the children called her, guided the institution's daily matters through the formative months.

It was well that she did, because George Hinckley simply did not have the time. Throughout Good Will's first year and a half, he preached and lived in Oakland, Maine, about eight miles away by carriage and twelve by rail. Finances dictated such an arrangement; he drew no salary from Good Will, and he could not afford to build a residence at the farm itself. Hinckley visited when he could but otherwise depended on the mails for news about the institution. In late October 1889, for example, he sat miserably through a religious conference more than a hundred miles from Good Will, listening to a cold rain that made the day even more dismal and wondering what was happening with the boys. In November he was shocked to hear rumors that he intended to make money rather than help children. "This hurts," he wrote.[32]

Precisely because he wanted to protect Good Will from such suspicions, he refused to take any money from the institution's funds, even to pay for his duties as supervisor. After he left Sunday School work and preaching, his only income for twenty years came from subscriptions to the *Good Will Record*, which sold initially for twenty-five cents, and later for fifty cents, annually. But the profits from the *Record*, including subscriptions and advertising, were less than $500 per year in those early days, and sympathetic members of the board and other supporters of Good Will kept Hinckley afloat financially. They voluntarily contributed to his personal account and in 1890 made it possible for him to move next door to Good Will Farm so that he could work there full time. With Hinckley as the example, it would have been difficult indeed to argue that there was money in child saving; for years he wore secondhand clothes and depended on the generosity of friends, some of whom he did not even know, to help support him and his famiy. Not until 1910 did he agree to accept a salary for his responsibilities as supervisor.[33]

Whatever the financial limits of his position, Hinckley found enormous gratification in the popularity of the farm. As requests to admit boys poured in, the need for more room quickly became apparent. By June 1890, the "family" of boys living under Jane Hinckley's care numbered eighteen. "God Help Us Save the Boys," the *Good Will Record* pleaded, as Hinckley launched a drive to get funds for another cottage. Soon he had added to the property a small house for six more boys. Shortly thereafter, nonetheless, he had to refuse six youths within five days for lack of room. "My heart is sick," he said. "I feel like condemning myself that I have not succeeded better in making people understand the need . . . to help save boys." By the fall of 1893, however, painstaking effort had provided facilities for fifty-one youngsters. Good Will was growing; it received favorable publicity from as far away as Chicago and New Orleans; and among its appreciative visitors were the wives of Maine's governor and of several state legislators. The *Record* expanded its format to keep pace with the institution's development.[34]

From another perspective, however, Good Will's future was still in doubt. "Our cash receipts to-day amount to fifty cents," Hinckley recorded on September 15, 1893. "It looks like a famine." Three days later he noted that "in the entire history of this work it never looked so dark." By September 22 he could not get the books to balance.[35] Yet despite these years of walking the knife's edge financially, the institution survived. Small contributions, however sporadic, covered day-to-day expenses; and the growing interest in Good Will on the part of several wealthy families eventually resulted in contributions large enough to purchase additional land and construct buildings.[36]

Looking back on all this in 1908, Hinckley conceded that he would not do it over again.[37] The raising of funds had rested almost exclusively with him while he had also served as "Supervisor of the entire work for both boys and girls, the personal friend and counsellor of each boy at the Farm, the Editor and Publisher of the paper ... the preacher on Sundays of the only religious service within miles, etc. etc." For a while in the early 1900s he kept monthly office hours in Boston and New York, besides traveling to numerous conferences. "I acknowledge," he wrote, "that the arrangements well-nigh cost me my life."[38]

Hinckley's concern for "endangered childhood" undoubtedly helped to sustain his efforts, but so too did his fears about the social costs of not helping the friendless youngster: "Who can tell how soon he may become the danger of *our* homes if some provision is not made for him?" According to statistics that Hinckley used in 1889, more than half the occupants of American prisons were under the age of twenty-two. The inaction of decent citizens was largely to blame for this social calamity: "If we leave the boys to themselves there are wicked men enough to take them where we leave them."[39]

In Hinckley's opinion, youths were necessary recruits in the great moral battles of the day. Just as boys during his own childhood had fought for the Union, young people of the new century should feel the call of "great conflicts." Disunion was no longer a threat, but the nation's future was still in jeopardy. Dangerous enemies continued to stalk the land in the form of liquor, tobacco, selfishness, and impurity. Hinckley reported incidents where immoderate smoking had allegedly driven a dozen California boys insane and had killed at least one Connecticut youngster, and he warned that tobacco was one of the causes of consumption—"the white plague." The boy who imbibed alcoholic beverages not only hurt himself but was "a traitor to a noble cause—the cause of home, and humanity and happiness." Crime, ruin, death, and a mother's broken heart were products of the same culprit: "Somebody's whiskey—that's all." In Hinckley's estimation, two-thirds of the homeless children owed their terrible plight to the liquor traffic. He urged youths to enlist in "the battle with self and selfish and wrong tendencies." A profane note that he found so disturbed him—"I did not care to have that hated piece of writing about my person"—that he quickly destroyed it lest someone see him with it and conclude that he liked "such an unclean bit of writing." Now was the time, he urged, to take a stand against such immorality. Convinced that the boy who fell victim to immoral temptations was "a traitor . . . an easy mark for the enemy," Hinckley sounded a call to duty: "The battle is on, my boy; the battle is on."[40]

This crusading temperament prompted him to support many of the moral campaigns of the progressive era. He had great respect for evangelist Billy Sunday's muscular brand of Christianity, which threw down the gauntlet to the forces of evil. He also approvingly quoted Washington Gladden, a well-known minister of the Social Gospel, who urged communities to recapture local governments from vice-ridden political factions. When President Theodore Roosevelt rejected a petition to pardon a man who had sent obscene literature through the mails, Hinckley cheered. Roosevelt's statement that he regretted the lack of "power to increase the sentence of the scoundrel" was, from Hinckley's viewpoint, striking "a nail on the head . . . with the force of a strong man."[41]

Hinckley hoped that Good Will in its own significant way would exert a moral influence by aiding penniless youths otherwise destined for "the army of the worthless." He wanted to be able to say, " 'It is well with the lad.' He is not on the city streets drifting; he is not at the mercy of the cruel and vicious. For the present he is safe."[42] Good Will's rural setting was absolutely basic to this task, as far as the supervisor was concerned. Poems and quotations regarding the advantages of country life appeared continually in the *Record*. In contrast to the farm's hills, forests, lake, and river stood "a sad world. If you don't believe it come with me to yonder city and look at the proof—saloons and dens, abodes of vice and crime, headquarters for filth and wickedness, down in the depths. Sad!" His comment when noting that New York City had the most densely populated block in the world was simply, "Alas for the children."[43]

While Good Will's setting was rural, its central social unit was the family. Hinckley instituted the cottage system from the very

183

beginning because he wanted to approximate as nearly as possible "the average New England Christian household." Each cottage contained a "family" of around fifteen boys or girls. There was no chronological grouping of the children, because in a real family siblings were of different ages. Regular household chores were part of the daily routine. At mealtime the children in each home sat at tables with places for no more than eight individuals.[44]

Hinckley admired the junior republic system, but at Good Will he preferred "home life and parental government." This meant that disciplinary matters were entirely the province of adults—not of children's courts and youthful politicians, as was the case at William R. George's Freeville, Edward Bradley's Allendale, or the Ford Republic. "Parental government" needed to be fair, reasonable, and firm; there should be no doubt about who controlled the home, because children could not respect a mother or father who refused to govern them. "You are in a place of discipline," Hinckley instructed Good Will's young residents. "You will be required to obey rules, but this you will want to do anyway. . . . you want to be controlled and we will help you to self-control." For recalcitrant youths, Hinckley had no aversion to "an old-fashioned spanking," which he carefully distinguished from whipping or the use of a ferule. A more common form of discipline at the farm was the denial of certain privileges, such as the Saturday afternoon break. Or a youngster might spend several days "in the Attic"—not really an attic but a third-floor room that isolated the child from peers and regular activities (except for some exercise). In 1914 the staff decided to punish theft by feeding the culprit three meals of bread and water and by posting the person's name in a conspicuous place. Although discipline was "strict," an early twentieth century resident emphasized that it was "always fair."[45]

Additional pressure for good behavior came from the presence of Hinckley himself. A man of medium build standing six feet tall with a large, drooping mustache that curled around the edges of a firmly set mouth, he seemed austere and formal, even "somewhat detached." To his face he was always "Mr. Hinckley"; only in his absence did the youths refer to him as "G. W." His frequent addresses at the farm, in the school, and on Sundays in the chapel were invariably moving, eloquent statements; they were delivered with such passion that tears sometimes seemed to be gathering in his eyes. These spellbinding orations, packed with human interest stories, had a powerful effect on his young listeners.[46] Moreover, they left no doubt about his values, expectations, and rules. Because Good Will was a place for needy but moral youths—not for delinquents—he felt free to ask troublemakers to leave. Once, when an orphan ran away, lied, and stole a farmer's watch, Hinckley concluded that the state reformatory was the answer: "George has had all the freedom he deserves for the present."[47]

Still, Hinckley could be compassionate and sensitive. He treated cases individually and flexibly, showing that beneath his stern exterior was a kindly, loving man. Although he was away a great deal of the time, he conscientiously visited the cottages and the school; he treated the youths "friend to friend," talking and playing games. One former resident, commenting on the "close bond between G. W. and every student," recalled fondly an ongoing dominoes tournament that he and the supervisor played as they baited each other with "caustic and humorous comments." Hinckley, in the words of one individual, "seemed a real father"; another described him as "very fatherly"; yet another saw him as "a grandfather figure," someone who "was always kindly, but never really intimate." "We just idolized him," remembered a 1909 graduate. Some of the older boys got to know him more closely than the younger ones, or the girls. On camping trips, for example, he was even more clearly "a remarkable man, a warm human companion, and an inspirational figure." One youth at the age of fourteen got the assignment of staying with Hinckley, then in his sixties, during late afternoons and evenings. He later regarded that association as the most important formative influence in his life. Said a 1923 graduate almost six decades later, "I will never forget him." And in 1982 Benjamin Drucker, who lived at the farm between 1909 and 1911, recollected touchingly on more than one occasion that Hinckley had personally given him a pair of ice skates.[48]

Although Hinckley took a firm position on moral behavior, he was not unyielding. One farm resident was a boy whose "specialty," as Hinckley euphemistically put it, "was lying." Good Will's founder, of course, despised such a habit, but he still felt genuine affection for the guilty youngster: "I like him. We are friends."

Hinckley, who kept working with the boy, did not believe that the youth's falsehoods sprang from malice; "the things which he says . . . are real to him." The supervisor also refused to banish another boy whose "weakness in character" was stealing; in this case it seemed that Good Will offered the best chance of saving him. Once, when someone broke into Hinckley's desk and stole two dollars, Hinckley asked none other than the suspect to solve the crime. "I have been robbed and I want you to be my detective and find the thief," he instructed the youth. Eventually the youngster confessed, implicating two others. The three boys had to earn and pay back double what they had stolen.[49]

Sometimes Hinckley bent his own rules about accepting only good children. Even though a half-orphan named Dick had wound up in truant school and acquired a reputation for making trouble, Hinckley admitted him. Dick responded by running away. When the supervisor visited the place where the boy showed up some ten days later, Dick sullenly steeled himself for a lecture. What followed caught him completely off guard. "Dick," Hinckley said, "I love you." The youngster broke into tears, and Hinckley held him close; then, turning to leave, he added, "I must go now. If you come back I'll be glad to see you; if you don't, then write to me once in a while, for I'll want to know where you are." The supervisor interpreted Dick's subsequent return as evidence that "the law is majestic; the dollar mighty; but love wins." Hinckley applied the same principle when dealing with a small boy who arrived at the farm following the death of his father and the hospitalization of his mother. Taking the desperately homesick child on his knee, Hinckley told him, "You know that I am not your father; I can't take your father's place exactly or fully but you may think of me as a man that loves you and you may come to me as you would to your father were he living."[50]

Although the supervisor set the tone for personal relationships at Good Will, on a daily basis it was the matron in each of the cottages who bore the largest responsibility for achieving the delicate balance between love and discipline. Hinckley once fired a matron who was not a good housekeeper as well as one who was "too good a housekeeper." In his opinion a good matron needed to gain the respect of the children without jeopardizing "the freedom of real home life." This assignment clearly required a special kind of temperament, but Hinckley emphasized that there was "no fixed type of matron" any more than there was a given personality for any family.[51]

If the recollections of former residents were accurate, he chose the matrons well. A number of them, perhaps most, had sons or daughters at Good Will. One of the favorites, Annie Pratt, came to the farm with two small daughters, following the death of her spouse in a railroad accident. She was "motherly, loving, and fair," according to one of the girls who lived under her direction. Another matron's spouse, a schooner captain, had died suddenly, leaving three children and a lapsed insurance policy. At Good Will the woman and the boys in her cottage developed a great affection for each other. While some of the matrons were predictably less popular than others, the general reaction of the youngsters toward them was positive. At the time, one of the boys viewed his matron as "a very stern taskmistress," but in retrospect he dubbed her "outstanding," a genuinely positive influence on him. The middle-aged married woman who ran the cottage where one youth lived from 1906 to 1912 was reportedly an "excellent person to mother the 14 youngsters." She had "a very clever method for handling youth" and looked out for them faithfully. "Perhaps I was more naive than some," wrote a 1909 graduate years later, "but I personally never knew of any serious cottage troubles."[52]

Hinckley made it clear that order and obedience at Good Will should never snap the close emotional ties of the individual family units. Life in each of the cottages needed to have its own characteristics, for a "home" was more than a building, three meals a day, and a place to sleep. A home was also a carefully constructed web of affection, loyalty, mutual respect, and tradition.[53] One of the biggest annual events at Good Will was "Home Night," on Thanksgiving, when all of the children gathered in the auditorium. They entered the hall as separate families, each cottage group giving its own cheer. "We are the Whit-ney Kids, rah, rah, rah," shouted residents of Whitney Cottage. Members of Bancroft Foote responded with "Win or bust, win or bust; / Bancroft Foote—yell we must." And the girls of Ryerson Hall sang, to the tune of "Good Night, Ladies," "Who's this coming? / The Jolly Ryerson Crowd." The program, often lasting more than three hours, included skits and songs from each group. When there were anouncements of what former residents were doing, current members of their various cottages cheered appropriately. "I would rather be Home tonight than anywhere else," wrote a Good Will graduate who spoke for many others: "A word from Good Will is, to me, a word from Home."[54]

Individual cottages held the spotlight at the Thanksgiving celebrations, but songs such as "Good Will Must Shine Tonight" underlined Hinckley's point that the families, taken together, formed a community.[55] Hinckley specifically compared Good Will to "any thrifty village—a collection of families under hospitable roofs," living near "well-conducted schools and a church," and displaying sound work habits. Again and again the ideal of small-town life surfaced at the farm. When the supervisor needed particular items for the youths, he adopted the message of country stores: "If you don't see what you want, ask for it." He listed in the *Good Will Record* things that the cottages needed—a clock, several yards of table linen, and soup plates, for example—and waited for cooperative citizens to respond. In a throwback to the old frontier house-raising projects, eight of the older boys helped to shingle the barn; upon completing the job one brisk November day, they stood on the roof in the gathering dusk and delivered the "Good Will Cheer."[56]

When Hinckley discussed the virtues of work, and when he stated Good Will's intentions of developing good industrial habits, he showed that his frame of reference was indeed the rural village. His sentiments were with common workers, not builders of corporate empires. Describing "A Sensible Ideal for Boys," he chose as models people he had known: one who rented a small farm until he was able to squeeze out payments for its purchase; another who was a carpenter; a third who learned a trade. All of them were devout, believed in public service, and exerted strong moral influence on their communities. They did not make newspaper headlines, but Hinckley felt that these individuals were real heroes. "Why glorify the millionaire before the multitudes of boys who can never attain millions?" he asked. "Why not make the position of such men as I have mentioned—the self-supporting, self-respecting, God-honoring men—the ideal for boys to imitate?"[57]

Given this perspective, it was not surprising that Hinckley approved of reforms aimed at placing business responsibility ahead of profits. He agreed with progressives who criticized railroad companies for overworking employees, and he applauded pure food laws. He hoped that "residents of communities which are blighted or whose homes are threatened by corporations" would stand up for their rights. However, although he was clearly suspicious of big business and angry at corporate arrogance, he stopped far short of radical measures. Instead, he placed his faith in the power of an awakened public conscience and applauded campaigns such as those of the New York Consumers' League, which urged Christmas shoppers to avoid the usual holiday rush and thereby to protect clerks from long, exploitative work schedules.[58]

He believed that Good Will could help to build responsible citizens by fostering a healthy respect for the dignity of honest labor and by providing useful training. "I am trying," he wrote, "to teach the boys of this community that the world does not owe them a living; that it is their business to pay their way through the world." He was irritated to read that a boy had "accepted a position." This implied that the job had simply been waiting for him, whereas in fact, employment went to the applicant who "hustled" the most: "the position accepts him." Hinckley had no doubts that the working boy always came out ahead of the idler. Because the children at Good Will came from disadvantaged backgrounds, it was especially important that they learn the principles of industry and self-reliance. "We are not adding to the army of tramps," Hinckley reassured the public.[59]

Good Will owed its existence to public benevolence, but Hinckley wanted the children to realize that the success of the farm really depended upon their own kinds of contributions. If they helped with the laundering, carpentering, and other daily tasks, and if they grew food for the tables, they could assist the institution financially. The supervisor made clear that it was a privilege to live at the farm and that everyone should expect to work. By rotating assigned tasks, which varied according to age, the youths earned some of their own clothes and supplies. It was possible to receive some spending money by undertaking jobs beyond the normal assignments, or by doing regular chores with special care. Some of the boys even "rented" small garden plots, selling their crops to the Good Will Association and keeping whatever profits remained after the rental deductions. At least one youth purchased pigs at $3.00 apiece and raised them for sale in the fall. "This spirit of enterprise is found on every hand among the Good Will Farm boys," reported one observer. "There are no drones in the hive."[60]

Because of the farm's needs and Hinckley's strong emphasis on the work ethic, life at Good Will was often Spartan. The usual day started around 6:30 A.M., but older boys who worked with the livestock and in the barn were up by 5:00 A.M., year round. One individual per cottage was responsible for bringing in five gallons of milk each morning. Other chores ranged from helping the cooks to cleaning the cottages and the school; the girls did not do outside farmwork but instead rotated household assignments. Four to six boys worked everyday but Sunday at the steam laundry. A soft-coal boiler provided heat for the laundry, so during the winter one youth slept on a cot in the boiler room, rising periodically to check the temperature so that pipes would not freeze. Another winter task involved cutting ice from a nearby stream; the blocks were then stored for icebox use in the summertime. School sessions ran for three hours in the morning and several more in the afternoons, although classes adjourned early in the spring to allow for planting and cleaning out the barns. A particularly undesirable assignment was that of loading the manure spreader, by hand, from beneath each barn. Major jobs during the fall included moving vegetables from the fields to the cellars and cutting wood for the fireplaces. Although the cottages had hot tubs for special use, showers—taken in the high school basement—were mandatory each Saturday. Upstairs bedrooms in the cottages were unheated and could become quite uncomfortable when winter temperatures plunged well below zero. "Life in the cottages served to toughen us up," recalled one individual who lived at the farm from 1914 to 1920. "It kept us together."[61]

While "a lot of gripes" provided evidence of at least some discontent in the cottages, a 1909 graduate remembered "a happy life" and high spirits: "most . . . liked being there." "We were not all angels by any means," wrote another Good Will product, but in learning the values of industry and trust, "we were absorbing some of the basic principles that would guide us later in life." Several other graduates subsequently confirmed that the work program was reasonable, balanced, and important in shaping character. "Never did the work overtax our strength or abilities, nor did it interfere with out schoolwork," wrote one. "Above all, I learned to take pride in doing a good job. In later years I heard from Good Will alumni over and over that such work or chore-doing was the most important aspect of Hinckley's school."[62]

Because Hinckley was intent on teaching the youths to appreciate the importance of labor and the value of earned property, he did not automatically pass on donated gifts to them. He reasoned that if donations supplied basic needs and taught a lesson as well, they were "of double value to humanity." The children needed to learn that they could not walk into a store and take what they wanted; this would "pauperize them all," and they would grow up failing to understand the value of money and how to support themselves. When someone gave seventy-five pairs of rubber boots to the farm, the boys had to work for them by cutting stipulated amounts of firewood. They reportedly came to appreciate the worth of the boots; for days afterward they were saying, "Look out for my boots. I worked and bought those, myself." But as Good Will enthusiasts proudly observed, this did not mean that selfishness prevailed. When "one little shaver" fell ill, several of his friends cut his share of wood so that he too could get a pair of boots.[63]

Hinckley was nonetheless well aware that employment in an increasingly complex economy depended on more than proper attitudes alone, so he continually tried to develop diversified educational opportunities at Good Will. At first, the boys attended the nearby district school (although for ten weeks during the midwinter months, they received instruction in their cottage). But in the early 1890s, as the number of farm residents grew and the public school could no longer handle them, Hinckley announced that, come fall, Good Will would have its own classrooms. At the end of July, however, there were still no desks or schoolbooks, and he began to wonder if disaster lay ahead. A local church salvaged the situation by pledging forty desks and some books. Shortly thereafter, in 1894, two sisters contributed enough money to erect a building specifically for classroom use; two years later the school opened. A carefully graded system emerged by the early 1900s, offering manual, agricultural, and domestic training, as well as college preparatory classes. By 1910 vocational training included ironworking, carpentry, patternmaking, bookbinding, basketry, mechanical drawing, freehand drawing, metalworking, and rug weaving; three boys passed examinations that year on the maintenance and operation of a ten-horsepower steam engine. Agricultural students had a greenhouse, as well as stock and poultry, to work with. And although preparing young people for college was not Hinckley's main priority, he made sure that those who had such aspirations received the best possible instruction. During the 1913–1914 academic year, ten former Good Will residents were enrolled in a variety of colleges, including Dartmouth, M.I.T., Yale, Brown, Syracuse, Maine, and Bowdoin.[64]

According to Ray Tobey, a 1906 Good Will graduate who completed a degree at Dartmouth, education at the farm was "superior." One of his instructors knew seven languages. Edward Brackett—class of 1909—who had no difficulty receiving admission to Brown University, said that "most [Good Will] teachers were well above average and all were dedicated." Earl Ormsby, who lived at the farm from 1906 to 1914, later took some courses at M.I.T., but it was at Good Will that he learned skills basic to his future employment. He converted his interest in working with the steamboilers at the farm (always under careful supervision) into a very successful business as a heating expert, which he pursued for decades in Brunswick, Maine. It was not simply specific training in mechanics that influenced him, however. A "well-balanced" education, he later said, had helped him "in each branch of life" and made him one of Brunswick's most active citizens—at town meetings, on the school board, and as a selectman. In retrospect, Ormsby had no doubt that Good Will "was probably one of the finest organized schools in the country at that time." Harry Harles, who came to Good Will in 1918 through the help of the Big Brother Association (because his widowed mother could not support her children), believed that Hinckley's teaching staff "was equal to, or better than," the instructors he had encountered at New York City's Speyer Junior High, an experimental school that reputedly had outstanding teachers for exceptional students. After graduating from Good Will, Harles received a degree from Georgia Tech and became a prominent North Carolina architect. Norman Palmer, who obtained a

Ph.D. from Yale before embarking on a long career in teaching political science at Colby College and the University of Pennsylvania, studied "English, math, history, and Latin every year" that he attended Good Will in the early 1920s. In his opinion he had received a fine education, one that prepared him not only for college but for life as well. Thomas Riley, a Harvard Ph.D. who taught German at Bowdoin College for years, recalled that because he "was a bookish boy, a great reader," he had gotten assignments at the Good Will library as janitor and assistant librarian. He could not praise Hinckley or his work and educational system enough.[65]

Hinckley's flexible and wide-ranging program squared nicely with the thinking of progressive educators, and this was no less true because of his belief in the need to instruct young people in the subject of sex. Here he stood with an expanding group of reformers who urged an end to "the conspiracy of silence" that had long characterized the topic. Confident that knowledge was the way to social purity, he recommended "The Self and Sex Series" by Sylvanis Stall and Mary Wood-Allen. One of those who were impressed by Hinckley's views on sexual instruction was none other than William Byron Forbush, a well-known student of "the Boy Problem" and a man who worried that sexual perversions were "the most common, subtle and dangerous foes that threaten American life." Forbush advocated a number of remedies for "impure thoughts" and masturbation—including exercise, busy schedules, judicious selection of reading materials, plain food, and early rising—but he particularly stressed candid, factual discussions that treated sex as a branch of science. The vigorous life-style at Good Will unquestionably pleased Forbush. So too did Hinckley's method of enlisting the boy in "a manly struggle with the sensual side of his nature." The supervisor took it upon himself, through informal conversations with individual boys, to provide information about the human body and, in Forbush's words, "the dangers of puberty." The subject received further attention only when it seemed necessary, but always in a manner that treated sexual organs as physiological facts, not shameful parts of the anatomy.[66]

Hinckley unquestionably agreed with the twin objectives of sex education that a speaker on social hygiene enunciated at a National Conference of Charities and Correction in 1914: on the one hand to help youths avoid feelings "of a false shame, or of disrespect, or vulgar innuendo and cheap witticism"; on the other hand to train youngsters "in purity, modesty, chastity and honor."[67] At Good Will, Hinckley and other adults not only carefully dispensed information on sex but also strove mightily to discourage sexual misconduct.

The social setting was quite rigid—in the words of former residents, "perhaps too narrow-gauged," "rather straight-laced," and "conservative socially . . . even for those days." This was due partly to the rather remote setting of the farm, but it also reflected moral concerns and judgments. Because more than a mile separated the cottages of the boys and girls, there was little intermingling between the sexes except in the high school classes or at closely supervised gatherings. When a silent movie was sometimes shown on a Saturday evening, males and females could not sit together (although as one early resident remembered wryly, "We could always look?"). Dancing was not permitted except in the form of occasional "marches" to piano music at "socials," and even then under the watchful gaze of chaperones—"no fun," as one woman laughingly recalled. At least some of the youths chafed, however quietly, at such strictness and wished for more knowledge "of the social graces," as one graduate later phrased it. But the rituals of dating, dancing, and interraction with the opposite sex were likely to be hard-won skills that came only after graduation from Good Will.[68]

Obviously, the willingness of many progressive educators, such as Hinckley, to disseminate information about sex hardly signaled a moral revolution. They endorsed scientific expertise and urged knowledgeable people to unveil the mysteries of sex in public forums or in serious, intimate environments where—in the words of one speaker—"the gymnasium teacher, the scout leader, swimming instructor, or the camp guide" could provide "wholesome counsel."[69] A key word, of course, was "wholesome." Education in sexual matters was very much supposed to buttress the traditional moral standards of restraint and social purity; less prudishness in talk was no green light for less prudishness in behavior. From this perspective, sex education in the progressive era resembled what historians Steven Schlossman and Stephanie Wallach have described as "a sexual counterrevolution." The result was a reaffirmation of "Victorian moral and sexual standards"—the moral equivalent of "the cleansing of corruption in the political and economic arenas."[70] It was thus perhaps not surprising that joking and wisecracking among Good Will's youths marked the day when a fourteen- or fifteen-year-old was summoned from school to discuss "the birds and bees" in Hinckley's office. The moment of greatest personal embarrassment may have come not while talking with Hinckley but during the kidding that followed the return to the peer group.[71]

While proper sexual instruction was considered important at Good Will, religious training was nothing less than pivotal. It included short religious services in school each day, grace before each meal, mandatory Sunday School attendance, and at least an hour of Bible study each Sunday morning. Hinckley insisted, however, that all of this was nondenominational. To outsiders who suspected that Good Will was transmitting sectarian ideas, he offered assurances that this could hardly be true. For one thing, he noted, there was his own diverse religious background. His father had been a Congregationalist and his mother a Methodist; he personally had belonged to the Congregational, Methodist, and Baptist churches. As further proof, he pointed out that members of Good Will's board of directors and its prominent donors had been Episcopalians, Quakers, Presbyterians, Universalists, Seventh-Day Adventists, Christian Scientists, Congregationalists, Baptists, and Methodists. There was the additional fact that graduates of the farm had joined a variety of denominations.[72] What, then, was the nature of religious training at Good Will? According to Hinckley, it focused on the worship of God and the belief in Christ, and did so without encouraging profound religious experiences (which the superintendent believed came only with maturity). It was also "void of cant, void of hypocrisy, void of priggishness." Because Hinckley had long believed that Christianity and salvation ultimately meant "service," he stressed that religion at the farm was intensely practical.[73]

Pared of specific theological doctrines, religion provided one of the four main pillars of life at Good Will. The other pillars, as Hinckley described them, were intellectual, social (with the home and industrial habits at the center), and physical (including work and recreation). The supervisor took the first syllable of each of the four key words and coined the term "Reinsophy"—which to the end of his life he saw as symbolizing the purpose and spirit that made Good Will unique, "not just another 'institution' to rise and flourish for a time and then to be forgotten."[74]

By 1909, when Theodore Roosevelt convened the White House Conference on Dependent Children, Hinckley was fifty-five years old; Good Will was ending its second decade; the original one hundred acres had increased to almost five hundred; and the institution was at last, in the founder's words, "well under way."[75] It was appropriate that he should decide to attend—unofficially—the White House gathering of some two hundred people who formed a virtual who's who in American child saving.

The importance of the conference was clear to Hinckley, who predicted that it would exert enormous national influence. Roosevelt's opening remarks obviously pleased him, especially those in which the president urged religious and philanthropic associations to continue their work. Hinckley shared the conference's sentiment—which took the form of a resolution—that the major goal should always be to keep children and worthy parents together. He believed firmly in the integrity of the family. "That the boy is imperilled we do not doubt," he wrote several years later, "but we have to be careful about doing anything that will encourage family quarrels, desertion of children by fathers and mothers, and several other things." The admittance to Good Will of a child whose father was guilty of desertion might actually encourage parental irresponsibility. For example, a neighbor, confident that "the Good Will Association will take his children under their roof," might conclude that he too should abandon his family. The dilemma had no easy resolution, as Hinckley was well aware. A fine line often existed between the needs of a troubled family and those of a suffering child; on a number of occasions Good Will had accepted children who in Hinckley's opinion "were in danger, in their home surroundings, of falling into evil ways."[76] The perplexing question of how to balance the claims of home and child continually plagued child savers, and Hinckley undoubtedly appreciated the resolve of the White House conferees to give highest priority to the sanctity of the family.

He nonetheless found very disturbing the strong anti-institutional sentiment that marked the Washington, D.C., meetings. Upon his return to Maine he contended that he personally was "not sensitive" about this animus; Good Will Farm, he said, was not in the category of institutions under attack.[77] Later, however, he admitted being upset. The conference had been "so radically anti-institutional" that he had come away pledging that "henceforth and forever Good Will is an institution; it will continue to be a protest against the old time institutionalizing of the young; at the same time it will demonstrate that an institution does not necessarily institutionalize."[78] He had no quarrel with the placement of dependent children in private homes, but he objected to suggestions that this was the only reasonable policy. "The wholesale attack on institutions," as he viewed it, simply betrayed a woeful ignorance of how far "modern institutions" had come from the old-style asylums.[79]

In his opinion, Good Will Farm stood as proud testimony against traditional children's institutions. Its purpose was "to build homes—real homes, in which family life is sheltered and each individual has opportunity to develop." Hinckley preferred to hire matrons who had not worked at other children's shelters, precisely because he felt they could more easily adjust to cottage life if they had not learned routines elsewhere. The tradition in old-style orphanages of letting visitors watch the children at mealtime repulsed him. For anyone who asked to observe the Good Will residents while they were eating, Hinckley had a stock answer: "Whenever you will be willing that a group of Good Will boys shall stand in the doorway and watch your family eat, I will be willing that you shall stand in one of the 'homes' and watch the boys."[80] Nor did Hinckley permit drills or uniforms; in fact, he preferred that not even two cottages look alike.[81] He prized self-reliance and individual initiative—not lockstep conformity and timidity. At one point he asserted confidently, "Among all the boys and girls who have spent a part of their life at Good Will, there is not one that has been institutionalized."[82]

People did not have to take his word for it. Visitors' accounts and newspaper stories were on his side. So too were Good Will graduates, who said that the Farm was always a home, not an institution. One beleaguered president of an Ohio orphanage, reportedly under

fire from individuals who opposed any kind of institution for children, gratefully assured Hinckley that Good Will was "the best
answer to . . . efforts to force us into a mere placing agency."[83] Such
opinions confirmed Hinckley's confidence that his beloved farm on
the banks of the Kennebec River stood as a powerful rebuttal to
arguments that the worst home was preferable to the best institution.

Another kind of criticism that seemed to make the supervisor
uneasy and somewhat defensive was the occasional complaint that
Good Will favored its boys more than its girls. From time to time,
letters arrived expressing disappointment because the girls received
little mention in the *Record*, because the Good Will seal featured
only a boy, and because it seemed that girls had fewer opportunities.
Hinckley insisted that such letters reflected erroneous impressions.
He reminded his critics that in the 1890s he had opened a girls'
home, despite warnings about the dangers inherent in housing
opposite sexes in the same area. To purchase the necessary land, he
had relied on the same strategies that had informed his earlier
efforts: namely, he had established "The Girls' Fund, Devoted to the
Interests of Girls in need of a Helping Hand," and had then awaited
contributions. (Two Good Will boys had made the first deposits, five
cents each.) In 1896 two Connecticut parents built a cottage in
memory of their daughter; a year later, the Granges of Maine erected
another home for girls. By the late 1890s, some thirty girls were in
residence at the farm. From Hinckley's perspective, "the existence
of the Good Will Homes for girls is our recognition of the equal
value of boys and girls to society."[84]

The girls' department had grown more slowly than that of the
boys, Hinckley explained, because of an imbalance of contributions.
On this matter he could not miss the chance to twit some of his
critics: "One cannot help wondering where these special friends of
the girls are in these days."[85] As for the complaint that only a boy
appeared on the institution's seal, Hinckley countered that it was
possible to see the young male as a generic symbol for both sexes:
"we will not insist that the boy in the design be used generically but
we are inclined to think he could be." The supervisor believed,
moreover, that the words "Home" and "Education" on the seal
certainly included "girlhood." The limited space that girls received

in the *Record* (one of every fourteen pages, according to one critic's tally in 1899) bothered him "a good deal," but he was unsure what to do about it because there were simply fewer gifts and activities to report. It seemed "obvious" to him why the boys got more publicity than the girls. His reasoning could come full circle, however, especially when he conceded that the girls' department had probably been slower to develop *because* "we have not said so much about the girls' home and schools."[86] The simple truth—which Hinckley may have sensed—was that however much he wanted girls to enjoy a happy home and receive a useful education at Good Will, his primary concerns were for the boys, with whom he went canoeing and camping, and whom he sometimes joined in the harvest fields.[87]

That fact aside, Hinckley correctly argued that finances were the critical factor in determining who came to Good Will. Because the farm was for needy children, little if any support arrived from their relatives.[88] In 1907, of some 180 boys and girls, the relatives (mainly brothers and sisters) of only three paid for their complete care—which averaged $200 annually. Between fifty-five and sixty received some family aid, often in the form of payments less than a dollar a week. Two-thirds received no support from relatives; their care rested entirely on contributions to the Good Will Association.[89] Hinckley adamantly rejected suggestions that he turn to the state for funds. From the beginning, his project had depended on the philanthropic contributions of citizens, many of whom sent small amounts from dimes to several dollars. The farm was supposed to attest to the charitable inclinations of God's almoners, not the power of the state over grudging taxpayers. "I have faith in the legislature," wrote Hinckley. "But I have more faith in God. . . . It shall never be said of the writer: 'In the beginning he trusted God; but a little later he turned to the State.'"[90]

Hinckley's efforts to obtain permanent endowments for the care of children never met with much success. A notable exception was an unsolicited contribution in 1904 from Edwin Bancroft Foote of New York City, who not only funded a new cottage but provided full support for ten to fifteen boys.[91] Larger financial support came in the form of designated cash gifts, whereby individuals or groups sponsored particular children. The task of making such arrangements proved so burdensome for the supervisor, however, that in the early 1900s the association finally hired a financial agent.[92] Hinckley consented to this arrangement reluctantly, and only at the urging of the board of directors; he agreed that it was "the ordinary method of modern institutions" but worried about abandoning his long-standing policy against soliciting money directly from specific individuals.[93] The agent at least took some of the wear and tear off Hinckley, who increasingly suffered from splitting headaches in hot weather and from occasional bouts with emotional exhaustion.[94] On the other hand, the results generally proved disappointing. John Boardman, who worked out of New York City for a while in 1912 raised expectations with a series of grandiose plans and prospective contributions that ultimately went aglimmering. In March, 1914, $11,262 worth of unpaid bills rested on Hinckley's desk, a "dispiriting" situation and one that forced a substantial reduction in the agricultural and manual training programs.[95]

By then, many of the Good Will children depended on earmarked contributions from individuals or groups, who often knew only by name the youths they were supporting.[96] The most important example of this was the Boy Conservation Bureau, headquartered in New York City. The Bureau was the creation of E. W. Watkins, who had worked as a traveling international secretary for the YMCA before establishing himself at the turn of the century as a successful Wall Street bond broker. His continuing interest in church and charitable work was evident in his involvement in the Big Brother movement, where he befriended several "little brothers," and in a men's Bible class that he taught for New York's Central Presbyterian Church. Intent upon making "Christianity as practical as possible," he organized the Bible class into committees to visit sick and needy strangers. During the early summer of 1911, his wife encountered a homeless boy at the Children's Court, and Watkins convinced his Bible class to find a family that would adopt the youth. Shortly thereafter, a court investigator for the Big Brothers told Watkins about a 12-year-old orphan destined for a public asylum. Again Watkins acted, this time convincing a banker to pay for the boy's support at Good Will Farm. The boy, upon learning that he was going to Maine, thanked the judge of the Children's Court for allowing him such an opportunity, and that gratitude impressed Watson as "quite a manly" response. Duly inspired, he committed himself full time to placing "homeless boys into boyless homes" or at farm schools such as Good Will. On April 10, 1912, he formally incorporated the Boy Conservation Bureau, advertised as having "the Modern Way of solving the problem of the homeless or imperiled boy."[97]

The bureau, with its marvelously progressive name, was a mixture of naiveté and practicality. For two decades it was under the direction of the ebullient Watkins, a distinguished-looking man with piercing eyes, short hair parted down the middle, small pointed beard, and full mustache. His enthusiastic reports—describing a boy with a "stay-out-late-at-night-habit" whom the bureau had "inspired . . . to accomplish something," or a half-orphan who "fell in with the gang" until the bureau placed him "where he will be taught to correct his ways"—underlined the idealistic side of the organization. So too did the sentiments of the New York banker, who volunteered to purchase a new suit of clothes for every boy whom Watkins placed in a rural setting. The banker believed that first impressions were basic to success; by sending youths into the countryside with neat clothes instead of their previously shabby garments, he thought that he was launching the careers of good citizens.[98]

On the practical side, the bureau raised pledges of $200 per year to support dozens of needy children at Good Will and elsewhere. By 1915, twenty-seven of some 160 boys at Good Will were under the sponsorship of the Bureau.[99] Watkins was pleased with Hinckley's institution and inquired now and again whether the farm might have room for more boys.[100] In turn, Hinckley looked to the bureau when he needed money for particular children. For example, in 1914, when the Big Brother movement could no longer raise money for three Good Will boys, Hinckley asked Watkins for help. The New Yorker, who was planning to visit the farm with a wealthy businessman, formulated the strategy: "'Our Boys'" (those whom the Bureau sponsored) should meet the train. The tactic duly impressed Watkins's wealthy companion, who agreed to add to the bureau's roster the three youths who previously had received support from the Big Brothers.[101]

Hinckley's growing contacts with child savers like Watkins helped to publicize Good Will and to bring the supervisor into contact with some of the top people in children's work. He was anxious to discuss "many things in boys' work" with leading child savers, such as Judge Ben Lindsey.[102] And he successfully brought to the farm William Byron Forbush, Hastings Hart, Booker T. Washington, Jacob Riis, Ernest Thompson Seton of the Boy Scouts of America, and others of substantial reputation.[103] In 1911, at a New York meeting on boys' work, he shared the speakers' platform with some of the most distinguished people in child rescue work: Hart, Edward T. Devine, Samuel McCune Lindsay, Charles Loring Brace, Jr., and R. R. Reeder.[104] Hinckley was also elected to the first executive council of the Boy Scouts of America, and he was a member of the committee that framed a Boy Scout rule against the acceptance of tips.[105] On at least one occasion he convened a four-day retreat in the Pennsylvania mountains, where twenty people discussed "The Less Fortunate Boy."[106] He visited settlement houses and missions in New York and Boston,[107] and in 1911 he interviewed Charles F. Powlison, general secretary of the New York Child Welfare Committee, about the committee's highly acclaimed Child Welfare Exhibit.[108] Hinckley, in turn, received considerable praise from his colleagues in youth work. Ernest K. Coulter, clerk of New York City's Children's Court and a founder of the Big Brother movement, spoke highly of Good Will Farm.[109] William R. George, who claimed to have read everything he could about Good Will, also touted it, adding, "To be perfectly candid, I do not know of more than one or two other places besides your excellent institution that I would recommend."[110] And Herman Smith, general manager of Beulah Land Farm for Boys, (a residence for homeless and neglected youths in Boyne City, Michigan), believed that "truly a great spirit" moved Hinckley.[111]

As Hinckley's personal connections grew, so too did the geographical area from which Good Will drew its children expand. Maine remained the dominant place of origin, but of the 182 boys and girls at the farm in 1912, 27 were from New York, 25 from Massachusetts, 12 from Michigan, 6 from New Jersey, 2 from Pennsylvania, and 1 from Georgia.[112] Surnames suggested that the ethnic backgrounds of the children were quite diverse,[113] although Good Will—at least through its first three decades—was not open to blacks.[114] Whatever the youths' geographical, ethnic, or racial origins, the overwhelming majority in the first several decades came from families in which at least one of the parents was dead.[115] From the Colorado boy whose father had died in a mine after being kicked by a mule, to the motherless Georgia youngster who traveled to Maine by himself for three days on the train (getting lost at one point), Good Will apparently provided exactly what Hinckley intended: a helping hand for needy children. Probaby most of them experienced, as one former resident recalled, the dread sense of "utter loneliness" as they first set foot in the "strange and unfamiliar environment" of the farm.[116] For most, those initial doubts and fears gave way rather quickly as they adjusted to life in the cottages with new "families." After leaving the farm, many continued to keep in close touch.

Hinckley could take much pride in this. Still, even after twenty-five years, Good Will remained extremely vulnerable to outside events. America's entry into the Great War in 1917 sent the institution reeling; the conflict exacted a considerable toll, emotionally and economically. One of Hinckley's sons was in the army, and a daughter worked with soldiers in France. By April 1918 the supervisor wrote that 111 former Good Will boys, who to him were "like my own sons," had put on uniforms; three had died. Hinckley himself wanted to go to France, but worried that at age sixty-five he would prove an "embarrassment." Finally, although he volunteered for YMCA work in Europe, he stayed at the farm, where he watched in dismay as the institution's debt soared.[117] By 1917, Good Will had expanded to the point of caring for 230 children, but it had never escaped financial uncertainty. Wartime inflation enlarged the problem. Faced with skyrocketing costs, Hinckley was reluctant to seek contributions; placing the farm's needs above those of soldiers would, he felt, be "almost like treason." Consequently, at the war's end Good Will's debt had mounted to $60,000. Three options seemed open at that point: closing the institution for several years until the debt had been paid; accepting only boys and girls whose friends could pay $325 a year support, a choice which would fundamentally alter the nature of the institution by turning it into "a boarding school at cost," rather than a home for needy children; or undertaking a major drive to raise money.[118]

Not surprisingly, Hinckley sought to raise funds. Tired and dis-

couraged, he personally assumed the onerous responsibility of soliciting contributions because he did not want to give up the usual
percentage that a financial agent demanded. In letter after letter he
described an institution worth saving. On one hand was the physical
setting of Good Will: 700 acres, valued at $400,000, and thirty-one
buildings (including eleven cottages for boys and three for girls, a
library of 14,000 volumes, and five barns). On the other hand was a
tradition of child saving that had not only helped endangered children become farmers, day laborers, college graduates, teachers,
YMCA secretaries, manufacturers, and clerks but had also contributed 154 service stars (and eight lives) to the recent war effort.
Hinckley hoped to remove Good Will's debt and then, if he lived
four more years, to step down at age seventy, leaving an institution
"second to none for . . . philanthropic and educational work."[119]

He need not have worried. Good Will recovered financially, and
he lived far beyond another four years. Although he turned the
supervisor's position over to his son Walter in 1919, he served as
president of the Good Will Association from 1927 until he resigned
in 1946, staying on for one last year as editor of the *Record*.[120]

In 1950, at age ninety-eight, he died. In his last several years, he
seemed to sense that Good Will might lose touch with its origins;
his resignation letter as president of the association contained an
appeal to the board not to forget the ideals upon which he had
founded the institution. From the beginning he had intended for
Good Will to provide underprivileged youths with a cottage-style,
family setting. He called attention to several other institutions, also
originally formed to care for poor children, which had subsequently
turned into preserves for the privileged—for people with money,
rather than those without. Good Will's history had been a study in
benevolence; he hoped its future would be the same. There were
warning signs, however. In 1943 the towns of Waterville and Skowhegan staged celebrations in honor of Hinckley's ninetieth birthday.
He was flattered, yet disappointed: not once at either occasion did
anyone mention Psalms 37:5, the inspiration underlying his entire
effort and the scriptural passage that he had included in every issue
of the *Good Will Record*. Perhaps the public had forgotten the
fundamental point—a discouraging thought for him indeed.[121]

Still, he had his memories. There was, for example, "Little

Charlie" Nutter's comment that Good Will had saved him from the fate of all his boyhood city friends: "police records and worse." And there was the statement of another youth that, except for Good Will, he "would have been on the street." Or Hinckley may have remembered a letter in 1915 from a youngster who was happy because at the farm "there is something I do in every part of the year, and I have a grudge against doing nothing." That recollection, thirty years later, may have caused Hinckley to smile and echo what he had said earlier: "I like that expression, 'I have a grudge against doing nothing.'"[122]

On Hinckley's successors devolved the question about how best to preserve the institution in a changing world. In the late 1950s the board of directors, after much study and consideration, transformed Good Will Farm from a home to a prep school—a substantial shift in which aiding poor youths was no longer the main concern. Dormitories replaced the cottage system.[123] Within twenty years, however, a major effort to salvage the original goals had started: in April 1977 the directors adopted a new name—Hinckley Home-School-Farm—to show that the institution was first and foremost a "home." Over the next few months, the directors embarked on a fundamental reorganization to bring Good Will "more in line with the goals of the founder." One result was the reinstitution of the cottage system, in which the residents had regular home chores and a family environment. Boys and girls, grades five through eight, who lacked a family life because of death, broken homes, or other circumstances were eligible for admission.[124]

The reorganization also included a significant attempt to rediscover and preserve the historical roots of Good Will through such steps as reopening and refurbishing the museum (which in 1978 received a place in the National Register of Historic Places). Such efforts attested to the continuing influence of Hinckley's dream; but the difficulty of trying to strengthen the connections between the institution's past and its future pointed up not only how many changes had occurred in Good Will's ninety years but also the importance of Hinckley himself. His successors perhaps appreciated more than anyone the comment of one of Good Will's first graduates, that the farm without Hinckley would be a little like "Hamlet without Hamlet."[125]

• 7 •

Epilogue

Looking back on his life, Edward Bradley in the 1930s described himself as a "Maker of Men" and claimed "1,800 foster children."[1] Such words conveyed marvelously the mood of an entire generation of child savers. At the turn of the century they had labored long and diligently to establish what they hoped would be a better world for children. Many, like Bradley, had been especially attentive to the needs of dependent youths and had dotted the landscape with new organizations, associations, and institutions.

The motives that drove them to "do good" were as different as the solutions they favored and the bases of support upon which they drew. Volatile combinations of fear and hope; of powerlessness and the desire to make a turbulent world orderly; of self-sacrifice and the quest for fame and attention; of humanitarian instincts and the urge to impose personal values on other individuals; of religious convictions and a concern with administrative and economic efficiency—these were some of the competing and contradictory elements that helped to define child rescue work.

While the child savers accomplished much, they also illustrated poignantly the difficulties of trying to establish community ties in a harshly competitive and individualistic society. Indeed, it was often evident that they had not made up their own minds about the nature of the emerging twentieth-century world or their own roles in shaping it. They agreed with Bradley "that there is a need of change,"[2] but they approached the rapidly shifting society around them tentatively and uneasily.

They confronted, for example, relentless nationalizing forces of modern transportation, communication, and administration that undermined the village world so familiar to most of them. Railroads, telephones, the telegraph, mail order businesses, and economic combinations that cut across local and state boundaries tipped the scale of human relationships overwhelmingly in favor of an urbanized, consolidated world. In the early twentieth century, inventions such as the automobile, motion pictures, and the radio quickened the pace of centralizing trends.[3] Child saving in the late 1800s and early 1900s was hardly free of these developments; indeed, it illustrated very well the tendency toward a more tightly organized, bureaucratized society. National conventions of social welfare organizations and the growing efforts to consolidate various groups were prime examples. An advertisement for the Associated Charities in Minneapolis portrayed this effectively: it showed a woman at "the charity switchboard," taking phone calls in behalf of numerous agencies—the Humane Society, settlement houses, charity homes and institutions, hospitals, schools, courts, the Salvation Army, and others.[4] Moreover, child savers talked increasingly of "scientific," "efficient," "professional" remedies to problems of dependency, neglect, and delinquency.

Nevertheless, in notable ways child rescue workers showed how vital the "island communities" of the rural, small-town culture still were. Again and again they tried to replicate as much of village America as possible. Just as Jane Addams and other settlement house people tried in crowded city slums to build small-scale communities reminiscent of agrarian America, so too did the founders of farm schools and junior republics seek to create environments that were heavily imbued with traditional, rural values. Such was clearly the case at Allendale Farm, Good Will Farm, the Wisconsin Home and Farm School, the Ford Republic, and a host of others.

Similarly, Bradley, G. W. Hinckley, Marion Ogden, John Gunckel, Mattie Younkin, E. P. Savage, and virtually the entire lineup of organizers of new associations and institutions felt uncomfortable in the increasingly professional setting that stressed formal training, certification, and credentials. If the emerging field of social work favored "professional altruists,"[5] this first generation of progressive child savers qualified as "amateur altruists." "I had no theory then, I have none now," wrote Bradley in 1926. In this respect he was certainly not alone.[6]

Hinckley, Savage, Bradley, and others also dramatized the continued appeal of the voluntaristic tradition in American reform. The dozens of farm schools, orphanages, and child rescue clubs that spring up at the turn of the century invariably received inspection and backing from voluntary private sources. Granted, the new institutions were subject to expanding state regulations and inspections,[7] and some states (such as Michigan and Minnesota) extended public responsibility for dependent and delinquent children. But private charity alone accounted for the development of the National Benevolent Association, the Home Societies, the Toledo Newsboys' Association, Good Will Farm, and a myriad of child rescue institutions and organizations. In fact, Hinckley's relative freedom to follow his own course at Good Will Farm may very well have flowed from the autonomous nature of a private—as opposed to a public—institution. Certainly that was a key reason why he did not seek public funding. Such autonomy may also have enlarged Homer Lane's maneuvering room for a while at the Ford Republic, and Bradley's at Allendale.[8]

Central to the upsurge of voluntary activity for dependent children was a vigorous religious impulse.[9] A remarkable number of the new societies and orphanages drew directly upon a swelling denominational interest in the plight of "waifs."[10] Even in the case of those institutions and associations that were not directly church-affiliated, the influence of religious ideas was strong indeed. Bradley, Hinckley, Savage, and J. P. Dysart were among those who were or had been ministers, or at least studied for the pulpit. Marion Ogden, a founder of the Wisconsin Home and Farm School, had taught Sunday School; her colleague Bert Hall, president of the farm school for twenty-five years, was a deacon in the Congregational Church.[11] Not surprisingly, emphasis on teaching "practical Christianity" ran deeply through the literature of nonsectarian institutions such as the Wisconsin Home. All of this provided ample evidence of the impact of the Social Gospel. Time and again, deeply religious people sought to channel their faith in constructive ways toward settling frightening social problems. Indeed, in an environment that too often seemed ready to fly apart, they almost desperately searched for moral ballast. As human relations became more impersonal, social ties more brittle, and urban disorder more threatening, it seemed imperative to revitalize the remembered values of mutual obligations, communal bonds, and Good Samaritanism. The alternative was apparently a splintered, chaotic society—a society composed of hostile strangers, rather than caring neighbors.[12]

Among at least some child savers, this quest for moral order undoubtedly encouraged tendencies to meddle, to pry, and to impose particular sets of values on "client" groups. Sometimes the results were mainly silly. For intance, during a 1906 discussion of dependent and neglected children, a volunteer from the Minneapolis Juvenile Protective League asserted that probation officers for the juvenile court might try a tactic that she used with poor families: distributing flower and vegetable seeds. "A small garden," she said, "has often resulted in uplifting and bettering all the inmates of the house."[13] Her choice of the word "inmates" to describe the members of a poor family was illuminating in itself. On other occasions, however, the results of "helping" unfortunate individuals were more insidious, as when a Milwaukee youth named Peter ended up in reform school, not so much for what he had done (exposing himself to a neighbor) but because the court decided that Peter's confinement might provide a salutary influence on his brother and sister. The early history of the juvenile court system contained numerous instances of reformers' trying to insinuate themselves into the lives of lower class, immigrant groups.[14]

For child savers, the "rescue" of unfortunate youths could be a heady calling. It cast them in the role of patriotic citizens battling for their nation's future. Sarah J. Bird, a widow who in 1897 founded the White Door Settlement in New York City, emerged in the settlement's literature as "noble-hearted" and "far-seeing, with the wide outlook upon humanity which was vouchsafed for her." Slum urchins reportedly "fairly swarmed" into the institution, whose motto was "For God and Home and Little Children." Not only did urban waifs gain important instruction, but they also returned "to their poor homes" with lessons in cooking, sewing, "neatness and order." In her own way, according to a settlement pamphlet, Bird was attempting to save her "beloved country" from the "deadly menace" of immigration. She was throwing her energies into aiding "the sin-sick, down-trodden creatues" of the ghettos who moved at night "like wild beasts from their lairs." She was teaching republican values to "superstitious, bigoted, ignorant" immigrants. As the literature reminded readers, Bird was no average person. She was almost saintlike in her idealism and her willingness to give of herself.[15]

Sarah Bird thus found in child saving more than personal satisfaction; she also enhanced her social status and gained public recognition.[16] Nor was she unique in this respect. For "Cap" Bradley, Hinckley, Gunckel, the women who founded the Christian Church's National Benevolent Association, and countless others, work with children gained public attention and praise. Just as certainly, their rescue operations gave them a sense of purpose and self-esteem.[17]

More than social control or a search for personal status and well-being was involved, however. So too was a keen sense of obligation and service. A key question was why they cared as much as they did.[18] There were, after all, easier roads to success (and far more prosperous ones) than child saving. Savage's experiences at the Minnesota Children's Home Society demonstrated how physically and emotionally draining the work could be and how it could elicit criticism as well as compliments. Aggie Hopkins, in 1911 a cofounder of the Orphan's and Children's Home in Creal Springs, Illinois, recalled that "the path was not always strewn with roses." Her husband Dan, a Methodist preacher, was dismayed when some of his own colleagues refused to support the orphanage. A few of them refused even to let him ask their congregations for contributions.[19] The initial opposition to Mattie Younkin and the other women who formed the National Benevolent Association showed that child saving was not always popular. And it was not monetary reward that drove Tena Williamson, matron at the St. Louis orphanage, to the point of exhaustion; strong feelings of compassion and duty surely helped to motivate such people.

Nor were their perceptions of a society in distress without basis in fact. Serious and deeply rooted social problems existed. John Gunckel did not imagine those two newsboys who huddled for protection in a vestibule, trying to ward off the freezing winds during that icy evening in 1885. Edward Bradley did not invent the thirteen-year-old boy whose mother had died and whose father had thrown him out of the house (a place so rodent-infested that the youth in one night had killed three rats in a homemade trap); or the youngster, orphaned at age four, who had lived in a farm bunkhouse for more than a year, doing chores for room and board until the local juvenile protective association placed him at Allendale. The miseries of Ignatius Dega, first resident at the Wisconsin Home and Farm School, were not fabrications. After Dega's mother had beaten the thirteen-year-old severely and even threatened him with a revolver to make him lie about his age and thus get a job, the battered youth ran away, freezing his feet while hiding on Milwaukee's wintry streets.[20]

Such genuinely harrowing aspects of lower-class living conditions did not spring from reformers' fantasies. Rats and fires and disease constituted an ugly part of tenement life, and slum landlords provided sufficient reminders of the corruption that hounded the poor.[21] Reformers not only recognized these problems but in many cases tried to deal with them in creative and humane ways. Child savers devised junior republics, farm schools, the cottage system, newsboys' clubs, and educational programs that emphasized individual needs and abilities. These strategies, however imperfect, were nonetheless defensible and sometimes even inventive.

On occasion, however, child savers seemed to wonder whether they were trying to square a circle. Sometimes, reform not only produced unintended results but also placed the reformers in ambiguous relationships with their society. At Allendale, the junior republic experiment provided a salient example. A major justification for the miniature commonwealth idea was that it built good citizens. By breaking from traditional institutional procedures, it supposedly allowed youths to develop individual abilities and interests, to forge independent spirits basic to democratic government, and to have a voice in their own affairs. At the same time, by rewarding effort and service, it stressed responsibility. Despite these much-heralded virtues of the little commonwealth, however, it also fostered certain tendencies that troubled Bradley.

Deep down, Bradley—no less than Daddy George at the Freeville junior republic—confronted a dilemma. Both men had difficulty deciding whether their experiments should reflect the outside world, or serve as a model by which to measure that larger environment and perhaps even help to shape it into a better place. Bradley could smile at the "frenzied finance" which at one point gripped the residents of the little lakeshore huts that some of the boys constructed, and also at the acquisitive spirit that stirred a "little gang" of citizens to sell the farm's cranberries for personal profit.[22] On the other hand he was uneasy that commercial tendencies could, perhaps all too easily, cross over the fine line that separated healthy enterprise from an exploitative system—a system that numbered among its victims the very kinds of children who arrived so pathetically at Allendale. Bradley, after all, was a man who emphasized that at Allendale "we have realized our larger selves through service." His own life did not feature the kind of productivity that, as a good friend noted, "counted in the market place." While Bradley found deep satisfaction in knowing that Allendale graduates were better equipped than before to deal with the outside world, he stressed that "the Allendale measure is always in terms of manhood and not in terms of wordly success or worldly standards."[23]

A basic question was involved. At what point did the goal of "recreating" boys suggest the need to recreate society as well? Bradley fretted when "the commercial spirit" seemed to press "better things" from the imaginations of his young charges. He expressed concern over the development in the Allendale court of those techniques and strategies that were often the very key to success in the outside legal system. One boy, for example, when bringing suit against another for assault and battery, used dramatic effects to move judge and jury; he had friends carry him into the court on a cot to emphasize his plight. A clever ploy it might have been, but did it suggest that the tiny judiciary was fostering what Bradley lamented as "the instinct of evasion and self-protection through the legal quibble"? To what extent was the daily boys' court—supposedly a training ground in good citizenship— encouraging habits of dissimulation as opposed to candor and honesty?[24]

Bradley found discouraging signs "that we were beginning to accentuate, and even produce, poor social types. The boss, the professional politician, the opportunist; and the ne'er-do-wells were being forced into a well-defined pauper class." The heart of the matter was simple: "We discovered that we were reproducing society, and it is a question with most of us whether society, as it is, is worth reproducing." That jarring insight pointed up an essential question not only for Bradley and for Daddy George but for the entire progressive generation.[25]

Bradley and George were not alone in their nervous assessments of a society that possessed many virtues but also created disturbing examples of injustice, innocent victims, and social turmoil. Many progressive reformers, wavering in the balance, placed considerable hope in the power of rhetoric and example to awaken and enlighten the larger public. The difference between a society that was unjust and exploitative and one that offered compassion, responsibility, and a sense of community seemed ultimately to depend on the attitudes which the citizens held. If the citizens were informed, if they respected the general welfare, and if a spirit of service motivated them, they would provide the essentials of good society. It was this faith in the redeeming qualities of an educated, public-spirited, morally aroused citizenry that galvanized many progressives in their appeals for uplift; in their major efforts through journalistic exposés and blue-ribbon commissions to gather the facts necessary to guide social action; in their evangelical appeals for a mobilized electorate to oust the forces of corruption and partnership; and in their tendency to believe in the ultimate success of right-thinking individuals to salvage traditional American ideals in the twentieth century.[26]

This faith in the rejuvenating power of a cooperative, united, educated people was the magnet that pulled such diverse individuals as Herbert Croly, Herbert Hoover, and Jane Addams into the progressive fold. It also stirred experiments—such as the settlement house movement, John Dewey's model classrooms, and junior republics—to forge the outlines of embryonic communities that might rescue victims of the emerging social order and provide them with the skills necessary to cope with the realities of that world. Such experiments might even go one step beyond, serving as beacons on the hill, drawing public attention to the possibility of orderly reconstruction so that society might become less susceptible to injustice and exploitation. Somewhat like the communitarian reformers of antebellum America who labored to produce "patent-office models of the good society,"[27] many social welfare progressives wanted to demonstrate what the outlines of that better society might be. There were inevitable tensions, however, between

213

the efforts to prepare individuals for the real world, thereby increasing their chances for success within it, and the hopes of improving upon institutions and practices. The debates between John Gunckel and his critics over the place of newsboys in society whirled around this very issue.

At the Wisconsin Home and Farm School, the directors were no less ambivalent when judging the world into which they sent their young people. They lamented that "our great industrial system is grinding up the energies of so many thousands of boys." But their stated aim of producing "healthy, manly boys, who, when they go out into life, will be able 'to work hard, think straight and play fair,'" hardly jeopardized the "great industrial system" that worried the directors. Indeed, they pointed enthusiastically to "desirable positions" open to young men of "pep": namely, as "presidents and managers of big, profitable business."[28]

Like the directors of the Wisconsin institution, Bradley (and William George, Hinckley, Gunckel, and others) chafed at reproducing a society whose rejects included ragged and deprived children—little "street arabs" trying to survive in a bleak underworld of poverty, squalor, and neglect. The larger society too often reduced to outcasts those who had "no market value"; Bradley wanted to include them among his "1,800 foster children." The difference was substantial. Child savers (and other progressive reformers) hoped to have the final word: the new age for children would be a new era for America as well.

Events seldom cooperated, however. Marion Ogden pointed to the juvenile court system as one example. She had helped to write the law that established Milwaukee's juvenile court and had served for several years without pay as the first probation officer. Years later she said that the ideals of probation work had foundered as early as 1907 when the position became salaried rather than voluntary. She regretted in 1974 that "probation officers today are too busy investigating and doing paper work to be a friend to a child."[29]

A major difficulty, as Ogden discovered, was that the sands upon which reformers built shifted so rapidly. The pace of change was itself a problem.[30] "Your society has done pioneer work and done it well," wrote one observer to Minneapolis's Juvenile Protective

League. But he added harshly that the league, "like the pioneer, finds itself left behind by the rapid development of . . . the attempts it has inaugurated." The writer took the league to task for "enormous" waste, and for not mapping out a larger organizational scheme for its work. "The Juvenile work in Minneapolis lacks coordination. It is like an army enlisted in a righteous cause, in which each company is waging a guerrilla warfare, and therefore a wasteful and ineffective one." The problem with boys' club work in Minneapolis and elsewhere was that it had depended too much on "the dynamic force of some one enthusiast, not the gently diffusive force of a committee." It was time, advised the league's critic, to shift child rescue work from the "heroic" to the "more prosaic."[31]

Father Peter Dunne learned somewhat sadly that it was apparently time for his News Boys' Home and Protectorate to move from its "heroic" initial phase. For the institution's first decade, Dunne had been virtually oblivious to the era's bureaucratic trends. He ran what amounted to a one-person operation and seemed to be in all places at once. His door was always open to the residents. According to one visitor, "the first time I saw him, he was in his office literally surrounded by his boys." Roger Baldwin, of St. Louis's juvenile court, marveled at Dunne's ability "to have a place for all the 'odd pieces' of the boy puzzle." But there were limits to what the priest could do. By the mid-1920s, one of Dunne's admirers, a Father O'Grady, wondered if he "is not trying to do too much himself." The recordkeeping was "meagre"; there was "no systematic follow-up for the boys discharged"; and there was inadequate supervision of the residents. Dunne reluctantly conceded that he had overreached himself. "He feels that he is dealing with too many different types of boys," wrote O'Grady. "In many ways he has been disillusioned. He has permitted his great, kind heart to get the better of him."[32]

As Dunne's experience illustrated, there were strong arguments in favor of the need to coordinate and streamline child saving. Various agencies and institutions often duplicated each other's work and competed unnecessarily for funds. Also, there was a definite necessity for better recordkeeping. Many superintendents and directors at first were notoriously casual about such details. It was equally imperative that the follow-up investigation of home placement receive as much energy as the placement process itself. In these respects it was essential that child saving enter a more "prosaic" era.

There were also good reasons for not letting some of the "heroic" aspects of child rescue work obscure its unsavory side. The Illinois State Charities Commission charged in 1911 that private institutions caring for dependent children in the state were generally "irresponsible and inadequately supervised."[33] Although the commission may have exaggerated in order to press its case for more direct state responsibility, it suggested that a definite gap existed between the progressive dream of a "square deal" for the child and actual practices. Hastings Hart, superintendent of the Illinois Children's Home and Aid Society and later director of the Children's Department of the Russell Sage Foundation, pointed to at least one Chicago group that conducted itself in ways "injurious to the general cause of the Child-Saving work"; and the Cook County Juvenile Court noted the large number of "baby farms" in Chicago where small children were "boarded at a meager price for the sake of profit by persons . . . often ignorant and sometimes cruel."[36] By 1916, in North Carolina several men were allegedly organizing orphanages simply to make money. According to one account, "A man with 12 or 14 boys at his disposal and a farm, and nobody to stop him and overlook him, is on the high road to prosperity." Members of the National Benevolent Association were reluctant to criticize any efforts on behalf of dependent children, but these reported developments in North Carolina suggested the "danger of overdoing a good work."[35]

Scandals also threatened to give child rescue work a bad name. In California several homes for dependent children were guilty of abusive practices and of misusing state funds. In 1903 the Howard Colored Orphan Asylum in Brooklyn faced investigation for nepotism, embezzlement, and sexual indignities against young female residents. When the New York Society for the Prevention of Cruelty to Children rebuked an organization for questionable financial procedures and for placing children in homes harmful to their moral and physical welfare, it observed that "in many cases [the children] were lost sight of entirely." One of the more shocking revelations involved a director of a boys' home in Chicago who was found guilty of sodomy and sent to the state prison. He had previously fled from England, where he faced charges of criminal conduct with boys; had traveled under an alias; had come to the attention of the New York Society for the Prevention of Cruelty to Children before he moved to Illinois; and at one point had stalked into the office of the Chicago Bureau of Charities (then investigating conditions at the home he directed) and beat up the superintendent.[36]

From the viewpoint of perhaps all too many of the young residents of institutions at the turn of the century, life fell far short of the reformers' expectations. One pathetic example involved a little girl, Irene, who by about age seven was living with her brother in a Kansas orphanage. "It was like an auction yard," she recalled. "People would come in and take us into the main room and look us over to see if we were what they wanted." Once, when her brother was crying for an orange, "I went to get one for him and one of the women there pulled my hair and slapped my face." A particularly vivid memory for her was the last time she saw her brother; as the three-year-old boy was leaving the orphanage with a man and woman, "he was looking back wondering where I was. . . . I never forgot the expression on his face. He was looking for me." When a tearful Irene fled to the bedroom and refused to come out, one of the women in the institution dragged her out by the hair. "They were so inhuman you can't imagine." Irene eventually moved to a foster home, but not because the adults loved her or wished to adopt her. "They needed a hired boy, but there weren't any, so I did the work."[37]

Irene's experiences were hardly unique, nor did they bode well for a generation that saw itself "answering the children's cry." Moreover, despite progressive criticism of traditional asylum life, a disconcerting number of state industrial schools continued to resemble military camps more than "homes," as the residents paraded in close-order drills with wooden rifles, kept their chairs in straight rows, lived in overcrowded conditions (sometimes spending up to twelve waking hours in one room), and thought of running away. As late as the 1940s, an Illinois social worker found that the superintendent at one home for wayward girls tied the hands of the girls to their beds out of fear that they would otherwise masturbate.[38]

Earlier, in 1912, one reform publication had asserted that "the

217

treatment accorded their dependent children is an index to the character of any people."[39] The record of child savers at the turn of the century was surely mixed. There was more than enough evidence of tragedy, cruelty, failure, arrogance, missed opportunities, discrimination, and manipulation of disadvantaged groups. But there was also evidence of genuine compassion, considerable personal sacrifice, awareness of suffering, sensitivity to the needs of less fortunate individuals, and a deeply felt desire to make the world a better place for children.

Good intentions and conscientious effort did not produce "the children's age" about which reformers talked so excitedly; but for some dependent youths a Tena Williamson, a Homer Lane, a Hinckley, or a Gunckel made a great deal of difference. Fred Bloman, the diminutive judge, enjoyed an inspired (although brief) career at the Ford Republic. Ignatius Dega, who came with frozen feet to the Wisconsin Home and Farm School, found shelter because of the labors of Marion Ogden and her associates; until his death in the mid-1930s he continued to communicate with the institution. The abandoned infant discovered in the Normal, Illinois, garbage dump would perhaps not have survived without the Baby Fold. Hundreds of children found homes with the aid of Savage and Dysart. Benjamin Drucker's first years, prior to his arrival at Good Will Farm in his early teens, were a catalog of miseries: after he—as a year-old-child—and his parents came to America, from Austro-Hungary around 1896, he got into trouble with the police on New York's Lower East Side, spent some time in a reform school, was placed on an Iowa farm (where the farmer clearly disliked this Jewish city boy), ran away, (riding in a cattle car and arriving in Chicago with frostbitten feet), and lived for a year near the Chicago stockyards. Good Will proved a welcome contrast; Drucker fondly remembered it as "a wonderful place" and described Hinckley as "a beautiful man." Another resident, Joseph Shea, recalled his debt to the Boy Conservation Bureau of E. W. Watkins in New York City. Shea had "thoroughly enjoyed" his years at Good Will Farm, courtesy of a benefactor at the bureau whom he did not meet until after he left the farm. An eight-year-old who had been to five institutions before arriving at "Cap" Bradley's junior republic declared, "Allendale is all right."[40] There was thus much of which turn-of-the-century child savers could be proud.

Years later, in 1938, Allendale Farm paid respects to Edward Bradley, who had died in an automobile accident. Numerous visitors and one hundred current residents gathered under a bright September sun in front of a wreath-covered monument. They stood solemnly for "Taps." The president of the Bradley Club (and one of the farm's first generation) spoke for "the sons of Allendale" and addressed "Cap" as if he were indeed present for the occasion: "Your real memorial is the spirit and soul of Allendale that goes marching on."[41]

To later generations, jaded and cynical, such tributes perhaps seemed effusive, as embarrassingly sentimental as had been the sending of rocks from miles around to place on John Gunckel's monument in Toledo several decades earlier. No doubt Allendale Farm, Good Will Farm, the Toledo Newsboys' Association, the Ford Republic, the orphanages of the National Benevolent Association, the Home Society movement, and numerous other turn-of-the-century examples of child rescue work were flawed. Nevertheless, in many respects they represented some of that era's finest achievements.

Notes

•

Chapter 1

1. Lillian Cousins, "The Fox Valley's Best Crop—Happy, Well-Trained Boys," *Fox Valley Free Press* (March-April 1954); quote from Edward Yeomans's guest foreword to Edward L. Bradley and Maud Menefee Bradley, *Allendale Annals* (Lake Villa, Ill.: Allendale Press, 1926), 3. Hereafter cited as *Annals*. Located some 50 miles north of Chicago, Allendale still maintains a rural setting. It is now called the Allendale School for Boys.

2. On Ogden, Milwaukee *Journal*, 21 April 1974. On her early support for a farm school "where grossly neglected boys might justly be sent until good habits are formed," see Ogden, "The Mission of Probation," *Wisconsin Children's Home Finder* 3 (Jan. 1902): 9. The Wisconsin Home and Farm School was located initially near Delafield, but moved in 1905 to Dousman. Ogden's handwritten minutes of board meetings 2 Feb. 1903, to 27 Dec. 1904, Wisconsin Home and Farm School Papers (at the institution, now known as Lad Lake).

3. Ben Lindsey to A. P. Bourland, 12 April 1906, Benjamin B. Lindsey Papers (Library of Congress, Washington, D.C.), Box 7.

4. Robert H. Wiebe, *The Search for Order, 1877–1920* (New York: Hill and Wang, 1967), develops this theme.

5. See, e.g., David J. Rothman, *Conscience and Convenience: The Asylum and Its Alternatives in Progressive America* (Boston: Little, Brown, 1980), 43–59.

6. The phrase is Richard Hofstadter's. *Anti-Intellectualism in American Life* (New York: Knopf, Random House, 1966), 363.

7. For a brief overview of some of the recent historiographical debate on the history of the family, see Lise Vogel, "The Contested Domain: A Note on the Family in the Transition to Capitalism," *Marxist Perspectives* 1 (Spring 1978): 50–73. On the growing "cult of childhood," Susan Tiffin, *In Whose Best Interest? Child Welfare Reform in the Progressive Era* (West-

port, Conn.: Greenwood Press, 1982), 15–33; George K. Behlmer, "The Child Protection Movement in England, 1860–1890" (Ph.D. diss., Stanford University, 1977); Lamar T. Empey, "The Progressive Legacy and the Concept of Childhood," in Empey, ed., *Juvenile Justice: The Progressive Legacy and Current Reforms* (Charlottesville: University of Virginia Press, 1979), 10–25; and T. J. Jackson Lears, *No Place of Grace: Antimodernism and the Transformation of American Culture, 1880–1920* (New York: Pantheon Books, 1981), 144–46, provide convenient syntheses of a burgeoning literature. Behlmer, "The Child Protection Movement in England," 132–33, and Keith Thomas, "The Beast in Man," *New York Review of Books*, 30 April 1981, 47, note the possibility that the economic marginality of children encouraged more indulgent views of them. Thomas writes that just as "middle classes regarded animals as pets, to be maintained for emotional gratification, not for economic purposes," so too did "indulgent attitudes to children become more widespread when child labor ceased to be an economic necessity."

8. Robert E. McGlone, "Suffer the Children: The Emergence of Modern Middle-Class Family Life in America, 1820–1870" (Ph.D. diss., University of California, Los Angeles, 1971) summarizes many of these trends. On the cult of domesticity and the true woman, see Barbara Welter, "The Cult of True Womanhood, 1820–1860," *American Quarterly* 18 (Summer 1966): 151–74; Barbara J. Berg, *The Remembered Gate: Origins of American Feminism—the Woman and the City, 1800–1860* (New York: Oxford University Press, 1978), 60–94; Carl Degler, *At Odds: Woman and the Family in America from the Revolution to the Present* (New York: Oxford University Press, 1980), 26-38, 52-85; and Kathryn Kish Sklar, *Catherine Beecher: A Study in American Domesticity* (New Haven, Conn.: Yale University Press, 1973). Kirk Jeffries, "The Family as Utopian Retreat from the City: The Nineteenth Century Contribution," *Soundings* 55 (Spring 1972): 21–41; Ronald Walters, "The Family and Ante-bellum Reform: An Interpretation," *Societas* 3 (Summer 1973): 221–32; Christopher Lasch, *Haven in a Heartless World: The Family Besieged* (New York: Basic Books, 1977), 4–8, and Lears, *No Place of Grace*, 15–17, are useful on the family. On the discovery of the child within the larger social and cultural context of nineteenth-century America, see Joseph M. Hawes, *Children in Urban Society: Juvenile Delinquency in Nineteenth-Century America* (New York: Oxford University Press, 1971); John Demos and Virginia Demos, "Adolescence in Historical Perspective," *Journal of Marriage and the Family* 31 (Nov. 1969), 632–38; and Degler, *At Odds*, 86–110. Ann Douglas, *The Feminization of American Culture* (New York: Knopf, 1977), discusses the

Victorian ideal of womanhood and the sentimentalized fictional child; for Litle Eva, see pp. 3–5, and Elsie Dinsmore, p. 72.

9. Joseph F. Kett, "Adolescence and Youth in Nineteenth-Century America," *Journal of Interdisciplinary History* 2 (Autumn 1971): 283–98; Kett, *Rites of Passage: Adolescence in America, 1790 to the Present* (New York: Basic Books, 1977), 62–211; David I. Macleod, "Good Boys Made Better: The Boy Scouts of America, Boys' Brigades, and YMCA Boy's Work, 1880–1920" (Ph.D. diss., University of Wisconsin, 1973); and regarding the antimodernist response and its importance for the strenuosity cult and the celebration of childhood vitality, Lears, *No Place of Grace*, esp. 27–47, 107–17, 142–49. See also Michael Katz, "Origins of the Institutional State," *Marxist Perspectives* 1 (Winter 1978): esp. 18.

10. E. E. Butterfield, "Citizen Building," *Juvenile Court Record* 12 (April 1911): 3.

11. Riis is quoted in a pamphlet, "The White Door Settlement" (c. 1906), Lindsey Papers, Box 8.

12. For the importance of children to progressive reformers, see Sheila Rothman, *Woman's Proper Place: A History of Changing Ideals and Practices, 1870 to the Present* (New York: Basic Books, 1978), 98; Steven L. Schlossman and Ronald D. Cohen, "The Music Man in Gary: Willis Brown and Child-Saving in the Progressive Era," *Societas* 7 (Winter 1977): 2. Walter Trattner, *From Poor Law to Welfare State*, 2nd ed. (New York: Free Press, 1979), 93–113, 117–89, and Elvena B. Tillman, "The Rights of Childhood: The National Child Welfare Movement, 1890–1919" (Ph.D. diss., University of Wisconsin, 1968), provide helpful overviews. In England, also, the issue of children's rights became "a major public preoccupation" in the late 1800s; see Behlmer, "The Child Protection Movement in England," 10, 136, 139.

13. Thomas L. Philpott, *The Slum and the Ghetto: Neighborhood Deterioration and Middle-Class Reform, Chicago, 1880–1930* (New York: Oxford University Press, 1978), 40–41.

14. Regarding progressive historiography, see David M. Kennedy, "Overview: The Progressive Era," *Historian* 37 (May 1975): 453–68; Arthur S. Link and Richard L. McCormick, *Progressivism* (Arlington Heights, Ill.: Harlan Davidson, 1983). Reform coalitions are prominent in David P. Thelen, *The New Citizenship: Origins of Progressivism in Wisconsin, 1885–1900* (Columbia: University of Missouri Press, 1972), and John D. Buenker's essay in Buenker, John C. Burnham, and Robert M. Crunden, *Progressivism* (Cambridge, Mass.: Schenkman, 1977), 42–59, 122–23.

15. For examples of tensions within progressivism, see David P. Thelen,

Robert La Follette and the Insurgent Spirit (Boston: Little, Brown, 1976), esp. 25–26, 50–51, 70–76, 83, 104–17; Thelen, "Collectivism, Economic and Political: Ben Lindsey against Corporate Liberalism," *Reviews in American History* 1 (June 1973): 271–76; Samuel Haber, *Efficiency and Uplift: Scientific Management in the Progressive Era, 1890–1920* (Chicago: University of Chicago Press, 1964); Jerold S. Auerbach, *Unequal Justice: Lawyers and Social Change in America* (New York: Oxford University Press, 1976), 74–101; and David B. Tyack, *The One Best System: A History of American Education* (Cambridge, Mass.: Harvard University Press, 1974), 126–76.

16. James R. McGovern, "David Graham Phillips and the Virility Impulse of the Progressives," *New England Quarterly* 39 (Sept. 1966): 334–55, and Otis L. Graham, Jr., *An Encore for Reform: The Old Progressives and the New Deal* (New York: Oxford University Press, 1967), 47–48, 84–88, are suggestive regarding this aspect of progressive thought.

17. See John W. Chambers II, *The Tyranny of Change: America in the Progressive Era, 1900–1917* (New York: St. Martin's, 1980), 107–13, 229–50, regarding "progressives as interventionists." The work of the "organizational" school of historiography is relevant here, especially Wiebe, *The Search for Order,* and Samuel P. Hays, *The Response to Industrialism, 1885–1914* (Chicago: University of Chicago Press, 1957).

18. Richard L. McCormick, "The Discovery That Business Corrupts Politics: A Reappraisal of the Origins of Progressivism," *American Historical Review* 86 (April 1981): 247–74, notes, e.g., that "often the results the progressives achieved were unexpected and ironical; and, along the way, crucial roles were sometimes played by men and ideas that, in the end, met defeat."

19. "Probation Work," *Juvenile Court Record* 10 (Sept. 1909): 8.

20. On the importance of voluntarism in the progressive era, Kenneth L. Kusmer, "The Functions of Organized Charity in the Progressive Era: Chicago as a Case Study," *Journal of American History* 60 (Dec. 1973): 657–78; John Burnham's essay in Buenker, Burnham, and Crunden, *Progressivism,* esp. 12–16; and Chambers, *The Tyranny of Change,* 119–25. Rothman, *Woman's Proper Place,* 63–132; Paul Boyer, *Urban Masses and Moral Order in America, 1820–1920* (Cambridge, Mass.: Harvard University Press, 1978), 162–276; and David J. Pivar, *Purity Crusade: Sexual Morality and Social Control, 1868–1900* (Westport, Conn.: Greenwood Press, 1973), esp. 131–280, convey a sense of the size and diversity of the progressive volunteer organizations.

21. According to Dominick Cavallo, *Muscles and Morals: Organized Playgrounds and Urban Reform, 1880–1920* (Philadelphia: University of

Pennsylvania Press, 1981), 2, "between 1880 and 1920, municipal governments spent over one hundred million dollars for the construction and staffing of organized playgrounds."

22. Mark H. Leff, "Consensus for Reform: The Mothers' Pension Movement in the Progressive Era," *Social Service Review* 47 (Sept. 1973): 397–417; Ellen Ryerson, *The Best-Laid Plans: America's Juvenile Court Experiment* (New York: Hill and Wang, 1978), 37–48; Steven Schlossman, *Love and the American Delinquent: The Theory and Practice of "Progressive" Juvenile Justice, 1825–1920* (Chicago: University of Chicago Press, 1977), 61–62, 180–82 (although Schlossman, p. 191, compares the courts' interventionism to Don Quixote rather than to George Orwell's Big Brother); Anthony M. Platt, *The Child Savers: The Invention of Delinquency* (Chicago: University of Chicago Press, 1969), 141–44; and Rothman, *Conscience and Convenience,* 216–23, 248–56.

23. See chap. 4.

24. Leff, "Consensus for Reform," 403–4; Tiffin, *In Whose Best Interest?* 126–29.

25. Hastings H. Hart, *Preventive Treatment of Neglected Children* (Philadelphia: William Fell, 1910), 217.

26. Helpful overviews of the various state systems are in Homer Folks, *The Care of Destitute, Neglected and Delinquent Children* (New York: Macmillan, 1902), esp. 72–114, 150–66; William P. Letchworth, "Dependent Children and Family Homes," *Proceedings of the National Conference of Charities and Correction, Toronto, July 7–14, 1897* (Boston: George Ellis, 1898), 94–105; Tiffin, *In Whose Best Interest?* 190–92

27. On Brace, see Tiffin, *In Whose Best Interest?* 190; for Ohio see Letchworth, "Dependent Children and Family Homes," 100; for Michigan see Folks, *The Care of Destitute, Neglected and Delinquent Children,* 97–99 (although Folks doubted that the Michigan record contrasted greatly in this respect with that of private institutions); on the Massachusetts plan see Hart, *Preventive Treatment of Neglected Children,* 225–26; "What a State Should Do for Its Children," *Survey* 29 (19 Oct. 1912): 64.

28. Thomas M. Mulry, "The Home or the Institution?" *Proceedings of the National Conference on Charities and Correction at the 25th Annual Session Held in New York City, May 18–25, 1898* (Boston: George Ellis, 1899) 362, 365.

29. Department of Commerce, Bureau of the Census, *Benevolent Institutions, 1910* (Washington, D.C.: Government Printing Office, 1913), 158–73. By 1908 there were at least 124 separate boys' clubs in cities across the United States, not counting the Boy Scout organization and its equivalents, or clubs attached either to settlement houses or the YMCA, or those

that had a strong denominational character. "Directory of Street Boys' Clubs," *Work with Boys* 8 (July 1908): 209–14.

30. Several generalizations emerge from the census figures. (1) Before the 1880s, Catholics clearly led the way in opening children's institutions, especially in the East. (2) In the next 30 years, the Catholics' rate of institution building remained strong; but between 1890 and 1910 Protestants set the pace, particularly in the Midwest and South. (3) Prior to the 1880s, institutions that were clearly sectarian—Protestant or Catholic—dominated heavily compared with institutions that claimed no religious sponsorship. (4) During the 1880s the growth rate of religiously affiliated institutions remained basically the same, while there was an upsurge in public institutions, especially in the form of county orphanages and state children's homes. (5) The building of public institutions leveled off in the 1890s, while private institutions—especially with Protestant connections—flourished. (6) By 1910 there were several dozen Jewish orphanages; most were established between 1890 and 1910, largely in the East but several in the Midwest and South. (7) A problem with census listings is that the large number of institutions under "private"—as opposed to specific religious—supervision can be misleading. Many presumably nonsectarian private institutions were actually rooted in Protestant voluntarism. Noted illustrations were Allendale Farm, Good Will Farm, the George Junior Republics, the receiving homes of the Children's Home Societies, and various local aid societies. *Benevolent Institutions, 1910,* 86–157.

31. Ibid. The 1910 census did not provide any clues as to how many orphanages from the pre-Civil War days had failed to survive into the twentieth century. Of those institutions for dependent children that emerged before 1870 and were still in operation by 1910, the chronological breakdown was as follows: 22 founded before 1820, 8 in the 1820s, 40 in the 1830s, 35 in the 1840s, 82 in the 1850s, and 108 in the 1860s.

32. Thomas E. Williams, "The Dependent Child in Mississippi: A Social History, 1900–1972" (Ph.D. diss., Ohio State University, 1976), 9–18.

33. The peak years were 1893 (32), 1898 (29), 1899 (28), 1900 (30). *Benevolent Institutions, 1910,* 86–157. These figures do not include institutions for both adults and children, such as the Florence Crittenton Mission homes or those for impoverished widows and their offspring.

34. Leonard Benedict, *Waifs of the Slums and Their Way Out* (New York: Revell, 1907), 23. In the words of a Chicago detective, the children who most deserved pity were "those who have father and mother and who are orphans nevertheless." "Does A Large City Breed Its Own Criminals?" *Juvenile Court Record* 12 (March 1911): 2.

35. *Christian Philanthropist* 24 (Sept. 1917): 72; "Detention Place for

Children," *Charities* 13 (12 Nov. 1904): 168–69; M. A. Covington, "The Child Welfare Problem and a State Program Therefor," *Proceedings of the Seventh Session of the State Conference of Charities and Correction, Centralia, Washington, June 2, 3, 4, 1914* (Centralia, Wash.: Hub Printing, 1914), 49–51; J. P. Dysart, *Grace Porter: A Jewel Lost and Found* (Milwaukee: published by the author, 1899), 133.

36. Rothman, *Conscience and Convenience*, 215. Invariably, state statutes prescribed that juvenile courts would deal with dependent, neglected, and delinquent youths. For specific figures of the categories of youths at particular times in the Chicago, Kansas City, and Philadelphia courts, see Annual Report, Chicago Juvenile Court, *Juvenile Court Record* 7 (Sept. 1906): 6; E. E. Porterfield, "Citizen Building," *Juvenile Court Record* 12 (April 1911): 3; "Philadelphia's Juvenile Court," *Charities* 8 (7 June 1902): 506–7.

37. The *Record* (published by the Chicago Visitation and Aid Society) appeared in the early 1900s and quickly gained a circulation of 35,000. William Byron Forbush to Homer Lane, 22 Sept. 1909, Ford Republic Papers (Collections of the Archives of Labor History and Urban Affairs, University Archives, Wayne State University). The *Record* disseminated "news and ideas helpful to such Handicapped, Dependent and Delinquent Children as come before the Juvenile Courts."

38. *Juvenile Court Record* 10 (Aug. 1909): 6.

39. According to one argument, ragged children saw "any man of good standing in the community" as "a model." "Are You a Big Brother?" *Juvenile Court Record* 8 (Aug. 1910): 7; printed again in 10 (Oct. 1912): 3. "The Big Brothers Movement," *Work with Boys* 8 (April 1908): 108–16, includes "Suggestions to Big Brothers."

40. Charles F. Ernst, "The Caddy Scheme as One Solution to the Summer Problem," *Work with Boys* 12 (April 1912): 201–7; Charles C. Keith, "The Caddie Camp," *Work with Boys* 14 (Oct. 1914): 319–24. According to Ernst, the South End House Settlement in Boston had by 1907 established a program to send young caddies to the Bretton Woods golf links, also in the White Mountains.

41. William P. Letchworth, *Homes of Homeless Children* (n.p., 1903), 20, 72–78—a reissue of his 1875–76 reports on orphans and paupers.

42. "Purity Industrial Home" pamphlet sent to Ben Lindsey, 19 June 1905, Lindsey Papers, Box 4.

43. Pamphlet on Good Will Institute in Lindsey Papers, Box 13; article on Buzzell's organizing efforts in Nashua (New Hampshire) *Telegraph*, 31 Oct. 1913, reprinted in *Good Will Record* 26 (Dec. 1913): 339. (Although G. W. Hinckley, founder of Good Will Farm in Maine, "heartily" endorsed

Buzzell's plan and believed the New Hampshire minister was "doing excellent work," he worried that people might confuse Buzzell's project with his own. On Hinckley and Good Will Farm, see chap. 6.)

44. Josie Dayton Curtiss, *The Defenseless Child* (Elgin, Ill.: Brethren, 1912), esp. 7–11, 33, 44–73. Curtiss Place was located in Marengo, Ill.

45. For an example of someone who did, however, see Byron C. Mathews, "The Duty of the State to Dependent Children," *Proceedings of the National Conference of Charities and Correction at the 25th Annual Session Held in New York City, May 18–25, 1898* (Boston: George Ellis, 1899), 373–74. Mathews, convinced that a majority of children were dependent because of "the ignorance, shiftlessness, or immorality of their parents," advocated stricter marriage laws that would "diminish the legalized propagation of paupers."

46. Pamphlet, "The Hershey Industrial School, Its Situation, Plan, and Requirements of Admission," Archives, Milton Hershey School (Hershey, Pa.). Hershey is quoted in Roy Bongartz, "The Chocolate Camelot," *American Heritage* 24 (June 1973): 92. On the importance of industrial training in many institutions, see Platt, *The Child Savers*, 59–60. The metaphor in one book on child rescue work was all too apt: " 'Industrial training is the key that is to unlock the street-boy problem,' and here tough boys are being 'put upon the anvil and hammered into shape.' " Benedict, *Waifs of the Slums*, 34.

47. Report of the Superintendent, 19 Nov. 1903, Wisconsin Home and Farm School Papers (the superintendent was James Melville, but the report was written in Marion Ogden's hand); "Safety First," *Our Boys* 8 (July 1914): 7; "He Saved the Flag," *Our Boys* 9 (July 1916): 6. At Lad Lake there is a fairly complete run of the early issues of this monthly publication of the farm school.

48. *Our Boys* 13 (Oct. 1913): 13.

49. "Allendale Farm Residents. Being the Record of Boys Resident in Allendale Farm, Lake Villa, Illinois, Together with Certain Views of Their Home and Home Life" (c. 1916), C. B. entry. This document is at the Allendale School for Boys. Hereafter cited as "Record," with initials indicating the specific entry.

50. On the Ford Republic, see chap. 5.

51. Jack M. Holl, *Juvenile Reform in the Progressive Era: William R. George and the Junior Republic Movement* (Ithaca, N.Y.: Cornell University Press, 1971); for George's own account, see *The Junior Republic: Its History and Ideals* (New York: Appleton, 1909).

52. George to E. Molenaar, 23 Aug. 1909, William R. George Papers (Olin Research Library, Cornell University), Box 5; Report for the National

Junior Republic Association, 1908, Box 4; George to Edward Lissner, 21 April 1911, Box 8, Judge Albert Matthewson to George, 27 July 1909, Box 5.

53. "Georgia to Have Juvenile State," *Charities and the Commons* 20 (25 April 1908): 131; pamphlet, "The Juvenile Protective Association: The Junior State" (c. 1910), George Papers, Box 78; and George to Frederick Almy, 29 Aug. 1910, Box 7.

54. George to Hastings H. Hart, 5 May 1910, George Papers, Box 7.

55. Bradley to Ben Lindsey, 29 April 1909, Lindsey Papers, Box 20.

56. *Benevolent Institutions, 1910,* 98–99; copy of letter from Julian W. Mack to George Higginson, Jr., president of the Allendale Association, 20 Nov. 1906, in "Record."

57. *Annals,* 8, 11, 65; "Record," R. F. entry.

58. "Record," passim; *Annals,* 13–14. On George's "Nothing Without Labor" policy, see George, *The Junior Republic,* 19–36; Holl, "Juvenile Reform in the Progressive Era, 4–6, 94–101.

59. *Annals,* 14–15; "Record," R. F. and G. C. entries.

60. George to Weber B. Kuenzel, 4 June 1910, George Papers, Box 7; Bradley to Ben Lindsey, 5 and 29 April 1909, Lindsey Papers, Box 20.

61. Julius F. Wengierski to Ben Lindsey, 26 Aug. 1907, and clipping from the Rockford *Daily Republic,* 13 Aug. 1907, Lindsey Papers, Box 10. A year later, Wengierski was caring for seven boys, ages 11 to 18; but he was struggling to keep the Winnebago Farm School afloat financially. He did not make clear whether he was in fact trying to run a junior republic with the seven youths. Wengierski to Lindsey, 20 July 1908, Box 16.

62. Lindsey to Bradley, 20 May 1909, Lindsey Papers, Box 20; Albert Matthewson to William R. George, 12 July 1909, George Papers, Box 5, and Harold Stephens to George, 1 June 1910, Box 7; Wisconsin Home and Farm School's Second Annual Report for Year Ending November 17, 1904, p. 10; "Fostering a Great Idea," *Our Boys* 4 (Jan. 1910): 10; *Our Boys* 11 (Oct. 1917): 18.

63. See chap. 4 on the Toledo Newsboys' Association.

64. Pamphlets, "Boys' Brotherhood Republic," and the "Constitution of the Boys' Brotherhood Republic," George Papers, Box 78; James E. Rogers, "'The State of Columbia' A Junior Republic," *Charities* 12 (5 March 1904): 245–50. See also Schlossman and Cohen, "The Music Man in Gary," 8, for information on Boy City, another summer camp along junior republic lines, located on Winona Lake in Indiana and subsequently moved to Charlevois, Mich. Boy City was a creation of the controversial child saver, Willis Brown. See "As to Judge Willis Brown," *Juvenile Court Record* 11 (Feb. 1910): 5. On Tacoma, F. S. D. Hughes to Esther B. George (c. 1909), George Papers, Box 5.

65. Robert M. Mennel, "'The Family System of Common Farmers': The Origins of Ohio's Reform Farm, 1840–1858," *Ohio History* 89 (Spring 1980): 125–56; "'The Family System of Common Farmers': The Early Years of Ohio's Reform Farm, 1858–1884," *Ohio History* 89 (Summer 1980): 279–322. On Townsend's home, which operated from 1863 to 1868, see Marcella C. Fisher, "The Orphan's Friend: Charles Collins Townsend and the Orphan's Home of Industry," *Palimpsest* 60 (Nov./Dec. 1979), 185–96.

66. See, e.g., Wayne Fuller, "The Rural Roots of the Progressive Leaders," *Agricultural History* 42 (Jan. 1968): 1–13. William L. Bowers, *The Country Life Movement in America, 1900–1920* (Port Washington, N.Y.: Kennikat Press, 1974), 34–40, discusses several reasons why country life appealed to many reformers.

67. Lyman Beecher Stowe, "Training City Boys for Country Life," *Outlook* 102 (9 and 16 Nov. 1912): 537–41, 584–91.

68. See the list of farm schools in *Work with Boys* 8 (July 1908): 202; pamphlet, "Are Boys Worth Saving?" (on Lake Farm), Lindsey Papers, Box 21; Oscar L. Dudley, "Saving the Children: Sixteen Years' Work Among the Dependent Youth of Chicago" (on the Illinois School at Glenwood), *Report of Committee on Child Saving, 1893,* 108–15; Arthur H. Shaw, "The Boys' Farm at Hudson," *Work with Boys* 12 (Sept. 1912): 395–97; George E. Marx, "Charlton Industrial Farm School," *Work with Boys* 12 (Sept. 1912): 368–69; Seymour H. Stone, "The Berkshire Industrial Farm," *Charities* 10 (7 Feb. 1903): 138–41; pamphlet, "Announcement of Junior Settlement," George Papers, Box 78.

69. "The Farm School Gives the Boys a Chance," *Our Boys* 11 (April 1917): 10–11; "The Hershey Industrial School."

70. Bradley was born in 1861 in Germantown, Pa., to a family which ran a small publishing business. A Princeton graduate, and then choirmaster and organist at St. Paul's Episcopal Church in Chicago, he also attended Western Theological Seminary, an Episcopal institution where he was reportedly not "high church" enough. In 1894 he started taking destitute city boys on summer outings to the northwestern Illinois lakes. *50 Year Record, Class of 1884, Princeton* (Princeton, N.J.: Princeton University Press, 1937), 31–33; *Chicago Tribune,* 28 Nov. 1937; *Who's Who in America, 1936–1937* (Chicago: A. N. Marquis, 1936), 369. For his views on city versus rural life, see "Record," L. J., L. D., N. R. entries.

71. *Annals,* 22, 34, 42.

72. See, e.g., Tiffin, *In Whose Best Interest?* 110–140; Schlossman, *Love and the American Delinquent,* esp. 69–78; Burnham's essay in *Progressivism,* 13; Lary May, *Screening Out the Past: The Birth of Mass Culture and the Motion Picture Industry* (New York: Oxford University Press, 1980),

46–52. A variety of progressive reforms focused on saving the family: antivice and purity campaigns against immorality and disease; labor laws regarding women and children; antiliquor crusades; and home economics programs, for example.

73. Mrs. David O. Mears, "The Home," *First International Congress in America for the Welfare of the Child held under the auspices of the National Congress of Mothers at Washington, D.C., March 10th to 17th, 1908* (National Congress of Mothers, 1908), 147–50; Sheppard's speech, 4 May 1911, quoted in *Good Will Record* 24 (May 1911): 146; on Mother's Day, Peter G. Filene, *Him/Her/Self: Sex Roles in Modern America* (New York: Harcourt, Brace, Jovanovich, 1974–75), 41–42.

74. Christopher Lasch, *Haven in a Heartless World*, 8–10; Filene, *Him/Her/Self*, 41–45; Philip Davis, *Street-Land: Its Little People and Big Problems* (Boston: Small, Maynard, 1915), 14; Martina Johnson, "The Child, the Family and the Community," *Proceedings of the Ninth Session of the Washington Conference for Social Welfare (State Conference of Charities and Correction) Walla Walla, June 1, 2, 1916* (Walla Walla, Wash.: Quick Print, 1916), 33–35.

75. "Commencement Day at the School," *Our Boys* 6 (July 1912): 11. "Our inventions multiply our dangers," said an agent of the Minnesota state training school as she described ways in which the bicycle had provided too much mobility for young people. "Too much freedom is allowed to the young in our country—a freedom that, unchecked, leads to license." Grace Johnston, "The Child and the State," *Proceedings of the Eighth Minnesota State Conference of Charities and Correction Held in Duluth, September 4–6, 1899* (St. Paul, Minn.: Pioneer Press, 1899), 65, 67.

76. "Difficulties That Face Us," *Our Boys* 9 (April 1915): 13; "Brief American Childhood," *Our Boys* 11 (April 1917): 11; "The First Juvenile Court," *Our Boys* 6 (April 1913): 8.

77. *Juvenile Court Record* 12 (Dec. 1911): 15; "Commencement Day at the School," *Our Boys* (July 1912): 9–10; "Record," H. P. entry. Another child saver estimated that in nine of ten cases a child received better care in an institution than "in the home of its parents." Rev. Samuel Langer, "A Defense of the Institution," *Charities* 8 (1 March 1902): 203.

78. Actually, by 1880, a majority of institutions housed fewer than 50 children, and the average was 42. Tiffin, *In Whose Best Interest?* 66.

79. "Echo Hills," *Charities* (2 May 1903): 441.

80. Matron's Diary, Children's Home of Detroit, 13 Feb. 1894, to 4 Aug. 1896, vol. D5, Children's Home of Detroit Papers (Burton Historical Collection, Detroit Public Library). Originally known as the Ladies Orphan Association of Detroit, the institution in 1889 became the Protestant

Orphan Asylum of Detroit. See "Memorial Minutes, Founders Day, May 17, 1900," Box 3, and *Year-Book of the Protestant Orphan Asylum of Detroit, Michigan, 1903*, Box 4. In 1932 the institution became the Children's Home of Detroit.

81. Mabel Potter Daggett, "Where 100,000 Wait," *Delineator* 72 (Nov. 1908): 773–76, 858–61.

82. "Record," E. I., L. R., A. K., and H. K. entries; *Annals*, 22, 54; *Allendale Alumnus* (May, Aug., Oct., Christmas 1926; April, May, Nov., Christmas 1927; Jan., Feb., March, April, May–June 1928; Spring, 1929). The *Alumnus* was published at the Allendale Press. Copies at the Allendale School for Boys. "Record," copy of T. H. Bushnell to Bradley, 10 Dec. 1906.

83. Holl, *Juvenile Reform in the Progressive Era*, ix–xi, 242–43, 247–56, 283–84; pamphlet, "Wisconsin Home and Farm School for Neglected, Destitute, Homeless and Orphan Boys" (1903), 9, Lad Lake Papers; typed ms. of Guy C. Weber (c. 1949), Archives, Hershey Industrial School.

84. Holl, *Juvenile Reform in the Progressive Era*, applies this concept to the Freeville republic.

85. R. R. Reeder, "Good Citizens from Institutional Children," *Charities* 11 (15 Aug. 1903): 147–54; "Echo Hills," 441–44; "An Orphanage and Its Vision," *Charities and the Commons* 17 (Oct. 1906–April 1907): 291–96; *Charities* 15 (7 Oct. 1905): 5–6; H. L. Crumley, "The Orphan Children of Georgia," *Charities* 10 (6 June 1903): 566.

86. "Record," passim; on Good Will Farm, see chap. 6.

87. Tiffin, *In Whose Best Interest?* 88–109, describes early home placement strategies.

88. Alden Fearing, "A Home and a Chance in Life," *World's Work*, 28 (June 1914): 193. On the home-finding movement, see chap. 2.

89. U.S. Congress, Senate, *Proceedings of the Conference on the Care of Dependent Children, held at Washington, D.C., January 25–29, 1909*, 60th Cong., 2d sess., S. Doc. 721 (Washington, D.C.: Government Printing Office, 1909), passim.

90. Letters from W. B. Sherrard and C. E. Lukens, *Delineator* 72 (Oct. 1908): 578–79; Mathews, "The Duty of the State to Dependent Children," 370–71.

91. For a good example of "mutual antagonism" between institutional and family defenders, see the heated debate following Rev. H. P. Nichols's talk on "Cooperation between Child-Saving Agencies," *Proceedings of the Fifth Minnesota State Conference of Charities and Correction Held in Red Wing, November 17–19, 1896* (St. Paul, Minn.: Pioneer Press, 1897), 37–48.

92. One study of the family backgrounds of dependent children in New York, Minnesota, Michigan, and Missouri concluded that by 1912 in well

over 40 percent of the cases, both parents were living; more than 40 percent of the other cases involved half-orphans. The actual percentage of real orphans was quite small—6 percent or less in Minnesota and Michigan, for example. In cases where both parents were still living, they were usually separated—by divorce, desertion, imprisonment, or illness. Sherman C. Kingsley, "The Dependent Child of Today," *Proceedings of the 22nd Minnesota State Conference of Charities and Correction Held at Minneapolis, October 25-28, 1913* (Stillwater, Minn.: Prison Mirror, 1914), 44–45.

93. Mrs. A. R. Colvin, "The Orphan Asylum," *Proceedings of the Thirteenth Minnesota State Conference of Charities and Correction Held at Faribault, November 16–18, 1904* (Stillwater, Minn.: Prison Mirror, 1905), 32–33. In another instance, at the Central Baptist Home in Chicago, the separated parents of a boy in the institution "met in the orphanage, and wept over the situation of their affairs." James P. Thomas, Superintendent, to Board of Directors, 20 Jan. 1909, Scrapbook, Central Baptist Children's Home Papers (Department of Special Collections, Chicago Circle Library of the University of Illinois).

94. William P. Letchworth, "Dependent Children and Family Homes," 103–4. Sarah R. Morris, "Work of the Protestant Orphan Asylum of St. Paul," *Proceedings of the Third Minnesota State Conference of Charities and Correction Held in St. Paul, January 14–16, 1895* (St. Paul, Minn.: Pioneer Press, 1895), 123–26, noted that in 29 years the St. Paul asylum had placed nearly 200 of 1,000 children.

95. See, e.g., Sherman Kingsley, "Child-Saving and the Standards of the Naturalist," *Charities* (10 Dec. 1904): 277–78. Some defenders of asylums, especially those with church affiliation, also expressed concern that home placement too often gave inadequate attention to proper religious instruction. Tiffin, *In Whose Best Interest?* 98.

96. Pamphlet of Wisconsin Home and Farm School (c. 1908), Lindsey Papers, Box 16.

97. On Dysart, ibid.; on Hall, see, "In Memoriam, Bert Hall, 1863–1933," *Our Boys* 27 (July 1933): 3–20; on Titsworth, ibid. 13 (May 1919): 8.

98. Hasting Hart's comments, *Proceedings of the Tenth Minnesota State Conference of Charities and Correction Held at Owatonna, November 19–21, 1901* (Stillwater, Minn.: Prison Mirror, 1902), 54.

99. Ibid.; "Whatever America may mean, it must be made to mean 'a square deal' to every child"—*21st Fractional Biennial Report of the Board of State Commissioners of Public Charities of the State of Illinois* (Springfield: Illinois State Journal, 1909), 658; Samuel McCune Lindsay, "Exploring the New World for Children," *Proceedings of the Child Conference for Research and Welfare Held at Clark University, 1909*, I (New York: G. E.

Stechert, 1910), 139; "The Children's Age," *Charities* 10 (16 May 1903): 501.

100. "Charlton Industrial Farm School," *Work with Boys* 12 (Sept. 1912), 368–73; George W. Wickstrom and Frances Gingerich, *Bethany Home: The Story of a Children's Haven* (privately published, c. 1952), 9–11, 48–51.

101. Pamphlets, "The Baby Fold: An Investment in Humanity" (1950, 1965); "Report of Inspection of Orphanages, Boarding Homes for Children and Maternity Homes," 3 March 1915—a 16-page report of the state visitation agency concerning the Baby Fold (copy in possession of the Baby Fold); interviews with Rev. William H. Hammitt, 27 April, 25 May, and 15 June 1972.

102. Rev. J.W. Gormley, *History of Father Dunne's News Boys' Home and Protectorate* (St. Louis: Father Dunne's News Boys, n.d.), 13–60; I. T. Martin, "'Little Jimmie,' Our First News Boy," reprinted in a special number of *Father Dunne's News Boys' Journal* (1919), 15–16, and Jean Peter Fleming to Dunne, 13 Dec. 1918, reprinted in *Father Dunne's News Boys' Journal* (1919), 7; Mary Barrett, "Home for Orphans for Half a Century," St. Louis *Globe-Democrat Magazine*, 5 Feb. 1966, 5–6. The home admitted boys without regard to race or creed. Indeed, of its 784 residents from 1906 to 1910, 238 were non-Catholics. "Financial Statement of Father Dunne's News Boys' Home and Protectorate from Time of Establishment February 6th, 1906 to February 1st, 1910." The figures for 1913 are in the "Seventh Annual Report, February 1, 1912 to February 1, 1913." Dunne very much sought to provide an anti-institutional atmosphere. According to one observer, the home was the "very antithesis of the old iron-bounded institution that dates centuries back. . . . The Home is in reality a home." William S. Bowdern, "An Unconventional Orphanage," *Father Dunne's News Boys' Journal* (1919), 1–2. All materials, except for Gormley's book, are in the possession of Father Dunne's Home for Boys. In 1946, Hollywood produced a movie, "Fighting Father Dunne," starring Pat O'Brien.

103. *Annals*, 7, 67.

104. W. B. Sherrard, "The Mission of the National Society," *Wisconsin Children's Home Finder* 1 (Feb. 1900): 7.

105. Edward T. Devine conceded that "modern social work calls for experts," yet warned that there was real danger in crowding out the volunteer. Even in the emerging new age of charity and social work, the voluntary friendly visitor remained in Devine's opinion "the true pioneer." The editor undoubtedly voiced the opinion of many child savers. "The Friendly Visitor," *Charities and the Commons* 21 (21 Nov. 1908): 321–22.

106. *Annals*, 8.

Chapter 2

1. "The Child at the Door," *Minnesota Children's Home Finder* 1 (Jan. 1900): 3. Hereafter cited as *Home Finder*. This and several other issues are in the possession of the Children's Home Society of Minnesota (St. Paul, Minn.).

2. "Children's Home Society Completes Quarter Century," *Charities and the Commons* 8 (18 July 1908): 480.

3. Rev. W. Henry Thompson, "Children and the National Conference of Charities and Corrections," *Juvenile Court Record* 7 (June 1906): 26–28.

4. Henry W. Thurston, *The Dependent Child: A Story of Changing Aims and Methods in the Care of Dependent Children* (New York: Columbia University Press, 1930), 92–140; Miriam Langsam, *Children West: A History of the Placing Out System of the New York Children's Aid Society* (Madison: University of Wisconsin Press, 1964). The exact number of children shipped westward is not clear. Brace's organization also sent older children to the country to work for wages and helped persons in poor families obtain rural employment. One source said that by 1914 the total number for the Children's Aid Society was over 116,000. Alden Fearing, "A Home and a Chance in Life," *World's Work* 28 (June 1914): 192–94. For a view of the Children's Aid Society from the perspective of one of its workers, see George C. Needham's impassioned book, *Street Arabs and Gutter Snipes* (Boston: D. L. Guernsey, 1884), esp, 237–81, 306–32, 409–12. The idea of placing city children in the countryside was not unique to the United States. England transplanted many street children to Canada, Australia, and South Africa. Regarding Brace, see Paul Boyer, *Urban Masses and Moral Order in America, 1820–1920* (Cambridge, Mass.: Harvard University Press, 1978), 94–107; Thomas Bender, *Toward an Urban Vision: Ideas and Institutions in Nineteenth-Century America* (Lexington: University Press of Kentucky, 1975), 131–57.

5. Jacob Riis, *The Children of the Poor* (New York: Scribner, 1892), 250–52.

6. Thurston, *The Dependent Child*, 141–45, and E. P. Savage, "The Origin, Early History and Spread of the Children's Home Society," an address delivered at the National Conference of the Children's Home Society at St. Louis, 21 Sept. 1904, and reprinted in *Home Finder* 5 (Nov. 1904): 7–8. Hereafter cited as Savage, "Early History." Where and by what means Van Arsdale gained custody of the children is not clear.

7. Thurston, *The Dependent Child*, 146–48. The initial name, "The American Educational Aid Society," pointed up Van Arsdale's hope of helping not only orphans but working-class girls, whom he wanted to

provide with a college education. While eventually the Van Arsdales did aid 28 girls in this manner, the major thrust of their work concerned placing dependent children with families. Given this primary interest, the subsequent shift in the organization's name was natural. For a brief discussion of Van Arsdale's unsuccessful effort in Missouri, see Savage, "Early History," 10–11, and Savage, "The Evolution of the Children's Aid Society," undated, typed manuscript in the Edward P. Savage Papers (Minnesota Historical Society), Box 1.

8. St. Paul *Pioneer Press*, 2 March 1921; Minneapolis *Tribune*, 2 March 1921. Savage and his father's Record & Sermon Book, Children's Home Society of Minnesota Papers (held by the society and hereafter cited as MHSP), gives some clues as to where the family lived in the early years. On Savage's Civil War experiences, see his alumni speech in the *University of Chicago Magazine* 10 (July 1918): 336–37; clipping in Savage Papers, Box 1; and his typed comments at the 13 Feb. 1907 dinner, MHSP.

9. Quoted in Rev. S. W. Dickinson, "History of the Children's Home Society of Minnesota, 1889–1927," a typed manuscript, MHSP. Dickinson succeeded Savage as superintendent of the society in 1908 and held the position until 1927. He knew Savage well.

10. Savage, "Early History," 9.

11. Quoted in Dickinson, "History of the Children's Home Society of Minnesota."

12. Savage, "The Evolution of the Children's Home Society." Other groups, of course, were also trying to aid dependent children in the state. Prominent among them were two large Catholic orphan asylums in the Twin Cities; Sheltering Arms, an Episcopal home in Minneapolis; the Children's Home in Duluth; and the Protestant Orphan Asylum in St. Paul.

13. Minutes of the Directors' Meetings, 11 Sept. 1889, MHSP (cited hereafter as "Minutes"); Savage, "Early History," 9–12, and "The Evolution of the Children's Home Society." Savage also credited his wife with convincing him that Minnesota should ally with Van Arsdale.

14. Hastings Hart, "The National Children's Home Society," address delivered 20 Sept. 1904 at the annual conference of the Society in St. Louis, reprinted in *Home Finder* 5 (Nov. 1904): 6. Figures for the year ending 31 May 1900 are in *Wisconsin Children's Home Finder* 1 (July 1900): 9. By then, the Minnesota Society was also fifth in terms of cash received for the year: Illinois, $31,643; Iowa, $17,720; Missouri, $14,212; Wisconsin, $12,911; Minnesota, $10,428. Most of the other state organizations were under the $5,000 mark. Early issues of the Wisconsin publication for several brief periods are in the possession of the Children's Service Society of Wisconsin (formerly, the Children's Home Society of Wisconsin) in Mil-

waukee. In 1897 the National Children's Home Society established a policy of representation at national meetings whereby each state organization received one at-large delegate plus additional delegates for every 50 children placed in homes over the preceding year. By this formula, Minnesota that year had three delegates. "Minutes," 13 May 1897.

15. W. B. Sherrard, "The Mission of the National Society," *Wisconsin Children's Home Finder* 1 (Feb. 1900): 7–8. Regarding progressive reform efforts to establish uniform national standards within a state-centered system, see William Graebner, "Federalism in the Progressive Era: A Structural Interpretation of Reform," *Journal of American History* 64 (Sept. 1977): 331–57.

16. Savage, "Early History," 9–10. For a short sketch of the Chicago troubles in the early 1890s, see "Some Chicago Child-Saving History," *Charities* 9 (9 Aug. 1902): 139–41.

17. Gioh-Fang Dju Ma, *One Hundred Years of Public Services for Children in Minnesota* (Chicago: University of Chicago Press, 1948), esp. 10–40, 63–67, and Esther Levin, "Fifty Years of Child Care, Children's Home Society of Minnesota, 1889–1939 (M.A. research project, University of Minnesota, 1939), 8–20, 28–29, are helpful on the legal backdrop and developments. In 1885, Minnesota, like Michigan several years earlier, opened a state public school for dependent children. The school was to provide temporary care until the state could find suitable families for the children, usually through indenture. See, e.g., Gioh-Fang Dju Ma, 36–40.

18. Gioh-Fang Dju Ma, *One Hundred Years of Public Services,* 10–14; Levin, "Fifty Years of Child Care," 85. For a discussion of indenture, free homes, and boarding-out, see Hastings H. Hart, *Preventive Treatment of Neglected Children* (Philadelphia: William Fell, 1910; 1971 reprint, New York: Arno Press, 1971), 225–27.

19. Typed document, "Historical Development of Adoption Agencies," n.d. but probably late 1950s, MHSP. The author may have been George V. Thomson, who served on the Board of Directors of the Children's Home Society from 1925 to 1971. The paper is filed with a copy of Thompson's 1958 speech, "Early History of the Children's Home Society."

20. Levin, "Fifty Years of Child Care," 24–25.

21. W. B. Sherrard, "A Correct View," *Wisconsin Children's Home Finder* 3 (April 1902): 12–13.

22. "Resolutions Passed by the National Children's Home Society, Indianapolis," *Wisconsin Children's Home Finder* 1 (July 1900): 12; Sherrard, "A Correct View," 12–13.

23. "A Remarkable Fact," *Wisconsin Children's Home Finder* 3 (Nov. 1901): 4.

24. *Modern Samaritan* 1 (March 1923): 3 (copy in the Children's Service Society of Wisconsin, Milwaukee); Mary Keith, "The History and Development of the Children's Aid Society of Wisconsin in Relation to State Authority" (M.A. thesis, University of Chicago, 1941), 12–13. Dysart was born in Bovina, New York, in 1841 and graduated from Union College in Schenectady. See also Harold W. Nickerson, "A Bit of History Written in 1894," *Wisconsin Children's Home Finder* 3 (April 1902): 21.

25. J. P. Dysart, *Grace Porter: A Jewel Lost and Found* (Milwaukee: published by the author, 1899). Within the next ten years, the book had a different title and publisher: *Second Hand Children* (Chicago: David R. Blyth n.d.).

26. Quoted in advertisement for *Second Hand Children* in *Juvenile Court Record* 11 (Nov. 1910).

27. Dysart, *Grace Porter*, 8, 54, 76, 99, 114.

28. Ibid., 53–54 on education; 174–76 on nonpartisan experts, rational methods, and optimism; 42–43, 78, on rural living; 76–77 on urban slums; 122–31 on liquor; 128 on the working class; 120 on "this social revolution"; passim regarding the virtues of the family and home placement, and the evils of institutions.

29. Quoted in advertisement in *Juvenile Court Record* 11 (Nov. 1910).

30. See, e.g., Dysart, *Grace Porter*, 36, 62, 70–75, 98–115, 178–83.

31. Titsworth, quoted in advertisement in *Juvenile Court Record* 11 (Nov. 1910). For information on Titsworth, see *Our Boys* 13 (May 1919): 8, copy in possession of Wisconsin Home and Farm School (now known as Lad Lake) in Dousman, Wis.

32. See, e.g., Savage, "Twenty-Five Years of the Work of the Children's Home Society of Minnesota," 3, typed manuscript in Savage Papers, Box 1, and *Home Finder* 2 (July 1901): 14, for flattering comments about Dysart.

33. Journal of the Superintendent, 1893–1898, report for year ending May 1, 1895, p. 68. The journal, comprising Savage's handwritten reports to the board over a five-year period, is in the possession of the Children's Home Society of Minnesota. Hereafter cited as "Journal."

34. Savage, "W. B. Sherrard," undated, typed manuscript in Savage Papers, Box 1. See also Dickinson, "History of the Children's Home Society of Minnesota." The superintendent's reports of the Minnesota Children's Home Society convey a sense of the relentlessness of Savage's schedule, and the rigor with which he struggled to keep pace.

35. Savage to D. R. Noyes, 16 Dec. 1903, Savage Papers, Box 1.

36. "Journal," report for Dec. 1893 to Jan.-Feb., 1894, p. 23; report for 1 June 1893 to 1 June 1894, pp. 32–33; report for quarter ending 1 Nov. 1895, pp. 80–82.

37. "Journal," report for 14 Dec. 1893, p. 15; typed description of the girl in Savage Papers, Box 1; "Journal," report for 14 Sept. 1893, p. 11; report for Sept.-Nov. 1894, p. 47; report for the year ending 1 May 1895, p. 65.

38. *Home Finder* 1 (Nov. 1899): 6.

39. "Some Reminiscences by Rev. E. P. Savage of the Children's Home Society," Savage Papers, Box 1; "Journal," report for 14 Sept. 1893, p. 12.

40. "Journal," report for Dec.-Jan. 1894–95, p. 57.

41. Quoted in "Historical Development of Adoption Agencies," MHSP.

42. On siblings, see, e.g., "Journal," report for Sept.-Nov. 1894, p. 48; other examples in letters to Savage, 28 Jan. 1901, 16 Jan. 1900, 12 Dec. 1900, 16 May 1901, and 12 July 1903, MHSP.

43. "Journal," report for quarter ending 1 Nov. 1895, pp. 85–87.

44. "Journal," report for Sept.-Nov. 1894, p. 46, and for Dec.-Jan. 1894–95, pp. 55, 57; "Historical Development of Adoption Agencies," MHSP.

45. Ellen Thompson's typed comments on the 13 Feb. 1907 dinner and handwritten statement, 1902, MHSP; "His Reward," *Home Finder* 2 (July 1901): 7–8.

46. *Home Finder* 5 (Nov. 1904): 4–5; "Journal," report for quarter ending 1 Aug. 1895; *Home Finder* 2 (July 1901): 8–9, 11; A. H. Tebbets, "*Service*, A New Years' [*sic*] Homily," 1 Jan. 1907, typed manuscript in Savage Papers, Box 1; *Home Finder* 2 (July 1901): 11.

47. "Journal," report for 1 June 1893 to 1 June 1894, p. 33; report for quarter ending 1 May 1895, pp. 62–63; report for quarter ending 1 Aug. 1895, p. 72; E. P. Savage, "Desertion by Parents," *Proceedings of the National Conference of Charities and Correction at the 22nd Annual Session Held in the City of New Haven, May 24–30, 1895* (Boston: George Ellis, 1895), pp. 213–15.

48. Unidentified clipping (1907), Savage Papers, Box 1. The law subsequently changed to a weaker version which Savage understood was worthless.

49. Savage's comments, *Proceedings of the Sixth Minnesota State Conference of Charities and Correction Held in St. Cloud, November 3–5, 1897* (St. Paul, Minn.: Pioneer Press, 1898), p. 82; Savage, "An Education Which Will Tend More to Lessen Pauperism and Crime—From the Viewpoint of Work for Dependent Children," *Proceedings of the Sixteenth Minnesota State Conference of Charities and Correction Held at Fergus Falls, November 9–12, 1907* (Stillwater, Minn.: Mirror Print, 1908), p. 42.

50. Typed comments delivered to the state legislature in 1907, Savage Papers, Box 1.

51. Savage to Theodore Roosevelt, 19 March 1907, and typed comments delivered to the state legislature in 1907, Savage Papers, Box 1. See also

typed comments delivered at 13 Feb. 1907 dinner, MHSP. Timberlake had moved from his native state of Indiana to Minneapolis in 1883, when he entered the insurance business. From 1897 to 1899 he was deputy state insurance commissioner. *The Legislative Manual of the State of Minnesota Compiled for the Legislature of 1907.*

52. Typed comments delivered to the state legislature in 1907, Savage Papers, Box 1.

53. Savage to Theodore Roosevelt, 19 March 1907, Savage Papers, Box 1; "Some Facts," a public statement, early 1907, signed by Savage and seven other individuals, Savage Papers, Box 1. Emphasis added.

54. Unidentified clippings (1907), Savage Papers, Box 1; Savage to Theodore Roosevelt, 19 March 1907, Savage Papers, Box 1. See also typed comments delivered at 13 Feb. 1907 dinner, MHSP.

55. See, e.g., typed comments, "A Law That Will Save Many Lives and Much Wealth" (1907), Savage Papers, Box 1.

56. Mabel Potter Daggett, "The Child without a Home," *Delineator* 70 (Oct. 1907): 505–10; Lydia Kingsmill Commander, "The Home Without a Child," *Delineator* 70 (Nov. 1907): 720–23, 830, and "The Delineator Child-Rescue Campaign," 715–19. The *Delineator* was a Butterick publication that had previously focused on women's fashion but in the early twentieth century began to probe social issues. On the journal's child rescue campaign, see Elvena B. Tillman, "The Rights of Childhood: The National Child Welfare Movement" (Ph.D. diss., University of Wisconsin, 1968), 114–29.

57. *Delineator* 71 (Jan. 1908): 97–98; *Delineator* 72 (Nov. 1908): 773–76, 781–82, 853–60.

58. *Delineator* 72 (Oct. 1908): 576; Savage, "W. B. Sherrard"; Sherrard to Editor, *Delineator* 71 (March, 1908): 429; Charles R. Henderson, "Home Finding: An Idea That Grew," *Delineator* 71 (April 1908): 609–11, and 72 (Nov. 1908): 781–82; conclusions of the 1909 Conference as summarized in a letter to Theodore Roosevelt from Hastings Hart and others, reprinted in *Charities and the Commons* 9 (20 Feb. 1909): 987–90, esp. point 3 on "Home Finding."

59. "Minutes," 11 Sept. and 10 Dec. 1889; "Journal," report for Aug.-Oct. 1897, p. 149, and report for year ending 30 April 1898, pp. 158–59.

60. "Journal," report for Aug.-Oct. 1898, pp. 172–74.

61. Letter to Savage, 10 July 1899, MHSP.

62. "Minutes," 10 Sept. 1891 and 15 Oct. 1903. See also Savage, "Twenty-Five Years of the Work of the Children's Home Society of Minnesota." Information about Kate Savage is extremely scanty, but see St. Paul *Pioneer Press*, 18 July 1920.

63. "Journal," report for year ending 30 April 1898, p. 160, regarding information that several other home societies had already established such receiving homes, "Minutes," 15 June 1893, 12 Nov. 1896.

64. "Journal," report for Aug.-Oct. 1898, p. 172; inspectors' letters recopied in "Minutes," 28 April 1904; Annual Report of Children, 1 April 1903 to 1 April 1904, in "Minutes," 28 April 1904.

65. Savage to D. R. Noyes, 16 Dec. 1903, Savage Papers, Box 1; "Minutes," 21 Dec. 1903.

66. "Minutes," 21 July 1904 and 20 Oct. 1904; Quarterly Report of Children, Oct.-Dec. 1904, in "Minutes,"

67. Savage, "The Evolution of the Children's Home Society." Emphasis added.

68. See "Minutes," from 1904 to 1908 as an example. Information on the children's ages is virtually nonexistent. In early 1909 there were 23 babies and 17 "older children." "Statement Adopted by the Board of Directors of the Children's Home Society, February 25, 1909," in "Minutes." Babies younger than three months, by resolution of the board, were not to be accepted. "Minutes," 18 July 1907.

69. Pamphlet, "Helping Hapless Children to Happy Useful Lives" (c. 1927), MHSP. As the brief typed "History" of the society phrased it in the late 1970s, "this building tended to become more than simply a receiving home as children were cared for many months at a time," MHSP.

70. "Journal," report for year from 1 May 1896 to 1 May 1897, p. 135. Kate Savage undoubtedly agreed. She had long been active in the Women's Christian Temperance Union. The St. Paul *Pioneer Press*, 18 July 1920. The Home Society intended to place children only "in Christian families" that were "strictly temperate and worthy of confidence for their honesty, morality and trustworthiness." See any copy of *Home Finder* for this statement. Hastings Hart, national secretary of the Home Societies, said also that the children must regularly attend Sunday School. "We are not willing to put a child into a home where the influences are irreligious." Hart, "The Care of Older Children," *Home Finder* 2 (Nov. 1901): 7.

71. Hastings Hart, et al., to Theodore Roosevelt, reprinted in *Charities and the Commons* 21 (20 Feb. 1909): 987.

72. "Minutes," 19 May 1894, 12 Nov. 1896, 11 Feb. 1897, 13 May 1897.

73. "Minutes," 28 April 1904, and 26 Oct. 1905; quarterly reports 1905–10.

74. Peter Tyor and Jamil S. Zainaldin, "Asylum and Society: An Approach to Institutional Change," *Journal of Social History* 13 (Fall 1979): 31, note the importance of a similar shift in Boston's Temporary Home for the Destitute. They see it resulting from "a new moralism" that focused on

keeping desperate families together, in contrast to an earlier policy that tended to exploit destitute parents in order to find adoptable children for middle-class families. Steven Schlossman, *Love and the American Delinquent: The Theory and Practice of "Progressive" Juvenile Justice, 1825–1920* (Chicago: University of Chicago Press, 1977), esp. chaps. 1–4, documents the growing commitment to keeping families intact.

75. For an interesting example, note the views of William Woodmansee, assistant superintendent of the Children's Home Society of Wisconsin at the turn of the century. See Keith, "The History and Development of the Children's Aid Society of Wisconsin," 17–18.

76. Typed rough draft, 9 Jan. 1909, of Savage's comments at a Minnesota conference concerning children. Savage Papers, Box 1.

77. "Journal," report for year ending 1 May 1896, pp. 99–101.

78. "Journal," report for year ending 30 April 1898, pp. 160–62.

79. Quoted in Henderson, "Home Finding: An Idea that Grew," 611.

80. *Juvenile Court Record*, 7 (Aug. 1906): 26–27.

81. *Home Finder* 1 (Jan. 1900) 9. Sherrard argued that thousands of childless homes in the country could provide more love and training than could natural parents. See *Juvenile Court Record* 7 (Aug. 1906): 26–27.

82. "Journal," report for Nov. 1897 to Jan. 1898, pp. 152–53; "Minutes," 30 Oct. 1902.

83. Typed rough draft, 9 Jan. 1909, of Savage's comments at a Minnesota conference concerning children. Savage Papers, Box 1.

84. "Journal," report for year from 1 May 1896 to 1 May 1897, pp. 132–33; report for Aug.-Oct. 1897, pp. 144–45.

85. Statistics on those children received, placed, returned, and replaced are scattered throughout the "Minutes" and the "Journal."

86. A. V. Burlvin to A. H. Tebbets, 20 Nov. 1908, MHSP.

87. On Jackson, see *Home Finder* 1 (Jan. 1900): 4, and Savage, "Twenty-Five Years of the Work of the Children's Home Society of Minnesota"; on Tebbets, see "Minutes," 20 July 1900.

88. Tebbets, Adams, and Lundgren to Board of Directors, n.d., but written Nov. 1908, filed with "Minutes," 21 Nov. 1908; ibid., Lundgren to Walter N. Carroll, 23 Nov. 1908, and Tebbets to Walter N. Carroll, 16 Nov. 1908.

89. "Statement Adopted by the Board of Directors of the Children's Home Society February 25th, 1909," printed as a small pamphlet; copy in "Minutes."

90. "Journal," report from Aug.-Oct. 1898, p. 173.

91. A. V. Burlvin to Tebbets, 20 Nov. 1908, MHSP; "Minutes," 9 Dec. 1908.

92. Savage to R. N. Adams, 15 April 1909, MHSP. The board made it clear that Savage had "honorably retired" as superintendent. R. N. Adams (president of the board), "To Whom It May Concern," 23 April 1909, Savage Papers, Box 1; Minneapolis *Tribune*, 2 March 1921.

93. "Statement Adopted by the Board of Directors of the Children's Home Society, February 25th, 1909."

94. S. W. Dickinson, "Is the American Home Declining in Influence?" *Juvenile Court Record* 10 (Oct. 1912): 10–12. The idea of having reform associations "supplement the family institution and furnish the requisite models of profitable suggestion," as Horace Fletcher, self-styed "Advocate for the Waifs," phrased it, was extremely popular during the progressive era. Fletcher, *That Last Waif or Social Quarantine* (Chicago: Kindergarten Literature, 1898), 158. Writing in behalf of the movement to establish kindergartens, Fletcher advocated a "National Quarantine Organization," in which a host of local groups of experts could "supplement the family." The National Congress of Mothers, which emerged in the late 1890s, exemplified the growing movement to bolster the family. For a later critique of this tendency of outside organizations to impinge on home life, see Christopher Lasch, *Haven in a Heartless World: The Family Besieged* (New York: Basic Books, 1977).

95. "Statement Adopted by the Board of Directors of the Children's Home Society, February 25th, 1909." For evidence that Home Societies generally were expanding their "aid work" by this time, see "Children's Home Society Completes Quarter Century," *Charities and the Commons* 15 (18 July 1909): 480–81.

96. Dickinson, "History of the Children's Home Society of Minnesota."

97. S. W. Dickinson, "The Adoption or Segregation of the Illegitimate Child," *Juvenile Court Record* (Feb. 1912): 3–4.

98. Dickinson, "History of the Children's Home Society of Minnesota"; Annual Report of the Superintendent, in "Minutes," 15 April 1909.

99. Dickinson, "History of the Children's Home Society of Minnesota." See also Levin, "Fifty Years of Child Care," 40–41.

100. Dickinson, "Is the American Home Declining in Influence?" 10, 12; S. W. Dickinson, *Rural Nursing, Its Development as a Part of the Public Health Movement, and Relation to Children's Work*, undated pamphlet, copy in Children's Service Society of Wisconsin; Dickinson, "The Adoption or Segregation of the Illegitimate Child," 4–5.

101. Dickinson, "The Adoption or Segregation of the Illegitimate Child," 4–5.

102. Quoted in Dickinson, "History of the Children's Home Society of Minnesota."

103. Annual Report of the Superintendent, in "Minutes," 15 April 1909. For another example of a tougher approach to home placement, see Irene V. Webb, "Should Every Home be Visited before a Child Is Placed in It?" a paper read at the annual conference of the National Children's Home Society at Louisville, 20 June 1906, reprinted in *Juvenile Court Record* 7 (Sept. 1906), 27–29, 31. Webb cautioned, e.g., about accepting too quickly a minister's recommendation, because pastors tended to support their church members. "It is right," Webb argued, "to go to church regularly, to pay your bills promptly, and to have a bank account. No home should fall short of this. But some homes having all these requisites will work absolute ruin to any child placed under their supervision."

104. Dickinson's comments at a program on "Standards in Child Placement," *Proceedings of the 25th Minnesota State Conference of Charities and Correction, Held at Stillwater, September 23–26, 1916* (Stillwater, Minn.: Prison Mirror), 137.

105. Savage to D. R. Noyes, 16 Dec. 1903, Savage Papers, Box 1; Henderson's address, Chicago, 11 June 1908, reprinted in *Juvenile Court Record* 9 (Oct. 1908): 7. Rev. W. Henry Thompson, superintendent of the Children's Home Society of Pennsylvania, hailed the "revolution" in "the attitude of all intelligent sociologists toward the child problem" in favor of "scientific theory" and "the most recent scientific methods." Thompson, "Children and the National Conference of Charities and Correction," *Juvenile Court Record* 7 (June 1906): 26–27. On the shift from voluntarism to professionalism in the progressive era, see Kathleen D. McCarthy, *Noblesse Oblige: Charity and Cultural Philanthropy in Chicago, 1849–1929* (Chicago: University of Chicago Press, 1982), 99–179.

106. Savage, "W. B. Sherrard," Savage Papers, Box 1.

Chapter 3

1. *Orphan's Cry* 6 (Sept. 1899): 3, on the children's march; *Christian Philanthropist* 9 (Feb. 1903): 25, for Ayar, and *Christian Philanthropist* 17 (Oct. 1910): 51, for the minister. Copies of the *Orphan's Cry* and the *Christian Philanthropist* (hereafter cited as *CP*) are in the National Benevolent Association Papers (Disciples of Christ Historical Society, Nashville), hereafter cited as NBA Papers.

2. Mrs. J. K. Hansbrough, "Then and Now," typed ms., 3 June 1935, NBA Papers, Box 6. The statistics are from the NBA Treasurer's Report for Year Ending 30 Sept. 1915, in *CP* 22 (Dec. 1915), 92–93.

3. Nathan O. Hatch, "The Christian Movement and the Demand for a

Theology of the People," *Journal of American History* 67 (Dec. 1980): 545–67, places the birth of the Disciples of Christ in a large cultural context. Hatch argues that "this new religious culture, which sanctioned the right of the individual to go his own way, would have been unthinkable apart from the crisis of authority in popular culture that accompanied the birth of the American Republic." The statement on the "crisis of confidence" is on p. 561. For discussions of grass-roots upheavals in medicine, see Joseph F. Kett's analysis of Thomsonianism in *The Formation of the American Medical Profession: the Role of Institutions, 1780–1860* (New Haven, Conn.: Yale University Press, 1968); in law, Richard E. Ellis, *The Jeffersonian Crisis: Courts and Politics in the Young Republic* (New York: Oxford University Press, 1971), esp. chaps. 8–9; in the theater, Robert C. Toll, *Blacking Up: The Minstrel Show in Nineteenth Century America* (New York: Oxford University Press, 1974), esp. chap. 1; and in mass culture, Neil Harris, *Humbug: The Art of P. T. Barnum* (Boston: Little, Brown, 1973), esp. chap. 3. W. J. Rorabaugh, *The Alcoholic Republic* (New York: Oxford University Press, 1979) also stresses the crisis of authority and the leveling tendencies of American society in the postrevolutionary decades. On the origins and beliefs of the Disciples of Christ, David Edwin Harrell, Jr., *Quest for a Christian America: The Disciples of Christ and American Society to 1866* (Nashville: Disciples of Christ Historical Society, 1966), esp. 1–90, is basic. On the mergers of the various Christian sects, see Harrell, *Quest for a Christian America*, 5n, and Hatch, "The Christian Movement," 548–51.

4. Harrell, *Quest for a Christian America*, 64–76, 78.

5. Ibid., 77–79, on the orphanages and the Missionary Society; for other reminders of the individualistic, anti-institutional temperament of the Disciples, see pp. 106–7, 179–80, 182–83, 212, 223. The Civil War, of course, provided issues that further divided the congregations and members. Fred Arthur Bailey, "The Status of Women in the Disciples of Christ Movement, 1865–1900" (Ph.D. diss., University of Tennessee, 1979), is very informative on postbellum divisions within the church. He quotes (p. 222) one member who in 1874 opposed "the formation of *any Society*" lest it imply "that the church is inadequate to do the work, which the society proposes to do." Don Harrison Doyle, *The Social Order of a Frontier Community, Jacksonville, Illinois, 1825–70* (Urbana: University of Illinois Press, 1978), 158–60, shows the impact of doctrinal clashes on one Disciples of Christ congregation in the 1850s and 1860s; see also Doyle, *The Social Order*, 167–68.

6. *1887–1937, Fifty Years March of Mercy of the National Benevolent Association of the Christian Church*, p. 5, pamphlet in NBA Papers, Box 6;

J. H. Mohorter's address, *CP* 12 (Sept. 1905): 44. Also Mrs. J. K. Hansbrough, untitled typed ms., 26 May 1936; Hansbrough to Dear Brother Clarkson, 29 Sept. 1936; and Hansbrough, typed undated ms., "The Beginning of the National Benevolent Association of the Christian Church," NBA Papers, Box 6.

7. Minutes of the First Annual Meeting, NBA Papers, Box 6.

8. Hansbrough's 26 May 1936 ms. and "The Beginning of the National Benevolent Association of the Christian Church," NBA Papers, Box 6; "Christian Orphans' Home, St. Louis," *CP* 13 (Sept. 1906): 36–37; and "Reminiscences," *CP* 23 (Nov. 1916): 144, are useful for these early years. On the Babies' Home and Hospital, *CP* 14 (July 1907): 1, 8, has a good overview.

9. See the monthly reports of the Cleveland Christian Orphanage in *CP* For a brief historical sketch, see *CP* 14 (Dec. 1907): 81, 89–90.

10. See the monthly reports in *CP*; clipping from the Atlanta *Constitution*, 3 May 1936, in NBA Papers, Box 9.

11. Monthly reports of the Juliette Fowler Home in *CP*; *CP* 13 (June 1907): 184, on "The Hoe Brigade." The children, fairly equally divided along gender lines, ranged in age from three to 15. *CP* 13 (Oct. 1906): 58, discusses some of the farm problems.

12. Pamphlet, *Golden Anniversary, Fifty Years of Service to Children*, NBA Papers, Box 12, and *CP* 13 (April 1907): 145, have brief overviews. See also monthly reports of the Colorado Christian Home in *CP*.

13. From 1892 until 1901, Clark called his orphanage the Boys and Girls Aid Society of Omaha. Useful brief histories of Clark's work and the NBA role appear in pamphlets, *First Half Century, Child Saving Institute*, NBA Papers, Box 10, and *Dedication Services, Improvement and Expansion of Child-Saving Institute, November 15, 1953*, Box 9; clipping from the Omaha *Sunday World-Herald Magazine*, n.d. but c. 1942, Box 9; "Third Annual Report of Child Saving Institute for the Year Ending October 31, 1900," Benjamin B. Lindsey Papers, Library of Congress, Washington, D.C., Box 7; monthly reports of the Child Saving Institute in *CP*, esp. 24 (Feb. 1918): 234–35. The other NBA homes were also closed to blacks, but in 1916 a *CP* editorial urged readers to respond positively to a request for financial support from the Virginia Christian Orphanage for Colored Children in Stuart, Virginia. The NBA, according to the editorial, had "served children . . . almost of every nationality. There is one class, however, to whose needs it has made no response—that of the negro, and perhaps no class is in greater need of assistance. . . . This . . . is a challenge to the catholicity of our profession. . . . What shall our answer be?" *CP* 22 (May 1916): 246–47.

14. In 1939 the Northwest Christian Home for the Aged relocated in Beaverton, Ore. Especially useful information for its early years appears in *CP* 16 (Oct. 1909): 49; *CP* 17 (July 1910): 3; *CP* 18 (July 1911): 12, and (Aug. 1911): 23; *CP* 20 (Jan. 1914): 115; copy of contract between Northwest Benevolent Association of the Churches of Christ and the NBA, 5 March 1910; and "Service of Dedication of the Northwest Christian Home for the Aged," 9 July 1939, NBA Papers, Box 9.

15. *CP* 20 (Dec. 1913): 100.

16. *CP* 18 (July 1911): 4, on "vast army"; *CP* 16 (Oct. 1909): 52.

17. Bailey, "The Status of Women in the Disciples of Christ Movement," 81, 231.

18. For Younkin and WCTU, see "A Short Sketch of Mrs. M. H. Younkin," 15 May 1896, Younkin Biographical File, Disciples of Christ Historical Society; for Hansbrough comment, her untitled 26 May 1936 ms., NBA Papers, Box 6; for Harrison, *CP* 23 (Nov. 1916): 144.

19. "A Short Sketch of Mrs. M. H. Younkin"; *Orphan's Cry*, 6 (Oct. 1899): 3; Mrs. J. K. Hansbrough to Clarkson, 29 Sept. 1936, NBA Papers, Box 6.

20. Typed ms., "Great Moments in the NBA," n.d., NBA Papers, Box 6. It is unclear why the police did not point to other orphanages which existed in St. Louis, most notably the well-established Protestant Orphans' Asylum founded in 1834. On the early history of that institution, see Susan Whitelaw Downs and Michael W. Sherraden, "The Orphan Asylum in the Nineteenth Century," *Social Service Review* 57 (June 1983): 272–90. According to Downs and Sherraden, p. 285, "The Roman Catholic Church established nine orphanages during the nineteeth century in St. Louis. German Protestants founded three homes between 1858 and 1877. The Episcopalian, Methodist, Baptist, Christian, and Church of the Messiah congregations also founded children's institutions, as did the Masons."

21. *CP* 10 (Feb. 1904): 116; *CP* 20 (March 1914): 146, regarding the opposition; *1887–1937, Fifty Years of Mercy*, 7–8, and "A Short Sketch of Mrs. M. H. Younkin" on her victory and death.

22. *CP* 20 (March 1914): esp. 145–49.

23. This is a concept that Allen F. Davis develops in *American Heroine: The Life and Legend of Jane Addams* (New York: Oxford University Press, 1973).

24. *CP* 20 (March 1914): 146–47.

25. *CP* 15 (Dec 1908): 85.

26. Author unidentified, typed ms., "Other Mothers," 1 Dec. 1934, NBA Papers, Box 6.

27. For information on Meier, see *CP* 12 (Jan. 1906): 102, and clipping,

St. Louis *Globe-Democrat,* 22 July 1935, NBA Papers, Box 6; on Ayars, *CP* 15 (Dec. 1908): 85; on Mason, *CP* 15 (June 1909): 185. Several men were active in the early organizing stages of the NBA, but as Estelle Freedman says in another context (when discussing the settlement houses of the progressive era), "the high proportion of female participants and leaders . . . as well as the domestic structure and emphasis on service to women and children, qualify" the organization as a female institution. Freedman, "Separatism as Strategy: Female Institution Building and American Feminism, 1870–1930," *Feminist Studies* 5 (Fall 1979): 518.

28. *CP* 16 (March 1910): 131.

29. *CP* 16 (May 1910): 161, 163.

30. Ibid.

31. Historians have devoted growing attention to the subject of gender roles, careers, and reform. On the antebellum era, see e.g., Anne Firor Scott, "What, Then, Is the American: This New Woman?" *Journal of American History* 65 (Dec. 1978): 679–703, and Kathryn Kish Sklar *Catherine Beecher: A Study in American Domesticity* (New Haven: Yale University Press, 1973). For the progressive era, see esp. Christopher Lasch, *The New Radicalism in America, 1889–1963* (New York: Knopf, 1965), chap. 1; Davis, *American Heroine;* Sheila Rothman, *Woman's Proper Place: A History of Changing Ideals and Practices, 1870 to the Present* (New York: Basic Books, 1978), 63–93, on "The Protestant Nun"; Jill Conway, "Woman Reformers and American Culture, 1870–1930," *Journal of Social History* 5 (Winter 1971–72), 164–77. Freedman, "Separatism as Strategy," 512–29, stresses the importance "of a separate, public female sphere" for American feminism during the progressive era. In this context, the NBA also deserves consideration. Unquestionably, it was an example of "female institution building"; the affectionate references to "sisterhood" in *CP* point up its significance for raising female consciousness. The NBA women also fit into the category of feminism that Anne M. Boylan discusses in "Evangelical Womanhood in the Nineteenth Century: The Role of Women in Sunday Schools," *Feminist Studies* 4 (Oct. 1978): 62–80. Indeed, Dowden's views of her role, and some of her statements, virtually mirrored those of Sunday School organizer Harriet Lathrop. On Lathrop, see Boylan, "Evangelical Womanhood," 66–67.

32. *CP* 12 (May 1906): 167.

33. *CP* 17 (Oct. 1910): 50, and 15 (March 1909): 132, are just two of many examples of such thinking. According to David Edwin Harrell, Jr., *The Social Sources of Division in the Disciples of Christ, 1865–1900* (Atlanta: Publishing Systems, 1973), 90, 94, "The Disciples moved to the left about as rapidly as the mainstream of the American social gospel movement. . . .

Proportionately, Disciples of Christ were probably about as active in the Social Gospel movement as were other evangelical churches."

34. See esp. J. H. Mohorter, "Christian Benevolence," *CP* 12 (Sept. 1905): 43; Ira Boswell, "The Greater Works," *CP* 21 (Nov. 1914): 69; A. D. Harmon, "The Supreme Apologetic," *CP* 20 (Dec. 1913): 99–100. See also "Who's the Heretic?" *CP* 24 (July 1917): 5, and comments of Fannie Shedd Ayars, *CP* 16 (March 1910): 131. Space in *CP* devoted to the "Society of Applied Christianity" also reflects this view. The society had formed in 1905 to carry the idea of organized benevolence to local churches. "Under the direction of our National Benevolent Association we are organizing Societies of Applied Christianity in our congregations," said *CP* 16 (Oct. 1909): 54.

35. On Snively, especially his effectiveness as a preacher, see the Biographical File and his scrapbooks, Disciples of Christ Historical Society. Reform ideas permeate his editorials. For examples of his views on Roosevelt, see *CP* 9 (April 1903): 49, and 9 (June 1903): 82; on Folks, *CP* 11 (Aug. 1904): 17, and 9 (Jan. 1903): 1; on the Senate, *CP* 12 (Jan. 1906): 101; on saloons, *CP* 13 (Oct. 1906): 51; on meat packers, *CP* 13 (Aug. 1906): 17; on trusts, *CP* 12 (May 1906): 165; on "child slavery," *CP* 9 (March 1903): 33; on labor, *CP* 11 (Sept. 1904): 33, and 11 (Aug. 1904): 17; on the world getting better, *CP* 12 (Jan. 1906): 101.

36. See, e.g., *CP* 16 (Oct. 1909): 54; *CP* 15 (Dec. 1908): 83; *CP* 15 (Sept. 1908): 46; *CP* 14 (March 1908): 136; *CP* 17 (Jan. 1911): 99.

37. *CP* 15 (Dec. 1908): 83; *CP* 23 (Aug. 1916): 43; see discussions of "Lodgeism" in, e.g., *CP* 12 (Aug. 1905): 22, and 15 (Jan. 1909): 99; the woman is quoted in *CP* 14 (Dec. 1907): 95.

38. *CP* 15 (Dec. 1908): 82, and 16 (March 1910): 131. See also, *CP* 15 (Nov. 1908): 65, and 15 (March 1909): 129.

39. Snively in *CP* 10 (Dec. 1903): 81; Minnick in *CP* 17 (Oct. 1910): 49; Rev. L. J. Marshall in *CP* 17 (Nov. 1910): 67; poem in *CP* 16 (April 1910): 145.

40. Poem, accompanied by a photograph of children at the Christian Orphans' Home, *Orphan's Cry* 6 (Sept. 1899): 1; *CP* 23 (May 1917): 323, and 21 (Jan. 1915): 98.

41. *CP* 17 (Jan. 1911): 99; *CP* 15 (Sept. 1908): 46; on immigration *CP* 14 (March 1908): 129, 134–36.

42. *CP* 15 (May 1909): 163; *CP* 17 (Sept. 1910): 33.

43. Editorial in *CP* 17 (July 1910): 2; *CP* 13 (Aug. 1907): 148, and 9 (April 1903): 50, on Cleveland home.

44. *CP* 14 (June 1908): 184; *CP* 15 (May 1909): 163; *CP* 12 (July 1905): 6. Some NBA supporters nonetheless worried that the Disciples were barely

touching the surface. In Jacksonville, Florida, a needy girl who had been in the Christian Church had received care from the Presbyterians and was thus preparing to become a Presbyterian deaconess. *CP* 15 (March 1909): 129.

45. On "the new interventionism," John W. Chambers II, *The Tyranny of Change: America in the Progressive Era, 1900–1917* (New York: St. Martin's, 1980), esp. chaps. 4 and 8. The Addams observation is on p. 113. Robert H. Wiebe, *The Search for Order, 1877–1920* (New York: Hill and Wang, 1967), is basic. For convenient discussions of the historical literature on the organizational revolution, see Louis Galambos, "The Emerging Organizational Synthesis in Modern American History," *Business History Review* 44 (Autumn 1970): 279–90; Robert Berkhofer, "The Organizational Interpretation of American History: A New Synthesis," in Jack Salzman, ed., *Prospects: The Annual of American Cultural Studies, 4* (New York: Burt Franklin, 1978), 611–29.

46. *CP* 12 (Sept. 1905): 42–44.

47. *CP* 15 (June 1909): 177, 181; *CP* 21 (May 1915): 163; Boswell in *CP* 21 (Nov. 1914): 70; Minnick in *CP* 12 (Oct. 1910): 49.

48. *CP* 11 (Jan. 1905): 98; Brown's address in *CP* 24 (Aug. 1917): 42–44; nurses' photo in *CP* 21 (March 1915).

49. *CP* 13 (July 1906): 198; *CP* 15 (May 1909): 162; *CP* 17 (Oct. 1910): 49–51. David Rothman, *Conscience and Convenience: The Asylum and Its Alternatives in Progressive America* (Boston: Little, Brown, 1980), esp. 56–59, 122–23, 267, discusses the medical model that so fascinated progressives.

50. E.g., *CP* 8 (Oct. 1906): 51, on liquor; *CP* 13 (Aug. 1906): 17–18, on food and drugs; *CP* 12 (May 1906): 165, on trusts; *CP* 9 (April 1903); 49, on arbitration; *CP* 11 (May 1905): 161, on municipal ownership.

51. "Put the Orphan in a State Home," *CP* 15 (March 1909): 130; *CP* 17 (April 1911): 151, and 23 (Sept. 1916), 70. For Harmon, see *CP* 20 (Dec. 1913): 99–101. See also "The Dependent Child the Victim of Politics," *CP* 22 (May 1916): 245–46.

52. Many *CP* editorials and articles dealt with this topic. The quotation is from *Juvenile Court Record* 10 (Sept. 1909): 8.

53. Among the many examples of this view, see *CP* 23 (Aug. 1916): 40; *CP* 14 (Dec. 1907): 85; *CP* 14 (May 1908): 161, 163.

54. *CP* 14 (April 1908): 146, quoted the critic. *CP* 15 (March 1909): 130; *CP* 17 (April 1911): 151, and 23 (Sept. 1916): 71, made the point about love. See *CP* 20 (Oct. 1913): 77 on the Colorado home.

55. *CP* 18 (Aug. 1911): 24.

56. *CP* 16 (April 1910): 146; *CP* 13 (Oct. 1906): 58.

57. See, e.g., *CP* 17 (Sept. 1910): 33; *CP* 16 (June 1910): 179; *CP* 16 (April

1910): 146; *CP* 8 (April 1907): 148; *CP* 21 (Jan. 1915): 98; *CP* 12 (Dec. 1905): 90; *CP* 18 (July 1911): 4; *CP* 17 (July 1910): 2.

58. See, e.g., *CP* 20 (June 1914): 194; *CP* 17 (Sept. 1910): 33; *CP* 14 (May 1908): 161, 163; *CP* 14 (April 1908): 146; *CP* 15 (March, 1909): 132; *CP* 15 (Feb. 1909), 115; *CP* 23 (Aug. 1916): 40.

59. See, e.g., *CP* 18 (Oct. 1911): 53; *CP* 15 (March 1909): 130; *CP* 21 (April 1915): 152–53; *CP* 22 (May 1916): 243; *CP* 23 (Sept. 1916): 69; and numerous monthly home reports—e.g., *CP* 12 (Oct. 1905): 63.

60. See, e.g., *CP* 17 (Feb. 1911): 121, on the St. Louis home; *CP* 16 (June 1910): 184, on the Cleveland home.

61. *CP* 21 (May 1915): 164–65; *CP* 10 (Jan. 1904): 103; *CP* 14 (March 1908): 136; *CP* 12 (March 1906): 139; *CP* 9 (March 1903): 40; *CP* 15 (Oct. 1908): 55; *CP* 10 (Feb. 1904): 119; *CP* 10 (April 1904): 150

62. *CP* 18 (Aug. 1911): 24.

63. *CP* 18 (Sept. 1911): 39.

64. *CP* 18 (Sept. 1911): 39, on the matrons' backgrounds; *CP* 11 (Oct. 1904): 54, on the St. Louis home; *CP* 16 (April, 1910): 158, on Brown; *CP* 12 (Aug. 1905): 29, on Bush. One of the best descriptions of life in the day of a matron is Tena Williamson's account, *CP* 9 (April 1903): 55–56.

65. *CP* 14 (Feb. 1908): 121; *CP* 15 (June 1909): 184; *CP* 10 (Feb. 1904): 118.

66. *CP* 10 (Dec. 1903): 86–87; *CP* 10 (April 1904): 149.

67. *CP* 10 (June 1904): 182; *CP* 10 (Jan. 1904): 100. The group accidentally encountered Ben some 14 blocks from where they had been shopping.

68. *CP* 11 (Oct. 1904): 54, and 11 (Nov. 1904): 70, for God's work; *CP* 9 (April 1903): 55–56, on the sick child; *CP* 11 (March 1905): 135, on the playroom.

69. *CP* 11 (April 1905): 151; 11 (May 1905): 167, and 11 (June 1905): 181–82.

70. *CP* 12 (Aug. 1905): 27, on Gordon; *CP* 12 (Sept. 1905): 45, on Maxson; *CP* 13 (Oct. 1906): 55, on her successor, a Mrs. Turley. Nervous strain and overwork were not unique to the St.Louis institution. In 1909 the matron of the Southeastern Christian Home resigned after a year because "the care and responsibility of the home proved too much" for her health. *CP* 15 (Jan. 1909): 100. Other homes had similar problems.

71. Matron quoted in *CP* 14 (Dec. 1907): 87; *CP* 17 (April 1911): 156, on the Georgia home.

72. *CP* 21 (Sept. 1914): 36, on Ivy Henderson; *CP* 17 (Oct. 1910): 56, and 15 (Aug. 1908): 25, on examples of appeals; *CP* 11 (Jan. 1905), Easter supplement.

73. *CP* 12 (Dec. 1905): 97.

74. *CP* 10 (Feb. 1904): 116.

75. On the issues involved in the controversy, see George Snively to "My Dear Sister," 11 Oct. 1902, and Mrs. J. K. Hansbrough to Arthur Dillinger, 16 March 1916, NBA Papers, Box 6; *CP* 10 (Feb. 1904): 116, and 16 (Oct. 1909): 54. Ayars quoted from *CP* 16 (Feb. 1910): 121.

76. *CP* 15 (May 1909): 162, and 15 (Sept. 1908): 33. DeWitt's address reprinted in *CP* 16 (Feb. 1910); see esp. *CP* 16 (Feb. 1910): 113–16.

77. For information on Ayars, sée *CP* 12 (Feb. 1906): 118. The split between her and the NBA is briefly described in several issues of *CP*. See, e.g., 18 (Dec. 1911): 83, and 20 (May 1914): 181. For further comments and a description of a fire in 1915 at Ayars's home, see *CP* 21 (May 1915): 163–64. The details of the disagreement between Ayars and the NBA are not clear. *CP* implied that Ayars left because she could not agree to "some changes in the methods and manner of conducting" the St. Louis homes. Nancy Wahonick, Director of Communications of the NBA, indicates that she and several other members of the organization have tried unsuccessfully to determine the exact nature of the disagreement. The fact that all the minutes of board meetings for the years between 1902 and 1911 were destroyed in a fire only complicates the matter. Ayars's new organization had no relationship to the Disciples of Christ. Wahonick to author, 19 Aug. 1980.

78. "The Twenty-Seventh Annual Report of the National Benevolent Association of the Christian Church," *CP* 20 (Oct. 1913): 66–73.

79. "The Report of the Commission on Benevolences," *CP* 21 (March 1915): esp.130, and 22 (Nov. 1915): 66.

80. *CP* 21 (March 1915): 66–67.

81. *CP* 23 (Feb. 1917): 228–29.

82. *CP* 9 (April 1903): 50; *CP* 23 (Aug. 1916): 40; *CP* 23 (Feb. 1917): 229.

83. *CP* 23 (Oct. 1916): 103; *CP* 23 (Jan. 1917): 196–97; *CP* 23 (June 1917): 355; *CP* 24 (July 1917): 4; *CP* 24 (Nov. 1917): 131–32; and 25 (Oct. 1918): 100–101.

84. *CP* 25 (Oct. 1918): 109.

85. In the 1980s, of course, the services of the homes have changed. Although the placement of dependent children is still a concern of several of the homes, many other services are available. The Child Saving Institute in Omaha gives particular attention to unwed mothers and single parents, providing day care and supportive training and jobs. The St. Louis Christian Home has become primarily a crisis intervention agency, looking out for abused and neglected children. Atlanta's Southern Christian Home works mainly with troubled children. Both the Cleveland Christian Home and the Colorado Christian Home are residential treatment centers for emotionally

252

disturbed children. And the Juliette Fowler Home in Dallas, after first becoming a residential care facility for children of working parents, has shifted its focus to dealing with neglected dependent children. See, e.g., the booklet, *All God's Children* (St. Louis: Christian Board of Publication, 1979), 24–31.

Chapter 4

1. Toledo *Sunday Times*, 11 Aug. 1946.

2. *Christian Philanthropist* 18 (Aug. 1911): 23.

3. Between 1890 and 1910, Toledo was one of the most populated cities in the United States. During those decades it more than doubled in size, from 81,434 to 168,497. Department of Commerce, Bureau of the Census, *Thirteenth Census of the United States Taken in the Year 1910*, I (Washington, D.C.: Government Printing Office, 1913), 80.

4. The exact number of newsboys in the United States or even in specific cities during these years is impossible to know. Census reports are apparently far from reliable. According to Philip Davis, who for a while was a supervisor of Licensed Minors for Boston Public Schools, census workers at one point in the early 1900s discovered only 427 newsboys in Boston, where "by actual account" the number was 2,200. Davis refused to believe official figures showing that Chicago, with a population triple that of Boston, had only 300 newsboys under age 16. In Davis's estimation, by 1915 there were perhaps as many as 300,000 youthful street workers across the nation. Philip Davis, *Street-Land: Its Little People and Big Problems* (Boston: Small, Maynard, 1915), 146–47. An informal count in New York City by interested philanthropists, c. 1915, found approximately 4,000 newsboys, aged 12 to 16, working the city streets. "Looking After the Newsboys," *Work with Boys* 15 (Oct. 1915): 309. At about the same time, the city of Milwaukee officially licensed 4,300 boys of 12 to 16 to sell papers on the streets. "The Milwaukee Republic," *Work with Boys* 14 (Jan. 1914): 21. The number of youths who sold or delivered newspapers prior to the state legislature's establishment of the licensing system in 1911 was probably considerably larger. And even after the system was in effect, there were presumably some unlicensed children who peddled papers illegally.

5. Frank T. Carlton, "The Toledo Newsboys' Association," *Commons* (Sept. 1905): 493. Copy in Toledo Newsboys' Association Papers (Toledo–Lucas County Public Library). Hereafter cited as TNBA Papers.

6. Scott Nearing, "The Newsboy at Night in Philadelphia," *Charities and the Commons* 17 (Oct. 1906–April 1907): 784, on "the embryo crimi-

nal"; Atkinson quoted in Leonard Benedict, *Waifs of the Slums and Their Way Out* (New York: Revell, 1907), 23. See Hine's photos in William R. Taylor, "Psyching Out the City," in Richard L. Bushman, et al., *Uprooted Americans: Essays to Honor Oscar Handlin* (Boston: Little, Brown, 1979), 269, and Judith Mara Gutman, *Lewis W. Hine and the American Social Conscience* (New York: Walker, 1967), 81.

7. Regarding the concept of "John Q. Worker," see Aileen S. Kraditor, *The Radical Persuasion, 1890–1917: Aspects of the Intellectual History and Historiography of Three American Radical Organizations* (Baton Rouge: Louisiana State University Press, 1981), esp. 10, 297–321.

8. Carlton, "The Toledo Newsboys' Association," 493; Ernest Poole, "Waifs of the Street," *McClure's* 21 (May 1903): 40, 48; Jacob Riis, *The Children of the Poor* (New York: Scribner, 1892), 245. As early as the 1850s, Charles Loring Brace, founder of the Children's Aid Society of New York, had drawn a connection between newsboys and "an army of orphans, regiments of children who have not a home or friend." "The Children's Aid Society of New York . . . Compiled from the Writings and Reports of the Late Charles Loring Brace," in *Report of the Committee on Child Saving, 1893* (Boston: George Ellis, 1893), 12.

9. "What of the Newsboy of the Second Cities?" *Charities* 10 (11 April 1903), 368–69.

10. Ernest Poole, "Newsboy Wanderers Are Tramps in the Making," *Charities* 10 (Feb. 14 1903): 159–60, and "Waifs of the Street," 40, 48.

11. Everett W. Goodhue, "Boston Newsboys, How They Live and Work," *Charities* 8 (7 June 1902): 530.

12. See unidentified clipping, "Help Us," c. 1915, in Jefferson D. Robinson Scrapbooks (Toledo–Lucas County Public Library).

13. See, e.g., *In Memory of John E. Gunckel*, 28, 51, in John E. Gunckel File (Toledo–Lucas County Public Library). This pamphlet was published at the time of Gunckel's death, 16 Aug. 1915.

14. On Gunckel's background, see ibid., esp. 7, 19, 22–24, 33; Toledo *Blade*, 16 Aug. 1915; other unidentified clippings, 16–17 Aug. 1915, in Gunckel File.

15. On Black, see Toledo *Blade*, 2 May 1903; for Black's recollections of Gunckel, Toledo *News-Bee* 14 April 1923. See also Toledo *Blade*, 13 Aug. 1946. The source of Gunckel's ideas on self-government are not clear; he gave no indication of having gotten the ideas from any one particular source. By the 1890s, of course, the subject of youthful self-government was much "in the air" and influenced a variety of child savers, such as William R. George and Edward Bradley.

16. John E. Gunckel, *Boyville: A History of Fifteen Years' Work among Newsboys* (Toledo: Toledo Newsboys' Association, 1905), 3–37; Toledo *Blade*, 20 Feb. 1909. See also Charles Perkins, "A Toledo Philanthropy," *New Era*, 1915 (clipping in Gunckel File).

17. Unidentified clipping, 27 March 1962, in Scrapbook, TNBA Papers.

18. Julius Wengierski to Ben Lindsey, 30 March 1909, Ben Lindsey Papers (Library of Congress, Washington, D.C.), Box 19.

19. Perins, "A Toledo Philanthropy."

20. Gunckel to Samuel M. Jones, 30 March 1898, and Jones's reply, 1 April 1898, Samuel M. Jones Papers (Toledo–Lucas County Public Library), Microfilm Reel 8.

21. Toledo *Blade*, 5–6 Jan. 1931; Toledo *Times*, 5–6 Jan. 1931.

22. Toledo *Blade*, 13 Aug. 1946. See also *In Memory of John E. Gunckel*, esp. 20; "'Gunck' the Newsboys' Friend," *Juvenile Court Record* 10 (Oct. 1909): 4.

23. Julius Wengierski to Ben Lindsey, 30 March 1909, Lindsey Papers, Box 19.

24. Brand Whitlock, "John E. Gunckel," *American* 69 (Nov. 1909): 63–64.

25. Gunckel, *Boyville*, 1, 73, 166, 169, 177–78, 211.

26. Ibid., 20, 214, 219. Conwell's "Acres of Diamonds," immensely popular as a speech and pamphlet, celebrated success and the pursuit of individual fortune. Gunckel's use of the title perhaps illustrated the progressive reformers' shift to a gospel of service rather than the Gospel of Wealth.

27. Copy of Christmas card in Robinson Scrapbooks.

28. Quoted from unidentified newspaper by Gunckel, *Boyville*, 47. On "The Popular Sunday School," see also pp. 44–46; Gunckel to Ben Lindsey,10 Jan. 1909, Lindsey Papers, Box 19.

29. J. E. Gunckel, "An Appeal to Sunday School Workers," n.d., in Robinson Scrapbooks.

30. Copy of Gunckel Report, 14 July 1913, Robinson Scrapbooks. At another point, Gunckel claimed to have "brought into the Sunday Schools over 400 boys." Gunckel memo to J. D. Robinson, n.d., Robinson Scrapbooks.

31. Gunckel, "An Appeal to Sunday School Workers."

32. Gunckel, *Boyville*, quoted on front page; see also p. 167.

33. Ibid., 80.

34. See, e.g., ibid., 12–13, 20; *In Memory of John E. Gunckel*, 35.

35. This was a point made by Albion E. Lang, president of the Toledo

Railways and Light Co. and a major financial backer of Boyville, at the dedication ceremonies of the Toledo Newsboys' Building in 1909. *Toledo Blade*, 22 Feb. 1909.

36. The card is in the Robinson Scrapbooks. On the lack of racial and religious restriction, see *Boyville*, 48; on the first girl to join, see *Toledo Blade*, 1 Nov. 1902; on later membership requirements, see, e.g., pamphlet, "Information about the Toledo Newsboys' Association [and] the National Newsboys' Association," p. 6, 9, undated but c. 1911, TNBA Papers, Toledo Vertical File. By 1911 a separate Girls' Auxiliary existed, comprising females under 16, a majority of whom were sisters of newsboys. The girls attended the regular Sunday afternoon meetings of the association, elected their own auxiliary officers, and held an annual outing at the Toledo Beach. In 1912 there were 250 members; in 1915 there were 735. When Gunckel decided that he was paying insufficient attention to this auxiliary, he turned to the Ursula Wolcott chapter of the Daughters of the American Revolution; by 1915 that group was sponsoring the Newsboys' Sisters' Association, open to girls between eight and 18. Members pledged their patriotism and resolved to keep their bodies "in cleanliness and decency; to avoid all objectionable places, not to run away from school or home." They received instruction concerning home and family. See "Information about the Toledo Newsboys' Association," 7; "Weekly Program of the Toledo Newsboys' Association," 21 Feb. 1915, and "Second Annual Outing of the Girls' Auxiliary . . . August First, 1912"; and clippings in Robinson Scrapbooks.

37. Gunckel, *Boyville*, 208; Ledger: "Auxiliary Officers, 1909–1915," 15 Oct. 1909 and 26 Dec. 1913, TNBA Papers.

38. See membership cards of Raymond Westfall in TNBA Papers.

39. Court of Investigation Minutes, 1910–13, 1923, entries for 22 Dec. 1910, 24 Aug. 1911, 16 Jan. 1913, TNBA Papers. Justice may have been less impartial in a special session of 25 Oct. 1911, which involved a fight between one of the judges and another boy: the judge escaped penalty, and his opponent received a 60-day suspension. The judge, of course, may have been an innocent victim, and the court's decision may have squared with the facts of the case. Still, at the least, there must have been a conflict of interest. For information on Gallagher, see Ledger, 1907–09, and auxiliary meeting minutes, 1910–12, TNBA Papers.

40. "Annual Report of the Toledo Newsboys' Association, as Submitted to the Members and Trustees, January 28, 1913," p. 3, TNBA Papers.

41. A. E. Winship, "John E. Gunckel of Toledo, The Newsboys' Evangelist," *World To-Day* 15 (Nov. 1908): 1171–72; unidentified clipping, 15 Aug. 1916, Robinson Scrapbooks.

42. "Official Report of the Probation Officers, Department Number

Seven, of the Toledo Newsboys' Association," c. 1912, and information pamphlet on "Juvenile Court Officers of the Toledo Newsboys' Association," c. 1914, Robinson Scrapbooks; Charles Morgan, "The Newsboys of Toledo," *Work with Boys* 14 (Sept. 1914): 289.

43. Poole, "Waifs of the Street," 46–47. The "Official Report of the Probation Officers, Department Number Seven," covering a 60-day period, showed that some 700 youths out of 1,108 stayed after the warning.

44. Clippings, 7 Nov. 1908, Ledger: 1907–09, TNBA Papers. Harmony returned before the meeting ended. The Toledo *News-Bee* pointed out that Gunckel's self-government plan had prevailed; the boys had selected their own officers—minus the suspended candidate—and agreed to cooperate to strengthen the association.

45. Gunckel, *Boyville*, 77–78, 100, 117–19.

46. "Information about the Toledo Newsboys' Association," c. 1911, p. 2, TNBA Papers; Winship, "John E. Gunckel of Toledo," 1171. Gunckel's own willingness to condone such physical force was hardly surprising. Many leading progressive reformers were quite ready to use violence in the name of virtue—to strike a blow for moral principles and to hold the muscular battlefield against the forces of evil. Examples range from Theodore Roosevelt's well-known pugnacity, to a reform journal's cheer that San Antonio's antiprostitution forces were "beginning to speak like 75 mm. guns," to Woodrow Wilson's pledge that he would "not cry 'peace' as long as there is sin and wrong in the world." See, e.g., newspaper quotation in Paul Boyer, *Urban Masses and Moral Order in America, 1820–1920* (Cambridge, Mass.: Harvard University Press, 1978), 211.

47. "Information about the Toledo Newsboys' Association," 2, TNBA Papers.

48. Gunckel, *Boyville*, 69–70, 79. Also Carlton, "The Toledo Newsboys' Association," 495.

49. Whitlock, "John E. Gunckel," 63; "Annual Report of the TNBA," 28 Jan. 1913; "Honor Roll" ledger, 1915–23; Raymond Westfall's certificate; unidentified clipping, 5 Jan, 1907, TNBA Papers. See also Carlton, "The Toledo Newsboys' Association," 494.

50. "Little Stories of Men of Action," *World's Work* 16 (Aug. 1908): 10524; also Winship, "John E. Gunckel of Toledo," 1169.

51. Gunckel, *Boyville*, 143; Perkins, "A Toledo Philanthropy,"; "Information about the Toledo Newsboys Association," 13.

52. Minutes of the Sellers' Auxiliary, 26 Dec. 1913, Ledger: Auxiliary Officers, 1909–15, TNBA Papers. The boys required that Gunckel appoint officers for the coming year, but he passed that unenviable task to a committee of the auxiliary vice-presidents. Ibid., 1 and 3 Jan. 1914.

53. John N. Mockett, "A Tribute to John Gunckel," copy in TNBA; Winship, "John E. Gunckel of Toledo," 1170; "Little Stories of Men of Action," 10524–25.

54. Unidentified newspaper clipping, 21 Dec. 1906, Gunckel File; "Little Stories of Men of Action," 10525.

55. Ibid., Winship, "John E. Gunckel of Toledo," 1170; Allen A. Stockdale, "Gunck," *In Memory of John E. Gunckel*, 27.

56. Paul Boyer, comments at session on "Capitalism and the Problem of Moral Order in the Nineteenth Century: Institutions, Values, and Control," Seventh Biennial Convention of the American Studies Association, Minneapolis, 28 Sept. 1979. Kraditor, *The Radical Persuasion, 1890–1917*, 297–301, vigorously addresses this issue, quotations from 301, 305. See also Herbert Gutman, "Labor History and the 'Sartre Question,'" *Humanities* 1 (Sept./Oct. 1980): 1–2. The relationship between middle-class and working-class values is still a subject that needs much analysis. In France during the nineteenth century, for whatever reason, many employees at the Bon Marché department store apparently embraced the expected manners and ethos of middle-class respectability. See Richard Cobb, "The Great Bourgeois Bargain," *New York Review of Books*, 16 July 1981, 35–40. Similarly, studies of Paris and of Oxford, England, suggest that youths from the laboring classes were genuinely attracted to the middle-class value system. See, e.g., Lenard Berlanstein, "Vagrants, Beggars, and Thieves: Delinquent Boys in Mid-Nineteenth Century Paris," *Journal of Social History* 12 (Summer 1979): esp. 544–45; John Gillis, "The Evolution of Juvenile Delinquency in England, 1890–1914," *Past and Present* 67 (May 1975): 119. T. J. Jackson Lears, *No Place of Grace: Antimodernism and the Transformation of American Culture, 1880–1920* (New York: Pantheon Books, 1981), esp. xiii–xvii, 10, 17, emphasizes the place of "private struggles" within the context of hegemony and class: "A change in cultural hegemony stems not only from deliberate persuasion by members of a dominant class but also from half-conscious hopes and aspirations which have little to do with the public realm of class relations."

57. See, e.g., William J. Reese, "'Partisans of the Proletariat': The Socialist Working Class and the Milwaukee Schools, 1890–1920," *History of Education Quarterly* 21 (Spring 1981): 3–50. Moses Rischin, "From Gompers to Hillman: Labor Goes Middle Class," *Antioch Review* 13 (Summer 1953): 191–201, draws upon C. Wright Mills's assertion that "socially and ideologically the wage workers are more middle class than has been assumed." Irving Howe, noting that Yugoslavia's Tito in his early years dressed "like a dandy" and described himself as an "engineer," contends that "the thought of upward mobility is nowhere more firmly planted than

in the minds of many an able, self-conscious, even rebellious proletarian." Howe, "The Boss," *New York Review of Books*, 22 Jan. 1981, 10. For other discussions of similarities between working-class and middle-class ideologies of success and mobility, see Boyer, *Urban Masses and Moral Order in America*, 59–60; Richard Fox, "Beyond 'Social Control': Institutions and Disorder in Bourgeois Society," *History of Education Quarterly* 16 (Summer 1976): 206; Ruth Rosen, *The Lost Sisterhood: Prostitution in America, 1900–1918* (Baltimore: Johns Hopkins University Press, 1982): 107.

58. "The Original 102," *Newsboys' Herald* 1 (March 1917): 3, TNBA Papers. The remaining 11 may have been unaccounted for, or they may have held less esteemed positions. Unfortunately, there is no way to authenticate the Association's statistics.

59. Gunckel, *Boyville*, 48, 55, 197.

60. Toledo *Times*, 12 Aug. 1908; Gunckel, "Instructions to G.A.R. Guides"; on "Clean Up Day," minutes of special officers' meeting, 28 April 1911, "Minutes of Auxiliary Meetings, 1910–12"; on the booster "movement," Gunckel to Officers of the TNBA, 22 May 1911. Organization minutes of the Information Bureau, 5 and 18 Sept. 1912, and Application for Membership form, Department Bureau of Information in Ledger: Information Bureau, Auxiliary No. 8; on the Business Men's Club, Ledger: Auxiliary Officers, 1909–15, p. 39. All in TNBA Papers.

61. The photo was the frontispiece of Gunckel, *Boyville*, and appeared in numerous other publications; for more information, see the caption in the Gunckel File. For a while it was also part of the National Newsboys' Association letterhead. See, e.g., Gunckel to Ben Lindsey, 28 May 1906, Lindsey Papers, Box 7.

62. "The Boys of Toledo," *Work with Boys* 14 (April 1914): 140–49; a photo of the band, with a proud Gunckel in the back row, is on p. 141. See also Gunckel, *Boyville*, 55–58.

63. "Editorials from Papers and Periodicals throughout the United States," *In Memory of John E. Gunckel*, 50–51; "'Gunck' The Newsboys' Friend," *Juvenile Court Record* 10 (Oct. 1909): 4; Gunckel, *Boyville*, 50–52, on the St. Louis fair; clipping, "Gunckel's 'Boyville,'" *Journal of Education* (14 Nov. 1907): 518, and other unidentified clippings: 21 Dec. 1906 in Gunckel File, 5 Jan. and 20 July 1907 in TNBA Papers; Lindsey to Gunckel, 17 Dec. 1907, Lindsey Papers, Box 13. See also Lindsey to Gunckel, 16 Jan. 1909, Box 19.

64. The law prohibited boys and girls under 12 from street sales, and boys under ten from delivering newspapers on routes. Women's organizations in Toledo failed in their efforts to establish 14 as the age limit for boys and 18 for girls. See clippings from Toledo *Blade* and Toledo *Times* for 1923

in TNBA Papers. In contrast, by 1909 New York City had prohibited children under age 11 from street trades; employers who knowingly hired younger children faced $200 fines. "New Rules for Street Trades," *Charities and the Commons* 21 (13 Feb. 1909): 953–54. Boston, as early as 1892, barred children under 11 from street vending, but the law was loosely enforced and even suspended for several years. In 1902, Boston toughened its regulations. See Pauline Goldmark, "What Boston Has Done in Regulating the Street Trades for Children," *Charities* 10 (14 Feb. 1903): 159–60. Fall River, Massachusetts, reportedly had a licensing law which, in the words of one enthusiast, required "that boys must have clean hands who sell papers." On Fall River, and for a discussion of the Boston licensing system, see Philip Davis, "Newer Ideas of Work among Newsboys," *Work with Boys* 8 (April 1908): 96–104.

65. Gunckel, *Boyville*, 175–82.

66. Ibid., 184.

67. *Juvenile Court Record* 10 (Nov. 1909): 7. See also the photo of the well-dressed woman buying a paper from a small newsboy and laying a helpful hand gently on his shoulder, *Juvenile Court Record* 23 (March 1911): 1. As late as the 1980s, this image of the inventive newsie as entrepreneur appeared in McDonald's hamburger advertisements.

68. *Newsboys' World* 1 (Dec. 1915): 2–4, 10. The organization even had its own cheer: "On Republic, Boys' Republic, / Eyes on manhood goal, / Every fellow for his brothers, / Everyone for all, / Ever steady, always ready, / Look not to left or right, / We'll lead our peaceful army, / For our country's might." Ibid., 9. Copy in William R. George Papers (Olin Research Library, Cornell University), Box 78.

69. Goodhue, "Boston Newsboys, How They Live and Work," esp. 529–30.

70. Nearing, "The Newsboy at Night in Philadelphia," 778–84.

71. William Hard, "'De Kid Wot Works at Night,'" *Everybody's* 18 (Jan. 1908): 25–37. See also Edward N. Clopper, *Child Labor in City Streets* (New York: Macmillan, 1912), which stridently recommended prohibition of child street work; Marcus Kavanaugh, "Scrapper Halpin," *Scribner's* 33 (Feb. 1903): 182–94, an account of how a seven-year-old orphan newsboy survived on Chicago's downtown streets; Poole, "Waifs of the Street"; and Myron E. Adams, "Children in American Street Trades," *Annals of the American Academy of Political and Social Science* 25 (May 1905): 23–26. While newsboy life sometimes resulted in success, wrote Felix Adler, head of the National Child Labor Committee, "more often it leads to ruin." Adler, "Child Labor in the United States and Its Great Attendant Evils," *Annals of the American Academy*, 427. "There is no other occupation so

devastating, so debasing to the mind, as street hawking or street running,"
argued Edwin Markham, Benjamin B. Lindsey, and George Creel, *Children
in Bondage* (New York: Hearst's, 1914), 217.

72. Florence Kelley, "The Street Trader under Illinois Law," in *The
Child in the City* (Chicago: Chicago School of Civics and Philanthropy,
1912), esp. 290–97.

73. See, e.g., "What of the Newsboys of the Second Cities," 368–71.
Goodhue, "Boston Newsboys, How They Live and Work," 527–32, is also
suggestive on this point.

74. Winship, "John Gunckel of Toledo," 1169.

75. Unidentified clipping, 21 Dec. 1906, Gunckel File.

76. On the Denver association, Ben Lindsey to Gunckel, 23 June 1905,
Lindsey Papers, Box 4; M. A. Delaney, Chief of the Metropolitan Police
Department, to Lindsey, 30 Sept. 1905, Box 5. On the Chicago conference,
unidentified clipping, 21 Dec. 1906, Gunckel File. On the adaptations,
unidentified clippings, 30 Sept. 1907, Ledger: National, 1906–11, TNBA
Papers.

77. Perkins, "A Toledo Philanthropy"; Winship, "John E. Gunckel of
Toledo," 1170.

78. See "Information about the Toledo Newsboys' Association and the
National Newsboys' Association," 9–12; "Annual Report of the Toledo
Newsboys' Association . . . January 28, 1913," 7; clippings and lists of
names and towns in Ledger Books: National, 1906–11 and 1909–15, TNBA
Papers.

79. Detroit *Free Press*, 24 Nov. 1907; "Newsboy Detectives," *Work with
Boys* 12 (Dec. 1912): 528, and 13 (Jan. 1913): 35, and 13 (Sept. 1913): 318;
letter from B. A. Dunn to editor, *Work with Boys* 13 (Oct. 1913): 365.

80. William Byron Forbush, "A Western Newspaper and Its Newsboys,"
Charities and the Commons 19 (5 Oct. 1907), 798–801; Edmund W. Booth,
"Welfare Work for Newsboys," *Fourth Estate* (4 Sept. 1915): 12–13, clipping
in Robinson Scrapbooks.

81. Toledo *Blade*, 20 and 22 Feb. 1909; Perkins, "A Toledo Philanthropy." See also the copy of a letter soliciting funds, Robinson Scrapbooks.

82. See especially the retrospective account in Toledo *Blade*, 13 Aug.
1946; *In Memory of John E. Gunckel*, 11–15, 49, 53; and clippings in the
Gunckel File.

83. On Robinson, see "Jefferson D. Robinson," in J. M. Killits, *Toledo
and Lucas County, Ohio 1623–1923*, vol. 2 (Chicago and Toledo: S. J.
Clarke, 1923), 298–301; *Newsboy Herald* (Nov. 1929), 1–2, in TNBA Papers,
Newsboy Herald Box; Toledo *Times*, 11 Nov. 1923 and 20 June 1928, and
other clippings in Robinson Scrapbooks. Fragmented records show that the

Court of Investigation still operated in the 1920s. See Court of Investigation Minutes, 1910–13, 1923; Ledger, 1923–29, 406–10; Toledo *News-Bee,* 14 April 1923; *Yearbook of Toledo Newsboys' Association, June 1, 1923 to May 31, 1924,* TNBA Papers.

84. On Mockett, see "Weekly Program of the Toledo Newsboys' Association" (20 Dec. 1914), 1, and several unidentified clippings in Robinson Scrapbooks.

85. See, e.g., Toledo *Times,* 16 Feb. 1936, 3 Dec. 1939, 6 Oct. 1940, and other clippings in TNBA Papers.

86. "Newsies at Gunckel's Grave," *Newsboys' Herald,* 1 (March 1917): 4; Toledo *Blade,* 13 Aug. 1917, and other clippings in Robinson Scrapbooks and Gunckel File. The monument was included among the 750 unusual monuments described in Charles L. Wallis, *Stories on Stone: A Book of American Epitaphs* (New York: Oxford University Press, 1954). On the movie, see the "Mitch Woodbury Reports" column in Toledo *Blade,* 8 April 1947, Mitch Woodbury Scrapbook (Toledo–Lucas County Public Library).

87. See, e.g., Toledo *Blade,* 16 Aug. 1915.

88. Poem in "Program for the Sixth Sunday Afternoon Entertainment of the Toledo Newsboys' Association," 30 Nov. 1913, Robinson Scrapbooks; Robinson's views in unidentified clipping, Robinson Scrapbooks.

89. "Survey of All Street Trades and Preindustrial Occupations of Boys of the Iowa Industrial School for Boys on December 1, 1916," *Proceedings of the Eighteenth Iowa State Conference of Charities and Correction, Ottumwa, Iowa, October 22–24, 1916* (no publishing information); *The High Cost of News,* Toledo Consumer League Pamphlet No. 22, 1919, Robinson Scrapbooks.

90. Grace Margaret Wilson, "An Appreciation," *In Memory of John E. Gunckel,* 17; Margaret C. Hockinberger, "The 'Newsies' Heartache," ibid., 44. Ernest Bourner Allen's poem, "John Gunckel—A Tribute," asked "Who gave his life unselfishly, / To make the newsboys happy, free?" *Toledo Christian Commonwealth,* 20 Aug. 1915, clipping in Gunckel File. There are numerous other examples.

Chapter 5

1. N. H. Bowen, "The Career of Former Street Arab Proves Worth of Boys' Home," *Detroit Saturday Night* (16 Sept. 1911), reprinted as pamplet; undated flyer, "Genius from the Gutters," from *Detroit Saturday Night,* Ford Republic Papers. Hereafter cited as FR Papers. The FR Papers are

currently in the Collections of the Archives of Labor History and Urban Affairs, University Archives, Wayne State University; but the author worked with them when they were still in the possession of retired Ford Republic superintendent Clyde Reed, Grosse Point, Mich.

2. Pamphlet, *The Ford Republic, A Boy Community* (1910), 3. The pamphlet carries no date, but its publication received notice in *Survey* 23 (26 Feb. 1910): 811–12, which focused specifically on the contention that there was no need to distinguish between caring for dependent and for delinquent boys. The Ford Republic formally listed its residents as "delinquent and homeless boys." Department of Commerce, Bureau of the Census, *Benevolent Institutions, 1910* (Washington, D.C.: Government Printing Office, 1913), 114–15.

3. Bowen, "The Career of Former Street Arab"; and "Genius from the Gutters."

4. Information on d'Arcambal is difficult to find. But see the Detroit *Journal*, 4 March 1898, clipping in the William Allen Pendry Scrapbook, Burton Collection, Detroit Public Library. Letter from Prison Boards, 10 Aug. 1896, in Minutes of the Home of Industry, FR Papers; on d'Arcambal's last request, see copy of Minerva Davis Rowley to Members of the Association, 12 April 1899 Minutes; for brief descriptions of d'Arcambal's influence on her "boys," see Gertrude Baldwin's recollection in 7 March 1900 Minutes, and Detroit *Journal*, 4 March 1898, clipping in Pendry Scrapbook. According to the *Proceedings of the Twentieth National Conference of Charities and Correction, Chicago, June 8–11, 1893* (Boston: George Ellis, 1893), 176, the released prisoners who lived at the home found temporary lodging, clothing, employment, and "a cheerful, healthy and moral atmosphere" in which "to regain their lost manhood." The home was formally incorporated on 7 May 1890 under the 1855 Michigan act for charities. Photostat of the articles of incorporation, FR Papers.

5. *Fourteenth Annual Report of the Home of Industry Association of Detroit, Michigan, for the Year Ending March 31, 1903*, esp. 4–5. The act establishing the probation system is reprinted on pp. 12–13. FR Papers.

6. Ibid. On the McGregor Mission, see, e.g., the *d'Arcambal Home of Industry Association Report, April 1 to December 31, 1904*, 3.

7. *d'Arcambal Association Reports*, 1904–06, FR Papers.

8. Copy of certificate of Amendment to the Articles of Association of the Home of Industry, 12 May 1906; motto in *Boys' Home and d'Arcambal Association Report for six months ending September 1, 1906*; figures in J. Morris Fisher's typed report, 1 March 1907.

9. Minutes of the Home of Industry, 7 March and 4 April 1900.

10. See the Fred M. Butzel File (Burton Historical Collection, Detroit

Public Library), especially Gordon Damon, "Fred M. Butzel," *Detroiter*, 9 July 1928, and Detroit *Free Press*, 6 March 1955.

11. W. David Wills, *Homer Lane: A Biography* (London: George Allen and Unwin, 1964), 71–72.

12. Ibid., 66–71.

13. "Homer Lane's Technique Won Boys—and a Job," *Boys Republic* (Sept. 1944), and Clyde Reed, "The Story of the Ford Republic," typed manuscript (Jan. 1935), FR Papers. This was, according to David Wills, Lane's first application "of 'self-determination' in the treatment of delinquency." *Homer Lane*, 73.

14. Wills, *Homer Lane*, 71–74. On Carney's background, see *Boys' Home and d'Arcambal Association Report for six months ending September 1, 1906*, FR Papers.

15. Quoted in Reed, "The Story of the Ford Republic."

16. Wills, *Homer Lane*, 24–65, is extremely helpful on Lane's early years.

17. See, e.g., David Noble, *The Progressive Mind* (Chicago: Rand McNally 1970), 65–71.

18. Cooley to Rollin H. Stevens, 27 Aug. 1907, FR Papers.

19. Wills, *Homer Lane*, discusses the competing aspects of Lane's personality and contends that his troubles at the Ford Republic and, later, at the Little Commonwealth in England had similar psychological sources.

20. Typed recollection of Ruth J. Colebank, n.d. but after 1948, FR Papers. Cited hereafter as Colebank Account. Colebank started working at the Ford Republic in February 1912, but first visited the institution in late 1911. She stayed on for some four decades. See also Wills, *Homer Lane*, 52, 56, 77–78.

21. Wills, *Homer Lane*, 69, 83.

22. Homer T. Lane, "Solving the Boy Problem," I, *Detroit Saturday Night*, 6 March 1909, 12.

23. Ibid., and "Solving the Boy Problem," II, *Detroit Saturday Night*, 13 March 1909, 4.

24. Quoted in Lane, "Solving the Boy Problem," II, 12.

25. Homer T. Lane, "The Story of a Boy Gang," I, *Detroit Saturday Night*, 17 April 1909, 27; II, 24 April 1909, 8; III, 1 May 1909, 11.

26. Ibid., III, 1 May 1909, 11.

27. See, e.g., Richard Slotkin, *Regeneration through Violence: The Mythology of the American Frontier, 1600–1860* (Middletown, Conn.: Wesleyan University Press, 1973); "The Hard-Boiled Detective: From the Open Range to the Mean Streets," paper delivered at the Sixth Biennial Convention of the American Studies Association, Boston, 28 Oct. 1977.

28. Homer T. Lane, "A Boy Gang Regenerated," *Detroit Saturday Night* 8 May 1909, 11.

29. Lane, "Solving the Boy Problem," II, 4.

30. On "cultural voluntarism," see Lawrence J. Friedman, "Abolitionists versus Historians," *Reviews in American History* 5 (Sept. 1977): 345–46; Ronald G. Walters, *The Antislavery Appeal: American Abolitionism after 1830* (Baltimore: Johns Hopkins University Press, 1976), esp. 55–56, 99–100.

31. Cooley to Rollin H. Stevens, 27 Aug. 1907, FR Papers.

32. Superintendent's Report for year ending 29 Feb. 1908, FR Papers.

33. See, e.g., pamphlet, *Definite Needs of the Ford Republic* (1909), FR Papers.

34. Lane to J. L. Hudson, 27 Oct. 1908, FR Papers.

35. Colebank Account, FR Papers.

36. See Colebank Account, FR Papers, and Wills, *Homer Lane*, 81, on Lane's appeal to the E. L. Fords. On Henry Ford's appointment to the d'Arcambal Board, see *Detroit Saturday Night*, 15 May 1909, 2. According to David R. Crippen, reference archivist for the Henry Ford Archives, "he contributed less than one thousand dollars to [the Ford Republic] over the years as a matter of record." Crippen to author, 28 June 1978.

37. Superintendent's Report for year ending 29 Feb. 1908, FR Papers.

38. Homer T. Lane, "Solving the Boy Problem," III, *Detroit Saturday Night*, 20 March 1909, 4, 12.

39. Wills, *Homer Lane*, 81.

40. Lane, "Solving the Boy Problem," III, 12. On Lane's visit to Freeville, see Colebank Account, FR Papers. The exact influence of William R. George's work upon Lane is unclear. Willis, *Homer Lane*, 108, says that Lane claimed to have heard about George's republic only after he had started his own miniature commonwealth outside Detroit.

41. State Meeting of the Commonwealth of Ford, minutes of meetings from 14 March to 17 July 1909, FR Papers. On the constitution, see Wills, *Homer Lane*, 81–82.

42. R. H. Stevens, "Democracy as an Educational Principle," *Public* 14 (19 May 1911): 464. Rollin H. Stevens, a distinguished Detroit physician, was on the d'Arcambal Association board. Allendale Farm in Illinois was another junior republic that had a relatively young population.

43. Minutes of State Meeting of the Commonwealth of Ford, 20 March 1909, on Lane being out of order; 24 March 1909, on the teacher, FR Papers. Stevens, "Democracy as an Educational Principle," 464.

44. Typed description of the citizens' legal rights, and power of the Citizens' and Supreme Courts, c. 1909–12, FR Papers.

45. *The Ford Republic: A Boy Community* (1912), 5; Lane, "Solving the Boy Problem," IV, *Detroit Saturday Night*, 27 March 1909, 19; Wills, *Homer Lane*, 84; minutes of State Meeting of the Commonwealth of Ford, 24 March 1909, FR Papers.

46. *The Ford Republic: A Boy Community* (1910), 6–8; Lane, "Making Boys Real Citizens," *Detroit Saturday Night*, 29 May 1909, 9.

47. Lane, "Solving the Boy Problem," III, 12.

48. *The Ford Republic: A Boy Community* (1910), 4–13.

49. Lane to editor, *Detroit Saturday Night*, 21 Aug. 1909, 8; Lane quoted in editorial, "Self-Government in the Ford Republic," *Detroit Saturday Night*, 15 May 1909, 2; descriptions of the Citizen's Court and legislature in Lane, "Solving the Boy Problem," IV, 18–19, and Stevens, "Democracy as an Educational Principle," 464. Stevens, who observed the court on numerous occasions, believed that it administered justice "in a very creditable manner."

50. Colebank Account; Wills, *Homer Lane*, 94–95.

51. Maurice Willows to Lane, 24 June and 24 Aug. 1909, FR Papers.

52. Lane to editor, *Detroit Saturday Night*, 21 Aug. 1909, 8. Editorials and articles on the Ford Republic, *Detroit Saturday Night*, 31 July 1909, 1; 18 Sept. 1909, 2; 22 Jan. 1910, 37; 18 Dec. 1909. Quotes and comparison of Lane and Lindsey, *Detroit Saturday Night*, 20 March 1909, 1; 21 Aug. 1909, 8.

53. "Experts on the Ford Republic," *Detroit Saturday Night* 17 July 1909, 1.

54. George to Frederick Almy, 29 Aug. 1910; to Hastings H. Hart, 5 May 1910; to L. S. Trowbridge, 14 June 1910, William R. George Papers (Olin Research Library, Cornell University), Box 7. George's plans in Illinois and Wisconsin never reached fruition.

55. George to Hastings H. Hart, 5 May 1910, George Papers, Box 7.

56. Jack M. Holl, *Juvenile Reform in the Progressive Era: William R. George and the Junior Republic Movement* (Ithaca: Cornell University Press, 1971), 215–16.

57. Superintendent's Report for year ending 29 Feb. 1908, FR Papers; *Detroit Saturday Night*, 18 Sept. 1909, 2.

58. Colebank Account, FR Papers.

59. Statistical Report to 6 Oct. 1910, FR Papers; L. S. Trowbridge to William R. George, 18 June 1910, George Papers, Box 7. The age breakdown for the period from March 1907 to October 1910 was as follows: 7 years (1), 8 (4), 9 (16), 10 (28), 11 (55), 12 (62), 13 (81), 14 (60), 15 (50), 16 (25), 17 (3), 18 (1).

60. *The Ford Republic, A Boy Community* (1910), 3; L. S. Trowbridge,

Jr., to William R. George, 18 June 1910, George Papers, Box 7. Trowbridge added, nonetheless, that "as far as we can determine our institution is doing very good work."

61. Boys' Home and d'Arcambal Association Minutes, 17 Jan. and 16 Oct. 1916, FR Papers.

62. See, e.g., John Gillis, "The Evolution of Juvenile Delinquency in England, 1890–1914," *Past and Present* 67 (May 1975): 133–83; Lenard R. Berlanstein, "Vagrants, Beggars, and Thieves: Delinquent Boys in Mid-Nineteenth Century Paris," *Journal of Social History* 12 (Summer 1979): 531–52; Steven Schlossman, *Love and the American Delinquent: The Theory and Practice of "Progressive" Juvenile Justice, 1825–1920* (Chicago: University of Chicago Press, 1977); Anthony M. Platt, *The Child Savers: The Invention of Delinquency* (Chicago: University of Chicago Press, 1969); Steven Schlossman and Stephanie Wallach, "The Crime of Precocious Sexuality: Female Juvenile Delinquency in the Progressive Era," *Harvard Educational Review* 48 (Feb. 1978): 65–94.

63. "From the Ohio Juvenile Law," in a pamphlet published by the Toledo Juvenile Court Association, Ben Lindsey Papers (Library of Congress, Washington, D.C.), Box 21. See also copy of proposed Kentucky law, sent by Bernard Flexner to Lindsey, 2 Jan. 1908, Box 13. On Willis Brown, Salt Lake City *Daily Reporter*, 21 June 1905, clipping in Lindsey Papers, Box 4. Lincoln Steffens, *Upbuilders* (Seattle: University of Washington Press, 1968 ed.), 136–37, describes Lindsey's response to the "weak" boy. The quotation is from Lindsey to Charles R. Henderson, 29 Aug. 1904, Lindsey Papers, Box 2.

64. Comments of "Mr. Whittier" in "Discussion," *Proceedings of the Fifteenth Minnesota State Conference of Charities and Correction Held in Red Wing, November 17–20, 1906* (Stillwater, Minn.: Mirror Print, 1907), 37–38.

65. Statistical Report to 6 Oct. 1910, FR Papers. During a three-month period in early 1910, the Juvenile Court accounted for 92 of the 98 Ford citizens. L. S. Trowbridge, Jr., to William R. George, 18 June 1910, George Papers, Box 7.

66. Superintendent's Report, 29 Feb. 1908, FR Papers. A woman in charge of New York City's truant school told Jacob Riis that of the 2,500 children she had supervised over a one-year period, fewer than 60 deserved the label of incorrigible, and even many of those were in her view quite capable of improving their conduct if the right circumstances prevailed. Jacob Riis, *The Battle with the Slum* (New York: Macmillan, 1902), 350.

67. Statistical Report to 6 Oct. 1910, FR Papers. Surnames of the youths most active in the citizen's legislature in its initial months suggested that

they were largely of new immigrant backgrounds: Bpjanczyk, Slovinski, Palizzolo, Laskowski, Schalkowski, Cohen, Klatt, Navrot, Schwab, Bloman, Rademacher, Levin, Brake, Ziviski, and Haight. Minutes of State Meetings of the Commonwealth of Ford 14 March to 17 July 1909, FR Papers. A detention report sent to Wayne County, 1 March 1910, listed the following names: Geering, Bartocewiecz, Kadetski, Kaminski, Kasparack, Lemanski, McDowell, Marowski, Dusseau, Novack, Parmantye, Rennie, Shoerman, Smolinski, Tonak, Tauby, Weisman, Wesnetski, Wood, Zagajewski, Borsle, and Smith. Ibid. "During the first years . . . many of the boys were of Slavic or Latin extraction and were Roman Catholic." Colebank Account. Several boys were black. The publicity photograph showing four or them eating watermelon in the garden and saying, according to the caption, "Golly! Dis yere's a fine place," reflected all too well the era's racial views. *The Ford Republic: A Boy Community* (1910), 8. More details on the residents during the first years are apparently no longer available. For the later period, 1916–17, the United Community Services Papers, Collections of the Archives of Labor History and Urban Affairs, University Archives, Wayne State University, have some information regarding several boys' families and situations. But the number of case files in the United Community Services collection is quite small—at least concerning the Ford Republic— and is not representative, because the organization was a kind of court of last resort, dealing with children who had already been in several institutions.

68. Thirty-five were sent to industrial schools, two to the State Public School, and one to the county jail. Statistical Report to 6 Oct. 1910, FR Papers. A substantial number of boys may simply have fallen between the cracks, especially given the difficulties of the Ford Republic's administrators in keeping touch with former residents.

69. Butzel, quoted in Wills, *Homer Lane*, 100.

70. "The Career of Former Street Arab Proves Worth of Boys' Home," FR Papers.

71. Quotation from unidentified clipping in FR Papers, which also include many letters and publicity notices about Boys Republic Day.

72. Lane's remarks are quoted from Superintendent's Report for year ending 1 Oct. 1908, FR Papers; Lane to editor, *Detroit Saturday Night*, 21 Aug. 1909, 8. Regarding the Wayne County payments, see Detroit *News*, 11 May 1909, and statement from d'Arcambal Association to County of Wayne for detention services, 1 March 1910, FR Papers. On Joshua Hill's contribution, see *Detroit Saturday Night*, 9 April 1910, 2. The FR Papers contain a limited amount of information regarding the contributions of the E. L. Ford

family and others. On the monthly deficit, see *Detroit Saturday Night,* 18 Dec. 1909, 25.

73. Clippings, 27 Feb. 1909, FR Papers. Lane meanwhile threatened to bring charges against a nearby storekeeper who, despite state law, had sold tobacco to some of the Republic's smaller residents. Lane to Prosecuting Attorney, Oakland County, 13 April 1909, FR Papers.

74. On Lane's departure from the Ford Republic, see Wills, *Homer Lane,* 103–4, 119–21. Curiously, the official minutes of the Boy's Home and d'Arcambal Association contain no mention of Lane's resignation. From 1913 until 1917 Lane directed the short-lived but much-publicized Little Commonwealth in England. Scandal continued to haunt him. Charges on the part of two young female residents that he had slept with them drove him from the superintendency. Until his death in 1925, he developed a career lecturing and even practicing psychotherapy. Once again there was considerable scandal when a female patient claimed to have had an affair with him. Through the last years of his stormy career, Lane nonetheless exerted an enormous influence on several notable thinkers, especially W. H. Auden and A. S. Neill. His biographer believes that Lane was a pioneer in psychotherapy and helped to develop such techniques as "group therapy." See Wills, *Homer Lane,* 19–21. Wills, 129–216, discusses very well the English part of Lane's life. E. T. Bazeley, *Homer Lane and the Little Commonwealth* (London: George Allen and Unwin, 2d ed., 1948), also treats the subject. See also Holl, *Juvenile Reform in the Progressive Era,* 210–22, regarding Lane's influence on English education.

75. Butzel quoted from *Detroit Saturday Night,* 8 April 1916, 20, and Butzel to Dr. C. P. Jones, 12 Jan. 1922, FR Papers.

76. Homer Lane's wife, Mabel, served as acting superintendent for seven months. She received $100 per month, and the board emphasized that "this arrangement is month to month." Boys' Home and d'Arcambal Association minutes, 11 April 1912. Subsequently, she took charge of a boarding house in Ann Arbor, Mich. According to Wills, *Homer Lane,* 121–22, Mabel was a patient, sensible woman whose "life with Homer Lane was one long grind of solid, hard and often monotonous manual work." She nonetheless eventually rejoined him in England.

77. On McIndoo's background, see especially J. M. McIndoo to G. Stanley Hall, 1 and 18 April 1908, G. Stanley Hall Papers (University Archives, Clark University). Several letters between McIndoo and Hall, from May 1908 to May 1909, discussed the scholarship. Hall seemed much impressed by the fact that McIndoo was "a former Antioch man." See, e.g., Hall to McIndoo, April 1908 and 8 May 1909. McIndoo's salary was $2,400

per year, plus room and board for himself and his wife, Susie, and their child. Boys' Home and d'Arcambal Association Minutes, 19 Nov. 1912, FR Papers. Mrs. McIndoo, who had attended Antioch for two years and several other colleges thereafter, also had teaching experience. See McIndoo to Hall, 20 Oct. 1918, Hall Papers. Susie McIndoo played an important role in the daily life of the Republic. See Colebank Account, FR Papers, and Margaret Hamilton Alden, "The Ford Republic—A Boy Community," *Detroit Saturday Night*, 12 Dec. 1914.

78. McIndoo to G. Stanley Hall, 21 Oct. 1913, Hall Papers. Hall, who claimed to "have heard all sorts of good and I may say excellent reports of your work," expressed "very much" interest in McIndoo's information "about peculiarities of Polish as contrasted with other boys interests." Hall to McIndoo, 24 Oct. 1913, Hall Papers.

79. Boys' Home and d'Arcambal Association Statement, 29 Feb. 1912; *The Ford Republic, A Boy Community* (1914), 8–15, FR Papers.

80. *The Ford Republic, A Boy Community* (1914), 15.

81. Ibid., 13; report of "a committee of the Ford Republic delegated by the Citizens thereof," c. 1913–17, FR Papers. The report indicated that the Republic had 8 cows, 3 calves, 5 horses, 75 chickens, and around 50 pigs.

82. Colebank Account; *The Ford Republic, A Boy Community* (1914), 19–22.

83. On the Worcester project, R. J. Floody, "The Garden City Solution of the Boy Problem," *Work with Boys* 13 (July 1913): 260–63; on New Britain, R. H. Crawford, "The Boy and the Garden," *Work with Boys* 14 (Nov. 1914): 346–51. The Boys' Dominion in Toronto, Ontario, also featured gardens; see *Work with Boys* 13 (Sept. 1913): 319. Jacob Riis, *The Battle with the Slum*, 366–67, noted the Stryker's Lane truck farming project in New York City.

84. Floody, "The Garden City Solution of the Boy Problem," 263; Crawford, "The Boy and the Garden," 349. For a discussion of the English counterparts, see S. Martin Gaskell, "Gardens for the Working Class: Victorian Practical Pleasure," *Victorian Studies* 23 (Summer 1980): 479–500.

85. Floody, "The Garden City Solution of the Boy Problem," 261; McIndoo to Hall, 21 Oct. 1913, Hall Papers. According to McIndoo, "In order that the boy be best fitted to become a member of a civilized community, he must, in a certain measure, travel the road over which the race in its evolution has come, by recapitulating in milder forms some of the traits of his savage forebears." Such traits were "instinctive tendencies," or "preestablished laws" of the nervous system, which "are the child's inheritance from the past." The process of education, by providing

"the proper stimuli for his innate tendencies," was supposed to help a child along "the genetic highway." John M. McIndoo, *Instinct as Related to Education* (Detroit: published by the author, 1914). The publication was McIndoo's doctoral dissertation.

86. *The Ford Republic, A Boy Community* (1914), 16–18; the Redford (Mich.) *Record*, 3 Feb. 1927, clipping in FR Papers.

87. Colebank Account; Health Officer's section in the report of "a committee of the Ford Republic delegated by the Citizens thereof," FR Papers.

88. Although McIndoo spurned repressive tactics, claiming that "directions and rules have little place in the education of the child," he nonetheless emphasized proper training. Hence he wrote that a boy at the advent of puberty "should be trained to habits of obedience. . . . He should be trained to habits of respect and reverence." The various instincts, "if not properly directed," could "often become criminal." But if, say, "the fighting instinct" were "properly purgated and sublimated," the result would eventually be a "man of grit, determination and courage." McIndoo, *Instinct as Related to Education*, 7, 18–19, 59. While Homer Lane assuredly tried in his own unorthodox way to channel the youthful gang's tendencies, and probably shared McIndoo's view that "moral training is the forming of right habits of conduct" (*Instinct as Related to Education*, 43), he was much more willing to follow the gang's lead and adapt to it. The difference in emphasis between Lane and McIndoo, however superficial at first glance, in fact made a great deal of difference in the Republic.

89. *The Ford Republic, A Boy Community* (1914), 18–19; Colebank Account; McIndoo to G. Stanley Hall, 21 Oct. 1913, Hall Papers.

90. *The Ford Republic, A Boy Community* (1914), 22.

91. Daniel Rodgers raises this point in "Socializing Middle-Class Children: Institutions, Fables, and Work Values in Nineteenth Century America," *Journal of Social History* 13 (Spring 1980): 363–64.

92. Like Joseph Lee and other advocates of the playground movement in the progressive era, McIndoo hailed the role of team athletics for youths. Team sports taught youngsters "to give up much for the sake of the group. . . . Through these group or cooperative games the juvenile learns many valuable lessons of self-control. He is being fitted to become a true member of society." McIndoo, *Instinct as Related to Education*, 50. And like Lee, Luther Gulick, and other champions of children's play, McIndoo favored the leadership of trained adult experts and administrators. Dominick Cavallo, *Muscles and Morals: Organized Playgrounds and Urban Reform, 1880–1920* (Philadelphia: University of Pennsylvania Press, 1981),

interprets progressive efforts to develop a "team player's personality" among city youths in order to make them ideal twentieth-century citizens; see esp. 4, 22, 34, 39–45, 88–106.

93. "A Statistical Study of One Thousand Consecutive Admissions to the Ford Republic," 2 June 1930, FR Papers. The author(s) of the report noted that "the incompleteness of the records" handicapped the study. There is a chance, of course, that the negative interpretation of self-government at the Republic may have told more about the author(s) than about the home itself. The report indicated, for instance, that many of the boys came from families who had been alien to "the American type of self-governing institution" or "American democratic theory." Such an assessment may have reflected the nativistic sentiments of the "Tribal Twenties." See, e.g., John Higham, *Strangers in the Land: Patterns of American Nativism, 1860–1925* (New Brunswick, N.J.: Rutgers University Press, 1955), chap. 10.

94. Minutes of Board Meeting, 12 Aug. 1943, FR Papers. According to Ruth Colebank, valiant efforts on the part of superintendent Clyde Reed in the 1940s "to revive the old spirit" of self-government could not surmount the obstacle of "too many disturbed boys, too preoccupied with their own problems to be able to feel concerned about community needs." Colebank Account, FR Papers.

95. Quoted in "Project Justification Boys Republic" (n.d. but after 1954), FR Papers.

Chapter 6

1. Mrs. Celia Jackson Rathbun to author, 10 April 1982; "Making Good Citizens of Left-Overs," *Technical World Magazine* 19 (March 1913): 25; "The Makers of Men," *Work with Boys* 15 (Dec. 1915): 392; "The Boy Conservation Bureau, Homeing Homeless Boys," *Working with Boys* 13 (May 1913): 201.

2. The *Boys' Fund* 1 (Feb. 1888): 1. Cited hereafter as *TBF*. Hinckley Home-School-Farm at Hinckley, Maine, has a complete set of *TBF*.

3. *Good Will Record* 27 (June 1914): 170, regarding the numbers of residents. During that time there had been only two fatal illnesses; one death was due to tuberculosis, and the other followed a tonsilitis attack. On the land and livestock, see *Good Will Record* 28 (June 1915): 164–65, and 28 (Oct. 1915): 300. Hinckley Home-School-Farm has a nearly complete set of the *Record* for its first 30 years. Cited hereafter as *GWR*.

4. "Making Good Citizens of Left-Overs," 25; Lewiston (Maine) *Journal Magazine*, 4–7 Oct. 1911, clipping in Good Will Farm Papers (Hinckley Home-School-Farm, Hinckley, Maine).

5. Lewiston (Maine) *Journal Magazine*, 4–7 Oct. 1911, clipping; Hastings Hart speech at Good Will, 23 Nov. 1916, reprinted in *GWR* 29 (Dec. 1916): 322.

6. Hart speech, *GWR* 29 (Dec. 1916): 322. Hinckley's scriptural quotation, every issue of *TBF* and *GWR*; Hinckley's 1929 address, Good Will Farm Papers.

7. George Walter Hinckley, *The Man of Whom I Write* (Fairfield, Maine: Galahad Press, 1954). Referred to hereafter as *Man*. Hinckley completed the book in 1943; it was published posthumously. See the preface for his disclaimers—"I am not an egotist; I am not a saint; I am not a scholar; I am not a philosopher"—and his reasons for rejecting the personal pronoun "I."

8. Portland (Maine) *Sunday Telegram*, 6 Dec. 1936, in Good Will Farm Papers, Montgomery File. For more on Hinckley's genealogy, see "Gee Double You" (G. W. Hinckley), *As I Remember It* 2 (Hinckley, Maine: Good Will, 1936), "Explanatory" page.

9. Hinckley, *Man*, 13–15, 31, 230; for the account of the boy in the field, *TBF* 2 (July 1889): 4. Hinckley's mother was a Methodist; his father, a Congregationalist. For several years they both attended one church, then switched to the other, then back. George was baptized in the Congregational church. Hinckley's 1939 anniversary sermon, typed copy, Good Will Farm Papers, Montgomery File. Hinckley was the second of five children. Except for his younger sister, Jane, who worked as a matron at Good Will Farm in its first years, Hinckley's siblings do not seem to have been a conspicuous part of his life. On Jane, see *GWR* 17 (March 1914): 65–70. In his autobiography, Hinckley told twice the story about his parents' refusal to let him go camping. *Man*, 45–46, 103–4.

10. *GWR* 4 (Feb. 1891): 2; *GWR* 18 (March 1905): 25; Hinckley, *Man*, 24–26, 32–33.

11. *GWR* 4 (Feb. 1891): 2.

12. Hinckley, *Man*, esp. 32, 40–41, 50–53, 60–61, 81, 100–101.

13. Ibid., 64–68.

14. See *TBF* 1 (Oct. 1888): 4; Hinckley, *Man*, 82–89; Hinckley's 1939 anniversary sermon.

15. See Milan James Kedro, "Autobiography as a Key to Identity in the Progressive Era," *History of Childhood Quarterly* 2 (Winter 1975): esp. 400–402, regarding Johnson, Ely, Darrow, and Howe in terms of an "identity crisis"; Robert M. Crunden, *Ministers of Reform: The Progressives' Achievement in American Civilization, 1889–1920* (New York: Basic

Books, 1982), esp. ix, 16–17, 25–26, for progressives and "a crisis of conversion." On Jane Addams, see Crunden, 16–25; Christopher Lasch, *The New Radicalism in America, 1889–1963* (New York: Knopf, 1965), 15–29; and Allen F. Davis, *American Heroine: The Life and Legend of Jane Addams* (New York: Oxford University Press, 1973), 24–52. Obviously, efforts to interpret the "identity" crises of individuals must avoid crude reductionism or simplistic "explanations" of motives. It is essential also to keep in mind that such crises are not limited to any one era, as studies of Jonathan Edwards in the colonial period and Charles Grandison Finney in the antebellum era make clear. See, e.g., Richard Bushman, "Jonathan Edwards as Great Man: Identity, Conversion, and Leadership in the Great Awakenings," *Soundings* 52 (Spring 1969): 15–46; William G. McLoughlin, *Revivals, Awakenings, and Reform* (Chicago: University of Chicago Press, 1978), chap. 4.

16. Hinckley, *Man*, 82, 84.

17. Hinckley's 1939 anniversary sermon; *GWR* 27 (March 1914): 74–75; Hinckley, *Man*, 89–95.

18. G. W. Hinckley, *The Story of Good Will Farm*, 3rd ed. (Hinckley, Maine: Good Will, 1909), 9 (hereafter cited as *Story*); *GWR* 27 (June 1914): 162; Norman D. Palmer to author, 20 Aug. 1980. Palmer lived at Good Will from 1921–26. Both he and Homer G. Rines, a Good Will resident 1914–20, used the word "devoted" to describe the Hinckleys' relationship. Rines to author, Aug. 1980. Ray Tobey, who graduated from Good Will High School in 1906 and returned to teach there 1913–20, agreed that Elma Hinckley was of great help to her spouse and provided him with essential time to build the farm. Author interview with Tobey in Hinckley, Maine, Oct. 1978. Elizabeth B. Ziesel (Good Will, 1924) recalled that although Elma Hinckley "seldom appeared in public," she was "a lovely, sweet woman always ready to help." Ziesel to author, 8 May 1982. Others described her as "gracious, warm," and "a motherly woman." Alice C. Bordeaux (Good Will, 1923) to author, 5 May 1982, and Barbara W. Larkin (Good Will, 1908) to author, 9 June 1982.

19. *GWR* 9 (Sept. 1895): 4–5.

20. Article from the Bangor (Maine) *Industrial Journal*, reprinted in *GWR* 3 (Feb. 1890): 1; on Ben, *GWR* 14 (May 1901): 4–5, and 27 (Sept. 1914): 257–64. Over the years Hinckley and Ben Mason lost touch. One of Hinckley's most rewarding moments came at a YMCA Boys' Conference, after Ben had died, when a young man introduced himself: "I am your Ben's boy."

21. *TBF* 1 (June 1888): 2.

22. George W. Hinckley's Scrapbooks, vols. 1 and 2, Good Will Farm Papers.

23. Hinckley, *Man*, 113, 119–20; notes from Hinckley's journal, 17 March 1884, 1 Jan. 1885, 31 Dec. 1886, as recorded in *TBF* 1 (March 1888): 2.

24. See Hinckley's *Daily Detail of Missionary Work for the American Sunday School Union, 1885,* Good Will Farm Papers.

25. *TBF* 1 (Feb. 1888): 1.

26. Quoted in *TBF* 1 (April 1888): 2.

27. *TBF* contained a running commentary on these developments.

28. *TBF* 2 (March 1889): 2, and 2 (April 1889): 1.

29. Hinckley, *Story*, 30–33; Carleton P. Merrill's "Brief History of Good Will," read at the 50th anniversary celebration (1939), copy in Good Will Farm Papers; Hinckley to J. Willard Hayden, 15 April 1941, Good Will Farm Papers.

30. Hinckley, *Story*, 34–43; *TBF* 2 (July 1889): 1, 5; *GWR* 2 (Aug. 1889): 1–5; *GWR* 2 (Sept. 1889): 1, 5; *GWR* 2 (Nov. 1889), supplement: 1.

31. On Jane Hinckley, see *GWR* 27 (March 1914): 65–70, 92–94. Ray Tobey confirmed G. W. Hinckley's appraisal of her personality and effectiveness at Good Will. Tobey interview.

32. From Hinckley's journal, 29 Oct. and 15 Nov. 1889, as recorded in *GWR* 2 (Dec. 1889).

33. *GWR* 27 (June 1914): 161–69; Hinckley, *Man*, 214–26. Hinckley even paid his own children's tuition in the Good Will schools. As late as 1913, one journal carried Hinckley's photograph with the caption, "Helps boys and takes no salary." "Making Good Citizens of Left-Overs," 25.

34. Supervisor's First Annual Report, 30 June 1890, in *GWR* 3 (July 1890): 2. *GWR* 3 (Aug. 1890): 4; *GWR* 3 (Dec. 1890): 3–4; *GWR* 4 (April 1891): 3; *GWR* 6 (Oct. 1893): 3. Hinckley often quoted from articles about the farm.

35. From Hinckley's journal in *GWR* 6 (Oct. 1893): 3.

36. Hinckley's *Story of Good Will Farm* is largely an account of which specific individuals financed which buildings and additional purchases of land. The prominent names were Edwin Bancroft Foote of New York City; Mary and Frances Moody of Bath, Maine, who built a cottage in memory of their recently deceased brother; C. M. Bailey of Winthrop, Maine; Hiram F. Fogg, a successful entrepreneur and politician who settled in Bangor after he had participated in the 1849 California gold rush; William G. Broadway of East Orange, New Jersey; Walter M. Smith, wholesaler of dry goods in New York City, Boston, and Chicago; A. N. Ryerson, manufacturer of neckwear, of Noroton, Connecticut; Edwin Gould of New York City, son of multi-

millionaire Jay Gould; Elisha S. Converse, president of a rubber company and mayor of Malden, Massachusetts; A. L. Prescott, manufacturer of shoe polish in New York City; Moses Giddings, one of the pioneers in the Maine lumber industry, in which he made a fortune; George H. Yeaton, president of the Ayrshire Breeders' Association who in 1894 gave the farm three choice head of cattle registered in the Ayrshire yearbook, and who added to the herd from time to time; and Andrew Carnegie. Carnegie provided $15,000 to help construct a library at Good Will, a donation that was reportedly his only departure from a policy of building libraries for towns, not for institutions. Information on these individuals is scattered through *GWR*.

37. *GWR* 21 (Sept. 1908): 15.

38. Hinckley to Edwin M. Bulkley, 29 April 1907, Good Will Farm Papers.

39. *GWR* 4 (March 1891): 4; *TBF* 1 (1 Feb. 1888): 2; *TBF* 2 (Feb. 1889): 3; *TBF* 1 (Aug. 1888): 3–4, and 1 (Dec. 1888): 4.

40. *GWR* 24 (March 1911), offers an excellent overview. On prohibition, see esp. *GWR* 16 (Dec. 1903): 13–15; *GWR* 17 (May 1904): 4–5. On tobacco, *TBF* 2 (May 1889): 4; *TBF* 2 (July 1889): 5; *GWR* 3 (March 1890): 4–5; *GWR* 20 (Sept. 1907): 17; *GWR* 18 (June 1905): 11. On swearing, *GWR* 19 (March 1906): 4–5.

41. On Billy Sunday, *GWR* 26 (June 1913): 162–63, and 28 (May 1915): 137–38; on Gladden, *GWR* 24 (March 1911): 83; on Roosevelt, *GWR* 15 (Sept. 1902): 29.

42. *GWR* 2 (Jan. 1890): 2.

43. *TBF* 2 (May 1889): 3; *GWR* 15 (Oct. 1902): 13, and 13 (Nov. 1900): 10.

44. *GWR* 3 (Jan. 1891): 6; photo of children eating in *GWR* 14 (May 1901): 18.

45. *GWR* 23 (Sept. 1910): 327, and *Story*, 220; Hinckley to Richard M. Hurd, 12 May 1915, Good Will Farm Papers, on spanking; staff minutes, 5 Oct. 1914, Good Will Farm Papers, Montgomery File; Edward T. Bracket (Good Will, 1909) to author, 24 Oct. 1981.

46. Norman D. Palmer (Good Will, 1926) to author, 20 Aug. 1980. Palmer, who has "heard many of the great pulpit orators of America and elsewhere," ranks Hinckley "on par with the best," including Harry Emerson Fosdick and Reinhold Niebuhr. Ray Tobey said that the three greatest speakers he had ever heard were William Jennings Bryan, Booker T. Washington, and Hinckley. Tobey interview. Ziesel to author 8 May 1982, and Larkin to author, 9 June 1982, agreed that he was an exceptional preacher. Larkin, who was Hinckley's secretary for a while, said that although he

sometimes seemed "unapproachable," it was nonetheless possible to express her opinions freely to him.

47. See, e.g., Hinckley to John R. Boardman, 5 July 1911, and to R. A. Jordan, 7 Nov. 1917, Good Will Farm Papers. Hinckley expelled one boy "for defacing the school-building, for obscenity and general misconduct." Ibid., individual card file; also *GWR* 8 (Oct. 1894): 4.

48. Tobey interview; Brackett to author, 24 Oct. 1980; Harry Harles (Good Will, 1914) to author, 20 Aug. 1981; Homer G. Rines (Good Will, 1920) to author, Sept. 1980; Earl Ormsby (Good Will, 1912) tape, 3 Sept. 1980, in author's possession; Palmer to author, 20 Aug. 1980; Thomas A. Riley (Good Will, 1924) to author, 22 Oct. 1980; Joseph W. Shea (Good Will, 1923) to author, 29 June 1982; Benjamin Drucker (Good Will, 1911) to author, 27 April and 10 May 1982. See also Boston *Sunday Globe,* 16 July 1911.

49. *GWR* 13 (Nov. 1900): 7–8, and 15 (July 1902): 6–7; Boston *Sunday Globe,* 16 July 1911.

50. *GWR* 16 (June 1903): 3–5, and 19 (Sept. 1906): 21. That Hinckley genuinely cared for his young charges was also evident in a moving eulogy that he wrote for a former Good Will resident who had drowned. The conclusion read, "And so I thank God that I knew John Porterfield Todd." *GWR,* 11 (Dec. 1898): 12–14. One youth arrived at Good Will, as he later recollected, "a frightened, inhibited, repressed little boy, emotionally off-balance." Over the previous six years, he had moved from one unloving family to another. But at Good Will, "within a year all memory of the past was wiped out so that I had the feeling that I had been born in Hinckley." Pamphlet (c. 1982), "One Man's Acknowledgement of His Debt to the Good Will Idea," with Thomas A. Riley's open letter.

51. Hinckley's 1929 address, Good Will Farm Papers.

52. Bordeaux to author, 5 May 1982; Ziesel to author, 8 May and 5 June 1982; Larkin to author, 9 June 1982; Harles to author, 20 Aug. 1980; Ormsby tape, 3 Sept. 1980; Brackett to author, 24 Oct. 1980. Also, Francis Conley (Good Will, 1918) to author, 8 June 1982; Rathbun to author, 10 April 1982.

53. See, e.g., *GWR* 23 (Sept. 1910): 326. "Home! What golden memories flood the mind, what hallowed influences stir the soul! Home; the greatest and most sacred institution of our land, the safeguard and hope of our nation," Hinckley wrote. "What shall we say of the one who rears a home where none existed before?" *GWR* 28 (Sept. 1915): 285–86.

54. See, e.g., *GWR* 23 (Dec. 1910): 426–28, and 26 (Dec. 1913): 320–30. Also Tobey interview.

55. See, e.g., Hinckley's 1929 address. "I have been asked," Hinckley said, "'What one thing does Good Will Farm stand for?' I have invariably answered that Good Will is a community." Boston *Sunday Globe*, 16 July 1911.

56. Hinckley's 27 July 1931 speech, Good Will Farm Papers, and Boston *Sunday Globe*, 16 July 1911; *GWR* 2 (Dec. 1889), and 3 (Dec. 1890): 5.

57. *GWR* 15 (March 1902): 7–8.

58. On public rights, *GWR* 20 (March 1907): 14; 18 (June 1905): 14; 20 (Sept. 1907): 28. His hostility to a company's proposal to elevate a dam on the Kennebec River, thereby flooding lower sections of farms along the water—including Good Will—certainly helped to shape his position on public vs. corporate rights. "Sometimes men will fight for their homes," he wrote, "and sometimes when they see blight coming to the community in which they live, they will at least ask, 'Must it be so?'" Regarding the need to conserve timber and to protect scenic areas, he asserted: "Lumbering operations which are against the public good must be prevented." *GWR* 28 (May 1915): 150–51. His opposition to the Shawmut dam was in vain. In 1915 he complained that the water, now seven feet higher, had damaged some of Good Will's woodland. Supervisor's Twenty-Sixth Annual Report, printed in *GWR* 27 (June 1915): 173. *GWR* 25 (Dec. 1912): 360, on Consumer's League.

59. Hinckley to George F. Evans, 20 March 1906, Good Will Farm Papers. *GWR* 14 (June 1901): 13–14; *GWR* 15 (March 1902): 9; *GWR* 10 (Dec. 1896): 5.

60. *GWR* 6 (Oct. 1893): 1; *GWR* 10 (Oct. 1896): 5; Boston *Sunday Globe*, 16 July 1911.

61. Rines to author, Sept. 1980, contains a lengthy description of the boys' daily life at Good Will 1914–20. Ziesel to author, 8 May 1982; Larkin to author, 9 June 1982, and Rathbun to author, 10 April 1982 are instructive about the girls.

62. Brackett to author, 24 Oct. 1980; Harles to author, 20 Aug. 1980; Riley to author, 22 Oct. 1980; also Ormsby tape. "We never wanted for anything and always had plenty to eat," recalled one individual. Rathbun to author, 10 April 1982. Joseph Shea was so happy at the farm that he chose to remain there during the summer rather than spend vacation time with his mother. Shea to author, 29 June 1982.

63. *GWR* 10 (Dec. 1896): 5–6, and 11 (April 1898): 4; Lewiston (Maine) *Journal* article, reprinted in *GWR* 8 (May 1894): 11.

64. See, e.g., *GWR* 3 (March 1890): 4; Supervisor's First Annual Report, *GWR* 3 (July 1890): 2; *GWR* 4 (Feb. 1891): 1; *GWR* 9 (Dec. 1895): 5; Supervisor's Annual Report, *GWR* 19 (Sept. 1906): 28; and Supervisor's

Twenty-First Annual Report, *GWR* 23 (June 1910): 224–25. In 1910 there were nine children in the second and third grades; 15 in the fourth; 19 in the fifth; 20 in the sixth; 28 in the seventh; 17 in the eighth; 18 freshmen, 10 sophomores, eight juniors, and seven seniors in the high school. See also Hinckley, *Story*, 80–82, 110–27, and "Back to the Land for Boys," *Literary Digest* 45 (Nov. 23 1912): 963. *GWR* 27 (June 1914): 175, on those in college.

65. Tobey interview; Brackett to author, 24 Oct. 1980; Ormsby tape, 3 Sept. 1980; Harles to author, 20 Aug. 1980; Palmer to author, 20 Aug. 1980; Riley to author, 22 Oct. 1980. Bordeaux to author, 5 May 1982; Ziesel to author, 8 May 1982; Conley to author, 8 June 1982, and Shea to author, 29 June 1982 also expressed satisfaction with the educational system. Shea believed that if he "hadn't been fortunate enough to have been sent to Good Will," he never would have completed high school.

66. William Byron Forbush, *The Boy Problem*, 8th ed. (Boston: Pilgrim Press, 1913), 159–64. For the progressive attack on "the conspiracy of silence," see John C. Burnham, "The Progressive Era Revolution in American Attitudes Toward Sex," *Journal of American History* 59 (March 1973):885–908, and David J. Pivar, *Purity Crusade: Sexual Morality and Social Control, 1868–1900* (Westport, Conn.: Greenwood Press, 1973). Regarding the series by Stall and Wood-Allen, see, e.g., *GWR* 11 (April 1898): 1; *GWR* 11 (Oct. 1898): 16; *GWR* 14 (Oct. 1901): 20. According to Pivar, p. 226, Mary Wood-Allen, Superintendent of Social Purity for the Women's Christian Temperance Union in the mid-1890s, fused "social reform with medicine." The matrons at Good Will apparently apprised the girls of sexual information.

67. Rabbi Henry Berkowitz, "Education the Largest Factor in the Awakening of a New Conscience," *Proceedings of the National Conference of Charities and Correction at the Forty-First Annual Session Held in Memphis, Tennessee, May 8–15 1914* (Fort Wayne, Ind.: Fort Wayne Printing, 1914), 209.

68. Rines to author, Sept. 1980; Brackett to author, 24 Oct. 1980; Rathbun to author, 10 April 1982; Bordeaux to author, 5 May 1982; Ziesel to author, 8 May 1982; Shea to author, 29 June 1982; Palmer to author, 20 Aug. 1980; Harles to author, 20 Aug. 1980.

69. Berkowitz, "Education the Largest Factor in the Awakening of a New Conscience," 210.

70. Steven Schlossman and Stephanie Wallach, "The Crime of Precocious Sexuality: Female Juvenile Delinquency in the Progressive Era," *Harvard Educational Review* 48 (Feb. 1978): 85–87, cautions against underestimating the hold of "older Victorian thinking" on progressive reformers, even those who adopted the "new secular, scientific language." Howard

I. Kushner, "Nineteenth Century Sexuality and the 'Sexual Revolution' of the Progressive Era," *The Canadian Review of American Studies* 9 (Spring 1978): 34–49, makes a similar argument.

71. Rines to author, Sept. 1980. Francis Conley, who arrived at Good Will around 1913, remembered that the first time Hinckley summoned him for a rare individual conference, it was to discuss "the birds and bees." Conley to author, 8 June 1982.

72. *GWR* 23 (Sept. 1910): 327; Hinckley's 1939 anniversary sermon, Good Will Farm Papers; *GWR* 16 (June 1903): 21; *GWR* 21 (Feb. 1908): 18; *GWR* 28 (May 1915): 148–49. "We could not give the denominational preferences of ten per cent of the boys and girls at Good Will now," Hinckley wrote in 1915. *GWR* 28 (Aug. 1915): 243–44. Thomas Riley, during his six years at Good Will, never knew exactly what Hinckley's own church preference was. Riley to author, 22 Oct. 1980. Benjamin Drucker was Jewish but was never made to feel that his religion was suspect at Good Will or that he was a marginal citizen. Drucker to author, 10 May 1982.

73. See, e.g., *GWR* 14 (May 1901): 3–4, and 27 (March 1914): 71; *Story*, 220–21. Perhaps to protect the nonsectarian atmosphere that he talked so much about, Hinckley candidly told one parent, "You will doubtless want to place your son where he will receive a Catholic training and he will not receive this at Good Will. We would advise you to place him in a regular Catholic school." Hinckley to Samuel White, 31 Oct. 1918, Good Will Farm Papers. Although Hinckley may not himself have been anti-Catholic, such sentiment was strong enough in Maine to make the Ku Klux Klan a force in Portland in the 1920s. See Kenneth T. Jackson, *The Ku Klux Klan in the City, 1915–1930* (New York, Oxford University Press, 1967), 182–83. At the least, Hinckley's nondenominational Protestantism may have been partly tailored to political realities. He insisted, nonetheless, that "we were not prejudiced against the Catholics, the Roman Catholic Church was strongly prejudiced against us." Once, a "priest had made a determined effort" to remove a Catholic boy whom Hinckley had admitted. Hinckley, *As I Remember It*, 15–16.

74. Hinckley to the Directors of the Good Will Association, 11 June 1946, Good Will Farm Papers. Hinckley talked about the concept of "Reinsophy" in this letter of resignation. One of the farm's earliest graduates, years later at age 90, immediately mentioned "Reinsophy" and defined its main characteristics in order to summarize what the Good Will experience was all about. Tobey interview.

75. *GWR* 22 (June 1909): 231.

76. *GWR* 22 (March 1909): 115; Hinckley to W. D. Hutchins, 4 Aug.

1915, Good Will Farm Papers; Hinckley quoted in Boston *Sunday Globe,* 16 July 1911.

77. *GWR* 22 (March 1909): 111.

78. Hinckley's 27 July 1931 address.

79. *GWR* 25 (Dec. 1912): 368; also *GWR* 22 (March 1909): 111.

80. Hinckley's 27 July 1931 address; *GWR* 26 (Dec. 1913): 331–32; Hinckley's 1929 address.

81. *GWR* 19 (Sept. 1906): 24. The board overruled him on this matter. By 1906 several cottages looked alike, but Hinckley emphasized that this violated one of his early principles.

82. Hinckley's 27 July 1931 address.

83. See, e.g., C. C. Robinson to Hinckley, 13 Nov. 1908, and clippings, Good Will Farm Papers; testimonials, c. 1937, of individuals who resided at the farm in the years before 1912, Good Will Farm Papers, Montgomery File; Rev. A. Elsworth Harford to Hinckley, 23 Nov. 1912, Good Will Farm Papers.

84. *GWR* 19 (March 1906): 18. For the origins of the girls' homes, see *Story,* 83–98. Also useful: *GWR* 9 (June 1895): 13, and 11 (Oct. 1898): 13–14.

85. *GWR* 17 (April 1904): 10. Hinckley kept the boys' and girls' funds separate. Unless contributors specifically gave donations to the girls, the money went to the boys' account. "This," Hinckley explained, "is because the work for the boys is older and better known, and we infer that general contributions are intended for it." *GWR* 10 (Dec. 1896): 9. Some backers of the girls' department might have thought that he could "infer" just as easily that the Good Will account was for both boys and girls, unless the donors specified one or the other group.

86. *GWR* 26 (March 1913): 91, on the seal; *GWR* 12 (Oct. 1899): 14, and 19 (March 1906): 18, on publicity; *GWR* 23 (Sept. 1910): 338.

87. The girls had regular sewing and homemaking classes, but their courses also included algebra, American history, English, bookkeeping, and physiology. When the girls in 1902 guessed what they would be doing in eight to 10 years, they listed not only cooking, dressmaking, and teaching, but medicine and bookkeeping as well. See *GWR* 15 (July 1902): 15, and 15 (Oct. 1902): 12. The Lewiston (Maine) *Journal* had a fairly long and informative essay on the girls' department which was reprinted in *GWR* 17 (July 1904): 26–28. One of the first girls to graduate from Good Will became an honors student at Colby College. *GWR* 14 (Dec. 1901): 4. According to Celia Jackson Rathbun, who lived at the farm for several years, starting in 1910, "the boys did have more opportunities than the girls." But she bore no resentment: "It really was nice up at Good Will. I liked it very much. . . .

Mr. G. W. was the best. Good and fair to all." Rathbun to author, 25 May and 10 April 1982. Elizabeth Ziesel guessed later that "Mr. G. W. Hinckley undoubtedly was more interested in the boys," but she emphasized that the girls respected him greatly and that she personally had no sense of being a second-class citizen at Good Will. Ziesel to author, 8 May and 12 June 1982.

88. The individual card files from the early days indicate, e.g., that one father pledged 50 cents per week to take care of his son, that a widow agreed to pay $1.00 per month and provide whatever clothes she could, etc. Few pledges were over $100 per year.

89. *GWR* 20 (June 1907): 18–19. See also typed excerpts of letter, Hinckley to Hastings Hart, 31 Aug. 1914, Good Will Farm Papers, Montgomery File. In 1911 Hinckley stated that "the annual amount paid by parents who are able to pay anything toward the support of the boys and girls here amounts to 10 per cent of the running expenses of the institution. . . . There are eighty-four boys now with us for whom nothing can be paid by relatives." Lewiston (Maine) *Journal Magazine*, 4–7 Oct. 1911. See also *GWR* 27 (June 1914): 184–85.

90. *GWR* 4 (March 1891): 5; also *GWR* 28 (March 1915): 94.

91. *GWR* 19 (March 1906): 12–13, 16, 19; Hinckley, *Story*, 136–37; pamphlet, "Facts about Good Will" (1937), 8, Good Will Farm Papers.

92. Hinckley to Edwin M. Bulkley, 29 April 1907, Good Will Farm Papers.

93. See, e.g., *GWR* 15 (Dec. 1902): 3–4. Hinckley's approach had been to publicize his efforts generally through *GWR*, speeches, and word-of-mouth, and then to await the public response.

94. In 1904, e.g., he teetered on the edge of an emotional collapse and finally took to the Maine woods for a long camping trip to recover. *GWR* 17 (July 1904): 20; *GWR* 17 (Aug. 1904): 4, 28; *GWR* 17 (Sept. 1904): 4. In 1911 he was again exhausted emotionally. John Boardman to Hinckley, 16 May 1911, Good Will Farm Papers.

95. Hinckley to William G. Broadway, 26 March 1914, Good Will Farm Papers, Broadway correspondence, contains a good summary of Boardman's failings, which stemmed from too much enthusiasm and ineffectiveness. A few letters from Boardman in the Good Will Farm Papers point this up. See, e.g., Boardman to Hinckley, 1 May 1911.

96. See, e.g., *GWR* 26 (March 1913): 87. Hinckley did not cite specific numbers.

97. New York *Herald*, 5 Nov. 1911; *GWR* 24 (Dec. 1911): 407–9; E. W. Watkins to Hinckley, 1 June 1911, and typed page regarding the "history of William Lester," sent to Hinckley from Watkins, and pamphlet, "The Modern Way of solving the problem of homeless or imperiled boys: A report

of the last six months' work of The Boy Conservation Bureau, May 1st, 1915," Good Will Farm Papers. Although the bureau focused most of its attention on boys ages seven to 16, it did take an interest in a few girls, mainly sisters of the boys.

98. "The Modern Way," 2, 4; New York *Herald*, 5 Nov. 1911.

99. Pamphlet, "What 'Our Boys' Are Doing in School," sent to Hinckley, 28 June 1915, Good Will Farm Papers. The bureau had also placed 64 boys in ten other home-schools, and 26 in private homes. See also Watkins's report, 5 May 1916, Good Will Farm Papers, and "The Boy Conservation Bureau, Homeing Homeless Boys," 200–211. By 1933, when Watkins retired, the Bureau claimed to have sponsored 1,561 boys and 105 girls. "The Boy Conservation Bureau, The Twenty-Second Annual Report, 1932–33," Good Will Farm Papers.

100. See, e.g., Watkins to W. P. Hinckley, 23 May 1916, Good Will Farm Papers.

101. Hinckley to Watkins, 4 June 1914; Watkins to Hinckley, 6 June 1914, and Watkins to W. P. Hinckley, 19 June, 6, 7, and 29 July 1914, Good Will Farm Papers. In 1941 Hinckley said that the Boy Conservation Bureau had sent "scores" of New York boys to Good Will. Hinckley to J. Willard Hayden, 15 April 1941, Montgomery File.

102. Hinckley to Judge Ben Lindsey, 23 Oct. 1907, Lindsey Papers (Library of Congress, Washington, D.C.), Box 11.

103. See, e.g., *GWR* 13 (May 1900): 5; 8 (May 1900): 5; 26 (Dec. 1913): 354; 25 (Sept. 1912): 268–71.

104. *GWR* 24 (Dec. 1911): 425–26.

105. Hinckley, *Man*, 195–97; *GWR* 24 (May 1911): 136–37.

106. *GWR* 24 (May 1911): 140–42.

107. See, e.g., *GWR* 19 (March 1906): 7–10, and 24 (Dec. 1911): 397–402.

108. *GWR* 24 (Sept. 1911): 286–93. Four years later, Powlison's son and daughter voluntarily worked at Good Will. *GWR* 29 (Sept. 1916): 246.

109. John Boardman to Hinckley, 26 April 1911, Good Will Farm Papers.

110. William R. George to Hinckley, 1 Feb. 1906, Good Will Farm Papers.

111. Herman Swift to Homer Lane, 18 Sept. 1909, Ford Republic Papers (Collection of the Archives of Labor History and Urban Affairs, University Archives, Wayne State University).

112. *GWR* 25 (July 1912): 221. Other states represented: Connecticut, 7; New Hampshire, 2; Delaware, 1; Vermont 1; Maine, 99.

113. The individual card files on the children in the first several decades contain virtually no information regarding ethnic or religious background.

A visitor in 1895 reported that the 76 boys were "really all . . . of American parentage." Kirk Monroe in *Harper's Round Table,* reprinted in *GWR* 9 (Sept. 1895): 7.

114. Department of Commerce, Bureau of the Census, *Benevolent Institutions, 1910* (Washington, D.C.: Government Printing Office, 1913), 108–9; Homer Rines (Good Will, 1920) to author, Aug. 1980. The fact that Good Will had no blacks may have indicated more about pressures on Hinckley than about his own inclinations, for he was apparently more racially tolerant than were many of his generation. At least twice, when he traveled to the South, he visited black church services. In Virginia he and his companion "were the only whites in the congregation." *GWR* 11 (June 1897): 3. In his autobiography, Hinckley referred to "the absence of racial prejudice in my own heart" and recounted his efforts to defuse anti-Chinese feelings at a boys' camp. Hinckley, *Man,* 105–7. The date when Good Will, now integrated, first accepted a black youth is not clear.

115. W. P. Hinckley to Raymond Cagon, 9 Feb. 1954, Good Will Farm Papers, Montgomery File. The individual card files also confirm this. According to Thomas Riley, "Most of us were children with no parents or only one." Riley to author, 22 Oct. 1980.

116. *GWR* 18 (Dec. 1905): 3–5; testimonials, c. 1937, in Good Will Farm Papers, Montgomery File.

117. Hinckley to Philip W. Wall, 25 April 1918; to Mrs. Llewellyn Brown, 14 June 1918, and to Byron Clark, 12 June 1918, Good Will Farm Papers.

118. Hinckley to Mrs. Llewellyn Brown, 26 March 1919, and to Amos L. Prescott, Nov. 22, 1918, Good Will Farm Papers.

119. Hinckley to Mrs. J. C. Stodder, 2 Jan. 1919; to H. T. Hayward, 17 January 1919; to Mrs. C. C. Converse, 18 Dec. 1918. Good Will Farm Papers.

120. Hinckley's 1929 address and Hinckley to Directors of the Good Will Association, 11 July 1946, Good Will Farm Papers, Montgomery File.

121. Hinckley, *Man,* preface.

122. Testimonials, c. 1937, Good Will Farm Papers, Montgomery File; *GWR* 18 (Dec. 1905): 4, and 28 (Dec. 1915) 382.

123. The Montgomery File in the Good Will Farm Papers has considerable information on this change.

124. The *Record* 4 (July, 1977): 2; the *Record* 5 (Aug. 1978): 3, 8; the *Record* 6 (March, 1979): 4. By Sept. 1981, the Home-School-Farm was accepting "any child between the ages of seven and fourteen who needs and could profit by the help that Hinckley can offer." The *Record* 8 (Sept. 1981): 10. The *Record* replaced *GWR.*

125. Testimonials, c. 1937, Good Will Farm Papers, Montgomery File.

Chapter 7

1. *50 Year Record, Class of 1884, Princeton* (Princeton, N.J.: Princeton University Press, 1937), 31.

2. Edward L. Bradley and Maud Menefee Bradley, *Allendale Annals* (Lake Villa, Ill.: Allendale Press, 1926), 8.

3. Robert Wiebe, *The Search for Order, 1877–1920* (New York: Hill and Wang, 1967), and Alan Trachtenberg, *The Incorporation of America: Culture and Society in the Gilded Age* (New York: Hill and Wang, 1982), make clear the immensity of the social, cultural, political, and economic changes that battered America in the late nineteenth century.

4. Pamphlet, "The Charity Switchboard" (1913), Minneapolis Humane Society Papers (Minnesota State Historical Society), 39-C-12-10F.

5. Roy Lubove, *The Professional Altruist: The Emergence of Social Work as a Career, 1880–1930* (Cambridge: Harvard University Press, 1965).

6. Bradley, *Allendale Annals*, 8. Some reformers helped to sketch the outlines of a professional, bureaucratic society, but no less prominent a child saver (and Bull Moose Progressive) than Ben Lindsey often took issue with advocates of efficiency, expertise, and corporate strategies. See David Thelen, "Collectivism, Economic and Political: Ben Lindsey against Corporate Liberalism," *Reviews in American History* 1 (June 1973): 271–76. See also Edward A. Purcell, "Brandeis and the Democratic Vision," *Reviews in American History* 1 (June 1973): 253–60, and Otis L. Graham, Jr., *An Encore for Reform: The Old Progressives and the New Deal* (New York: Oxford University Press, 1967), regarding progressive resistance to modernizing trends. Such resistance was invariably uneven, however; Lindsey worked anxiously to pull champions of the juvenile court under one organizational umbrella, the Juvenile Improvement Association. See, e.g., Lindsey to Willis Brown, 26 March 1906, Lindsey Papers (Library of Congress, Washington, D.C.), Box 7.

7. This was not always a welcome trend. At the Baby Fold in Normal, Illinois, e.g., the superintendent and administrative board "were dead set against the state butting into their business. . . . The whole idea of licensing, of any type of supervision or investigation, was anathema to the whole organization." Sometimes, in fact, when the state people came, they found the door locked. Interview with Rev. William H. Hammitt, 25 May 1972. Hammitt, superintendent of the Baby Fold from 1939 until the mid-1970s, was well acquainted with the first superintendent, whom he replaced.

8. Peter L. Tyor and Jamil S. Zainaldin, "Asylum and Society: An Approach to Institutional Change," *Journal of Social History* 13 (Fall 1979): 23–48, suggests that "the private/public distinction may well be of the

utmost importance" in the history of asylums. Private funding may have allowed more autonomy to follow "an ever-expanding anti-institutional policy" (p. 39). Of course, such autonomy can cut in several directions. By the 1960s, public agencies and institutions were more open and flexible on, say, racial issues than were many of their private counterparts.

9. See, e.g., Susan Tiffin, *In Whose Interest? Child Welfare Reform in the Progressive Era* (Westport, Conn.: Greenwood Press, 1982), 55–56.

10. Examples beyond the National Benevolent Association and the Children's Home Societies are legion. In 1896 the Evangelical Lutheran Kinderfreund Society of Wisconsin, inspired by the work of the Wisconsin Children's Home Society, opened its own home placement operation; by 1910 there were 14 other Kinderfreund societies. The Catholic Home Bureau for Dependent Children, the first Catholic placement agency for destitute, neglected, and dependent children, opened in New York City in 1898. For these organizations and others, see Hastings H. Hart, *Preventive Treatment of Neglected Children* (Philadelphia: William Fell, 1910), 5, 147, 149, 174, 193.

11. Milwaukee *Journal,* 21 April 1974; "Bert Hall," *Our Boys* 27 (July 1933): 4.

12. In this sense the progressive child savers were spiritual kin of the Jacksonian era's urban reformers; see Paul Boyer, *Urban Masses and Moral Order in America, 1820–1920* (Cambridge: Harvard University Press, 1978), esp. 54–64.

13. "Discussion," *Proceedings of the Fifteenth Minnesota State Conference of Charities and Correction Held at Red Wing, November 17–20, 1906* (Stillwater, Minn.: Mirror Print, 1907), 32–38.

14. Anthony M. Platt, *The Child Savers: The Invention of Delinquency* (Chicago: University of Chicago Press, 1969); David J. Rothman, *Conscience and Convenience: The Asylum and Its Alternatives in Progressive America* (Boston: Little, Brown, 1980) and Steven Schlossman, *Love and the American Delinquent: The Theory and Practice of "Progressive" Juvenile Justice, 1825–1920* (Chicago: University of Chicago Press, 1977), all stress this theme. The example of Peter is in Schlossman, pp. 176–77.

15. Pamphlet, "The White Door Settlement" (c. 1906), Lindsey Papers, Box 8.

16. See, e.g., Harriet Mashburn Stewart to Dear Friend, Dec. 1906, Lindsey Papers, Box 8.

17. Boyer, *Urban Masses and Moral Order in America, 1820–1920,* 61, regarding the "impulse toward self-definition" among reformers. In 1920, Princeton awarded Bradley not only an honorary master of arts degree, but

what was reportedly the most "spontaneous and enthusiastic applause by a Commencement audience" in the memory of those familiar with the institution. *50 Year Record, Class of 1884*, 33.

18. Bertram Wyatt-Brown, "The Mission and the Masses: The Moral Imperatives of the City Bourgeoisie," *Reviews in American History* 7 (Dec. 1979): 527–34, raises this question of nineteenth-century reformers.

19. Dan Hopkins, himself orphaned at ten, and Aggie had long been sympathetic to the needs of poor, dependent children. The Southern Illinois Conference of the Methodist Episcopal Church gave him permission to establish the home—at his own risk—and he was superintendent from 1911 to 1917. The institution, relocated in Mt. Vernon, Ill., is now the United Methodist Children's Home. See handwritten reminiscences of Aggie Hopkins (1955) and typed document, "Orphan's and Children's Home" (1950s), in possession of the Home.

20. "Allendale Farm Residents. Being the Record of Boys Resident in Allendale Farm . . ." (Allendale School for Boys), S. T. and W. H. entries. Cited hereafter as "Record." On Dega, *Our Boys* 8 (Jan. 1914): 11–12.

21. David Thelen, "Urban Politics: Beyond Bosses and Reformers," *Reviews in American History* 7 (Sept. 1979): 406–12, provides a forceful reminder of this.

22. "Record," R. F. and E. I. entries.

23. "Record," C. B. entry; Rev. Clyde Hay's address, *Dedication Services in Memory of Our Beloved Founder "Captain" Edward L. Bradley* (Lake Villa, Ill.: Allendale Press, 1938), 9; Bradley, *Allendale Annals*, 34.

24. Bradley, *Allendale Annals*, 14–15.

25. Ibid., 15; Jack M. Holl, *Juvenile Reform in the Progressive Era: William R. George and the Junior Republic Movement* (Ithaca, N.Y.: Cornell University Press, 1971), 31–33, 335–36, on George's dilemma; Tiffin, *In Whose Best Interest?* 54–55, on other reformers.

26. Robert M. Crunden, "George D. Herron in the 1890s: A New Frame of Reference for the Study of the Progressive Era," *Annals of Iowa*, 42 (Fall 1973): 102–6, 111–13, and Richard L. McCormick, "The Discovery That Business Corrupts Politics: A Reappraisal of the Origins of Progressivism," *American Historical Review* 86 (April 1981): 272–73, on progressive rhetoric.

27. Arthur E. Bestor, Jr., "Patent-Office Models of the Good Society: Some Relationships between Social Reform and Westward Expansion," *American Historical Review* 58 (April 1953): 505–26.

28. "Outdoors for Boys," *Our Boys* 11 (April 1917): 8.

29. *Milwaukee Journal*, 21 April 1974.

30. "Progress was the new century's chief problem," writes Richard M. Abrams, *The Burdens of Progress, 1900–1929* (Glenview, Ill.: Scott, Foresman, 1978), 31.

31. James P. Johnson to Juvenile Protective League of Minneapolis, 17 June 1915, Minneapolis Humane Society Papers, 39-C-12-10F.

32. William S. Bowdern, "An Unconventional Orphanage," Special Number of *Father Dunne's News Boys' Journal* (1919), 1; Roger Baldwin to Dunne, 22 Sept. 1910; "Father O'Grady's Report of His Study of Father Dunne's Newsboys' Home," c. 1926, at Father Dunne's Home for Boys.

33. *Second Annual Report of the State Charities Commission to the Honorable Charles S. Deneen* (Springfield: Illinois State Journal, 1912), 8–12. Some 60 private institutions had by then received State charters.

34. Hastings H. Hart to John G. Shortall, 24 May 1901, Illinois Humane Society Papers (Illinois State Historical Society Library), Box 53; "Report of Juvenile Court for Cook County, Illinois, for the year ending June 30 1900," Box 59.

35. "The Abuse of a Good Thing," *Christian Philanthropist* 24 (July 1916): 6–7.

36. Rino J. Patti, "Child Protection in California, 1850–1966" (Ph.D. diss., University of Southern California, 1967), 112–13; "Orphan Asylum Scandal," *Charities* 19 (Nov. 1903): 458; E. Fellows Jenkins to John G. Shortall, 22 May 1901, Illinois Humane Society Papers, Box 53; Jenkins to Shortall, 21 July 1903, and *Record-Herald* newspaper clipping, 14 March 1903, Box 62; *Eighteenth Biennial Report of the Board of State Commissioners of Public Charities of the State of Illinois* (Springfield: Illinois State Journal, 1905), 149–50.

37. Grand Junction (Colo.) *Daily Sentinel*, 15 March 1981.

38. Edward A. Halsey, "Answering the Children's Cry," *The World To-Day* 20 (June 1911): 735–40; Rothman, *Conscience and Convenience*, 268–82, for a grim description of the "precipitous" decline "from the rhetoric to the reality of juvenile institutions in the early twentieth century"; interview with Emma S. Blackman in Normal, Ill., 13 March 1972.

39. *Juvenile Court Record* 10 (Nov. 1912): 3.

40. "First Farm School Boy Dies," *Our Boys* 30 (July 1936): 1, on Dega; Benjamin A. Drucker to author, 27 April and 10 May 1982; Joseph W. Shea to author, 29 June 1982; Bradley, *Allendale Annals*, 129.

41. *Dedication Services*, photographs, and remarks of Robert A. Canon, all in possession of Allendale School for Boys.

Bibliographical Note

•

Primary Sources

Manuscripts and turn-of-the-century publications of various children's institutions and organizations provided the bulk of material for this study, but the collections of Ben Lindsey (Library of Congress, Washington, D.C.), and William R. George (Olin Research Library, Cornell University) were extremely helpful. The Lindsey Papers, besides containing many informative letters written by the "Kid's Judge" himself, serve as a virtual clearinghouse for material on progressive child saving activities; child rescue people from across the nation not only wrote to Lindsey but sent pamphlets and clippings as well. The George Papers are excellent on the junior republic idea, not just as George implemented it himself, but also on its adaptations and popularity elsewhere. For the purposes of this study, the small Sophonisba Breckinridge collection (Library of Congress) and the large Daniel Carter Beard Collection (Library of Congress) were disappointing.

The Children's Home Society of Minnesota (St. Paul) has a relatively small but exceptionally rich assortment of materials from its initial years. The handwritten Journal of the Superintendent, for the years 1893 to 1904, is a series of quarterly and annual reports to the board of directors, but it often reads like a diary and conveys very well a sense of what child saving was like at the grass-roots level. The Minutes of Directors' Meetings supply more good information. Also in the possession of the Home Society are some revealing letters to and from the superintendent, plus some brief typed histories by E. P. Savage, and S. W. Dickinson, the first superintendents. Unfortunately, only a few of the early issues of the society's official publication, the *Minnesota Children's Home Finder*, still exist. The collection of Edward P. Savage Papers (Division of Archives and Manuscripts, Minnesota Historical Society), although quite small, is indispensable regarding Savage. On J. P. Dysart and the Wisconsin Children's Home Society, the Children's Service Society of Wisconsin (Milwaukee) has all the issues of the Wisconsin edition of the monthly *Home Finder* from 1899 to mid-1902, scattered copies of other issues, a few clippings, and other documents, including Dysart's last report to the board in 1922.

The National Benevolent Association Papers (Disciples of Christ Historical Society, Nashville) contain only several issues of the *Orphan's Cry* (1894–1903) but virtually a complete run of its successor, the *Christian Philanthropist*. These monthly publications are loaded with information on NBA child-saving. Besides numerous essays and reprinted speeches and sermons, there are the matron's and superintendent's monthly reports from each of the institutions. The quality of the reports varies, given the different personalities of the people who wrote them; but some are outstanding, especially those of Tena Williamson in St. Louis. The NBA Papers also include some limited correspondence, clippings, and a number of pamphlets. The biographical file at the Disciples of Christ Historical Society has information on several key figures, especially Matilda Hart Younkin. The scrapbooks of George Snively are helpful mainly for appreciating his energy and popularity as a speaker.

The Toledo Newsboys' Association Papers, Jefferson D. Robinson's Scrapbooks, and the John E. Gunckel Files (Toledo–Lucas County Public Library) provide splendid material on the newsboys' organization and Gunckel. The materials are varied and fascinating, although the minutes of meetings and of the "Court of Investigation" are fragmented and few in number. The Samuel M. Jones Papers (Toledo–Lucas County Public Library) contain only a few communications between the mayor and Gunckel. Gunckel's own account, *Boyville: A History of Fifteen Years' Work among Newsboys* (Toledo: Toledo Newsboys' Association, 1905), is basic on the association and Gunckel's perspectives.

The Papers of the Ford Republic (Collections of the Archives of Labor History and Urban Affairs, University Archives, Wayne State University) are quite rewarding on the institution's formative period. They include minutes of the board meetings, numerous published reports, the typed recollections of Ruth J. Colebank (who worked at the institution from 1912 until the 1950s), several clippings, and some correspondence. The G. Stanley Hall Papers (University Archives, Clark University) include some illuminating correspondence between Hall and J. M. McIndoo regarding the shift in tone at the republic following Homer Lane's departure. McIndoo's published Ph.D. dissertation, *Instinct as Related to Education* (Detroit: published by the author, 1914), shows Hall's influence on McIndoo and documents the latter's point of view at the time he became superintendent. The Fred M. Butzel File (Burton Historical Collection, Detroit Public Library) is helpful on Butzel. There is apparently no collection of Homer

Lane manuscripts, but his 19_
is crucial for understand__

The Hinckley H__
almost all issues o_
the basis for any his_
George W. Hinckley.
School-Farm but are ve_
ence, although clustered __
Hinckley's scrapbooks, mai_
interest in aiding needy child_
ed. (Hinckley, Maine: Goodwil_
velopment of the institution and n_
His autobiography, *The Man of Wh_
Press, 1954), is disappointing (in ten_
suggestive (in terms of what he chose to_
it).

Most of the papers concerning Allendale_
before World War I. Nonetheless, the sever_
constitute "Allendale Farm Residents. Being the_
Allendale Farm, Lake Villa, Illinois, Together wit_
Home and Home Life" (Allendale School for Boy_
exceptionally fine. Some sense of what life was li_
emerges in scattered copies of the *Allendale Alumnus* fo_
1929. Edward L. Bradley and Maud Menefee Bradley's A_
(Lake Villa, Ill.: Allendale Press, 1926) is both charming and_
the junior republic's early years.

A strikingly poignant illustration of a matron's life in a la_
asylum is available in Matron's Dairy, 1894–96, Children's Home o_
Papers (Burton Historical Collection, Detroit Public Library). Fathe_
ne's Home for Boys (St. Louis) holds copies of several of its prewar an_
reports, the special issue in 1919 of *Father Dunne's News Boys' Journal,* a_
Father O'Grady's report (c. 1926)—all of which, though scanty in number,
are quite useful on Dunne's institution. The Central Baptist Children's
Home Papers (Department of Special Collections, University of Illinois at
Chicago Circle) contain minutes of the board of managers and superintendent's reports, but these are disappointingly thin. The United Methodist
Children's Home (Mount Vernon, Ill.) has a smattering of documents on its
early history, especially the brief handwritten memoir by one of the founders, Aggie Hopkins. Although the archives of the Milton Hershey School are
closed, the directors made available several items of interest, particularly

nuscript (c. 1949) of Guy C. Weber, one of the first five
Hershey Industrial School, and a copy of the institution's
t Lad Lake (Dousman, Wis.) there are several fine sources
ut the founding and development of the Wisconsin Home
ool: the Minutes of the Board, including superintendent's
-04; a fairly complete set of the monthly journal *Our Boys*
; and publicity pamphlets.

rs of the Illinois Humane Society (Illinois State Historical
rary) are voluminous—including mainly thousands of individual
hat provide a depressing catalog of human misery and abuse; for
the small amount of correspondence involving such individuals
ngs Hart, E. Fellows Jenkins, and John Shortall was useful. The
on of the Minneapolis Humane Society (Minnesota Historical Soci-
elded several good items. A number of collections in the Social
re History Archives (University of Minnesota Libraries)—those of the
ey Associates, Inc., the Child Welfare League of America, Paul Kellogg,
Child Study Association of America, C. C. Carstens, and Gertrude Folks
nand—have much that is important regarding social welfare in
entieth-century America but are generally disappointing on the pre-
World War I period, especially in the matter of children. Moreover, a
common problem is that many institutions no longer have historical
records for their formative years, or have only isolated documents. This is
the case, for example, of the Baby Fold in Normal, Illinois; the Seybert
Institute in Philadelphia; the Washburn Home in Mineapolis; and Starr
Commonwealth in Albion, Michigan. Efforts to locate historical materials
for places such as the Purity Industrial Home in Missouri were also
unproductive.

Government publications with essential information on progressive
reformers and dependent children are Department of Commerce, Bureau of
the Census, *Benevolent Institutions, 1910* (Washington, D.C.: Government
Printing Office, 1913), and U.S. Congress, Senate, *Proceedings of the Conference on the Care of Dependent Children, held at Washington, D.C.,
January 25–29, 1909*, 60th Cong., 2d sess., S. Doc. 721 (Washington, D.C.:
Government Printing Office, 1909). An important and very well-selected
collection of primary documents, government and others, is Robert H.
Bremner, ed., *Children and Youth in America: A Documentary History*,
vol. 2, 1866–1932 (Cambridge: Harvard University Press, 1971).

Several journals with considerable material on progressive child saving
include *Charities, Charities and the Commons*, the *Survey*, the *Juvenile
Court Record, Work with Boys*, and the *Delineator*. The *Juvenile Court
Record* was published "in the interest of homeless and dependent children."

Work with Boys, edited by William Byron Forbush, focused mainly on boys' clubs but featured other useful articles as well; it also includes helpful listings of child saving organizations and new publications in the field. For several years, starting in 1907, the *Delineator* was a major voice for the home placement movement.

Other basic sources regarding progressives and dependent children are the various conference proceedings of charities and correction organizations. Invariably, the annual gatherings included sessions on orphans, waifs, and neglected youngsters. (This study draws primarily upon the publications of the national meetings and those of Minnesota, Washington, and Illinois.) Contemporary studies of particular value are Homer Folks, *The Care of Destitute, Neglected and Delinquent Children* (New York: Macmillan, 1902); Hastings Hart, *Preventive Treatment for Neglected Children* (New York: Charities Publication Committee, 1910); and Hastings Hart, *Cottage and Congregate Institutions for Children* (New York: Russell Sage, 1910). Books that express superbly the mood and perspectives of progressive child savers include Jacob A. Riis, *The Children of the Poor* (New York: Scribner, 1892); Leonard Benedict, *Waifs of the Slums and Their Way Out* (New York: Revell, 1907); Jane Addams, *The Spirit of Youth and the City Streets* (New York: Macmillan, 1909) Ernest K. Coulter, *The Children in the Shadow* (New York; McBride, Nast, 1913); and Phillip Davis, *Street-Land: Its Little People and Big Problems* (Boston: Small, Maynard, 1915).

Secondary Sources

This study owes much to the growing body of literature on progressivism and American social welfare history. Helpful on progressive historiography are David M. Kennedy, "Overview: The Progressive Era," *Historian* 37 (May 1975): 453–68; Robert H. Wiebe, "The Progressive Years, 1900–1917," in William H. Cartwright and Richard L. Watson, Jr., eds., *The Reinterpretation of Amercian History and Culture* (Washington, D.C.: National Council for Social Studies, 1973), 425–42 (stressing the "modernization" theme); and Dewey W. Grantham, "Review Essay: The Contours of Southern Progressivism," *American Historical Review* 86 (Dec. 1981): 1035–59. Peter G. Filene, "An Obituary for 'The Progressive Movement,'" *American Quarterly* 22 (Spring 1970): 20–34, effectively shows the diversity of interpretations.

In the past two decades a number of historians have emphasized the social control aspects of progressive reform. The elitist, "professional" efforts to defuse democracy and remove debates from the streets to board rooms and committees of experts emerge clearly in James Weinstein, *The Corporate Ideal in the Liberal State, 1900–1918* (Boston: Beacon Press, 1968); Samuel Haber, *Efficiency and Uplift: Scientific Management in the Progressive Era, 1890–1920* (Chicago: University of Chicago Press, 1964); and Samuel P. Hays, "The Politics of Reform in Municipal Government in the Progressive Era," *Pacific Northwest Quarterly* 55 (Oct. 1964): 157–69.

For more on the social control interpretation generally, see especially Frances F. Piven and Richard A. Cloward, *Regulating the Poor: The Functions of Social Welfare* (New York: Pantheon Books,1971), and "Reaffirming the Regulation of the Poor," *Social Service Review* 48 (June 1974): 147–69; Lois W. Banner, "Religious Benevolence as Social Control: A Critique of an Interpretation," *Journal of American History* 60 (June 1973): 23–41; William Muraskin, "The Social-Control Theory in American History: A Critique," *Journal of Social History* 9 (Summer 1976): 559–69; and Richard Fox, "Beyond 'Social Control': Institutions and Disorder in Bourgeois Society," *History of Education Quarterly* 16 (Summer 1976): 203–6. An excellent recent addition to the debate is Walter I. Trattner, ed., *Social Welfare or Social Control?* (Knoxville: University of Tennessee Press, 1983), a collection of essays critiquing *Regulating the Poor* and including a rebuttal from Piven and Cloward, as well as a useful introduction and brief bibliography essay. Lawrence Stone, in an exchange with Michel Foucault, *New York Review of Books*, 31 March 1983, 42–43, emphasizes the need to distinguish between "socialization," common to all societies, and "social control"—between as he puts it, training children to brush their teeth and jailing dissenters.

In terms of child saving, the social control interpretation received vigorous expression in Anthony M. Platt, *The Child Savers: The Invention of Delinquency* (Chicago: University of Chicago Press, 1969), a provocative work that probes the social roots of the "rule makers." A similar approach to the growth of public education, although focusing on an earlier era, is Michael B. Katz, *The Irony of Early American School Reform* (Cambridge, Mass.: Harvard University Press, 1968). Steven Schlossman, *Love and the American Delinquent: The Theory and Practice of "Progressive" Juvenile Justice, 1825–1920* (Chicago University of Chicago Press, 1977), is an illuminating book that makes social control tendencies clear but carefully notes other factors. See also the insightful essay by Schlossman and Stephanie Wallach, "The Crime of Precocious Sexuality: Female Juvenile Delinquency in the Progressive Era," *Harvard Educational Review* 48 (Feb. 1978): 65–94.

David J. Rothman's *Conscience and Convenience: The Asylum and Its*

Alternatives in Progressive America (Boston: Little, Brown, 1980), is a major study, along with his earlier pathbreaking work, *The Discovery of the Asylum: Social Order and Disorder in the New Republic* (Boston: Little, Brown, 1971). Rothman is well aware of the progressive desire to "do good," but stresses that considerations of "convenience" ultimately prevailed. Rothman's "Doing Good," in Willard Gaylin, Steven Marcus, and Rothman, *Doing Good: The Limits of Benevolence* (New York: Pantheon, 1978), is a superior essay showing how progressive concerns with the "needs" of disadvantaged groups tended to come at the expense of the "rights" of the poor and the powerless.

In the past several years there has been a tendency once again to see the progressive reformers in a sympathetic light. Paul Boyer, *Urban Masses and Moral Order in America, 1820–1920* (Cambridge: Harvard University Press, 1978), is a splendid book on the evolving urban, middle-class reform mentality. Boyer is alert to social control themes, but his interpretation, rich and diverse, is sensitive to matters of nuance and ambiguity. David P. Thelen, one of the most perceptive scholars of progressivism, has warned convincingly of the dangers of turning history upside down and seeing genuine social problems as the imagined creations of power-hungry reformers. Thelen, "Urban Politics: Beyond Bosses and Reformers," *Reviews in American History* 7 (Sept. 1979): 405–12, is a good example, but see also his *New Citizenship: Origins of Progressivism in Wisconsin, 1885–1900* (Columbia, Mo.: University of Missouri Press, 1972). John W. Chambers II, *The Tyranny of Change: America in the Progressive Era, 1900–1917* (New York: St. Martin's, 1980), is a balanced treatment that is favorable to the progressives. For a fine recent synthesis, see Arthur S. Link and Richard L. McCormick, *Progressivism* (Arlington Heights, Ill.: Harlan Davidson, 1983).

Among the host of other significant studies that students of progressivism must consider are Otis L. Graham, Jr., *An Encore for Reform: The Old Progressives and the New Deal* (New York: Oxford University Press, 1967), especially useful in understanding the several varieties of early twentieth-century reform; Robert H. Wiebe, *The Search for Order, 1877–1920* (New York: Hill and Wang, 1967), a seminal examination of the organizational tendencies of progressivism; David P. Thelen, *Robert La Follette and the Insurgent Spirit* (Boston: Little, Brown, 1976), which probes the struggle between the insurgent and modernization wings of the reform movement; and Richard M. Abrams, *The Burdens of Progress, 1900–1929* (Glenview, Ill.: Scott, Foresman, 1978), which shrewdly notes the problems that "progress" posed for reformers. Two outstanding collections of essays are John D. Buenker, John C. Burnham, and Robert M. Crunden, *Progressivism*

(Cambridge, Mass.: Schenkman, 1977), and Lewis L. Gould, ed., *The Progressive Era* (Syracuse, N.Y.: Syracuse University Press, 1974); both collections offer positive assessments of progressivism. A thoughtful analysis of the progressive temperament is Clyde Griffen, "The Progressive Ethos," in Stanley Coben and Lorman Ratner, eds., *The Development of an American Culture* (Englewood Cliffs, N.J.: Prentice-Hall, 1970).

On social welfare themes, two places to start are Walter I. Trattner, *From Poor Law to Welfare State: A History of Social Welfare in America*, 2nd ed. (New York: Free Press, 1979), and James Leiby, *A History of Social Welfare and Social Work in the United States* (New York: Columbia University Press, 1978). Robert H. Bremner, *From the Depths: The Discovery of Poverty in the United States* (New York: New York University Press, 1956), is a pioneering work regarding progressive reform. Also admirable are Allen F. Davis, *Spearheads for Reform: The Social Settlements and the Progressive Movement, 1890–1914* (New York: Oxford University Press, 1967), and *American Heroine: The Life and Legend of Jane Addams* (New York: Oxford University Press, 1973). Kenneth Kusmer, "The Functions of Organized Charity in the Progressive Era: Chicago as a Case Study," *Journal of American History* 60 (Dec. 1973): 657–78, warns convincingly against dismissing voluntarism and private control as retrogressive, when in fact private charities played a major role during the progressive era.

On the rise of children's issues among reformers, two impressive overviews that supply a wealth of information are Joseph M. Hawes, *Children in Urban Society: Juvenile Delinquency in Nineteenth-Century America* (New York: Oxford University Press, 1971), and Joseph F. Kett, *Rites of Passage: Adolescence in America, 1790 to the Present* (New York: Basic Books, 1977). Susan Whitelaw Downs and Michael W. Sherraden, "The Orphan Asylum in the Nineteenth Century," *Social Service Review* 57 (June 1983): 272–90, takes issue with the social control thesis and David Rothman's argument that institutions were primarily supposed to create islands of order and discipline in a disorderly world. Downs and Sherraden believe that children's institutions proliferated in the nineteenth century as substitutes for the old indenture system and, even more, as a "response to the social and economic problems of transiency." Robert M. Mennell, *Thorns and Thistles: Juvenile Delinquents in the United States, 1825–1940* (Hanover, N.H.: University Press of New England, 1973), and Schlossman, *Love and the American Delinquent*, are very informative, along with Hawes, regarding the various trends that led to the establishment of the juvenile court system. Also good on the court is Ellen Ryerson, *The Best-Laid Plans: America's Juvenile Court Experiment* (New York: Hill and Wang, 1978). Jack M. Holl, *Juvenile Reform in the Progressive Era: William*

R. George and the Junior Republic Movement (Ithaca, N.Y.: Cornell University Press, 1971), is excellent, not merely on George but on a range of topics bearing on progressives and children. Steven L. Schlossman and Ronald D. Cohen, "The Music Man in Gary: Willis Brown and Child-Saving in the Progressive Era," *Societas* 7 (Winter 1977): 1–17, shows how the study of a relatively unknown figure can provide considerable insight into the progressives' "child-centered search for order."

On child labor reforms during the progressive era, see especially Walter I. Trattner, *Crusade for the Children: A History of the National Child Labor Committee and Child Labor Reform in America* (Chicago. Quadrangle, 1970), and Jeremy P. Felt, *Hostages of Fortune: Child Labor Reform in New York State* (Syracuse, N.Y.: Syracuse University Press, 1965). On the playground movement, see Dominick Cavallo, *Muscles and Morals: Organized Playgrounds and Urban Reform, 1880–1920* (Philadelphia: University of Pennsylvania Press, 1981). Susan Tiffin, *In Whose Best Interest? Child Welfare Reform in the Progressive Era* (Westport, Conn.: Greenwood Press, 1982), is insightful and wide-ranging concerning dependent children.

Two striking recent efforts to interpret the evolution of institutions and asylums in the nineteeth and early twentieth centuries are Michael B. Katz, "Origins of the Institutional State," *Marxist Perspectives* 4 (Winter 1978): 6–22, and Peter L. Tyor and Jamil S. Zainaldin, "Asylum and Society: An Approach to Institutional Change," *Journal of Social History* 13 (Fall 1979): 23–48, which includes a very complete listing of relevant literature concerning prisons and crime, insanity, education, charity, and children. Good Will Farm, Allendale, and the other primary examples in this study fit what Katz describes as the "early voluntarist stage of institutional development," but they came later than Katz's essay would seem to allow. On the other hand, Good Will and its counterparts lend credence to Tyor and Zainaldin's point that it is essential to distinguish between kinds of institutions. They note, for example, that the conclusions of historians such as David Rothman, Gerald Grob, and Christopher Lasch concerning asylums are "based almost entirely on the history of the public asylum." Among the variables that Tyor and Zainaldin recommend for consideration, the issue of autonomy clearly affected the Ford Republic, Allendale, Good Will, and, presumably, numerous other examples.

Index

Adams, Anna, 61
Addams, Jane, ix, 82, 87, 175, 207, 213
Adoption, as goal, 5. *See also* Home placement
Albany Orphan Asylum, 30
Alger, Horatio, 6, 172
Allendale Farm, 19, 33, 36, 184, 207, 218–19; as "anti-institutional" institution, 29–30; autonomy of, 208; family setting of, 25, 29–31; farm setting of, 23–25; founding of, 3; interest of William R. George in, 20–21; as junior republic, 18, 20–22, 211–13; western branch of, 20
Allendale School for Boys, 221 n. 1. *See also* Allendale Farm
Almy, Frederick, 11
American Christian Missionary Society, 72
American Educational Aid Society, 40
American Sunday School Union, 178, 179
"Anti-institutional" institutions, 5, 29, 31, 92–94, 197–98
Anti-liquor, 46, 182–83
Apprenticeship, 31
Asher, Tompie Witten, 35
Arthur, Timothy Shay, 6
Asylums. *See* Orphanages
Associated Charities in Minneapolis, 207
Atkinson, J. F., 105

Ayars, Fannie Shedd, 69, 79–80, 82, 84, 85, 99–100, 252 n. 77
Babies' health contests, 4
Babies' Home and Hospital (St. Louis), 72, 80, 99, 100
"Baby farms," 65, 216
Baby Fold, 35, 218, 285 n. 7
Baby Welfare Association (St. Paul), 65
Baker, Ray Stannard, 9
Baldwin, Roger, 215
Baptist Orphanage (Hopeville, Ga.), 30
Barkan, Max, 112
Beecher, Catherine, 81
Bethany Home, 35
Berkshire Farm School, 24
Beulah Land Farm For Boys, 202
Big Brothers, 4, 15, 192, 200, 201, 202
Big Sisters, 4, 15
Bird, Sarah J., 209–10
Birmingham Boys' Club, 154
Black, Moses, 107–8
Blacks: and Ford Republic, 268 n. 67; and Good Will Farm, 284 n. 114; and NBA, 246 n. 13
Blake, William, 6
Bloman, Fred, 162, 169, 218; background of, 134; as citizens' judge, 133, 159–60; death of, 133, 160; honored, 133, 160–61
Blum, Isador, 113
Boardman, John, 200

Bootblacks' and Newsboys' Union, 108
Booth, William, 59
Boston Farm and Trades School, 24
Boswell, Ira, 83, 88
Boy City, 229 n. 64
Boy Conservation Bureau, 13, 218, 200–201, 283 n. 99
Boyer, Paul, 119
Boys' Brotherhood Republic, 22
Boys' Busy Life Club, 46
Boys' Club Association of New York, 107
Boys' Club of Toledo, 130. *See also* Toledo Newsboys' Association
Boys' clubs, 225–26 n. 29
Boy Scouts, 4, 161, 202
Boys' Fund, 178, 180
Boys' Home and d'Arcambal Association, 136–69 *passim*
Boys Republic Day, 161
Boyville. *See* Toledo Newsboys' Association
Brace, Charles Loring, 12, 39, 41, 127
Brace, Charles Loring, Jr., 202
Brackett, Edward, 192
Bradley, Edward L., 36, 184, 206, 207, 210, 286–87 n. 17; anti-asylum views of, 29–31; anti-urban views of, 25; background of, 230 n. 70; death of, 219; dilemma of, 211–14; and family ideal, 25, 27, 30–31; and founding of Allendale Farm, 3, 19; and junior republic, 18, 20–21, 211–13; and religion, 208; and tradition, 36, 37; and village values, 4, 5, 25, 211–12; and voluntarism, 4; and "western

Allendale," 20; and work ideal, 18
Bremner, Robert, x
Brown, Betty R., 88, 95
Brown, Willis, 158
Brucker, Jake, 113
Bush, Emma, 95
Bushnell, T. H., 30
Butzel, Fred: background of, 137; compared with Lane, 137–38; contributions of, 161; praise of Bloman, 160; views about Lane, 138–40, 162–63
Butzel, Henry, 137
Butzel, Magnus, 137
Buzzell, G. W., 16–17

Caddie camps, 15, 227 n. 40
California, scandals in, 216
Callaway, W. R., 108
Campbell, Alexander, 71
Carnegie, Andrew, 276 n. 36
Carney, C. S., 139
Catholic Bureau of Dependent Children, x, 12
Charities, 124
Charlton Industrial School, 24
Chicago Boys' Club, 105
Chicago Bureau of Charities, 217
Chicago Commons settlement, 139
Child guidance clinics, 4
Childhood, discovery of, 5–7, 222 n. 7
Child labor laws, 4, 83–84, 89; reformers divide over, 11, 105, 122–26, 130–32. *See also* Newsboys
Child placement. *See* Home placement
Children: abnormal, 46, 66–67;

boarding of, 32; deserted, 51–52; as future citizens, 7, 85; illegitimate, 50, 56, 59, 63; as innocents, 6, 104–5; as symbols, 7–8; as threats, 7, 85, 105–7. *See also* Dependent children

"Children's Age," 218

Children's Aid Society of New York, 12, 31, 39

Children's Friend Society of Boston, 179

Children's Home Societies, 13, 38, 39, 81, 219; early turbulence of, 42; founding of, 40; in Illinois, 42; in Iowa, 42, 81; and laws concerning placement, 44–45; in Missouri, 40, 42, 81; in Montana, 81; in North Dakota, 42, 47; and Protestantism, x, 44, 241 n. 70; shift toward "exact science," 67–68; in South Dakota, 42, 47; structure of, 42; in Texas, 81; transition of, 67–68; and voluntarism, 45, 208; in Wisconsin, 33, 42, 45, 47. *See also* Children's Home Society of Minnesota

Children's Home Society of Minnesota, x, 33, 210; and aid to needy families, 58; and churches, 44, 61, 64; crisis of, 61–64; and deserted children, 51; difficulties concerning placement, 49–50, 57–59, 61, 67; founding of, 41–42; and health problems, 55–56; and infant deaths, 56–57, 62; legal status of, 43; and number of children placed, 42, 61; and nursing babies, 52–53; and receiving home, 55–58; and temperance, 58; and

transition under Dickinson, 65–67. *See also* Savage, E. P.

"Child Rescue Department," 54. See also *Delineator*

Child saving: and amateurs, 4, 37, 67–68, 173–74, 207, 215, 234 n. 105; ambivalence concerning change, 36–37, 206–7, 211–16, 231 n. 75, 285 n. 6; and bureaucratization, 70, 87, 89, 207, 214–16, 243 n. 105; as career, 82; and Catholics, x, 84–85, 226 n. 30; and "doing good," x, 37, 83, 85–86, 104, 181, 206, 210–11, 218–19; and efficiency, 70, 88, 100–102, 206–7, 285 n. 6; and environmentalism, 5, 59–60, 142–43; excitement of, 34, 82, 206; and family ideal, 5, 25–27, 30, 32–33, 58–59, 64–65, 93–94, 196; and feminism, 79–82, 248 n. 31; goals of, 5; and government, 10–13, 37, 44–45, 89–90, 93, 208, 285 n. 7; and individualism, 5, 145, 146, 148, 156, 197, 211; institutional growth of, 13–14, 226 n. 30; and modern world, 4, 37, 65–68, 70, 84, 87–89, 206–7, 211–16, 285 n. 6; nineteenth-century roots of, 4, 84, 171, 193–95, 206–7; and opposition to asylums, 5, 27, 30, 33, 45–47, 53, 148, 197; organizational growth of, 13; and patriotism, 18, 209; and personal status, 210; and professionalism, 4, 37, 65–68, 70, 88–89, 168, 207, 214, 234 n. 105; and religious benevolence, 47–48, 50–51, 63, 208–9, 226 n. 30, 286 n. 10 (*see also* National Be-

nevolent Association); sacrifices of, 34, 50–51, 181; scandals of, 216–17; and scientific solutions, 38, 65–66, 87–89, 207, 244 n. 105; and search for order, 206, 208–9; and social control, x, 11, 15–18, 59–60, 66, 85–86, 111–12, 164–68, 209–10; and world of suffering, 34, 47–50, 60–61, 210–11. *See also* Cottage system; *Delineator*; Farm schools; Garden movement; Home placement; Junior republics; Newsboys
Child Saving Institute, 74–75, 79, 252 n. 85
Child study movement, 7
Child Welfare Exhibit, 202
Christian Church. *See* Disciples of Christ
Christian Orphan's Home (St. Louis), 69, 70, 80, 95, 96–97, 252 n. 85. *See also* National Benevolent Association
Christian Philanthropist, 76–102, passim, 104
Christian Woman's Board of Missions, 99
Christian Woman's National Benevolent Association, 100
Civilization versus savagery, theme of, 144–45
Clark, A. W., 74–75
Cleveland Christian Orphanage, 73, 95, 252–53 n. 85. *See also* National Benevolent Association
Cohen, Ben, 109
Colorado Christian Home, 74, 252–53 n. 85. *See also* National Benevolent Association
Colored Orphan Asylum, New York City, 30

Columbia Park Boys' Club, 22
Consumer protection, 10
Cooley, Charles, 140, 141, 145, 154
Commonwealth of Ford, 149. *See also* Ford Republic
Confessions of a Reformer, 175
Conwell, Russell, 110
Cottage system, 30–31, 211. *See also* Good Will Farm
Coulter, Ernest K., 202
"Country life" movement, 23
Crane, H. W., 154
Croly, Herbert, 213
Crunden, Robert, x
"Cultural voluntarism," 145
Curtiss, Josie, 17
Curtiss Place, 17

Daggett, Mabel Potter, 54
d'Arcambal, Agnes L., 134–35
d'Arcambal Home of Industry Association, 135–36, 146, 155
Darrow, Clarence, 175
Darwinian theory, 84, 85
Dega, Ignatius, 211, 218
Delineator, 29, 53–55, 92, 240 n. 56
Delinquency: and d'Arcambal Association, 135–37; and Washington state, 14. *See also* Dependent children
Dependent children: defined, ix, xi, 14; and delinquency, xi, 14–15, 37, 133–34, 157–59, 168, 263 n. 2, 267 n. 66; in Michigan, 11–12, 208, in Minnesota, 43–44, 208, 237 n. 17; in Mississippi, 13; in New Jersey, 12; and newsboys, 106–7, 254 n. 8; numbers of, xi, 232–33 n. 92; in Ohio, 12; in Pennsylvania, 12

Depression of 1890s, 48
Detroit Saturday Night, 154
Detroit Women's Club, 161
Detroit's Associated Charities, 161
Devine, Edward T., 11, 202
Dewey, John, 213
Dickens, Charles, 91
Dickinson, S. W.: background of,
    64; on decline of families, 64-65;
    and eugenics, 66; and "scien-
    tific" approach, 65–68; and sex
    education, 66; and social classes,
    66. *See also* Children's Home
    Society of Minnesota
Dinsmore, Elsie, 6
Disciples of Christ: anti-elitism of,
    71, 72; anti-institutionalism of,
    70–72, 77, 87; growth of, 71;
    and NBA fund-raising, 98–99;
    origins of, 70–71; and Social
    Gospel, 82–84, 248–49 n. 33;
    and views concerning charity,
    71, 78; and views concerning
    New Testament, 71; and views
    concerning women's roles, 77;
    and voluntarism, 71. *See also*
    National Benevolent Association
Domesticity, ideal of, 6
Dowden, Isadora E., 80–81
Dreiser, Theodore, 53
Drucker, Benjamin, 185, 218
Dunn, B. A., 127
Dunne, Father Peter Joseph, x, 35–
    36, 215–16
Dysart, J. P., 42, 45–47, 208

Education: compulsory, 11; and re-
    form in Milwaukee, 119–20. *See
    also* Ford Republic; Good Will
    Farm
Elizabethan poor laws, 43
Ely, Richard T., 175

Eugenics, 17, 66
Evangelical Lutheran Kinderfreund
    Society of Wisconsin, 286 n. 10

Family: as ideal, 6; as social issue,
    59–60, 64–65
Farm schools: at Hershey In-
    dustrial School, 17; at Juliette
    Fowler Home, 74; popularity of,
    23–25. *See also* Ford Republic;
    Good Will Farm
Father Dunne's News Boys' Home
    and Protectorate, 36, 215–16,
    234 n. 102
Fleming, Jean Peter, 35–36
Flynt, Josiah, 9
Folk, Joseph, 83
Foote, Edwin Bancroft, 199
Forbush, William Byron, 127, 193,
    202
Ford, E. L. family, 147, 161
Ford, Henry, 147
Ford Republic: autonomy of, 208;
    changes name, 147; and Citi-
    zens' Bank, 166–67; and Citi-
    zen's Court, 150–51, 153, 159–
    60; and cleanliness campaign,
    167; compared with Freeville,
    151, 154–56; and dependency
    versus delinquency, 133–34,
    157–59, 168–69; early difficul-
    ties of, 146–47; economy of,
    151–52, 156; education at, 148,
    156; evaluated, 156–59; as farm
    school, 23, 139, 141, 146, 149,
    164–66; financial problems of,
    161; fire at, 147; and fly war,
    167–68; and gardens, 165–66;
    and good citizenship, 151–53;
    and absence of jails, 155; and
    absence of lawyers, 153, 160;
    origins of, 134–39; population

of, 146, 149, 156–59, 163, 168–
69, 267–68 n. 67, 272 n. 93; and
psychological testing, 169; and
race, 268 n. 67; relocation of,
139; reputation of, 133, 154–55;
and safety, 146–47, 156, 163;
and self-government, x, 19, 22,
134, 141, 145–46, 146–56, 159–
60, 163, 168–69, 272 n. 93, 272
n. 84; as temporary shelter, 135–
36; and "tobacco parties," 161;
transition under McIndoo, 134,
163–68, 271 n. 88
Foster, Joel, 23
Foster placement, 5
Freeville Republic, 19, 21, 149,
155, 184, 211
"Fresh-air" camps, 23
Friedman, Bennett, 108
Friedman, Flora, 108

Gallagher, Edward, 108, 113
Gangs, 143–45, 48, 163, 168, 271
n. 88
Garden City, 165–66
Garden movement, 165–66, 209
George, Henry, 175
George Junior Republic, 34, 149,
184. See also Freeville Republic
George, William R., 19, 22, 151,
184; and Allendale Farm, 20, 21;
and "anti-institutional" in-
stitutions, 30; and child labor
laws, 37; dilemma of, 211–14;
and family ideal, 31; and Ford
Republic, 149, 155–56; and
Good Will Farm, 202; and Junior
State, 20
Germann, Gottlied, 35
Girl Scouts, 4

Glennon, Archbishop John J., 36
Gladden, Washington, 83, 183
Good Will Association, 180, 199
Good Will Farm, xi, 34, 207, 218,
219; after Hinckley, 205, 284 n.
124; and blacks, 284 n. 114; and
Boy Conservation Bureau, 200–
201; Carnegie Library at, 276 n.
36; and Catholics, 280 n. 72;
children's views of, 170, 187–88,
190–95, 203, 205, 218, 277 n.
50, 278 n. 62, 281–82 n. 87;
cottage plan at, 30, 31, 171,
183–84, 186–88, 197, 204; daily
life at, 190; discipline at, 184,
185–86; and education, x, 171,
190–94, 279 n. 65; as farm
school, 24, 183; and finances,
181–82, 199–200, 203–4, 275–76
n. 36, 282 n. 89; and girls' department, 180, 198–99, 281–82
n. 87; growth of, 170–71, 181,
196, 203–4; matrons at, 186–87,
197, 279 n. 66; and needy children, 170, 178–82, 183, 185, 203,
204; origins of, 178–80; population of, 185, 199, 202–3, 279 n.
64, 283–84 n. 113; praised, 171,
202; and "Reinsophy," 195–96,
280 n. 74; and religion, 195, 280
n. 72; seal of, 198–99; and self-
government, 184; sexual instruction at, 193–95, 279 n. 66; social
life at, 194; and voluntarism,
180–82, 199–201, 208; and
World War I, 203–4. See also
Hinckley, George W.
Good Will Institute, 16
Good Will Record, 180, 181, 183,
188, 198, 199, 204
Gordon, Nannie, 97

Government: progressive views of, 9–13

Grace Porter: A Jewel Lost and Found, 45–47, 54

Grand Rapids, Mich.: and *Evening Press*, 127; and newsboys, 127

Griffen, Clyde, ix

Guardian Angels, 120

Gunckel, Alice, 107, 109, 129

Gunckel, John Elster, 5, 207, 210, 218, 219; background of, 107; and child labor laws, 11, 37, 105, 122–23, 125–26, 130–31; and Christian example, 110; death of, 128–29; disagreement with Hull House group, 105, 125–26, 214; fears of social disorder, 110; founds Boyville, 107–8; as "Gunck," 104, 109, 119, 128, legacy of, 130–32; monument to, 130, 219, 262 n. 86; opposition to economic injustice, 122–23, 214; praised, 109–10, 212–22, 128; proposed movie on, 130; relationships with newsboys, 113–14, 118–19; and self-government, 112, 254 n. 15; and social control, 11–12; starts National Newsboy's Association, 126. *See also* Toledo Newsboys' Association

Gunckel, Will, 107, 129

Hall, Bert, 33, 208

Hall, G. Stanley, 7, 143, 163, 166

Hannah Schloss settlement house, 137, 141

Hansbrough, Mrs. J. K., 70, 77, 80, 94, 99

Hard, William, 124–25

Harles, Harry, 192

Harmon, A. D., 83, 90

Harrison, Mrs. W. D., 77

Hart, Hastings H., 12, 33–34, 42, 171, 202, 216

Hawley, John S., 34

Hegemony, concept of, 119, 358 n. 56, 358–59 n. 57

Henderson, Charles Redmond, 67

Henderson, Ivy, 98

Herrick, Myron T., 121

Herron, George, 83

Hershey Industrial School: and anti-institutionalism, 30; and cottage plan, 30; and social control, 17–18

Hershey, Milton S., 17, 24

Hexter, Maurice, 131

Hill, Joshua, 161

Hinckley, Elma Palmer, 176, 274 n. 18

Hinckley, George W., 37, 207, 210, 218; anti-institutionalism of, 31, 178, 197; background of, 172–78, 273 n. 9; and Boy Scouts, 202; and Boys' Fund, 178–79; children's views of, 170, 185, 276–77 n. 46; and cities, 183; compassion of, 185–86, 277 n. 50; and contacts with child savers, 202; and crisis of conscience, 174–76; death of, 204; and delinquents, 185–86; educational views of, 191, 193–94; and family ideal, 31, 178, 183–84, 186–87, 196–98, 204, 277 n. 53; fear of social disorder, 182; and founding of Good Will Farm, 179–80; and Girls' Fund, 198; and home placement, 197–98; and idea of service, 171, 188, 195; and morality, 171, 178,

182–83, 193–95; and obsession with saving children, 177–78; personality of, 174, 176, 184–86; praised, 170, 202, 218; progressive views of, 188–89, 278 n. 58; and race, 284 n. 114; and "Reinsophy," 195–96; religious views of, 171, 172, 195, 199, 208, 273 n. 9, 280 n. 72; resignation of, 204; salary of, 180–81; uneasiness with modern world, 171, 173–74, 183, 188–89, 194–95, 204, 214; and vice, 182–83; and village ideal, 188; and White House Conference, 196–97; and work ethic, 171, 188–91. *See also* Good Will Farm

Hinckley, Jane, 180

Hine, Lewis, 8, 105

Home of Industry for Discharged Prisoners, 135, 136, 137, 263 n. 4

Home placement, x, 5, 13, 31–33, 44, 53–54, 168. *See also* Children's Home Societies; Children's Home Society of Minnesota

Hoover, Herbert, 213

Hopkins, Aggie, 210, 287 n. 19

Hopkins, Dan, 210, 287 n. 19

Howard Colored Orphan Asylum, 216

Howe, Frederick C., 175

Hudson Boys' Farm, 24

Hudson, J. L., 161

Humane Societies, 13, 207

Hull House group, 105, 125–26

Hunter, Robert, 8

Illinois Children's Home and Aid Society, 33, 64

Illinois Industrial School for Girls, 33

Illinois School of Agriculture and Manual Training for Boys, 24

Illinois State Charities Commission, 216

In Darkest England, 59

Indenture, 43–44

Industrial training, 16, 17–18, 164, 228 n. 46

In His Name Orphanage, 73

Industrial Farm School (Charlton, N.Y.), 34

Institution versus home placement debate, 31–33, 92–93, 196–97

Iowa Industrial School for Boys, 131

Islam, 83

"Island communities," 4, 207

Jackson, Celia, 170

Jackson, Daniel B., 61

James, William, 9

Jewish orphanages, x

"John Q. Worker," concept of, 105, 119

Johnson, Tom, 175

Jones, Edgar DeWitt, 99

Jones, Samuel M., 109, 110

Juliette Fowler Home, 74, 95, 253 n. 85. *See also* National Benevolent Association

Junior republics, 18–22. *See also* Allendale Farm; Ford Republic; Freeville; George, William R.

Junior Settlement, 24

Junior State, 19–20

Juvenile courts: 4, 113, 135, 139, 146, 148, 157, 158, 200, 209, 214; dependency versus delinquency in, 15, 227 n. 36; and

social control, 11, 209; as substitute parents, 26–27
Juvenile Court Record, xi, 10, 15, 26, 90, 123, 227 n. 37
Juvenile Improvement Association, 285 n. 6
Juvenile Protective Association (Atlanta), 19-20

Kelley, Florence, 122, 125
Kelso, J. J., 125–26
Kerby, Monsignor William J., x
Kerns, Sophia Robertson, 78
Kindergartens, 4
Knights of the Round Table, 138
Kraditor, Aileen, 119
Kurn Hattin Homes, 24

Lad Lake, 221 n. 2. *See also* Wisconsin Home and Farm School
Lake Farm, 24
Lane, Homer, 134, 167, 218; anti-institutionalism of, 148; background of, 139–40; Butzel's evaluation of, 162–63; character of, 137–41, 162–63; child-saving techniques of, 138–45, 148–49, 152–54, 161–62, 167, 168, 271 n. 88; educational views of, 148, 156, 159; and William R. George, 149, 155–56; influence of, 269 n. 74; and Little Commonwealth, 162, 269 n. 74; and moral training, 271 n. 88; praised, 140, 154; resignation of, 162; schedule of, 157; views on self-government, 145–46, 150, 153, 155–56, 162, 168; and smoking incident, 161–62; views of youthful wrongdoing, 142–43, 148. *See also* Ford Republic

Lane, Mabel, 141, 162, 269 n. 76
Larsen, Gustav, 140
Letchworth, William P., 16, 32
Lettice, Margaret, 65
Lewis, John L., 120
Lincoln Agricultural School, 24
Lindsay, Samuel McCune, 34, 202
Lindsey, Ben, ix, 9, 154, 202; and Allendale Farm, 22; and bureaucratic trends, 285 n. 6; and "gospel of child saving," 4; and Gunckel, 109, 122, 126; and manliness and unchastity, 158
Lipscomb, David, 77
London, Jack, 9
Lone Scouts, 4
Lowell, Josephine Shaw, 11
Lundgren, E. E., 61, 62

McDonald's hamburgers, and newsboy advertisement, 260 n. 67
McGregor Mission (Detroit), 135
McIndoo, J. M.: and athletics, 271 n. 92; background of, 163, 269 n. 77; and cleanliness, 167–68; creates Citizens' Bank, 166–67; emphasis on farm life, 164; garden strategy of, 165–66; and G. Stanley Hall, 163, 166; and moral training, 271 n. 88; and recapitulation theory, 270–71 n. 85; views on self-government, 163–64, 168. *See also* Ford Republic
Mack, Julian, 20
Man of Whom I Write, 172
Manual training. *See* Industrial training
Mason, Ben, 177, 274 n. 20

Mason Deaconess Home and Baby Fold. *See* Baby Fold
Mason, Nancy, 35
Mason, Rowena, 80
Massachusetts plan, 12
Matrons, 27–28, 94–97, 186–87
Matthewson, Albert, 22
Maxson, Sadie, 97
Meier, Emily Ivers, 80
Mettray, 23
Michigan plan, 11–12, 208
Million Egg Farm, 23
Minneapolis Juvenile Protective League, 214–15
Minnesota: and crime, 48; and desertion, 51; and laws concerning children, 43–44, 208; and state training school, 158
Minnesota Children's Home Finder, 47
Minnick, Henry, 88
Mississippi, and dependent children, 13
Mockett, John N., 129
Mohorter, J. H., 87, 91–92
Moody, Dwight Lyman, 40
Morgan, J. P., 84
Mothers' Day, 25
Mothers' pension laws, 11, 65
Mulry, Father Thomas, 12–13

National Baby Show, 6
National Benevolent Association (NBA), 14, 34, 210, 216, 219; aid to widows and working mothers, 93; ambivalence concerning government, 89–90, 93, 101; attacks on congregate asylums, 90–91; and blacks, 246 n. 13; bureaucratization of, 70, 87–89; and Catholic benevolence, 84–85, 87; children's responses to, 91, 94; and family model, 93–94; finances of, 70, 103; founding of, 69, 72; and fraternal benevolence, 84, 87; and fund raising, 97, 99; goals of, 69–70; growth of, 70, 72–76, 82; and home placement, 90, 91–93; and homes for elderly, 70, 72–73, 76; and hospital for the poor, 70; matrons of, 94–97; and narrowing of goals, 100–102; nostalgia of, 84; optimism of, 84; and organizational revolution, 87–89; and professionalism, 88–89; and progressivism, 83–84; protective network of, 70, 89; and Protestant benevolence, 69, 84–87; and relationship with Christian Church, 70, 76, 78–79, 84, 98–100, 102–3; and role of women, 69, 72, 76–82, 210, 248 n. 31; and search for converts, 85–87; and social class, 84, 86, 102; training school for nurses, 70, 89; transition of, x, 70, 87–89, 100–103, 252–53 n. 85; and voluntarism, 89–90, 208. *See also* Babies Home and Hospital; Child Saving Institute; Christian Orphans' Home; Cleveland Christian Orphanage; Colorado Christian Home; Disciples of Christ; Juliette Fowler Home; Northwestern Christian Home; Southern Christian Home
National Conference of Charities and Correction, 51
National Congress of Mothers, 25, 243 n. 94

National Farm School, 24
National Home-Finding Society, 31. *See also* Children's Home Societies
National Junior Republic Association, 19, 20, 155
National Newsboys' Association, 126–27
National Quarantine Organization, 243 n. 94
Neale, William R., 109
Nearing, Scott, 124
New Britain, Conn.: and Boys' Club, 165; and gardens, 165
New England Association, 171
New England Home for Little Wanderers, 39
"New interventionism," 87
New Jersey, 12
Newsboys, xi, 136, 140; adaptability of, 120; as entrepreneurs, 105, 120–21, 123–24, 130–31, 260 n. 67; images of, 104–7, 123–24, 130–32; as "John Q. Workers," 105, 119; national organization of, 126–27; and "Newsies at Skeeter Branch," 105; numbers of, 153 n. 4; and pursuit of respectability, 119; laws concerning, 259–60 n. 64; and social class, 105, 119–21; and Martin Van Buren Van Arsdale, 40; as victims, 124–25, 131, 260–61 n. 71; and vaudeville stage, 121; as waifs, 106–7, 125. *See also* Toledo Newsboys' Association
Newsboys' Day, 122
Newsboys' Lodging House (New York City), 127
Newsboys' World, 123

Newsboys' Republic (Milwaukee), 123–24
New York Child Welfare Committee, 202
New York Consumers' League, 189
New York Juvenile Asylum, 27
New York Orphan Asylum, 30
New York Society for the Prevention of Cruelty to Children, 216, 217
Northrup, Cyrus, 41
Northwestern Christian Home, 75–76. *See also* National Benevolent Association
Nurses: and home nursing, 66; training of, 65–66, 70, 76
Nutter, Charlie, 205

O'Donnell, Judge O'Brien, 114
Ogden, Marion, 18, 37, 207, 218; and founding of Wisconsin Home and Farm School, 3–4; and juvenile court, 214; as Sunday School teacher, 208; and views on rural environment, 5
O'Grady, Father, 215
Ohio, delinquency laws in, 158
Ohio plan, 12
Ohio Reform School, 23
O'Kelly, James, 71
Ormsby, Earl, 192
Orphanages: and boarding children, 32; as congregate institutions, 27–28; defended, 32–33; and matrons, 27–28, 94–97; as missionary agencies, 86–87; and Minnesota law, 43; in Mississippi, 13; oppposition to, 5, 27–30, 33, 45–47, 53, 90–91; overview of, 226 n. 30; in St.

Louis, 247 n. 20; and saving families, 32–33. *See also* National Benevolent Association
Orphans and Children's Home (Creal Springs, Ill.), 210, 287 n. 19
"Orphan trains," 31, 39
Orphan's Cry, 69, 80, 82
Orphans' Home of Industry (Iowa City), 23
Osborne, Chase, 154

Palmer, Norman, 192–93
Parks, Henry L., 143–45, 150, 159. *See also* Homer Lane
"Patent-office models" of reform, 213
Pennsylvania, and dependent children, 12
Perry, J. W., 80
Philadelphia House of Refuge, 30
Phillips, David Graham, 9
Playgrounds, 4, 11, 137, 271 n. 92
Poe, John T., 77
Poole, Ernest, 106, 115
Powlison, Charles F., 202
Pratt, Annie, 187
Prison reform, 134–35
Private institutions, autonomy of, 208, 285–86 n. 8
Progress and Poverty, 175
Progressivism: ambivalence concerning modern world, 9, 84, 171; characterized, 8–11, 213; and children, 7–8; and coalitions, 8, 119–20; and crises of conscience, 175–76; and democracy, 8, 18; and elitism, 8; and humanitarianism, 8–9; and the family, 25–26, 64–65, 93; and fears, 9, 84; and *Grace Porter*,

46; and localism versus nationalism, 42; and medical analogies, 89; and moral campaigns, 183; optimism of, 9, 84, 213; and organizational revolution, 87; and rhetoric, 213; and role of government, 9–10; and "sexual counterrevolution," 193–95; and social class, 105, 119–20; and social control, x, 9; and social problems, 210–11; tensions within, 213–14; and violence, 257 n. 46; waning of, 102
Protestant Orphan Asylum of Detroit, 27–28
Protestant Orphan Asylum of St. Paul, 32, 33, 55
Psychological testing, 67
Protestantism: and child saving, ix; and progressivism, ix; and voluntarism, ix. *See also* Children's Home Societies; Children's Home Society of Minnesota; Good Will Home; Hinckley, George W.; National Benevolent Association; Savage, E. P.
Psalms 37:5, 171, 178, 204
Purity Industrial Home, 16, 17

Quincy, George Henry, 179, 180

Rauschenbusch, Walter, 83
Recapitulation theory, 166, 270–71 n. 85
Reeder, R. R., 30, 202
Regeneration as theme, 144–45, 159
Reform: and antebellum era, 145, 213; and crises of conscience, 175–76; and "cultural voluntar-

ism," 145; and gardens, 166; and nostalgia, x; strategies of, 145. *See also* Child saving; Progressivism

"Reinsophy," 195–96

Richmond, Mary, 11

Riley, Thomas, 193

Riis, Jacob, 7, 8, 39, 105, 202

Robins, Raymond, 9

Robinson, Jefferson D., 129, 131

Rockefeller, John D., 84

Romanofsky, Peter, x

Roosevelt, Theodore, 9, 23, 83, 121, 196; appeals from Savage, 53; on birth rate, 25; and government, 10; as quoted by Gunckel, 111–12; Hinckley praises, 183

Rousseau, 6

Sage, Mrs. Russell, 128

Salvation Army, 207

Savage, Edward P., 207, 218; ambivalence of, 38-39, 57–58; as amateur, 67–68; background of, 40–41; and Brace, 41; and Christian benevolence, 47–48, 50–51, 63, 208; death of, 64; and desertion, 51–52; and difficulties of child saving, 38–39, 47–50, 54–55, 60–61, 210; and dilemmas concerning home placement, 59–61; and fears concerning social disorder, 47–48, 59–60; and founding of Children's Home Society of Minnesota, 38, 41–52; and illegitimacy, 50, 56, 59, 63; and infant burial issue, 56–57, 63; and receiving home, 57–58; removed as superintendent, 64, 243 n. 92; and scandal, 61–64;

and sick babies, 62; and social class, 59–60, 63; and Martin Van Buren Van Arsdale, 41; and "wet nurse" bill, 52–53, 63. *See also* Children's Home Society of Minnesota

Savage, Kate Snoad, 55–56, 241 n. 70

Savagery versus civilization issue, 144–45

Schlossman, Steven, 194

Self-discipline, 145, 148, 156, 184

Seton, Ernest Thompson, 202

Settlement houses, 207

Sex education, 66, 193–95

Shea, Joseph, 218

Sheppard, Morris, 25

Sherrard, W. B., 42, 45, 54, 59–60

"Sloyd" system, 140

Smith, Elias, 71

Smith, Herman, 202

Snivley, George, 83–84, 96, 99

Social class: as child-saving issue, 48, 59–60, 66, 209–10; and newsboys, 105. *See also* Hegemony

Social control: and G. W. Buzzell, 16–17; and Caddie camps, 15; and juvenile courts, 11; and mother's pensions, 11; and newsboys, 111–12; and orphan asylums, 15–16; and Purity Industrial Home, 16, 17; and Edward P. Savage, 60; and W. B. Sherrard, 59–60; and Wisconsin Home and Farm School, 18. *See also* Child saving; Progressivism

Social Gospel, 82–83, 183, 208, 248–49 n. 33

Social purity, 10

Solvey Guild Association, 147

"Sons of Allendale," 219

Southern Christian Home (Atlanta), 73–74, 252 n. 85. *See also* National Benevolent Association

St. Louis: and origins of National Benevolent Association, 72, 78; orphanages in, 247 n. 20; and 1904 World's Fair, 96, 122, 126

St. Mary's Training School for Girls, 33

Stall, Sylvanus, 193

Starr Commonwealth, 30

"State of Columbia," 22

Stevens, Rollin, 161

Stone, Barton, 71

Stowe, Harriet Beecher, 6

Stowe, Lyman Beecher, 23–24

"Street arabs," 5, 7, 134, 214

Sunday, Billy, 183

Taylor, Graham, 139

Tebbets, A. H., 50, 61–64

Tenement Conditions in Chicago, 8

Thomas, Danny, 130

Thompson, Ellen, 50

Timberlake, Byron H., 52, 240 n. 51

Titsworth, Rev. Judson, 33, 46–47

Tobey, Ray, 192

Toledo: and Clean Up Day, 121; and laws concerning newsboys, 122; and youth crime rate, 117

Toledo Consumers' League, 130, 131

Toledo Newsboys' Association, 13, 219; anti-vice viewpoint of, 113–15; changes name, 130; and Clean Up Day, 121; and "Court of Investigation," 113; different nationalities of members, 117; expanding influence of, 126; girls' auxiliary of, 256 n. 36; "Honor Roll" of, 116–17; "insurrection" in, 115; and lower crime rate, 117; membership of, 112; and Newsboys' Band, 121; and original members, 120–21; origins of, 107–8; and "Popular Sunday School," 111; praised, 116–17, 121; probation officers of, 114–15; receives endowment, 129; and return of lost goods, 116–17; and self-goverment, x, 22, 112–13, 115–18; and social class, 115, 117–21; and voluntarism, 208. *See also* Gunckel, John Elster

Toledo Newsboys' Building, 127–28, 129

Toledo Newsboys' Business Men's Club, 121

"Town of Home," 22

Townsend, Charles Collins, 23

Tracy, Spencer, 130

"Tramp's Roost" (Kalamazoo), 134

"True womanhood," 6

Twist, Oliver, 106

United Methodist Children's Home, 287 n. 19

Uncle Tom's Cabin, 6, 46

United States Children's Bureau, 4, 10–11, 89

United States of Tacoma Junior Republic, 22–23

Van Arsdale, Martin Van Buren, 54, 67, 235–36 n. 7; background of, 39–40; and founding of Children's Home Societies, 40; death of, 42

Voluntarism, ix, 4, 5, 10, 45, 71, 89, 181–82, 199–201, 207–8, 214

Wallach, Stephanie, 194
Warren, J. W., 74
Warren, Mary, 74
Washington, Booker T., 202
Watkins, E. W., 200–201, 218
Wengierski, Julius, 21–22
"Wet nurse bill," 52–53, 63
White Door Settlement, 209–10
White House Conference on Dependent Children (1909), 31, 38, 54, 58, 65, 92, 196
Whitlock, Brand, 109, 116, 122
Widows' pensions. *See* Mothers' pensions
Willard, Emma, 81
Williams, J. S., 154–55
Williamson, Tena, 94, 96–97, 210, 218
Willows, Maurice, 154
Winn, Courtland S., 20
Winnebago Farm School, 22
Wines, Frederick, 48
Wisconsin Home and Farm School,

46, 207, 211, 218, 221 n. 2; ambivalence of, 214; anti-institutionalism of, 30; and family ideal, 26, 27, 33; as farm school, 24; founded, 3–4; as junior republic, 19, 22; and patriotism, 18; and "practical Christianity," 208; praise for, 33; and social control, 18. *See also* Ogden, Marion
Women, and child saving, 76–82
Women's Christian Temperance Union, 75, 77
Women's Society of Georgia Missions, 73
Wood-Allen, Mary, 193, 279 n. 66
Worcester, Mass., "Garden City Plan," 165–66
Work with Boys, 121
World War I, 100–101, 203–4
World's Fair of 1904, 96, 122

Younkin, Edwin, 77
Younkin, Martha Hart, 77–79, 82, 207, 210

American Civilization

A series edited by Allen F. Davis

Gospel Hymns and Social Religion: The Rhetoric of Nineteenth-Century Revivalism, by Sandra S. Sizer

Social Darwinism: Science and Myth in Anglo-American Social Thought, by Robert C. Bannister

Twentieth Century Limited: Industrial Design in America, 1925–1939, by Jeffrey L. Meikle

Charlotte Perkins Gilman: The Making of a Radical Feminist, 1860–1896, by Mary A. Hill

Inventing the American Way of Death, 1830–1920, by James J. Farrell

Anarchist Women, 1870–1920, by Margaret S. Marsh

Woman and Temperance: The Quest for Power and Liberty, 1873–1900, by Ruth Bordin

Hearth and Home: Preserving a People's Culture, by George W. McDaniel

The Education of Mrs. Henry Adams, by Eugenia Kaledin

Class, Culture, and the Classroom: The Student Peace Movement of the 1930s by Eileen Eagan

Fathers and Sons: The Bingham Family and the American Mission, by Char Miller

An American Odyssey: Elia Kazan and American Culture, by Thomas H. Pauly

Silver Cities: The Photography of American Urbanization, 1839–1915, by Peter B. Hales

Actors and American Culture, 1880–1920, by Benjamin McArthur

Saving the Waifs: Reformers and Dependent Children, 1890–1917, by LeRoy Ashby

A Woman's Ministry: Mary Collson's Search for Reform as a Unitarian Minister, a Hull House Social Worker, and a Christian Science Practitioner, by Cynthia Grant Tucker